Protecting
RESEARCH
CONFIDENTIALITY

CAUT Series titles

Academic Freedom in Conflict: The Struggle over Free Speech Rights in the University, ed. James L. Turk (2014)

Universities at Risk: How Politics, Special Interests and Corporatization Threaten Academic Integrity, ed. James L. Turk (2008)

Free Speech in Fearful Times: After 9/11 in Canada, the U.S., Australia, & Europe, eds. James L. Turk and Allan Manson (2006)

Time's Up! Mandatory Retirement in Canada, eds. C. T. (Terry) Fillin, David MacGregor, and Thomas R. Klassen (2005)

Disciplining Dissent, eds. William Bruneau and James L. Turk (2004)

Let Them Eat Prozac by David Healy (2003)

Counting out the Scholars: How Performance Indicators Undermine Colleges and Universities by William Bruneau and Donald C. Savage (2002)

The Oliviery Report: The Complete Text of the Report of the Independent Inquiry Commissioned by the Canadian Association of University Teachers by Jon Thompson, Patricia Baird, and Jocelyn Downie (2001)

The Corporate Campus: Commercialization and the Dangers to Canada's Colleges and Universities, ed. James L. Turk (2000)

Universities for Sale: Resisting Corporate Control over Canadian Higher Education by Neil Tudiver (1999)

PROTECTING RESEARCH CONFIDENTIALITY

What happens when law and ethics collide

Ted Palys and John Lowman

James Lorimer and Company Ltd., Publishers
Toronto

Notice to educators:
This book is available for purchase in print and ebook form. Copies can be purchased from our website at www.lorimer.ca. Copies of individual chapters or portions of the full text in print or digital form are also available for sale at reasonable prices. Contact us for details at rights@lorimer.ca.

The publisher and the author of this work expect that portions of this work will be useful for education, and expect reasonable compensation for this use. This can be readily achieved by arranging to purchase these portions from the publisher. Contrary to the view of university administrators and their legal advisors, it is unlikely that use of a chapter or 10% of this work for educational purposes with no payment to the publisher or author would be found to be fair dealing under the Canadian Copyright Act.

James Lorimer & Company Ltd., Publishers acknowledges the support of the Ontario Arts Council. We acknowledge the financial support of the Government of Canada through the Canada Book Fund for our publishing activities. We acknowledge the support of the Canada Council for the Arts which last year invested $24.3 million in writing and publishing throughout Canada. We acknowledge the Government of Ontario through the Ontario Media Development Corporation's Ontario Book Initiative.

The Canada Council | Le Conseil des Arts
for the Arts | du Canada

Cover design: Tyler Cleroux
Cover image: Shutterstock

Library and Archives Canada Cataloguing in Publication

Palys, T. S. (Theodore Stephen), author
      Protecting research confidentiality : what happens when law and ethics collide / Ted Palys and John Lowman.

Includes bibliographical references and index.
Issued in print and electronic formats.
ISBN 978-1-4594-0703-9 (pbk.).--ISBN 978-1-4594-0704-6 (epub)

      1. Confidential communications--Canada. 2. Disclosure of information--Law and legislation--Canada. 3. Research--Law and legislation--Canada. 4. Privacy, Right of--Canada. 5. Confidential communications--United States. 6. Disclosure of information--Law and legislation--United States. 7. Research--Law and legislation--United States. 8. Privacy, Right of--United States. 9. Law and ethics. I. Lowman, John, 1950-, author II. Title.

KE8468.P34 2014	342.7108'58	C2014-904327-9
KF1262.P34 2014		C2014-904328-7

James Lorimer & Company Ltd., Publishers
317 Adelaide Street West, Suite 1002
Toronto, ON, Canada
M5V 1P9
www.lorimer.ca

Printed and bound in Canada.

MIX
Paper from
responsible sources
FSC® C004071

To Russel Ogden, Anthony McIntyre, Ed Moloney, Chris Bruckert, and all those other researchers who have gone the distance for an ethical principle. Thanks for your courage and perseverance.

"Never do anything against conscience, even if the state demands it."

— Albert Einstein

Table of Contents

Foreword

Many of the most interesting and important questions about human behaviour arise in relation to behaviour that is socially disparaged, results in harm to the participants or others, or threatens the interests of powerful institutions. We are fascinated with what motivates a serial killer or how Jim Jones' cult could have induced more than 900 people to commit mass suicide by drinking cyanide-laced Kool-Aid. We are puzzled by the intense emotions that fuel the hatred between Catholics and Protestants in Northern Ireland, Singhalese and Tamils in Sri Lanka, that lay behind the eruption of mass murder of Tutsis and moderate Hutus in Rwanda or the vicious warfare among ethnic groups in the former Yugoslavia – groups that had lived harmoniously for decades.

We display great interest in sex work, why young people join gangs, why individuals commit suicide, why some risk HIV/AIDS by having unprotected sex, what prompts a seemingly typical North American teenager to join al-Shabaab in Somalia, or how it is possible that errors by hospital medical staff are one of the leading causes of death in the United States and Canada. We want to know about major corporations distorting scientific work to falsely claim the safety and efficacy of their products, about corruption in government, and about the secret arrangements of social media networks and internet service providers to turn over information and records they have on all of us to national security agencies.

Learning about these things has one common element: They require researchers gaining information from individuals who put themselves at risk by participating in the research. Gang members who talk with researchers risk exposure to the police as well as retribution by their fellow gang members. Hospital staff who help researchers understand how medical colleagues and they, themselves, made errors that proved fatal put their jobs at risk and could face criminal prosecution. Employees who disclose malfeasance on the part of their employers can be fired and, in the case of civil servants or military personnel, can be prosecuted.

For the socially important research on such subjects to be conducted, the solution has been for researchers to promise confidentiality to their research participants – pledging that if they participate in the research, the confidentiality of their information will be protected. In the absence of such a promise, the research would be impossible, just as in the absence of lawyer-client privilege the legal system would founder. Confidentiality is what makes many socially important relationships possible: lawyer-client, priest-confessor, physician-patient, investigative journalist-informant, and researcher-research participant.

The problem is that there is no such thing as absolute confidentiality. Journalists, physicians, priests, and even lawyers, can be ordered by a court to divulge confidential information and be held in contempt of court should they refuse to do so. In deciding on such matters, courts weigh the social benefit of protecting confidential relationships against the social cost of denying police, the court or the public access to a particular piece of confidential information.

Solicitor-client privilege has been part of common law since the 1500s and only under the most extraordinary circumstances can it be breached.[1] On the continuum of protection of confidential relationships, solicitor-client is at one end. It is recognized by courts as a privilege that makes the legal system possible. No other relationship has been accorded the same status. The best that has been achieved in the case of physician-patient, priest-confessor and journalist-source is case-by-case privilege.

The nature of such privilege was described in a Supreme Court of Canada ruling on a demand for disclosure of confidential information held by a *National Post* Reporter:

It is in the context of the public right to information about matters of public interest that the legal position of the confidential source or whistleblower must be located. The public has an interest in effective law enforcement. The public also has an interest in being informed about matters of public importance that may only see the light of day through the cooperation of sources who will not speak except on condition of confidentiality. The role of investigative journalism has expanded over the years to help fill what has been described as a democratic deficit in the transparency and accountability of our public institutions. There is a demonstrated need, as well, to shine the light of public scrutiny on the dark corners of some private institutions. The appellants and their expert witnesses make a convincing case that unless the media can offer anonymity in situations where sources would otherwise dry-up, freedom of expression in debate on matters of public interest would be badly compromised. Important stories will be left untold, and the transparency and accountability of our public institutions will be lessened to the public detriment.

In appropriate circumstances, accordingly, the courts will respect a promise of confidentiality given to a secret source by a journalist or an editor. The public's interest in being informed about matters that might only be revealed by secret sources, however, is not absolute. It must be balanced against other important public interests, including the investigation of crime. In some situations, the public's interest in protecting a secret source from disclosure may be outweighed by other competing public interests and a promise of confidentiality will not in such cases justify the suppression of the evidence.[2]

The status of promises of confidentiality made by academic researchers is less clear. Ethically bound to minimize harm to research participants, academic researchers have sought assurances from the universities, under whose auspices their research has been undertaken, for support and protection of the promises of confidentiality they must made to do their research.

11

But university administrations have proven surprisingly reluctant to offer such support, despite being obligated to do so by the policy of the federal granting councils that provide the funding for research in Canada and despite requirements of the universities' own research ethics boards that insist upon protection for research participants when there is a risk to them.[3]

The university administrations' hesitancy is puzzling at first. Every university professes commitment to academic freedom, a central tenet of which is that scholars must be free to explore questions and pursue issues they think important and have the protected right to publish what they find. But when researchers' work takes them into areas that are illegal, socially maligned or that can expose questionable behaviour by governments or important societal institutions, their university administration's support often wavers or disappears altogether. This leaves the academic researchers alone to deal with the protection of the confidentiality of their research participants.

The contrast with the behaviour of media companies is noteworthy, as the latter have historically gone to great lengths to protect and defend the confidential relationships between journalists and their sources. Media companies' aggressive defence of journalistic privilege has helped lead to court recognition of the importance of that privilege, as in the Canadian *National Post* decision cited above.

The curious failure of university administrations, in a similar manner, to support their own academic staff and the confidentiality on which their staff's research depends has been consequential – imposing a chill on doing sensitive research and forcing researchers who confront the chill to take do so at their own risk. This may not be so curious after all given, despite their almost universal policies in support of academic freedom, university administrations have a less than enviable record in defending their academic staff s' academic freedom when there is a true price to be paid for doing so.[4] There have been exceptions, but too often university administrations are reluctant to offend governments, powerful donors, prospective corporate partners or local elites.[5] With the increasing corporatization of universities, they have become more concerned with what they now call their "brand." This has only intensified their risk-aversion and disinclination to offend powerful interests in the society.

The academic freedom to explore behaviour that requires research participants to put themselves at risk is undermined not only when university administrations fail to defend a researcher under attack, but also when they fail to help create the circumstances under which such research can be safely undertaken. That means helping ensure the judicial recognition of researcher-research subject privilege and the introduction of laws that protect it.[6] In the case of journalists, judicial recognition of privilege arose from the demand for it, from the explanations of its necessity, and from media corporations and journalists going to court to challenge attempts to obtain material gained through the promise of confidentiality.

In the pages that follow, Ted Palys and John Lowman examine the pivotal struggles for the recognition of research confidentiality in Canada. The centre was Simon Fraser University in Burnaby, British Columbia, and the first major case involved a graduate student, Russel Ogden, studying assisted suicide. The details of Ogden's determination to do his work, the roadblocks put in his way, the battles with the university administration, the coroner and the courts are both fascinating reading and a case study in how important rights are won.

Along the way, Palys and Lowman do many things. They provide an overview of the law on evidentiary privilege. They look at the efforts of the federal granting councils to define human research, to articulate to the ethical duty of confidentiality which researchers must uphold, and to specify the obligation of institutions to support researchers in protecting participant confidentiality. Perhaps most importantly, Palys and Lowman explore whether a researcher's obligation to protect participant confidentiality is simply up to the limit that the law allows, or whether it extends beyond that to an ethical commitment that means accepting the consequences of defying a legal order so as to protect the confidentiality that was promised research participants. They make clear that much depends on which standard is chosen.

They also examine a more recent case at the University of Ottawa. Criminologists Chris Bruckert and Coleen Parent refused to turn over confidential research information demanded by the Montreal police in a high profile murder case. Bruckert and Parent took the matter to the Quebec Superior Court where they won the first judicial recognition of research privilege in Canada. This was made possible by their courage and determination, supported by the Canadian Association of University Teachers, not their university administration.[7] Palys and Lowman discuss how this case led to a clarification and toughening of the federal funding agencies' requirements for academic institutions to support their academic staff in protecting confidentiality promised research participants.

Palys and Lowman's book is important reading for anyone concerned with how rights can be won through determined struggle, how universities operate, and the importance of confidentiality in much human research. It is also a vital exploration of ethical obligations when ethics and law collide.

— James L. Turk

CHAPTER I
Threats to Research Confidentiality

Many professional relationships involve an expectation of confidentiality. Journalists and their sources; lawyers/social workers/accountants and their clients; therapists/physicians and their patients; police and their informants, all involve persons providing information confidentially.

For the most part, professionals can maintain confidentiality without a hitch. However, occasionally someone else's interests intervene, threaten confidentiality, and lead us to question the values that underlie our duty and the threat. These issues play out in many forums, the most public and documented of which is the courtroom. Journalists often promise confidentiality to whistleblowers, but what if police or an aggrieved corporation seek a source's identity with an eye to prosecuting or suing them? Lawyers promise confidentiality to their clients, but what if a wrongful conviction will result unless a lawyer shares some secret that a client divulged under the promise of lawyer-client privilege? Although therapists can only be effective when their patients are willing to share their most private thoughts, what if a third party seeks to discover what a patient said during therapy in the belief that it would constitute material evidence advancing his or her criminal or civil case? When push comes to shove and a court weighs competing interests, the challenge forces professionals to consider their duty of confidentiality in light of another person's competing rights and interests. Judges then have to weigh the competing claims.

On May 25, 1994, for the first time in Canada, a lawful challenge to research confidentiality occurred when a coroner subpoenaed Simon Fraser University (SFU) criminology graduate student Russel Ogden and ordered him to attend an inquest. The coroner sought the identity of two research participants who had provided Ogden with information about the death of an "unknown female" discussed in his master's thesis on euthanasia and assisted suicide.

A Twenty-Year Journey

Ogden's subpoena and the university's response to it triggered a debate about research confidentiality and ethics policy at SFU that coincided with, and in large part anticipated, a national debate that was just beginning in the context of an initiative of the federal granting agencies to develop a national trans-disciplinary policy statement on ethics in research involving human participants. What are the researcher's ethical obligations in this situation? Must a subpoena lead to disclosure or can the researcher challenge it? What are the legal options for challenging a subpoena? What obligations does the researcher's institution have? Does it have an ethical obligation to support the researcher? Does it have a legal obligation? What if the researcher exhausts every avenue open to him or her and the court decides that, notwithstanding any ethical commitments, it still wants the information? In this last instant, the competing values underlying ethics and law come to a head. Researchers must choose between their ethical commitment to protect research participants from harm regardless of the fact this would mean taking the consequences of defying a legal order — which we refer to as the "ethics-first" approach — or adhering to the law in violation of their ethical duty — the "law-of-the-land" or "law-first" approach. Should the university support the researcher regardless of which choice he or she makes? These questions are the subject of this book.

Our examination of these questions constitutes a case study in which we happen to have been centrally involved for reasons that will become apparent. Because of our involvement in these issues, the book is a form of ethnography. We entered the fray with a clear ethical position, but understood little about the law in relation to confidentiality. In our view, the answers to the questions posed above were relatively simple; they are the same as Ogden's answers when he was resisting the coroner's subpoena. They reflect the ethical standards of our discipline: criminology. For us, the bigger question was why it took twenty years to resolve these issues. It is only by recounting our journey — one that began locally but ended up with national and international dimensions — that we can show how the debate about research confidentiality was a proxy for bigger issues. These issues include diverse visions of the university's role in contemporary society, respect for disciplinary and epistemological diversity, the role of academic freedom in inquiry, and the responsibility of university administrators and federal agencies to govern fairly and support diversity rather than ignore or suppress it. Accordingly, the intent of this book is not simply to pose questions and suggest answers, but to illustrate the challenges that arose and the resistance we encountered, consider what this revealed about the various actors and the institution in which we work, and outline how a resolution was achieved.

The book begins with a description of Ogden's case and our subsequent efforts — first at SFU, then nationally, and then internationally — to fight the doctrine of limited confidentiality at the heart of what we refer to as the *culture of disclosure*. We integrate into this account a description of the statutes and common law pertaining to evidentiary privilege — the exemption of certain communications from use as evidence in criminal and civil proceedings — and an analysis of the numerous US and two Canadian cases where a court, grand jury, congressional committee, or other legal body has challenged research confidentiality. We also tell a story about how university administrators exercise power and how to resist their power by holding them accountable to the policies they are supposed to uphold.

The book's thesis is that, if universities really do believe confidentiality is crucial to research on sensitive topics, they must fight to protect it. At the very least, that fight should involve doing everything legally possible to protect research confidentiality. In instances where there is no legal protection, universities must allow researchers to engage in civil disobedience by refusing to comply with a court order to violate research confidentiality.

Lawful Threats to Research Confidentiality

In Canada, there are three classes of potential lawful threats to research confidentiality:

1. court-ordered disclosure of confidential research records that might provide evidence in a criminal, civil, or other legal proceeding;
2. the possibility that there is a tort "duty to warn" a third party if a research participant discloses in confidence that he or she intends to harm that third party; and
3. mandatory reporting laws, such as the requirement that all citizens report child abuse.

Our story focuses on the development of policy regarding the first two of these potential legal threats, and the threat to academic freedom that a policy of "limited confidentiality" represents. We use the regime of limited confidentiality that SFU's research administration tried to impose on researchers following the Ogden subpoena as the exemplar of this threat. According to the architects of SFU-style limited confidentiality, "the problem" was not the challenge to research confidentiality that the coroner's subpoena represented, but Ogden's REB-approved[1] pledge of "absolute confidentiality" and the potential liability it incurred. Rather than fight the coroner's subpoena, the administration offered Ogden minimal support. At the behest of the VP-research, the SFU research ethics committee — which the VP-research chaired — then began requiring researchers to warn research participants that a court might order disclosure of confidential research information, implying that, if ordered to, the researcher would disclose it. One of our primary purposes in writing this book is to reveal the problems this culture of disclosure creates.

If we acquiesced, limited confidentiality would end criminology as we know it. Many criminological classics — Howard Becker's *Outsiders*, Richard Ericson's *Reproducing Order*, William Foote Whyte's *Street Corner Society* — could not have been written under a regime of limited confidentiality. What offender would discuss offences he or she had committed knowing that the researcher might end up serving as a witness for the prosecution? What police officer would tell us about his or her violation of a citizen's civil liberties if he or she thought we would share this information with a disciplinary board? If our research participants thought that, for any purpose, courts, commissions, or inquiries would be inclined to order information to be disclosed about their past crimes or discreditable conduct, which they provided to us in confidence, they would not have participated in our research. Even if they decided to participate, who could trust the veracity and completeness of research information collected based on a promise of confidentiality that a researcher may not keep?

The disciplines for which these issues are germane extend far beyond criminology. Researcher experiences suggest, and research-ethics codes confirm, that participant confidentiality is vitally important to any research that involves participants divulging information that could cause them serious harm or embarrassment if a third party discovered that it pertained to them. This includes research on: sexual attitudes, preferences, or practices; HIV/AIDS and other STIs; the use of alcohol, drugs, or other addictive products; illegal conduct; psychological well-being and mental health; genetic information, including biological samples stored for future use; epidemiological information; and any other information that could be damaging to a participant's financial standing, employability, or reputation within the community or might lead to social stigmatization or discrimination if it were to be disclosed.[2]

While some research is critical of a particular community or practice, a core ethical responsibility is to protect the identity of persons to whom we promise confidentiality as a condition of their participation. This ethical responsibility applies even in research that is potentially critical of the communities from which researchers recruit participants. Limiting confidentiality *a priori* compromises researchers' ability to protect research participants from harm.

SFU happens to be where our story began, but SFU was not alone in attempting to impose limited confidentiality on researchers. As we document in later chapters, it is still the requirement of some universities; the culture of disclosure has washed across the Canadian academy. There are signs that a similar culture is developing in the United Kingdom.[3] In contrast, in the US — the country where the vast majority of court, grand jury, and congressional committee challenges to research confidentiality have actually occurred — a variety of federal and state laws formally protect research confidentiality. Although not all research is eligible for such protection, for much US research, a *culture of protection* prevails.

Despite the fact that there has never been a case of court-ordered disclosure of a research participant's identity in Canada, the fear of court-ordered disclosure is nonetheless blowing a chill wind on research involving sensitive topics. Ironically, the fact that there has never been a single case may explain why Canada's three national research-funding councils[4] have not lobbied for the enactment of some kind of confidentiality research shield law in Canada. The granting agencies' collective act of omission has allowed the culture of disclosure to flourish.

In the process of describing the ethics and law of research confidentiality, this book has three goals:

1. to ensure that when researchers follow a "law-first" or "law-of-the-land" doctrine that absolutely subjugates ethics to law, the institutions housing their research must defend confidentiality to the *full* extent permitted by law;

2. to assert the academic freedom of researchers to follow an "ethics-first" doctrine that subordinates law to ethics, including civil disobedience if necessary to protect research confidentiality; and

3. to encourage the presidents of Canada's granting agencies to walk their talk about protecting research participants by lobbying for the enactment of a research-confidentiality shield law in Canada, and, in the interim, to inform researchers about the common-law mechanisms — particularly the Wigmore criteria, which we describe below — that can be used to assert research-participant confidentiality privilege.

What Is at Stake?

As we were writing *Protecting Research Confidentiality*, two new important cases started to unfold. First, in the summer of 2011, the Police Service of Northern Ireland (PSNI), using the provisions of the British–US Mutual

Legal Assistance Treaty, sought disclosure of certain interviews archived in the "Treasure Room" of the Burns Library at Boston College. The interviews were conducted as part of the 'Belfast Project,' an oral history of paramilitaries involved in armed conflict in Northern Ireland." Ostensibly, PSNI wanted the interviews in relation to its investigation of a 1972 murder. This is the first time, to our knowledge, that a third party has resorted to an international treaty to obtain confidential research information housed in another country.

Second, in the summer of 2012, Montreal police contacted two University of Ottawa researchers seeking the transcript of an interview they had conducted with "Jimmy" (a pseudonym). A research assistant told police that "Jimmy" is the alias of Luka Rocco Magnotta, a man charged with murder and several other serious crimes. On hearing that police wanted a copy of the confidential interview, the researchers handed it over to lawyer Peter Jacobsen for safekeeping. In response, Montreal police obtained a warrant authorizing seizure of the audio recording and interview transcript from Jacobsen's office. As far as we know, this is the first time a legal authority has used a warrant to seize confidential research material rather than issuing a subpoena.

Although these two cases occurred a decade after the conflict *Protecting Research Confidentiality* describes, it was the anticipation of situations like them that motivated us to write this book. The two cases share one feature — the failure of universities to defend research confidentiality — but they had diametrically opposed outcomes. The Belfast Project turned into a disaster when a judge ordered Boston College to release seven oral history interviews to the PSNI to facilitate a murder investigation. Although it is highly unlikely these interviews will have any probative value or lead to any convictions, the damage to oral history and other kinds of research may take years to undo. In contrast, the seizure of the "Jimmy" interview turned into a precedent-setting case, the protection of confidential research information, and the formal recognition in Canadian law of researcher-participant privilege.

The Belfast Project

The Belfast Project began soon after the Good Friday Agreement of 1998 initiated a fragile peace plan to end the decades-long conflict in Northern

Ireland known as "the Troubles." In the absence of a truth-and-reconciliation process, Boston College and the researchers hired to conduct the project hoped it would provide a more complete view of history than is contained in official accounts, which often are heavily sanitized and self-serving, written by those in command. The Belfast Project aimed to record the experience of the Troubles through the eyes of the foot soldiers involved, and to throw light on how individuals one otherwise might know as plumbers or school teachers ended up planting bombs to advance their political cause. There is no way such information could be gathered unless those being interviewed felt they could trust the researchers and Boston College to abide by the terms of the Donor Agreement they signed, which promised their interviews would remain confidential as long as they lived or until they gave permission for them to be released. The Belfast Project represented the quintessential example of research in which a cast-iron guarantee of confidentiality was indispensable. Which paramilitary would divulge information if he or she knew the researchers would turn it over to the authorities so he or she could be prosecuted?

The PSNI became interested in the archive ostensibly to help investigate the 1972 abduction and unsolved murder of Jean McConville, who certain IRA members alleged was an informer. The divisions the subpoenas have created are palpable. In the United States, conflict erupted between Boston College and the Belfast Project researchers. The researchers — project director Ed Moloney, Irish Republican Army (IRA) interviewer Anthony McIntyre and Loyalist interviewer Wilson McArthur — followed an "ethics-first" approach to research confidentiality, whereby the researchers use every legal avenue open to them to protect confidentiality, but in the absence of appropriate research shield laws, are prepared to go to jail to protect research-participant identities. In contrast, although it appears that representatives of Boston College originally assured the interviewers the archive would be safe from British legal authorities once it was in the United States, more recently the college has argued that it extended its pledge of research confidentiality only to the "the extent American law allows." Whether the college met that criterion is open to dispute.[5]

A primary victim in this episode is oral history itself. Other researchers have abandoned plans for parallel oral histories that would have involved interviewing police and British soldiers because prospective participants withdrew.[6] Columbia University researchers who sought to interview guards and former Guantanamo Bay detainees watered down their research protocol to avoid attracting the attention of US legal authorities. Researchers encouraged participants who spontaneously mentioned incidents that might be the subject of legal action to withdraw their comments.[7] The implications of such a state of affairs are staggering for anyone who takes seriously the university's mission to try to understand all aspects of society. We return to the details of this sorry saga towards the end of our story. For the moment, we want to focus on the issues the Belfast Project subpoenas and other lawful challenges to research confidentiality raise for researchers more generally.

Is academic freedom at an end when researchers can only ask questions that the state approves? Does the academy serve the greater good when it produces knowledge that only state-approved research participants provide? Do state authorities expect researchers to function as informers? Should research participants who share their innermost secrets today expect to see researchers on the witness stand for the prosecution tomorrow? What is the proper relationship between researchers, universities, the courts, and the state? These same questions arose when police seized the research interview with sex worker "Jimmy," who it transpired is accused murderer Luka Rocco Magnotta.

The "Jimmy" Interview

Concordia student Lin Jun was murdered on either May 24 or 25, 2012. Subsequently, someone mailed parts of his dismembered body to the Conservative and Liberal party headquarters, and to two schools in Vancouver. His head was found in a park, his torso in a suitcase in an alley.

The last time anyone saw Lin Jun alive was on May 24, the day before a video that depicted the stabbing and dismembering of a naked man, followed by acts of necrophilia and cannibalism, was uploaded to an Internet site.[8] Allegedly, the video depicts Lin Jun's demise. Several days later, a janitor found his torso in a suitcase outside a Montreal apartment building. Video surveillance from inside the building showed a man carrying several garbage bags out to the alley. When police began to investigate the building's residents, they came upon Magnotta's empty apartment. Evidence at the scene made him the prime suspect.

On May 31, police obtained a warrant for Magnotta's arrest on suspicion of murder, interfering with a dead body, publishing obscene material, distributing obscene material by mail, and criminally harassing the prime minister and other members of parliament.[9] When police learned that Magnotta had travelled to Europe, Canadian authorities requested Interpol detain him and extradite him to Canada. On June 4, 2012, German police apprehended Magnotta in Berlin. He was flown to Canada on June 18. His preliminary hearing began on March 11, 2013.

On reading that Magnotta was a suspect in Lin Jun's murder, research assistant Adam McLeod informed Montreal police that he had conducted an interview with Magnotta in 2007 under the pseudonym "Jimmy" as part of University of Ottawa professors Colette Parent and Chris Bruckert's study of sex workers and their clients. The University of Ottawa REB had approved the unlimited guarantee of confidentiality Bruckert and Parent proposed to give research participants. The warrant executed on June 21, 2012, to seize the interview from lawyer Peter Jacobsen's office was authorized because of McLeod's revelation. McLeod told police the interview focused on all aspects of Magnotta's personal and professional life. Given that Magnotta likely did not meet Lin Jun until after the latter arrived in Canada in 2011, the 2007 interview presumably does not contain evidence relevant to establishing who murdered Lin Jun. Instead, the prosecution declared an interest in any evidence that might shed light on Magnotta's personality and experience should he plead not guilty by reason of insanity.[10]

Anticipating the Crown's argument about the potential material relevance of the Jimmy interview to Magnotta's mental state five years later, Bruckert and Parent submitted an affidavit by Dr. Scott Woodside giving his opinion on the likely value of the interview for ascertaining whether Magnotta is "not criminally responsible" (NCR) as per section 16 of the *Criminal Code of Canada*. Woodside is a forensic psychiatrist and head of The Sexual Behaviours Clinic of the Centre for Addiction and Mental Health, Canada's largest mental health and addiction teaching hospital, and one of the world's leading research centres on addiction and mental health.[11] Woodside also is a member of the Ontario Review Board, which assesses the competence of accused persons to stand trial. The gist of Woodside's affidavit was that a social science interview conducted five years prior to the commission of Lin Jun's murder would have little probative value.

Part of the evidence the court considered was an affidavit from one of us (Lowman) concerning "researcher-participant confidentiality privilege" and the importance of confidentiality for interviews with sex workers. Lowman described the cost to criminological research in particular and research on sensitive topics more generally should the court establish that the researchers could not make a reliable guarantee of confidentiality:

> *The effect of a disclosure of the interview with "Jimmy" could have a decidedly chilling effect on all Canadian research on sensitive topics. If researchers studying sensitive topics cannot give enforceable guarantees of confidentiality, many prospective participants will decline to participate in research. . . If the subjects of my research thought that, for any purpose, courts would be inclined to order information to be disclosed about their past potential crimes or discreditable conduct that they provided to me in confidence, they would not have participated.*
>
> *Criminologists could be left in a position where only a small pool of potential participants who believe they have nothing to lose by disclosing potentially criminal or discreditable conduct would participate in research.*
>
> *Ironically, the cost of pursuing this information would likely be the closing down of many research opportunities into crime and criminality that could, among many other benefits, help to make Canada a safer country.*[12]

In response to Parent and Bruckert's arguments, the Crown held that neither the general nor the specific interest in maintaining research confidentiality outweighs the court's need for evidence to aid its search for the truth given the serious nature of the charges against Magnotta.[13]

The Belfast Project and Jimmy interview cases raise important issues about the ability of research to contribute empirical evidence to some of the most important and often controversial issues of our time; the role of research confidentiality in the production of evidence; and the role of researchers, research ethics boards, and university administrators in the protection of research confidentiality, research participants, and academic freedom. This book recounts how in 2014 two very important principles were established:

1. the formal recognition in Canadian common law of researcher-participant privilege; and
2. the presidents of the granting agencies asserting that, as a minimal standard, they require *both* researchers and universities to protect research participants to the extent that law permits.

CHAPTER II
Ogden's Research on Euthanasia and Assisted Suicide

SFU Criminology

SFU is a relatively new university, born in the baby-boom higher education expansion years of the 1960s, and very much a product of the thinking of that era. SFU's School of Criminology opened in 1975. The school's faculty have always represented a broad spectrum of disciplines and epistemological and political persuasions. By the early 1990s, the school had grown to twenty-four members whose academic roots lay in criminology, geography, law, mathematics, political science, psychology, and sociology. Some faculty engage in qualitative field research. Others deal with aggregate databases involving hundreds or thousands of cases. Some do both.

Contrary to a stereotype that criminologists often encounter when being introduced as such at a party, most of our faculty do not teach FBI or RCMP investigative techniques, nor do they only study crime and criminals. They investigate the making, the breaking, and the reaction to the breaking of laws, as well as how criminal and other laws interact with other social-control mechanisms. In addition to studying offenders, some faculty study social controllers, including police, probation officers, prison guards, lawyers, and judges. Others study related systems of social control, such as Aboriginal justice processes, private security, the mental health system, and gender socialization in order to understand how justice and social control are practised.

Explaining the sociology or psychology of crime, or trying to understand how the justice system works or does not work, or how law and justice may aspire to coincide but sometimes are at odds, are valuable pursuits in their own right. Such research allows criminologists to offer advice to governments that seek to formulate public policy, to courts when empirical research helps to inform their search for truth, and to journalists when they phone and ask for insights about crime and justice. As a discipline, criminology shares with other social and natural sciences the view that this understanding must come from gathering information about the world by directly interacting with it, posing questions, recording information, and interpreting the results.

Russel Ogden Enrolls at SFU

The Criminology Master of Arts (MA) graduate program was already well established when Russel Ogden enrolled in September 1991. He was a more mature student than most, returning to his studies after several years as a social worker. His application proposed a study of assisted suicide among persons with HIV/AIDS for his thesis.

Among Ogden's first courses were criminological theory and research methods. Dr. Bill Glackman taught the methods course and used a pre-publication draft of *Research Decisions: Quantitative and Qualitative Perspectives*[1] as required reading. *Research Decisions'* chapter on research ethics included descriptions of several codes of ethics, including those of the American and Canadian Psychological Associations (APA and CPA)[2] and the American Sociological Association (ASA).[3] A core principle of each concerns the researcher's obligation to protect participant confidentiality.

Social research is quite different from many other professions where an expectation of confidentiality occurs. For example, in medicine, law, the church, and counselling psychology, normally the patient, client, or penitent seeks out the professional for healing, advice, or absolution. Without compelling reasons to the contrary, what you tell a doctor, priest, lawyer, or therapist should remain between you and him or her.

In contrast, researchers normally seek out prospective participants and ask them to share personal information with the intention of broadcasting it to the world, hopefully for the greater good. Researchers believe their findings are most beneficial when they are open to critical scrutiny. The researcher thus has a duty to protect research-participant identities, not to ensure the information remains secret. Researchers create risks when they enter participants' lives; participants normally receive nothing beyond a thank you or a small token of appreciation. This asymmetry magnifies the ethical obligation researchers have to protect research participants from harm.

At one level, the researcher's obligations are straightforward. If we want to find out why people commit crimes the most obvious way to begin is by talking to the people who commit them. If we want to find out how the justice system operates and whether it is just, then surely we should talk to the police officers, prison guards, lawyers, and judges who run it.

The easiest way to protect participant identities is to gather information anonymously; if researchers do not know the identities of those involved in their research, they cannot divulge them. Much survey research proceeds this way, as does much observational research where there is little or no interpersonal connection between the researcher and individual participants. However, many kinds of research cannot proceed that way. For example, longitudinal research, which involves going back to the same group of people repeatedly in order to follow the participants' progression through school, adolescence, marriage, the justice system, or whatever, requires the researcher to maintain some way of reconnecting with participants in successive phases of the research. Similarly, when researchers want to link two different databases — such as health records and responses to a general social survey — there must be some way to link the information for specific individuals across the two databases. Anonymity also is often difficult to achieve in qualitative field research as researchers often establish long-term relationships with people, communities, and organizations. While it is easy to anonymize quantitative research records, qualitative field researchers often know the identity of the people they talk to and often remember what they said. Consequently, researchers must consider how far they are prepared to go to protect the confidentiality of their sources. Research-ethics codes offer guidance on how far that should be.

At the time Ogden began his MA studies at SFU in 1991, the American Society of Criminology (ASC) — an international organization to which many Canadian criminologists belong — did not have its own ethics code. Instead, it referred researchers to other relevant disciplinary ethics codes, a practice that continues to this day. The American Sociological Association

(ASA) and American Political Science Association (APSA) codes of ethics stated:

> Confidential information provided by research participants
> must be treated as such by sociologists, even when this
> information enjoys no legal protection or privilege and legal
> force is applied.[4]

> [S]cholars also have a professional duty not to divulge
> the identity of confidential sources of information or data
> developed in the course of research, whether to governmental
> or non-governmental officials or bodies, even though in the
> present state of American law they run the risk of suffering an
> applicable penalty.[5]

Marvin Wolfgang — who the *British Journal of Criminology* once described as "the most influential criminologist in the English speaking world"[6] — also considered that very issue in a series of articles:[7]

> The traditional research response . . . is that [the researcher]
> is a neutral, disinterested recipient of data collected only for
> scientific research purposes. The purpose for obtaining the
> information is to aid the scholarly enterprise and to provide
> guidance for a rational social policy. Data obtained that could
> have direct untoward consequences to subjects are not the
> possession of the state but of science . . . [T]he social scientist
> is not a representative of any branch of government with an
> obligation to execute certain police or judicial duties.[8]

In a subsequent section entitled "What should a research center do if the police, prosecutor or court requests the files?" Wolfgang stated unequivocally:

> [W]e would not honour the request. We would make every
> effort, short of using aggressive force, to prevent the files

from being examined or taken from the Center's premises.
We would, if necessary, enter into litigation to protect the
confidentiality of the records.[9]

Wolfgang added that, even if charged as an accessory or with contempt of court, ". . . we would still maintain a posture of unwillingness to reveal names." The Academy of Criminal Justice Sciences (ACJS) *Code of Ethics* still takes this position:

Confidential information provided by research participants
should be treated as such by members of the Academy, even
when this information enjoys no legal protection or privilege
and legal force is applied.[10]

A researcher's primary ethical responsibility is to protect research participants. Protecting them entails not revealing their identities, even when no legal privilege or protection exists and legal force is applied.

Investigating a Controversial Social Practice

Ogden's thesis research examined assisted suicide, a crime that was receiving media attention at the time, but about which there was little Canadian research. His research focused on assisted suicide among persons with HIV/AIDS. Although there have been tremendous strides in the treatment of AIDS since then, being HIV-positive in the early 1990s turned a person into a pariah. AIDS often involved many years of degenerative illness ending in a lonely death.

Undertaking systematic field research on assisted suicide and euthanasia in the HIV/AIDS community required considerable compassion and sensitivity. The criminal prohibition of the behaviour Ogden wanted to study made the research even more taxing given the consequences for those he hoped to interview if he disclosed their involvement in an assisted suicide. A conviction for assisting a suicide could result in up to fourteen years imprisonment and life imprisonment for first-degree murder.

In keeping with his scholarly interests and the ethical standards of criminology, Ogden stated that he would maintain "absolute confidentiality" in his research. He further stated he would tell prospective research participants they did not need to supply identifying information, but that even if he did learn their identities, he would safeguard them by keeping any incriminating information locked in a location known only to him. He promised to remove any identifying information from interview transcripts and to destroy audiotapes immediately after he transcribed them. Although at that time no researcher in Canada had ever received a subpoena and been ordered to violate a research confidence, Ogden proposed to inform participants that it was conceivable a Crown attorney or the coroner might try to wrest the names of research participants from him. If they did, he pledged to maintain their confidence nonetheless.

Ogden's thesis supervisory committee approved his proposal.

The SFU Ethics Policy

SFU's research ethics policy in effect in 1992 — R20.01, the *University Research Ethics* policy — required that all research involving human subjects undergo ethics review. Accordingly, once Ogden satisfied his thesis supervisory committee that his proposal met disciplinary standards, he next submitted it to the University Research Ethics Review Committee (hereafter the ethics committee) for review.

The version of the policy the ethics committee followed, in effect from 1987 until its revision in 2001,[11] comprised six sections. Sections Two (Rationale) and Four (Ethical Policy Considerations), the most germane to our story, read as follows:

> *2. RATIONALE*
>
> *There is a professional responsibility of researchers to adhere to the ethical norms and codes of conduct appropriate to their respective disciplines. When researchers are employed by a University, the institution may, in some circumstances, be liable for research conducted by these researchers. In the interests of protecting them and itself, the University provides insurance protection for those research projects which receive ethics approval. Furthermore, most funding agencies require ethics review of research proposals which involve the use of*

human subjects. For these reasons, policy and procedures are required to ensure that appropriate safeguards are provided. . .

4. ETHICAL POLICY CONSIDERATIONS

The purpose of ethics review of research is to consider the risks to physical and psychological well-being, and the cultural values and sense of propriety of the persons who are asked to participate in and/or be the subject of research. A research proposal must demonstrate that appropriate methods will be used to protect the rights and interests of the subjects in the conduct of research. In general, the primary ethical concerns respecting research on subjects relate to: informed consent; deception; privacy; confidentiality; and, anonymity . . .

Where research may involve invasion of privacy of a subject, the research proposal must contain provisions that the subject will be fully informed, in advance, of the nature of information required and the subsequent use to be made of that information. Each subject is to be given the freedom to decide for himself or herself what information which is not already in the public domain or available to an ordinary member of the public and which relates to his or her physical and mental condition, personal circumstances and social relationships should be communicated to or withheld from others.

When submitting proposals for ethics review, researchers also had to sign a form that listed five conditions to which the researcher must agree in order to receive ethics approval:

1. secure the informed consent of subjects who participate in the project;
2. allow subjects to withdraw participation, in part or in full, at any time;
3. maintain in strict confidence the responses of individual subjects;

4. Carry out the research strictly in accordance with the proposal and the documents that accompany it, as well as any conditions imposed by the ethics review committee; and

5. Permit relevant chair, director or dean to observe the conduct of the research and to verify that procedures are followed.

The ethics policy required that the ethics committee comprise:

> *The Vice-President, Research, or his/her delegate as Chair; the Director of University Medical Services; the University Safety Officer; and, six members of faculty appointed by the Vice-President, Research . . . Faculty membership is to be drawn primarily from Departments or Faculties whose members frequently conduct research with subjects.*[12]

Prior to submitting the proposal to the ethics committee for review, Ogden approached two members of the committee for advice. One was Dr. Peter Harmon, then-director of SFU's Medical Services, who told Ogden he believed his proposal met the university's requirements. The other was Dr. Ray Corrado, the Criminology Department's representative on the committee, who graduate students routinely called on to comment on the ethical probity of their research.

An independent panel that would later examine the review process made the following comments about Ogden's interchange with Corrado:

> *As a result of his discussion with Corrado, Ogden prepared a covering letter as part of his application, dated September 14, 1992, addressed to the URERC.*[13] *Corrado reports that he urged Ogden that he seek legal advice about possible legal complications and about the question of accountability, since, as Ogden notes in his covering letter to the URERC, his research "may result in my learning of criminal behaviour such as aiding suicide or murder – how might I, or the University, be held accountable." Neither Corrado nor anyone else, as far as we can determine suggested to Ogden that he write the letter. In*

addition no one saw the letter before Ogden submitted it as part
of his application of ethical approval to the URERC, including
Corrado or Burtch, Ogden's thesis supervisor at the time.[14]

Ogden's covering letter explained that no legal precedent required individuals to share information about crime with Crown counsel. Nor was there any statutory requirement that citizens report crimes to the police. The letter then made a statement that would have profound implications for Ogden's subsequent interaction with the SFU administration:

> *It is a remote possibility that Crown Counsel or the Coroner's*
> *Office may request cooperation with an investigation. In such*
> *a circumstance, I accept full responsibility for any decision I*
> *make with respect to the sharing of information.*

Ogden submitted his proposal to the ethics committee on September 18, 1992. The one deviation from routine processing of his application involved a phone call from SFU's research grants officer on September 23. She asked Ogden to modify his proposed snowball sampling method because it could jeopardize confidentiality. Apart from this minor change, the ethics administration approved Ogden's proposal, including his undertaking to maintain in *absolute* confidence the identities of his research participants.

While the research grants officer would later testify that the project's ethical sensitivity rated a "ten" on a scale of one to ten, with ten being the highest, Ogden's proposal covered all the ethical bases and did not require review by the committee as a whole.[15] On September 24, 1992, VP-research Dr. Bill Leiss sent a letter on behalf of the ethics committee to Ogden approving his proposal.

CHAPTER III
The Coroner, the Media, and SFU

Assisted Suicide in the News

When researchers become engrossed in a project, they often begin tracking everything pertaining to it — TV programs, films, newspaper reports, court cases, and so on. Although Ogden's formal research involved interviews with persons in the HIV/AIDS community about euthanasia and assisted suicide, he also tracked media reports and other events related to his research. One sequence of events was set in motion by an article that appeared in the *Province*, a Vancouver newspaper, a few months before Ogden entered the SFU criminology graduate program. Entitled "An Act of Courage,"[1] Lyn Cockburn's article described how an unnamed man with AIDS had helped another AIDS victim end her life. The article reported the man's description of the woman's plight when he visited her in hospital:

> *"I heard her before I saw her," he says. "I got off the elevator in the hospital and I could hear her screaming with pain. . ."*
>
> *"She was lying tiny in that hospital bed; she was no larger than a child. I wasn't ready for how little she was. She told me that medical personnel sometimes came into the room and sometimes they didn't.*
>
> *"Sometimes they'd leave her food tray at the door and of course she couldn't get out of bed to get it. Sometimes, she'd get a pain killer and sometimes she wouldn't."*

The situation was intolerable; the woman wanted to leave. She implied that she wanted to die at home. The doctor understood, wrote a prescription for "enough Seconal to kill half of B.C.," and walked away. The article went on to describe how the man found the woman a foam mattress and took her home to help her die. However, things did not quite turn out the way they expected. Instead of initiating a quick death, taking all the pills in one gulp only led to her throwing up the Seconal and continuing to breathe. What could her friend do?

> *He looks past me into a place I cannot see. "I took a plastic bag and I held it over her face until she stopped breathing," he says.*

Mr. Larry Campbell, who at that time was the Vancouver coroner, read the article.

The Canadian coroner performs two main functions. The first is to identify each deceased person and ascertain when, where, and by what means the person died. This function ensures that no death is concealed, overlooked, or ignored. The second is to learn from that death in order to make practical recommendations about preventing similar deaths.[2]

Upon reading "An Act of Courage," and in keeping with a coroner's responsibilities, Campbell asked Cockburn for information about the death of the "unknown female." Cockburn similarly followed her professional ethics — in her case as a journalist — and refused to name the deceased woman or the man who helped her die. Her refusal posed a problem for Campbell; he had a story about a tragic death, but no name and no location. He did not even have a body.

On June 7, 1991, Campbell submitted a report to B.C.'s chief coroner, Vince Cain, reporting the situation and seeking advice about whether to call an inquest. Cain would indeed convene an inquest, at which point he sent subpoenas to Cockburn, Brian Butters, the *Province*'s editor-in-chief, and Patricia Graham, the editorial page editor who also knew the source's identity. With the full support of their publisher, Pacific Press Ltd., all refused to name Cockburn's source.

Given his interest in the case of the "unknown female" and with his thesis almost complete, Ogden attended the inquest when it reconvened on

December 10, 1993, after two years of procedural wrangling over whether the coroner could hold an inquest into a death where there was no name and no body, and which may have occurred outside British Columbia. Again, Campbell asked the assembled journalists to reveal the source of the information reported in Cockburn's "An Act of Courage." Cockburn and the other journalists again refused to disclose his name. They were not, they explained, an investigative arm of the coroner's office. Not being able to guarantee confidentiality to their sources would compromise the vital role journalists play in a free and democratic society. They held that journalists enjoy a special evidentiary privilege, one that section 2(b) of Canada's *Charter of Rights and Freedoms* protects.[3]

In response, the coroner asserted that the inquest served the greater good of society by ensuring the investigation of every death, and that people should not have to die in the circumstances described in Cockburn's article. He would find them in contempt of court if they did not name their source. In turn, Vincent Orchard, counsel for Brian Butters and Patricia Graham, questioned whether the Coroner had the power to find contempt. The coroner agreed to adjourn the proceedings so a higher court could answer that question.

The Media and Ogden

By the time Ogden defended his thesis in February 1994, assisted suicide and euthanasia were making front-page news across the continent — especially the cases involving Sue Rodriguez[4] and Robert Latimer[5] in Canada and Jack Kevorkian in the United States.[6]

Journalists were looking for an expert who could offer an informed opinion on these cases. Having just emerged from two years of research into the law surrounding assisted suicide and interviews with persons who had assisted, Ogden was the ideal expert. Canadian and US newspapers lined up to interview him. A Canadian Senate Committee on assisted suicide invited him to testify about his research.

A *New York Times* article called Ogden's research, "one of the rare studies of assisted suicides in a terminally ill population." It focused on his unanticipated finding that a large proportion of assisted suicides are "botched," owing largely to the lack of medical knowledge of those who assist death and the difficulty of obtaining the appropriate drugs to end a life. Ogden said his study showed "that in the absence of regulation and medical supervision, euthanasia is occurring in horrific circumstances, like back-street abortions."[7] The article also reported health-policy makers' reactions to the research:

> "[Ogden's research has] fundamentally altered the way the situation is looked at," said Elke-Ilenner Kluge, professor of philosophy at the University of Victoria and a member of the Special Ethics Advisory Committee of the British Columbia Ministry of Health. "We've long been familiar with the fact of assisted suicides. What we weren't aware of was that the number of botched cases was so great. This has shocked the community into awareness."[8]

SFU revelled in the international attention that Ogden's research brought. SFU Media Relations offered to help him handle requests for interviews and proudly announced in its bi-weekly publication *Simon Fraser Week*, "SFU Research on Euthanasia and AIDS Attracts International Media Attention." The article noted, "Ogden and SFU's media relations office, switchboard and criminology department received almost 100 requests for interviews."[9] Ogden used the occasion to highlight his major findings and underline the important role that university research plays in informing public debate:

> The issue of euthanasia has reached the "emerging policy" stage of development in Canada and must be informed by solid research," notes Ogden. "Research is required to move beyond speculative viewpoints and opposing ethical views. The introduction and incorporation of facts will make a significant contribution to the morals and ethics of law and medicine, as well as provide important data for policy development and law reform.[10]

Ogden was the poster boy for social research, a walking affirmation of the importance of the academy in shedding light on fundamental social practices about which we know little.

The Coroner's Subpoena

All went smoothly until the Vancouver coroner read an article by *Vancouver Sun* ethics columnist Douglas Todd entitled "Mercy Killing Secret World Revealed."[11] Todd reported that Ogden's thesis had "uncovered two independent sources, including a doctor, who confirmed an assisted suicide first reported in the *Province* newspaper by former columnist, Lyn Cockburn." Campbell wondered whether Ogden might be of assistance in helping him identify the "unknown female" and/or the man who had caused her death. On February 25, 1994, Campbell requested a copy of Ogden's thesis. On May 13, 1994, he informed Ogden by telephone that he would subpoena him to appear at the inquest when it reconvened; on May 25, 1994, the subpoena arrived.[12]

Ogden and the SFU Administration

As soon as they heard of the coroner's intention to send a subpoena, Ogden and his supervisor, Dr. Simon Verdun-Jones, approached Dr. Bruce Clayman — a physicist who was serving in the multiple roles of dean of graduate studies, VP-research, and chair of the ethics committee — requesting "that SFU assist with [the] legal costs associated with the inquest."[13] Rather than make the decision himself, Clayman sent President John Stubbs an e-mail, which began, "although this is nominally a grad studies matter, I think the required decision should be made at your level in view of all implications."[14]

The VP-research was correct when it came to his assessment of the subpoena's broad implications. The coroner made Ogden the first researcher in Canada ever to receive a subpoena, asked to reveal the identity of a research participant,[15] and faced with a charge of contempt for refusing to comply. The implications for academic freedom, the integrity of research, the moral authority of the ethics committee, and the lives of the research participants were substantial.

Ogden's study was on a solid legal foundation thanks to his attention to detail and the advice of his senior supervisor, and his thesis exemplified the value of research to public policy debate. As such, it offered an opportunity to assert research participant rights, the social value of research, and the importance of confidentiality to it. However, this was not how the

VP-research and other university administrators viewed the case. Later in the same e-mail, VP-research Clayman explained to President Stubbs:

> *Simon asks that we assist with his legal bills. Mr. Ogden*
> *himself hasn't been in contact with me. He's a social worker,*
> *presumably of modest means. Whether we do or not, we will*
> *be drawn into the controversy surrounding the matter since*
> *the work was done as part of his thesis research with approval*
> *of our Ethics Committee. The committee of course did not*
> *approve his withholding information from the court or coroner,*
> *so I don't think there's any legal liability on our part.*
>
> *We might wish to offer to assist with his initial legal*
> *expenses, say, up to $2,000, on compassionate grounds or*
> *possibly based on support for his academic freedom. Other*
> *external groups will undoubtedly rally 'round him in his*
> *refusal to divulge names. I'd like to be able to help him. But*
> *what worries me though is that our offer to provide $ will be*
> *interpreted by media (et al.) as SFU support for his position*
> *. . . supporting assisted suicide.*

Clayman's email reveals the potential for conflict of interest among the three institutional positions he held simultaneously — vice-president-research, chair of the ethics committee, and dean of Graduate Studies — and his interpretation of the responsibilities of each position.

As the VP-research who would subsequently use the slogan "Research Matters" on promotional buttons and brochures, Clayman apparently did not see this challenge to academic freedom as an opportunity to make precisely that point: research matters. Instead, he framed it as an issue of liability and image management. Would the chair of the ethics committee, whose primary duty is to protect research participants — including protecting them *from* the university, if necessary — frame the issues at stake the same way? Could a person wearing both hats distinguish the two roles? Is it possible for the same person to occupy both positions without the appearance of an institutional conflict of interest?

Further, it is difficult to understand the VP-research's claim that "The

committee of course did not approve [Ogden's] withholding information from the court or coroner." In his capacity as ethics committee chair,
Clayman must have been familiar with the SFU ethics policy's requirement that "Each subject will have the choice to decide what information
not already in the public domain or available to the public relating to
physical and mental condition, personal circumstances and relationships
shall be conveyed or withheld from others." The policy affirmed it was up
to the research participants to allow disclosure, not Ogden or the coroner.
Clayman also was familiar with the ethics committee's requirement that
researchers sign a form whereby they agree "to maintain in strict confidence
the responses of individual subjects." The ethics policy did not identify any
limitation to confidentiality; nor did the form researchers were required to
sign. And finally, it is difficult to see how Clayman could reconcile his statement that "The committee . . . did not approve his withholding information
from the court or coroner" with Ogden's quite unambiguous statement,
which the ethics committee had approved, that "Absolute confidentiality
of all participants will be assured."[16]

The most perplexing aspect of Clayman's email to Stubbs was its lack of
consideration of Ogden and the university's *ethical* obligations to research
participants. The purpose of the SFU ethics policy was to protect the "rights
and interests" of research participants. Surely, the main issue should have
been how to protect their identities from court-ordered disclosure? No SFU
administrator — including the VP-research/ethics committee chair — asked
how ethically appropriate it would be for the university to wash its hands
of Ogden's research participants at exactly that moment when their rights
needed protecting.

On May 24, 1994, on the advice of his vice-presidents and advisors,
Stubbs decided that the university had no legal obligation to defend
Ogden's research participants and no assistance would be forthcoming. The
VP-research informed Ogden of the decision. Ogden replied with an impas-
sioned letter that attempted to re-frame the issues:

> *The legal representation that I seek has nothing to do with*
> *euthanasia, and everything to do with academic freedom and*
> *support of the research that SFU members conduct . . . In*

my case, this is an issue of academic freedom . . . SFU [has]
assume[d] a cowardly position, abandoned a 'former student',
and [foregone] the opportunity to be a part of what may
crystallize the legal definition of academic freedom.[17]

The following day Ogden's supervisor, Simon Verdun-Jones, visited Stubbs. He pressed the president to do more to defend Ogden's research participants and academic freedom. Stubbs agreed to provide $2,000 to Ogden on "compassionate grounds"[18] — thereby avoiding any precedent that might imply liability — but that was it. The same day, Ogden received a subpoena requiring him to appear in Coroner's Court for a hearing. If Ogden's research participants, academic freedom, the standards of his discipline, and the integrity of research required protecting, the university administration wanted no part of it. Ogden would have to do it himself.

When Ogden appeared at the inquest, he was prepared to assist the coroner in whatever way he could as long as he identified none of his sources. At one point, Coroner Campbell asked him whether the two persons referred to in his thesis were in addition to the person Cockburn interviewed. Ogden said, "I believe so." The ensuing interaction between Ogden and the coroner's counsel, John Bethel, constituted the first occasion that a Canadian court came anywhere close to requesting a researcher reveal confidential information:

> Q: *Did they claim — we're not talking about identity — did*
> *they both claim to have been there at the time of the*
> *death?*
> A: *No . . . one claimed to have been present at the death and*
> *the other was not.*
> Q: *The physician was not present?*
> A: *The physician was not present at the death.*
> Q: *Did the one who claimed to be present at the woman's*
> *death participate with you in terms of confidentiality and*
> *anonymity?*
> A: *Yes.*
> Q: *What about the physician?*

A: Yes.

Q: Presumably you know who these individuals are?

A: Yes, I do.

Q: All right. Who are they? Who is, first of all, the doctor?

A: I cannot answer that.

Q: Why not?

A: It is a matter of conscience and a matter of respecting the principles that were outlined in this study to assure the confidentiality and anonymity of participants.

Q: And what about the person who was there at the time of the death, but not assisting, who was that?

A: I cannot answer that.

Q: Why not?

A: It's a matter of protecting the anonymity of the source and the confidentiality of the source as outlined in the procedure of the study.[19]

Coroner Campbell then intervened:

> Well, it's my position that, as with members of the press, that there is no basis in law for you be [sic] able to offer this anonymity and confidentiality and while I respect both your view on this and also the view of the press, I believe that you are a compellable witness and must answer that question. So, in fact, by not answering, you are in contempt.[20]

At this point, Ogden's council, Mr. E. David Crossin,[21] asked for an adjournment so that he could adduce evidence that Ogden had a right to claim privilege in this instance.

CHAPTER IV
Defending Research Participants

Understanding Evidentiary Privilege: An Introduction

The Anglo-American legal tradition holds that, in their search for truth, courts are entitled to everyone's evidence. However, that principle is not absolute. Rules of evidence determine what is admissible and what is not. Indeed, one of the court's roles is to referee debate about admissibility when the rules are not clear, or when external values are more important than the court's need for evidence. One such value involves "privilege" — the protection of certain confidential communications against compelled disclosure:

> *When information is privileged a witness may not be compelled*
> *to testify about the information and may not be compelled*
> *to disclose documents or other materials which contain the*
> *information. Under the privilege rules, relevant information is*
> *excluded in order to further social values external to the trial*
> *process such as fostering confidential relationships.*[1]

The courts consider some confidential relationships — such as that between a lawyer and client — to be so important that the normal expectation that everyone should give evidence is set aside. Courts grant such privilege in the interest of public policy and the good order of society. Because privilege can interfere with a court's search for truth, courts and legislatures grant it sparingly. There are two sources of privilege: statute and common law. We review them briefly here to provide the context for Ogden's defence of his research participants; Chapter 19 provides a more detailed discussion of the various types of privilege.

Statutory Privileges

The protection of certain types of communication is so important that they have been enshrined in law. For example, the *Canada Evidence Act* demarcates Queen's Privy Council and ministerial privilege (s.37–39).[2] The Act protects Privy Council and ministerial communications because requiring ministers to testify about their discussions would undermine their ability to do their work. In the research realm, the *Statistics Act*[3] protects information that Statistics Canada researchers collect.

Privilege in Common Law

Legislatures are not the only source of privilege. The courts also create privileges via the common law, i.e., through their decision-making in particular cases. There are two categories of common law privilege: class and case-by-case. The location of the onus of proof distinguishes them.

Class privileges are *de facto* privileges that courts have recognized repeatedly. The most commonly cited example of a class privilege involves the lawyer-client relationship. It is easy to see why it is important: What accused person would seek legal advice from a lawyer who the prosecutor could call the next day to testify against him or her? Protecting the sanctity of the lawyer-client relationship is crucial to the functioning of the legal system. However, cases have arisen where a third party challenged the privilege owing to a unique set of circumstances. In the case of a class privilege, the onus is on the third party to establish why the court should set it aside and permit disclosure.

In instances where neither a statute-based nor a class privilege exists, but where someone in a confidential relationship believes the court should protect it nonetheless, that person can assert a public-interest privilege. Courts adjudicate such claims case by case. Ogden found himself in exactly that situation when the Vancouver coroner subpoenaed him. Because his was the first case in Canada where a legal body subpoenaed a researcher and ordered him to divulge the identities of research participants, it was the first opportunity to assert researcher-participant privilege. It was the only legal strategy available to protect Ogden's research participants.

Asserting Privilege Case by Case: The Wigmore Criteria

In the absence of a statutory or class privilege, the onus is on the person claiming privilege to demonstrate to the court why it should be recognized in that particular case. To evaluate such a claim, Canadian courts employ the Wigmore criteria, which the Supreme Court of Canada has recognized as the appropriate mechanism for evaluating on a case-by-case basis the competing values that are at play in any given situation:

> *Confidential relationships have a long history of being protected through the common law doctrine of privilege. The "Wigmore test" sets out the generally accepted criteria for determining whether, in a particular case, the communications at issue should be privileged and therefore excluded as evidence at trial.*[4]

The Wigmore criteria refer to the common-law test former Northwestern University Dean of Law Henry Wigmore distilled from legal decisions throughout the British Commonwealth and the United States. All four criteria must be satisfied for the court to grant privilege:

1. the communications must originate in a *confidence* that they will not be disclosed;
2. this element of *confidentiality must be essential* to the full and satisfactory maintenance of the relation between the parties;
3. the *relation* must be one that in the opinion of the community ought to be sedulously *fostered*; and
4. the *injury* that would inure to the relation by the disclosure of the communications must be *greater than the benefit* thereby gained for the correct disposal of litigation.[5]

Ogden's lawyers looked to these criteria to construct his defence. It is instructive to review their strategy[6] as it reveals the way SFU and the ethics committee could have contributed to the defence of Ogden's research participants.

1. The communications must originate in a confidence that they will not be disclosed.
The first criterion requires a shared expectation of confidentiality regarding any communications. That was clearly the case in Ogden's research. He explicitly designed his procedures to assure research participants that he would not reveal their identities. When questioned about whether the issue of a subpoena ever came up in his conversations with prospective participants, Ogden explained:

> *The issue of subpoena arose in that I explained to the participants that I was aware that there was a remote possibility that I could be subpoenaed to provide information that was not already published in the thesis . . . I promised to the participants that in the event that I was subpoenaed to court, that I would still maintain my pledge of anonymity and confidentiality to them.*[7]

Ogden's pledge of confidentiality was unambiguous and shared. His behaviour was consistent with that understanding — wherever possible he did not record names, he anonymized interview transcripts at the first opportunity, and he kept materials in locked cabinets at unidentified locations.

2. This element of confidentiality must be essential to the full and satisfactory maintenance of the relation between the parties.
Evidence on the second criterion normally addresses two concerns. First, is there a *general* expectation of confidentiality? Clearly, there is such an expectation in research, as every disciplinary ethics code confirms. Second, because confidentiality is not essential to all research — such as market surveys that ask whether consumers prefer a glossy or matte coating on their

chocolate-covered raisins — Ogden had to demonstrate that confidentiality was essential to the research *in this case.*

Ogden's research proposal did just this by stating that complete confidentiality was a prerequisite to his gathering valid and reliable information. It is exactly on this point that the VP-research's testimony would have been helpful. Clayman could have clarified that the objective of SFU's ethics policy was to protect research participants from harm, that the ethics committee was the SFU body specifically authorized to examine the ethical probity of the research proposed to it, and that it had approved Ogden's unambiguous commitment to confidentiality in SFU-authorized research on a controversial social issue. But he did not.

In lieu of assistance from the SFU administration or ethics committee, Ogden took the stand. He distinguished two components of the study. The first involved interviews with "persons with AIDS" about their views on euthanasia and assisted suicide. The second component involved interviews with persons who had been involved in assisted suicides or had direct knowledge of them. Ogden explained that many of those in the first group did not particularly care whether he provided them confidentiality, but that every individual in the second group — which included the two participants whose identities the coroner was seeking — indicated they would participate only if he guaranteed he would not reveal their identities.

Several expert witnesses testified on Ogden's behalf. Eminent Canadian criminologist Dr. Richard Ericson testified about the fundamental importance of confidentiality to the academy's research mandate. He stressed the importance of confidentiality in research that asked participants to divulge their criminal behaviours:

> *I think that if you didn't ensure confidentiality, you would not*
> *have access to the information you require to conduct social*
> *science research. I think it's as fundamental as that.*[8]

When asked what would happen if confidentiality could not be assured, Ericson stated, "Most research just simply would not be conducted."

Ogden also sought evidence on criterion two from Mr. Andrew Johnson, a community health nurse who had worked with persons with

HIV/AIDS in palliative care and the author of *Living with Dying, Dying at Home: An AIDS Care Team Resource Manual*. When asked how important he felt confidentiality was for research on euthanasia and assisted suicide within the HIV/AIDS community he replied:

> *It has taken us ten years to get to a place where we can provide a sense of trust in the relationship between client and professional, whether it's a physician, a nurse, a social worker, or whatever . . . The way that we would develop that trust was by guaranteeing and providing confidentiality in our relationship with that person, in the research that we do, in the way that we record and document our interactions with people . . .*
>
> *So, it's not just an issue of death and dying. It's an issue that we deal with in every aspect of a person's life. HIV, the disclosure of that kind of diagnosis, could result in someone losing their home, their job, their insurance, their health insurance, their life insurance. A whole number of losses can result from disclosure. Confidentiality is key to the relationship that we have with people that we are caring for.*[9]

There simply was no way to do Ogden's research without a trustworthy guarantee of confidentiality.

3. The relation must be one that in the opinion of the community ought to be sedulously fostered.
It is relatively easy to give examples of the different kinds of relationships that satisfy the first two Wigmore criteria, i.e., where those involved share a commitment to confidentiality and where one of the participants would not take part if he or she thought the other would divulge his or her identity to any third party. Criterion three draws the court's attention to the social value "the community" attaches to the relationship. It requires the relationship to be so highly valued that it needs special measures to ensure its sanctity. But what "community" was Wigmore referring to?

David Crossin, Ogden's lawyer, addressed this criterion by presenting evidence regarding several communities of interest. First was the academic community, for which he argued the researcher-participant relationship was of crucial importance, particularly for the social sciences that rely heavily on volunteer participants to supply sensitive personal information that, if disclosed to a third party, could cause them harm. This was demonstrably the case with Ogden's research. It looked at activity that no one had previously scrutinized, and it earned him a Master's degree that led to several peer-reviewed publications.[10]

Crossin argued that Ogden's research also was valuable to those whose jobs included responding to euthanasia and assisted suicide, and to other people suffering from terminal illnesses. In relation to the former community of interest, the government and various health-care organizations that previously had operated in an informational vacuum had shown considerable interest in his research. Crossin argued that, until the publication of Ogden's research, terminally ill patients and their caregivers and families had similarly been making painful decisions in an informational void. His research provided a safe vehicle for people to tell their stories.

The final community Crossin addressed was the Canadian public at large. One might have hoped SFU's VP-research would have brought some of his "Research Matters" buttons and talked about the need for research on controversial social issues to help highlight the moral, ethical, and pragmatic issues involved in assisted suicide. He might have explained how, given the huge international media interest in the Sue Rodriguez case, journalists everywhere were looking for an expert, and how lucky SFU was to have a graduate student conducting such innovative research. The VP-research might have added that Ogden's research was a clear example of why "Research Matters," and why courts should recognize researcher-participant privilege. The VP-research did none of these things.

4. The injury that would inure to the relation by the disclosure of the communications must be greater than the benefit thereby gained for the correct disposal of litigation.

The first three Wigmore criteria deal with the nature of the communication and the social value of the relationship that gave rise to that communication. Criterion four is where the greatest challenge arises. It is the moment where the judge weighs the competing interests at stake and the values underlying them. In the context of the Ogden case, the coroner had to decide which weighs more heavily on the scales of justice: a) the negative impact that an order for disclosure would have on research; or b) the benefit to the coroner's inquest if Ogden were to name the physician who prescribed the Seconal and the person who assisted the suicide.

Although researchers should always ask themselves about the social value of their research, the problem for researchers who have to claim privilege case by case is that they do not know exactly what kind of argument they might encounter until they receive a subpoena; the law is effectively made after the fact using the scales of justice. Researchers can sometimes anticipate who might be interested in the confidential research information they gather, just as Ogden did in his research proposal.[11] However, the researcher can never know for sure who will make what claim until a claim arises. Nevertheless, in the interest of achieving informed consent, researchers are obliged to tell prospective participants how far they are prepared to go to protect research confidentiality in court.

The more researchers can understand and prepare for the crucible into which they could be thrown, remote though that possibility may be, the better the protection they will provide for their research participants by having "good facts" for their day in court. The evidence of eminent researchers and university administrators will be most helpful in meeting the challenges of the balancing exercise that criterion four requires.

The Coroner's Decision

Coroner Campbell held that all three witnesses — Ogden and the two *Province* journalists — who were claiming privilege in his investigation of the death of the unknown female had satisfied the first three Wigmore criteria. The fourth criterion was the distinguishing consideration.

Upon considering Ogden's carefully planned research protocol in light of the Wigmore criteria, the coroner agreed that, were it not privileged, research on euthanasia and assisted suicide would not be possible. The only reason Ogden had the information the coroner wanted in the first place was because of the pledge of confidentiality he made, which he was now ethically bound to maintain. With respect to the fourth criterion, the coroner ruled that Ogden's need to maintain research confidences outweighed the coroner's need for the information to investigate the death of the unknown female. Consequently, he ruled that Ogden's communications with his research participants should be privileged:

> *Mr. Crossin called witnesses who testified to the public good that has flowed from Mr. Ogden's publication. His witnesses detailed the steps required to ensure confidentiality, the necessity of this confidentiality and the contribution this document has made to the society as a whole and to persons with AIDS in particular. I am convinced after listening to the testimony and the arguments of Mr. Crossin that, in fact, Mr. Ogden should not be compelled to answer questions that would breach his promise of confidentiality. It is my finding that Mr. Ogden has fulfilled the fourth requirement under the Wigmore Test.*[12]

The coroner's conclusion regarding the journalists was quite different. He rejected the Pacific Press argument that Canada's *Charter of Rights and Freedoms* protects confidentiality between a journalist and a source. As to Wigmore criterion four, the coroner concluded:

> *[S]ociety's best interests are served by determining the identity of the deceased. It is my finding that the injury to society would be greater than the injury suffered by these parties by allowing them relief from testifying. I therefore find that Mr. Butters, Ms. Graham and Ms. Cockburn are compellable witnesses in regards to the challenged questions.*
>
> *Having found that Mr. Ogden fits the common law exception to compellability in this matter, I release him from any stain or suggestion of contempt.*
>
> *The opposite is true, however, of Ms. Cockburn, Ms. Graham and Mr. Butters. Having found that they do not fit the Wigmore test, their refusal to answer is contempt.*[13]

Although it turned out a coroner does not have jurisdiction to find a witness in contempt, his view that Ogden's research communications should be privileged bears comment.

Ogden's Accomplishment

There would be debate as to whether Ogden's victory was "precedent setting." Commentators like Bruce Clayman argued that because the coroner's court is a quasi-judicial proceeding, it does not set a precedent that other courts have to follow; winning the case was not much of a victory. While technically correct, that conclusion misses the point.

Looking at it from an ethical perspective, the case was the first test of the ethical reasoning embodied in the ethics-first perspective. Although Ogden framed his arguments to meet certain legal criteria that Wigmore identified, the criteria pose a series of tests that researchers must meet. Ogden met the first criterion — whether there was a mutual expectation of confidentiality — in the process of gaining informed consent by pledging "absolute confidentiality." He met the second criterion in his proposal to the ethics committee by outlining why he thought confidentiality was essential for fulfilling his obligation to protect research participants. The people he interviewed who had attended an assisted suicide confirmed this when they said they would only agree to Ogden interviewing them if he assured them confidentiality. The third criterion assesses the social value of research on the controversial issue of assisted suicide. The coroner agreed such information was important for helping society in general and several specialist communities to go beyond mere stereotype and speculation and find out what really goes on in this particular niche of life. While the third criterion assessed the value accorded social research on its own, the fourth criterion pitted the value of social research unfettered by legal intrusion against the specific benefit the coroner would have realized had he ordered disclosure. Looked at from a purely legal perspective, the significance of the coroner's decision is not that it sets a precedent for higher courts, but that it follows the reasoning illustrated in precedent by higher courts in which the Wigmore criteria are seen as the appropriate vehicle for evaluating the competing values involved in case-by-case claims of privilege.[14] For this reason the *Lawyer's Weekly* described Ogden's victory as, "a precedent setting ruling on privilege and confidentiality," and "an excellent example of how the Wigmore test can be used to protect confidentiality."[15]

Although Ogden's ethics-first perspective involved him placing his liberty on the line — reminding us that researchers are by no means "above the law" — by being prepared for the legal challenges his ethical compass would lead him to encounter, Ogden was rewarded with his work being judged both ethical *and* legal.

An independent legal opinion by Professors Michael Jackson, Q.C., and Marilyn MacCrimmon of the Faculty of Law at the University of British Columbia, on which we base much of our analysis of the Wigmore criteria in the Ogden case, concluded it was likely the coroner's decision would have withstood judicial review:

> [I]n Russel Ogden's case there was a legally sufficient
> evidentiary basis upon which to ground the application of the
> Wigmore principles and Coroner Campbell's decision would
> have withstood appellate review. We would add that in light
> of subsequent developments in cases such as Ryan the case
> for privilege could be enhanced in accordance with "Charter
> values", in this particular case the need to protect AIDS
> patients' rights to privacy and to secure equal treatment before
> the law without discrimination.[16]

Whatever ends up being the historical value of the case, Ogden's tenacious and principled commitment to go the distance was in keeping with established criminological tradition. By identifying the Wigmore test as the appropriate vehicle for researchers to assert their ethics-based claims to a researcher-participant privilege, he secured a victory for academic research participants as a whole.

For this victory, the SFU administration could not take one crumb of credit. Its abdication of responsibility to Ogden's research participants was a dark day for SFU and the Canadian academy.

It was not to be the last.

CHAPTER V

Protecting Research Participants, or Protecting the University from Research Participants?

Institutional Conflict of Interest

As the controversy surrounding the SFU research ethics policy (R20.01) is central to our story, it is worth highlighting three of its key features when Ogden did his research. The first two involve a built-in institutional conflict of interest that opened the door for extra-ethical criteria, such as liability and public image management, to contaminate the ethics review process. The third involves the ethics committee's power to design its own operating procedure.

The first way the appearance of institutional conflict of interest contaminated SFU's research-ethics administration was through the membership of the committee, which the VP-research controlled.[1] The second conflict was enshrined in the ethics policy "rationale."

The rationale started reasonably by affirming that the "purpose of ethics review is to consider the risks to physical and psychological well-being, and the cultural values and sense of propriety of the persons who are asked to participate in and/or be the subject of research." Like all research-ethics codes, it required that researchers "demonstrate that appropriate methods will be used to protect the rights and interests of the subjects in the conduct of research." However, while recognising that researchers have a professional obligation to adhere to their respective disciplinary ethics codes, the policy's rationale delineated a potentially conflicting interest: the university's *liability*:

> *When researchers are employed by a University, the institution*
> *may, in some circumstances, be liable for research conducted by*
> *these researchers. In the interests of protecting* them and itself,
> *the University provides insurance protection for those research*
> *projects which receive ethics approval. [emphasis added]*[2]

These words built the appearance of institutional conflict of interest into the policy. From whom was the policy protecting researchers and the university? Instead of emphasizing the protection of research participants, the phrase opened the door to the university protecting itself *from* research participants in the name of preventing negative publicity and minimizing the university's liability.

The third key feature was the way the policy allowed the committee "to establish its own operating and appeal procedures." In practice, this procedural flexibility rolled out the red carpet to extra-ethical criteria.

Its architects might have built some degree of independence into an appeal procedure as a check and balance against an administratively chaired and appointed committee. At SFU, however, they kept the appeal process in the administrative realm. If the VP-research did not sit as chair of the ethics committee, then the policy specified that s/he was the sole mechanism of appeal if the committee declined to approve a research protocol. If the VP-research did sit as chair, then the VP-academic would hear the appeal.

To top it off, the policy left resolution of any disagreement about interpretation of the ethics policy to the president, whose ruling was "final." In the case of graduate students, who have no mechanism for grieving the decisions of faculty and administrators outside the collective bargaining agreement for teaching assistants, the decision really would have been final, unless they had the resources to finance a judicial review. Faculty at least could resort to the grievance procedure in the *Framework Agreement* between SFU faculty and the administration.

SFU Ethics in Action: The ACE-Inhibitor Study

There is evidence in its meeting minutes that the ethics committee began incorporating non-ethical criteria into its decision-making at least as early as January 1994 on a project proposed in 1993 entitled, "Adaptive

Response to Exercise and ACE-Inhibitor in Hypertensive Subjects." A major pharmaceutical company was funding the research.

A memorandum dated July 15, 1993, to the researcher from the SFU research grants officer indicates she circulated the ACE-Inhibitor proposal to all members of the ethics committee for comment prior to their meeting to discuss it. Subsequent minutes show the project received extensive discussion in at least two meetings (in October 1993 and January 1994). This degree of attention to a proposal was unprecedented. An examination of its minutes for the years 1992 through 1997 revealed the ethics committee met as a whole on only eight occasions — not much more than once per year during a period when between 1,000 and 2,000 ethics applications were processed. The Office of the VP-research dealt with all but two of those applications without the ethics committee ever meeting to discuss them; the ACE-Inhibitor study was one of those two.

Part of the reason the ACE-Inhibitor study received the attention it did was because the drug to be tested had a "long and alarming list of side effects" that, according to the pharmaceutical company's own report, included renal failure and death. Ethics committee members expressed concern that neither of these side effects appeared in the experimenter's informed-consent statement, which noted only that, "The drugs do have some side effects." They noted numerous other ethics concerns as well, such as whether the researcher wrote the informed-consent statement in language that was comprehensible to lay subjects, and whether it was sufficiently clear that participation was voluntary, and not part of a medical referral.[3]

While much of the committee's initial discussion emphasized the rights of human subjects,[4] by January 19, 1994, they were considering liability concerns as part of the ethics approval process:

> The Acting Chair asked Dr. [name deleted][5] to describe
> what [name deleted] will do when the physician is away. The
> concern of liability and the use of waivers was also raised. If
> waivers are not used, why not? Dr. [name deleted] replied
> that [name deleted] perceived the Informed Consent form
> to be a form of waiver. The Chair questioned if having a

> *physician two floors away could constitute negligence . . .*
> *The Acting Chair indicated that the Informed Consent*
> *form does not constitute a waiver. If a waiver is not carefully*
> *worded, it could be challenged in a court of law. The Acting*
> *Chair said that the use of a waiver, in this experiment, needs*
> *to be discussed with the University's insurance officer.*[6]

Liability waivers, informed-consent statements as liability waivers, avoiding findings of negligence, insurance coverage — what do these have to do with the ethics policy requirement that "A research proposal must demonstrate that appropriate methods will be used to protect the rights and interests of subjects"? The question had shifted from the ethical issue of "What should be done to ensure that research subjects are protected?" to the liability issue of "What do we have to do to ensure research subjects cannot sue us?" Both are legitimate questions for a university to consider, but there is an appearance of conflict when the committee charged with the responsibility of protecting research participants also is responsible for protecting the university from liability.

Dr. Peter Harmon, the SFU medical officer, is the only ethics committee member recorded as finding the tenor of the discussion problematic. After another member suggested that "the committee needed to talk to the university's lawyer" and the acting chair questioned whether availability of the 9-1-1 emergency number constituted sufficient medical help when a physician was unavailable, the minutes note:

> *Again the committee's medical officer reminded the committee*
> *that this is an experiment. The subjects are coming to SFU as part*
> *of an experiment. This is not the same as paying a membership*
> *at Gold's Gym. Dr. [Name deleted] told the committee that*
> *[referent deleted] has a CPR certificate. Again, the medical*
> *officer said SFU is not in the medical field, yet is about to embark*
> *in medical research. Are these safeguards adequate?*

Harmon consistently expressed concern about protecting research participants rather than dressing up liability as ethics. Either way, the discussion surrounding the ACE-Inhibitor proposal shows that the inter-mingling of research participant protection and liability considerations was already occurring when Ogden's case landed on the VP-research's desk six months later.

The Absolute Subordination of Ethics to Law

Even before the coroner released his findings, the VP-research — a physi-cist with no expertise in social research — set about re-writing the ethics policy to address the problem he saw subpoenas posing. Rather than "threats that would undermine research confidentiality, the integrity of research and academic freedom," the VP-research saw the problem as "researchers who make unlimited guarantees of confidentiality." Accordingly, he designed the policy changes he brought to the ethics com-mittee before Ogden's case was resolved to force researchers to limit their confidentiality pledges.

A few weeks after Ogden appeared in Coroner's Court — but before the Vancouver coroner made a decision about Ogden's assertion of researcher-participant privilege — the VP-research placed "limited confidentiality" on the agenda of the meeting scheduled for September 9, 1994.

Although the ethics policy required that the VP-research appoint six faculty members to the Committee, the meeting minutes reveal he had appointed only three members at that time, only two of whom attended the meeting. Although he had not properly constituted the committee and did not have a quorum, the chair forged ahead. Under agenda item four, "Limited Confidentiality Issues," the minutes reported:

> The Committee reviewed the issues raised in the types of cases in which information gathered from subjects in a research project is about activities that are potentially in violation of criminal or civil law. The question was raised as to what the Ethics Committee can do to protect the interests of the subjects, the researcher and the University.
>
> It was agreed that in cases where it can be foreseen that the researchers may not legally be in a position to ensure confidentiality to their subjects, these researchers must

be required to provide only limited confidentiality in the wording of the consent form. It was recognized that limited confidentiality might serve to discourage participation of some subjects, and conceivably even prevent the research from taking place at all due to lack of subjects. Nevertheless, it was agreed that causing the researchers to provide limited confidentiality in appropriate cases would protect the subjects, the University, and the researchers.

Action

A question #9 will be added to the checklist as follows: Does information to be obtained from subjects include information on activities that are or may be in violation of criminal or civil law? Yes or no.

Requests for Ethics approval which give an affirmative answer to question #9 on the checklist will be provided to the full Committee for approval.[7]

Up to 1997 when one of us submitted an application, we do not know how many ethics applicants answered affirmatively to question nine. Apparently, there were several applications from criminology. However, there is no indication in subsequent minutes that the ethics committee met to discuss any of them, as the new procedures required; they were handled by the office of VP-research on behalf of the committee and, in turn, by an administrative assistant on behalf of the VP-research.

The Limited-Confidentiality Consent Statement

More than a year passed before the committee revisited its decision to impose limited confidentiality at SFU. On November 23, 1995, policy revisions again were on the agenda. At this meeting, the Committee decided to introduce a "limited-confidentiality consent statement."

According to an account that VP-research Clayman published years later in the *Simon Fraser News* in response to criticism of the ethics committee's actions,[8] "The university research ethics review committee approved a large number of proposed changes to the policy in 1995." Given that the committee met only once in 1995 (on November 23),

Clayman presumably was referring to that meeting. Item six concerned research on illegal activities:

> 6. *Consent Form – "Illegal" activities.*
> *This is a very sensitive issue. One Committee member will forward to the Chair an example of what is used by the Faculty of Education where disclosure is required by law. An example of wording to use when subjects report information about activities that may be in violation of civil or criminal law will be incorporated into the draft policy and the consent form.*
> *Action: Dr. Horvath will supply wording used in psychological interviews.*

Under item nine, "Approval of Revised Policy R 20.01," the minutes concluded:

> *After seeking Dr. Corrado's opinion on the wording of the "illegal activities" paragraph on the Consent Form, the Chair will incorporate all these agreed upon changes and distribute the Draft Policy to the university community to seek out comments or concerns. The goal is to launch this policy in 1996.[9]*

The wording Dr. Horvath provided shortly after the meeting was as follows:

> *Any information that is obtained during this study will be kept confidential to the full extent permitted by law . . . However, it is possible that, as a result of legal action, the researcher may be required to divulge information obtained in the course of this research to a court or other legal body.*

We do not know what interaction occurred between criminologist Dr. Ray Corrado and the VP-research following this meeting, but we do know that Corrado resigned from the ethics committee shortly thereafter — the next meeting was on June 11, 1996, at which time the secretary recorded his resignation in the minutes. Corrado has since told us that both he and Harmon held that the SFU community should discuss *all* major wording changes, such as the change from "confidentiality" to "limited confidentiality," and that Senate and the Board of Governors should approve them *before* they were put into effect. This is consistent with a first-hand account of the meeting prepared some time later by Dr. Philip Hanson from the Department of Philosophy.

Hanson was a new appointee to the ethics committee at the time it was discussing the limited-confidentiality protocol. The first meeting Hanson attended was in December 1994. A second meeting was not scheduled until November 1995. Prior to the November 1995 meeting, the secretary provided Hanson with a copy of the September 9, 1994, minutes, the meeting at which the VP-research had first discussed "causing the researcher to provide limited confidentiality."

In December 1997 when we met with the committee to discuss the limited-confidentiality consent statement, Hanson wrote a memo describing the November 1995 meeting at which the committee adopted that statement:

> It is worth noting that the Nov. '95 meeting was poorly
> attended, barely a quorum,[10] and on the issue of revisions
> to the consent form wording discussion was dominated by
> the one person on the committee who already had a strong
> and confident opinion on the matter. That person was not
> me. Whereas most of the committee members come from
> departments whose members make extensive use of the offices
> of the Ethics Review Committee, I do not, and had been
> largely unaware of its procedures until my appointment to the
> committee, and had no basis in experience for strong opinions
> about policy matters. Why was I asked to be on the committee
> in the first place? Presumably because as a philosopher I know
> something about ethical theory. But actually applying ethical
> theory to concrete situations also requires a familiarity with

*the salient complexities of those situations, a familiarity that
I didn't as yet have with respect to the issues of informed
consent and confidentiality. I say all this to underscore that
the committee chair got rather limited, one-sided input
from the committee that day, and I am partly to blame,
because I was unaware at the time of, e.g., some of the legal
ramifications of the consent form wording.*

Indeed, its champions appeared to be either oblivious to or unconcerned about the broader ramifications of limited confidentiality and its threat to academic freedom.

CHAPTER VI
Ogden v. SFU

Testing the University's Contractual Obligations

Ogden did not accept SFU abandoning research confidentiality and academic freedom. Nor did he accept the university's decision as the last word on its obligations to graduate students. The university had imposed certain requirements on him — to undertake a thesis, to submit a proposal for ethics review, and so on — and Ogden had met those requirements to the letter. In his mind, the university had implicitly entered into a contractual obligation with him as a graduate student, in which case SFU should defend him when the Coroner challenged the university policies that required him to do what he did. Ogden resolved to hold the university accountable. His legal fees totalled $11,367.38. President Stubbs' offer of $2,000 on "compassionate" grounds left Ogden with a legal bill of $9,367.38. The maximum allowable award in British Columbia's Small Claims Court in 1996 was $10,000, thus making it the perfect venue in which to sue SFU for breach of contract.

Although all the rules of evidence that govern all courts apply in Small Claims Court, because of the relatively small sums of money at issue, it is set up to help plaintiffs represent themselves. An added benefit of bringing the case forward was that it gave Ogden, who represented himself, the power to subpoena Dean of Graduate Studies/VP-research/Ethics Committee Chair Bruce Clayman and SFU President John Stubbs and ask them to explain their decision to abandon his research participants in Coroner's Court.

Eileen Vanderburgh of Alexander Holburn Beaudin & Lang of Vancouver represented SFU. She initiated two actions early in the process. First, she told Ogden that, as his claim was baseless, SFU would give up any claim for costs if he withdrew the action before the trial began.

Ogden declined.

Ironically, her second action was to move to have the Stubbs subpoena quashed. The court denied this motion. The president would have to testify.

The Trial: Day One

The trial began on June 20, 1996, with Judge Daniel Steinberg presiding. Steinberg made clear Ogden's procedural obligations from the start:

> Let me explain the ground rules . . . I have read the materials
> that are in the file, including all the email and letters that
> have gone back and forth. The case will be decided only on the
> evidence that's in court.[1]

Steinberg began by emphasizing the difference between moral and legal claims:

> THE COURT: . . . what might properly be done is often
> different from what a legal obligation . . . is. Much of your
> pleadings seem to say they had a moral responsibility or they
> ought to have, in the name of the defence of academic freedom
> . . . supported me financially . . .
>
> . . . this is a courtroom, which has a much more narrow
> focus than life in general . . .[2]

The distinction Steinberg affirmed is at the very heart of this book, i.e., there is an important distinction between what is ethical and what is legal; they overlap to varying degrees, but are distinct. Ogden was facing a situation where he had an ethical obligation to maintain the confidence of his research participants, but where the law might demand that he give it up. When ethics and law conflict, what do universities expect researchers to do? Do researchers have an obligation to do what they think is ethical, or must they always do what the law commands? Does a university have the right to *require* its researchers to take one or the other of those positions, or must the university leave it to their consciences?

There was little dispute with respect to the facts of the case. The primary exception arose during cross-examination about what came to be referred to as Ogden's "waiver" letter, i.e., the letter in which Ogden said "I accept full responsibility for any decision I make with respect to the sharing of information . . ." SFU seized on this line, arguing that it constituted Ogden waiving his right, assuming he had one, to legal assistance.

> THE COURT: I guess the problem is it doesn't sound very ambiguous . . . It just says, "I take full responsibility for any decision. If there's any fallout from any decision I make, that's my responsibility."
>
> MR. OGDEN: That certainly wasn't my intent as a twenty-odd-year-old researcher that was attempting to follow the university's rules . . .
>
> Certainly, I wasn't intending to waive any right to anything. I was merely trying to be honest with the university and I was engaging in a process that I believe existed not just to protect research subjects, but also to afford the equivalent level of protection to researchers . . . I was looking to the university for guidance . . . why they have an Ethics Committee is to provide guidance in research.
>
> It is not the custom of the university . . . to grant approval to projects if they believe that a waiver or a release has been given to them. That would undermine the very purpose of an ethics review committee . . .
>
> MS. VANDERBURGH: . . . Your Honour, I don't know how this witness can testify as to the policy of the university.
>
> MR. OGDEN: I have a letter —[3]

The letter to which Ogden referred was a signed and witnessed affidavit that ethics committee member Dr. Peter Harmon prepared because he was unable to attend court. Although the ethics committee as a whole never considered Ogden's proposal — the chair, Dr. William Leiss, signed it on the Committee's behalf — Ogden had consulted Harmon about the ethics of his research while preparing his proposal. Because of this interaction, his membership on the ethics committee when Ogden submitted his proposal, and his independence from Ogden's supervisory committee, Harmon was in unique position to shed light on the meaning of the phrase that SFU was now portraying as a waiver of liability.

Unfortunately, Ogden discovered too late that Harmon would be unavailable to appear to testify. The affidavit was a last-ditch effort to make the court aware of Harmon's interpretation of Ogden's letter. However, because of the lateness of its preparation, Ogden's legal obligation to divulge all evidence to SFU's lawyer in advance so that she could prepare SFU's defence meant that she would have had to agree to submit the affidavit into evidence. She did not agree.

Although the adversarial system is designed to ascertain truth, the debate over the letter is a reminder that trials are complex battles where competing principles must be resolved, and where truth is sometimes the victim. In this instance, SFU's lawyers argued that Ogden should have submitted the affidavit to them because of the perfectly reasonable principle that a defendant is entitled to a full opportunity for defense. Claimants should not ambush defendants with surprise evidence. SFU's lawyer did what any good lawyer would do in these circumstances: use the rules of court to prevent the affidavit's admission. In this instance, the process of obeying law compromised the truth.

Day Two

On the second day, Ogden called several witnesses, including VP-research and Ethics Committee Chair Bruce Clayman. Because of his multiple roles and centrality to the issues that Ogden's subpoena raised, Clayman's testimony is worth examining for the insight it provides into the way the administration conceptualized the issues.

Ogden understood the issues to consist of living up to the ethical standards established by his discipline and SFU policy, fulfilling the researcher's duty to protect research participants from harm, and defending academic freedom. If the SFU administration shared some of these concerns, they were not the ones it prioritized. When Ogden asked Clayman whether the original decision not to provide him with any financial support reflected a consideration of the ethical probity of his research, Clayman responded that it did not. When Judge Steinberg inquired what principles the administration considered, Clayman responded:

> *The primary consideration had to do with the overall welfare of the university and that, of course, included the research enterprise, but it also included the potential financial and other liability that the university would incur if it were to offer unlimited support to every student researcher . . . you have to look at, as we did, look at the specifics of the case. Mr. Ogden provided what we considered to be a very clear acceptance of responsibility for the outcome of exactly the scenario that had played out, and in that context we felt that our responsibility was, well, initially zero in terms of dollars and eventually a modest sum of dollars. But it doesn't mean that a similar case with slightly different detail wouldn't have been decided differently.*

When asked what other consideration played a role, Clayman responded:

> *[I]n some of the written material that we have, the possibility of, well, what I will say crudely as bad press for the university and being associated in the public mind using public funds to support a strong advocate of a very controversial issue.*[4]

In sum, the administration's main concerns were liability and image management. Ogden next asked Clayman about the puzzling statement from his email to President Stubbs asserting, "The committee, of course, did not approve his withholding information from the court or the coroner, so I don't think there is any legal liability on our part." Ogden asked whether the ethics committee's approval came with the understanding that he would defy a court order for disclosure in order to protect research participant identities. When Clayman responded that the proposal "was silent on the question," Judge Steinberg interrupted:

> THE COURT: *Well, just a second. If we look at that paragraph in the appendix to the proposal that deals with absolute confidentiality and goes on to talk about "the researcher will advise participants of the possibility of court action, ordering the researcher to produce a list of participant names," when I read those two sentiments, it seems to me that there is only one way to reconcile those, and that is to defy a court order . . . [I]s there any other way to reconcile absolute confidentiality with the possibility the court will order the researcher to produce the names, which is a breach of confidentiality? The fact that a court orders something doesn't actually make it happen . . . [I]s there anywhere any statement that he would comply with the court order? . . .*
>
> DR. CLAYMAN: *No, there isn't.*
>
> THE COURT: *Well, then is there any other way to reconcile those two statements that are within the same paragraph, other than defiance, other than by the implication of defiance of a court order?*
>
>   . . .
>
> DR. CLAYMAN: *Part of my problem is that I cannot read what was going on in Bill Leiss's mind when he reviewed the whole thing.*
>
> THE COURT: *I'm just looking at the wording.*
>
> DR. CLAYMAN: *And I'm not disagreeing with you.*[5]

It is not clear how knowing what was in former VP-research and Ethics Committee Chair Bill Leiss's mind would help in this situation. Surely, the answer lay in the ethics policy that was in place when Ogden submitted his research proposal. That policy made no mention of limits to confidentiality.

Day Three

President Stubbs was the only person to appear on the third and last day of the trial. His recollections about the administrators' meetings confirmed liability and image management had been their main considerations. A primary consideration was how the media would portray SFU if it defended Ogden:

> DR. STUBBS: *Well the threat ultimately to the university is that we end up . . . taking a position where we're supporting someone who is not willing to give information that is required . . . in a court proceeding and so the university could be perceived as taking a position that is . . . challenging the legal process . . . that kind of publicity is something that doesn't . . . necessarily do the university a lot of good.*[6]

With the testimony finished, all that remained was closing arguments and the judge's decision. Judge Steinberg was non-committal about when his ruling might be expected, suggesting that it might take some time. He encouraged both sides to use the intervening period to try to find some basis for settling out of court. The judge concluded that if there was no settlement, that the case raised

> *a problem that deserves and will get some close scrutiny. There's some pretty important issues . . . especially in the modern day where things are increasingly litigious, and researchers and people that associate with universities are getting increasingly exposed and so are universities getting increasingly exposed, and there's a very real question about academic freedoms and protections.*[7]

Indeed, the issues went to the heart of what universities stand for and the role they play in generating knowledge and debate in a democratic society. No one would have guessed at the time that it would be more than two years until Judge Steinberg released his decision.

CHAPTER VII
The Federal Government's Research Ethics Agenda

Developing a Canadian Research Ethics Code

As Judge Steinberg retired to consider his ruling and the debates over limited confidentiality at SFU continued, changes were brewing concurrently on the national scene that would have implications for SFU. In 1996, the federal government released the first draft of a policy statement on research with human subjects. The Tri-Council Working Group (TCWG)[1] wrote the draft, which would apply to all research involving human research participants in Canada and other institutions that wished to receive funding from any of the three national granting agencies, i.e., the Medical Research Council (MRC),[2] the Social Sciences and Humanities Research Council (SSHRC), and the Natural Sciences and Engineering Research Council (NSERC).

The TCPS First Draft

In March of 1996, "Approximately 14,000 copies of a first draft *Code* were distributed to every Council-funded institution and to all the academic groups that could be identified."[3] Reactions to the draft *Code of Ethical Conduct for Research Involving Humans* were extensive and vigorous. TCWG chair Jean Joly later noted that:

> We received over 250 responses, totalling 3,000 pages, to
> the draft document published in 1996. Some were signed by
> multiple authors, including entire university departments. We

> *also received comments from private industry, the Pharmaceutical*
> *Manufacturers Association of Canada, from governments, and*
> *from almost any other type of group you can imagine.*[4]

Of particular relevance to this book was the TCWG draft code's discussion of the relationship between ethics and law. At one point the TCWG appeared to understand that law and ethics constitute distinct, albeit overlapping, normative systems:

> *Justice is the ethical principle the law aims to serve. Conduct*
> *is not necessarily ethical because it is legal. Similarly, conduct*
> *that can be justified ethically is not necessarily legal.*[5]

However, a later section on "privacy and confidentiality" was ambiguous about what the TCWG envisioned should happen in the event that ethics and law conflicted. The TCWG did anticipate the possibility that legal authorities might challenge research confidentiality:

> *Subjects should be told of any significant shortcomings in*
> *privacy and confidentiality safeguards (including, for example,*
> *the right of authorities to subpoena research records).*[6]

But was the TCWG imposing a course of action or merely outlining a possibility? In a segment dealing with "compulsory reporting," the TCWG stated:

> *Subjects must be made aware during the consent process*
> *that information will be kept confidential except when*
> *required by law.*[7]

Was this assertion specific to situations where there was well-defined law, as in the case of mandatory reporting statutes, or did the TCWG intend to impose it as a more general requirement? The similarities were sufficiently close to the SFU ethics committee's new policy of limited confidentiality that Palys confronted it directly:

These assertions are similar to SFU research policy R20.01,
which was formulated immediately following the controversy
over Russel Ogden's M.A. thesis. Those researchers whose
proposals are now flagged because they deal with "deviant"
subcultures . . . are now required to tell research participants
that . . . it is possible that, as a result of legal action, the
researcher may be required to divulge information obtained in
the course of this research to a court or other legal body . . .

That both the TCWG and SFU would seem to make
ethical desiderata subservient to law suggests the TCWG might
have joined SFU in advising Russel Ogden to cooperate fully
with the court, even though doing so clearly would have put
Ogden's research participants at risk, would have undermined
the trust that respondents have for researchers in general, and
effectively would have closed the door for such marginalized
persons ever to have a voice through the medium of research.[8]

SFU's treatment of Ogden also highlighted the problem of institutional
conflicts of interest. Two points seemed important to make. First was the
"protecting the university" clause in SFU's ethics policy. Instead of protecting research participants, this proviso opened the door to decision-
making that would protect researchers and the university from research participants.[9] A second and related point concerned the relationship between
a university's administration and its ethics committee. Palys questioned

whether senior university administrators are appropriate
heads of REBs, since, in my understanding of "conflict of
interest," many of the constraints of their roles (such as
risk management) may well conflict with the appropriate
execution of their ethical responsibilities broadly defined. My
own suggestion is that there be some separation of roles in
which REBs and their members are separate and apart from
the university administration, with the sort of independent
decision-making status that is accorded offices such as
Ombudsperson.[10]

Faced with a barrage of critique from researchers across the country, the TCWG withdrew to digest the feedback and prepare a second draft.

The TCPS Second Draft

The TCWG submitted the second draft to the granting council presidents in May 1997. With respect to the ethics and law of research confidentiality, two aspects of the 1997 draft are noteworthy. First, there was no clear statement of the relationship between ethics and law. Legal standards were mentioned frequently in sections pertaining to biomedical topics, but were absent in the more general portions of the draft. It included a straightforward statement of the importance of confidentiality to research and of the importance of maintaining privacy and confidentiality. However, there was no mention of potential third-party challenges other than to affirm that information belonged to the research participant; researchers should not share it without the research participant's consent:

> When a research participant confides in a researcher,
> unless laws are in place to protect the public interest (e.g.,
> mandatory reporting of child abuse), the researcher is
> obliged not to share this information with others without
> the participant's agreement. Breaches of confidentiality may
> result in irreparable harm to the trust relationship between
> the researcher and the research participant as well as to other
> individuals and collectivities.[11]

A second encouraging aspect of the 1997 draft was its elaboration of "institutional conflict of interest":

> The REB must act independently from the parent organization.
> Therefore, institutions must respect the autonomy of the REB
> and ensure that the REB has the appropriate financial and
> administrative independence to fulfill its primary duties.
> Situations may arise where the parent organization has a
> strong interest in seeing a project approved before all ethical
> questions are resolved. As the body mandated to maintain high

> *ethical standards, it is essential that the REB maintain an*
> *arms-length relationship with the parent organization to avoid*
> *a conflict of interest, real or apparent.*[12]

If this definition of institutional conflict of interest survived the process of subsequent revisions, the days that the same individual could be both vice-president of research and chair of a research ethics committee were numbered.

As a commentator on the 1997 draft, Palys was ambivalent.[13] On the one hand, the idea of federal authorities intervening in research through the creation of a one-size-fits-all federal ethics code represented bureaucratic overkill and a threat to the ethical diversity and autonomy of academic disciplines. As US historian Louis Menand ironically and prophetically (given the disciplinary background of SFU's VP-research) argued in his edited anthology on academic freedom:

> *Academic freedom, as it is now structured, depends crucially*
> *on the autonomy and integrity of the disciplines. For it is the*
> *departments, and the disciplines to which they belong, that*
> *constitute the spaces in which rival scholarly and pedagogical*
> *positions are negotiated. Academic freedom not only protects*
> *sociology professors from the interference of trustees and public*
> *officials in the exercise of their jobs as teachers and scholars; it*
> *protects them from physics professors as well. It mandates that*
> *decisions about what counts as good work in sociology shall be*
> *made by sociologists. And, practically speaking, "sociologists"*
> *means the department of sociology. That is the self-governing*
> *professional community.*[14]

On the other hand, if the production of a federal code was inevitable, then at least the changes from the 1996 to 1997 draft showed the TCWG was attempting to address the critical feedback it had received from the social science and humanities communities. Weighing the various advantages and disadvantages, Palys's commentary concluded, "Thanks, but no thanks," a sentiment that, according to Michael McDonald, a co-author of the 1997 draft, reflected the general reaction of Canada's social science and humanities research communities, which still saw the second draft as espousing a singularly biomedical ethos.[15]

Notwithstanding these reservations, for better or worse the TCWG had fulfilled its mandate. In May 1997, it submitted the second draft to the funding council presidents, who apparently were eager to approve and implement it.

CHAPTER VIII
Justice for Ogden

The School of Criminology Speaks Out

Up to this point, the narrative on Ogden's research at SFU has focused almost exclusively on his relationship with the SFU administration. What was the School of Criminology's reaction to the subpoena? As soon as it learned of the threat to research confidentiality, the school sent a letter to the SFU administration calling for its support.

Penned by then-director Neil Boyd on October 11, 1994, the letter to the dean of Graduate Studies read in part:

> As faculty members of the School of Criminology, we wish to
> express our strong support for Russel Ogden in his attempt to protect
> the confidentiality of his research subjects. We strongly endorse the
> right and duty of researchers to give guarantees of confidentiality
> to those who participate in criminological research which focuses
> on behaviours that may be considered criminal under Canadian
> law. We also wish to place on record our view that such research is
> essential to the academic enterprise of criminology.[1]

The letter also called on the university to support Ogden:

> As a graduate student who prepared a research protocol that
> received the university's ethical approval, he is accordingly

entitled to the strong support of the university in his principled
refusal to reveal the identities of those research subjects
to whom he gave promises of confidentiality . . . [S]uch
guarantees of confidentiality constitute a vital component
of many types of criminological research; indeed, without
such guarantees, the ability to conduct research into illegal
behaviours would be severely impaired and society would be
deprived of knowledge that may be vital to the evolution of
public policy.[2]

Boyd and sixteen[3] of the twenty criminology faculty members at that time signed the letter, and copied it to President Stubbs, Dean of Arts Evan Alderson, and Ogden.

Colleagues in Arms

Neither of us had been directly involved with Ogden as he went through the process of completing his MA in the School of Criminology. Neither of us instructed him in a graduate-level course and neither was on his thesis committee. We listened to updates on his situation at faculty meetings, and signed the school's letter urging the university to support Ogden's defence of his research participants, academic freedom, and research confidentiality.

Our more intense involvement in Ogden's case and our resistance to SFU's regime of limited confidentiality began a few years later, almost by accident. Palys teaches research methods courses in the School of Criminology. During 1996 and 1997, he taught Advanced Research Methods (Criminology 320), an undergraduate lecture course on qualitative and quantitative research methods. As always, his lectures included a section on research ethics, but in this version of the course, Palys used Ogden's case as an exemplar of how to defend research confidentiality and to lament how the university administration had fumbled the ball when it failed to support him in court.

Several students suggested there must be more to the university's position than Palys was letting on, because no university could be so short-sighted and unethical as to cut one of its researchers — and his research participants — loose when so much was at stake. They asked Palys for further details about the university's rationale. However, Palys had not attended any of the court sessions and did not have copies of the trial transcripts. Consequently, he wrote to VP-research Bruce Clayman and SFU President John Stubbs relaying to them his students' questions and inviting them to attend his class to explain their side of the story. On behalf of both him and Stubbs, Clayman declined the invitation.

As we explain later, in 1997 Stubbs resigned as president over a controversy that had no direct connection with the Ogden situation, but rather with its mishandling of the SFU harassment policy. The incumbent vice-president Harbour Centre and Development, Dr. Jack Blaney, who was nearing retirement, agreed to act as SFU president *pro tem* until he retired, during which time SFU would launch a formal search for a new president. It was thus Blaney who presented the 1997 SFU Sterling Prize in Support of Controversy to John Lowman for his research on prostitution law in Canada. Lowman used the occasion to read an open letter to the president encouraging him to reconsider the university's treatment of Ogden. Published in the *Simon Fraser News*[4] under the heading "Pay Legal Fees, Urges Professor," the letter stated:

> *In 1994 Russel Ogden, an MA student in criminology studying assisted suicide, was subpoenaed to appear at a Coroner's inquest into the suicide of a woman suffering from AIDS. He was faced with the prospect of being held in contempt if he did not divulge the identity of certain research subjects. As he was determined to protect the confidentiality of his subjects — an absolute requirement of SFU ethics policy at that time — Russel could easily have ended up in prison. His research and subsequent legal defence of it won him the 1995 Sterling Prize for controversy.*
>
> *In a precedent-setting case, Coroner Campbell ruled that Russel's research was so important to society that he was not required to disclose his confidential sources. Although the entire academic community would have suffered had he not won this case, SFU paid only a small fraction of Russel's legal expenses. He is now suing the university to reclaim the balance.*

If SFU expects graduate students to abide by its ethics policy, it has an ethical responsibility to support them in cases such as this.

Although a decision on Russel's suit against SFU has not yet been rendered, I request that President Blaney reverse the university's decision, and reimburse in full Russel's legal fees. After all, they were sustained in defending the interests of all researchers working with human subjects. Failing this, I cannot see how any of us can, in good faith, encourage students to apply to SFU graduate programs if we know the university will abandon them when controversy looms.

John Lowman, Criminology (Recipient of the 1997 Sterling Prize for controversy)

Sometimes one chooses one's future, and sometimes events choose it for you. We had been friends and colleagues for many years, but it turned out that our decision to seek justice for Ogden and resist SFU's limited confidentiality regime would result in a collaboration that altered the trajectory of both our careers. Our conception of the subpoena problem at this point was that we could file it in the drawer marked "No-brainer." How much more obvious could it be that SFU's treatment of Ogden was unjust and that the ethics committee's imposition of limited confidentiality was beyond its jurisdiction and a violation of academic freedom? How long could it possibly take to reverse two no-brainers and bring the university back on course?

The VP-Research Reviews the Ogden Decision

President *pro tem* Jack Blaney responded to Lowman's request by asking the VP-research to reconsider the university's position on the Ogden subpoena. The appearance of conflict of interest in the choice of the VP-research to review a decision for which he was largely responsible was conspicuous, to say the least. According to President Stubbs's testimony in Small Claims Court, Clayman was a central member of the group that made the initial decision, largely on his interpretation of the situation and his recommendation. Responding to Lowman's request this way was not the first time, nor would it be the last, that the administration would circle the wagons, restrict decision-making to an administrative in-group, and deflect any call for an independent review.

Even so, much water had passed under the bridge since that day more than three years before when the vice-presidents and former president Stubbs first decided to offer Ogden nothing, followed by the president offering $2,000 on compassionate grounds. If the SFU administration was worried about creating a bottomless pit of legal financing, its fears had not materialized. Ogden's legal fees were $9,367.38 beyond the $2,000 that SFU provided. A drop in the bucket for SFU, it was a large sum for a graduate student. If there were any question about the legal reasonableness of Ogden's claim of privilege — an issue on which the university administration had not sought formal legal advice — surely Ogden's victory in Coroner's Court laid that issue to rest as well.

Ogden's lawsuit against the university the previous year, while still without a decision, would be useful for any reconsideration of the case. The VP-research and president were required to articulate under oath the basis for their decisions, which turned out to be image management and liability. Broader questions about the purpose of the university, the importance of confidentiality, and the ethical treatment of research participants did not figure into their accounts. Might the university reconsider its decision about whether to support Ogden in light of these broader considerations?

It was clear from the Small Claims Court testimony that two of the most significant elements of Clayman's justification for SFU abandoning Ogden — i.e., that the ethics committee had never considered whether Ogden might defy a court order and that Ogden had signed a liability "waiver" — were on shaky ground.

Ogden's questioning of Clayman as to what exactly the phrase "absolutely confidentiality" might have meant to the ethics committee, followed by Judge Steinberg's questioning on that point, led Clayman himself to acknowledge that "absolute confidentiality" must have included defying a court order.

As to whether Ogden had signed a "waiver of liability," although the Small Claims Court ruled that Dr. Harmon's affidavit was inadmissible, there was nothing to stop Clayman from considering it. After all, it was the testimony of a member of the ethics committee who approved Ogden's research.

In October 1997, Clayman met with the two of us for an hour and subsequently completed the review. Clayman's report, addressed to Lowman, delivered the following conclusions:

> I have given very careful consideration to the information provided in these materials and by all parties. Mr. Ogden has performed pioneering, valuable research in an area of importance to society. For that, he has my admiration and respect. However, based on the specifics of the case (as outlined below), I have decided that there is no basis upon which to alter Dr. Stubbs' original decision. I would be happy to discuss this matter again with you and your colleagues if any clarification of my reasons is required.
>
> 1. Mr. Ogden designed his research protocol in 1992, with the expert advice of faculty members in the School of Criminology;
> 2. He was fully aware at that time that he might learn of criminal activities in the course of his research.
> 3. He assured his research subjects, via the subject consent form, of confidentiality and that ". . . no identifying information is required." In Appendix B of his Request for Ethics Approval, he repeated this and added that it would be sufficient that they give him only a pseudonym; he also said there that he would "advise participants of the possibility of court action ordering him to produce a list of participant names."
> 4. He advised subjects via the consent form that, in the event of his learning their identities, such information would be secured in locked storage and that, at the completion of the study, all identifying details would be destroyed.
> 5. He was aware that no privilege exists under Canadian law for communication between researcher and subject.
> 6. He knew that, if he learned the identities of his subjects,

> *he could be requested by Crown Counsel or the Coroner to*
> *cooperate with an investigation.*
>
> 7. *He stated that in such a circumstance he would ". . .*
>   *accept full responsibility for any decision I make with*
>   *respect to the sharing of information." [This is a direct*
>   *quotation from his letter of September 14, 1992,*
>   *addressed to whom it may concern and submitted with*
>   *his application.]*
> 8. *He repeated in that same letter that subjects would be*
>   *under no obligation to disclose identifying information —*
>   *serving to protect both the subjects and himself.*

Before concluding, Clayman reaffirmed the core role of the putative "liability waiver" letter:

> *In Mr. Ogden's testimony before small claims court*
> *and in your discussion with me, it was asserted that*
> *the intent of Mr. Ogden's statement that he would*
> *". . . accept full responsibility for any decision I make*
> *with respect to the sharing of information" was not an*
> *acceptance of any financial responsibility, but of some*
> *other type of responsibility. I cannot accept this and*
> *must interpret "full responsibility" as meaning just that*
> *— especially in view of Mr. Ogden's well-informed,*
> *detailed knowledge of the legal situation and possible*
> *consequences of his actions. Therefore, the legal expenses*
> *that Mr. Ogden incurred without any authorization from*
> *the University remain his responsibility.*[5]

The report was as noteworthy for what it did not say as for what it did. It was as if the debate in the intervening years about the issues the subpoena raised had never happened. The report merely restated the reasoning that the administration had used previously to defend its position. It did not consider any of the arguments about academic freedom and the integrity of research that critics of the university administration found compelling.

Ogden wrote to President Blaney denouncing the report, especially its assertion that he had waived liability.[6]

Faculty in the School of Criminology also voiced their collective displeasure about the process whereby Blaney charged Clayman with reviewing his own decision. Twenty[7] of twenty-three criminology faculty members in residence at the time signed a letter calling for an independent review of the administration's response to the Ogden subpoena.

CHAPTER IX

Challenging Institutional Conflict of Interest

Institutional Conflict of Interest in Action

Clayman's reconsideration of the Ogden decision was disappointing. The dialogue now became more public. A pair of articles appeared in *Simon Fraser News*[1] shortly after Clayman released his review of the Ogden decision — one by Ogden entitled "An Insult to Free Inquiry" the other by Clayman entitled "The Law of the Land."

Ogden's article explained how the ethics committee's limited confidentiality policy would sound the death knell for confidentiality by inviting legal intrusion:

> *The draft policy's escape clause retreats from any commitment [to] protecting confidential data and undermines researchers whose personal ethics lead them to challenge orders to violate confidentiality. If, as per R20.01, research subjects are informed that promises of confidentiality are limited, the door is opened for courts or "legal bodies" seeking access to data to argue that both the researcher and subject anticipated the possibility of forced disclosure and therefore waive any claim to a legal privilege. What appears to be a safety valve could easily lend itself to systematic legal invasions of research subjects' privacy. Can academe afford this kind of blank cheque?*[2]

Clayman's article addressed none of the issues Ogden raised. However, Clayman did explain his law-of-the-land doctrine:

> *It was the belief of the [ethics] committee that, since we live in a society governed by laws, enacted through democratic means, we are obligated to obey those laws or be prepared to suffer the consequences of violating them. It was also the opinion of the committee that researchers may not be prepared or able to bear the legal consequences of offering participants protection beyond that sanctioned by law. In any event, the university itself could not be placed in the situation of requiring one of its employees or students to refuse to comply with lawful process.*
>
> *I quote a committee member, upon considering this issue: "As a public institution, it would be morally and ethically wrong to assume that our research activities are above the law of the land." Hence, the warnings to researchers and to potential subjects of these limits.[3]*

In defending limited confidentiality, Clayman and the committee member misrepresented researchers like Ogden, who do not consider themselves to be above the law. Ogden attended the legal proceedings when required. He understood that he was subject to the law and faced imprisonment if the court were to find him in contempt.

Clayman's statement that no policy can *require* a researcher to disobey a court order and go to jail was another straw man. Neither Ogden nor the two of us had ever argued that universities should require researchers to violate a disclosure order. Our disagreement is with the opposite position, i.e., that a university would require a researcher to violate confidentiality when a court orders him or her to do so, a doctrine that absolutely subjugates ethics to law. All researchers have the ethical obligation to protect research participants to the extent that law permits. It is only in the last instant, when and if all legal efforts fail, that researchers should have the academic freedom to choose between the law-of-the-land and ethics-first approaches to research confidentiality. To require otherwise at SFU would be a violation of the academic freedom clause of the *Framework Agreement* between the administration and the faculty association:

> *1.2 Academic Freedom*
>
> *Academic freedom is the freedom to examine, question, teach and learn, and it involves the right to investigate, speculate and comment without reference to prescribed doctrine, as well as the right to criticize the University, Faculty Association, and society at large. Specifically, academic freedom ensures:*
>
> 1. *Freedom in the conduct of teaching;*
> 2. *Freedom in undertaking research and publishing or making public the results thereof;*
> 3. *Freedom from institutional censorship.*
>
> *. . . The parties agree that they will not infringe or abridge the academic freedom of any member of the academic community.*

The ethics committee's limitation of confidentiality was a doctrine that absolutely subjugated research ethics to law. If imposed on researchers who would subjugate law to research ethics, it thus would comprise a violation of their academic freedom to conduct research "without reference to prescribed doctrine."

Further problems arose with the way the Committee worded the limited-confidentiality consent statement. Neither the VP-research nor the ethics committee acquired a formal legal opinion to find out exactly what the law of the land is when it comes to testimonial privilege — a disturbing omission given that their limited-confidentiality doctrine had the potential to change the face of criminology and other social science disciplines at SFU. When the ethics committee began to require that researchers inform participants that research information provided "will be kept confidential to the full extent permitted by law," the committee never explained to researchers, or asked them to explain to research participants, what exactly that meant. The meaning is anything but self-evident. Did "full extent permitted by law" mean a researcher could throw in the towel as soon as a subpoena arrived? Or did it mean using common law to assert researcher-participant privilege all the way to the Supreme Court of Canada if necessary?

In this light, consider the SFU administration's reaction to the Ogden subpoena. If the university approves a promise to protect confidentiality "to the full extent permitted by law," would it condone a researcher not even contesting a subpoena? Would research participants feel adequately informed if the university promised to protect confidentiality "to the full extent permitted by law" only to have their confidences betrayed without a fight? If the "full extent of the law" is the lowest height the bar should be set, the SFU administration did not even meet its own criterion when it failed to defend Ogden's research participants against the coroner's subpoena, the alleged Ogden liability waiver notwithstanding.

A further problem with the limited-confidentiality protocol was that, when it came to asserting privilege using common law, it had the potential to shoot the researcher in the proverbial foot. Recall that the first Wigmore criterion required that "the communications must originate in a confidence that they will not be disclosed." The ethics committee was requiring researchers to say that, "as a result of legal action, the researcher may be required to divulge information obtained in the course of this research to a court or other legal body." Would this warning undermine the researcher's ability to claim privilege on the research participant's behalf? The court could say, "Participants were told that a court might want the information when they agreed to participate in the research, in which case please disclose it."

Surely, before limiting confidentiality the VP-research and the ethics committee should at least have sought a formal legal opinion about the best way to word any limitations so as not to undermine a researchers' ability to protect confidentiality "to the full extent permitted by law."

But they did not.

When Roles Conflict

If we were to achieve justice for Ogden and a retraction of the "limited confidentiality" policy, the administration would have to address the institutional conflicts of interest that were permeating these issues. In the wake of Clayman's reconsideration of the Ogden decision, we prepared two briefs for President Blaney presenting our view of the problems besetting limited confidentiality.

Under the heading *When Roles Conflict: Research Ethics at SFU,*[4] the first brief outlined how institutional conflicts of interest were continuing to contaminate the administration of the ethics policy, and how they were continuing to impede resolution of the conflict over limited confidentiality. The meeting between President Stubbs and the vice-presidents exemplified the way that liability and image management became the paramount issues. Although the ethics committee chair and VP-research was the same person, only the VP-research persona showed up at the meeting. Judge Steinberg asked if the administration decision not to support Ogden in Coroner's Court was "independent of whether he was completely ethical or not." Clayman replied, "That's correct."[5]

When Roles Conflict asserted that, to prevent the appearance of institutional conflict of interest, university policies should not permit university administrators to chair a research ethics committee. The most recent draft of the TCPS at that time affirmed as much:

> *The REB must act independently from the parent organization.*
> *Therefore, institutions must respect the autonomy of the REB*
> *and ensure that the REB has the appropriate financial and*
> *administrative independence to fulfill its primary duties . . .*
> *As the body mandated to maintain high ethical standards, it*
> *is essential that the REB maintain an arms-length relationship*
> *with the parent organization to avoid a conflict of interest,*
> *real or apparent.*[6]

Palys then reported the response to a question he had asked at a TCWG consultation held at the University of British Columbia to gauge the research community's reaction to its 1997 draft *Code.* Palys explicitly asked the TCWG whether SFU's ethics committee structure — where the VP-research is also the chair of the ethics committee — would qualify as "independent" and an "arms-length relationship." The response was an unequivocal "no." Two members of the VP-research's staff who attended the session heard this response.

A Law unto Itself

Our second brief to President Blaney, *SFU's Ethics Review Committee: A Law unto Itself*,[7] argued that the VP-research-chaired ethics committee was single-handedly rewriting university policy in a manner that went far beyond its jurisdiction. In the process, the committee was undermining researchers' ability to protect research participants, making it impossible for some researchers to follow their disciplinary ethics codes, and violating academic freedom.

The VP-research insisted that the changes to the ethics review process were merely procedural and not substantive. We countered that the changes produced a regime of administration by fiat. *Law unto Itself* argued that if the changes were merely procedural, they would not affect

1. the type of research that is viable;
2. a researcher's ability to comply with the ethics policy requirement that they "adhere to the ethical norms and codes of conduct appropriate to their respective disciplines";
3. a researcher's ability to adhere to the ethics policy expectation that researchers and the members of the ethics committee respect "the cultural values and sense of propriety of the persons who are asked to participate in research"; and
4. the type of research that can be approved.

With respect to the viability of particular types of study, crime and justice researchers talk to persons on both sides of the law who are engaged in illegal or stigmatized behaviour. While both criminals and law enforcers are often willing to share their experiences with researchers, their biggest concern is being "outed," which could result in their being either fired for their on-the-job behaviour, or prosecuted because they have disclosed their own criminal behaviour. These participants take "confidentiality as limited by law" to be no guarantee at all. Researchers are supposed to be motivated by their desire to understand a particular phenomenon, not to be surreptitious agents for the police or other state authorities.

With regard to disciplinary standards, we asserted that the limited-confidentiality doctrine places some researchers in a catch-22 where they would be required to violate that portion of the SFU research ethics policy that stated, "There is a professional responsibility of researchers to adhere to the ethical norms and codes of conduct appropriate to their respective disciplines." When the ethics committee imposed limited confidentiality, the American Sociological Association's ethical code of conduct held, "Confidential information provided by research participants must be treated as such by sociologists, even when this information enjoys no legal protection or privilege and legal force is applied." The same sentence appears in the *Code of Ethics* of the Academy of Criminal Justice Sciences. Limiting confidentiality *a priori* required criminologists to violate the ethical codes they are obliged to observe.

We held that the ethics committee's limited-confidentiality policy violated the existing SFU ethics policy dictum that "The purpose of ethics review of research is to consider the risks to physical and psychological well-being, *and the cultural values and sense of propriety of the persons who are asked to participate* in and/or be the subjects of research" [emphasis added]. When it changed the informed-consent form, did the ethics committee consider how police officers and offender populations' cultural values and sense of propriety might shape the research enterprise? In both cultures, "ratting" or "snitching" on a person with whom you are in a relationship of trust is a serious offence, the commission of which could have dire consequences for the health of the researcher, and for the integrity of research more generally.

Ironically, by following the ethics committee's requirement to limit confidentiality, researchers in criminology and sociology would place themselves in the position of violating other aspects of the policy, thus creating the situation where the ethics committee would reject research that previously it had approved.

Informing Ourselves about Law

Law unto Itself marked the first time that we had ventured into the legal aspects of limited confidentiality beyond emphasizing the importance of the Wigmore criteria for protecting research participants. Because the VP-research and ethics committee did not commission a formal legal opinion in that regard, we started scouring the legal and social science literature for references to cases where research confidentiality ended up in court.

Among our first discoveries was lawyer Mary Marshall's article, "When Is a Secret Not a Secret?"[8] The article drew attention to the Supreme Court of Canada's decision in *R. v. Gruenke*,[9] which involved Adele Gruenke, a 22-year-old reflexologist accused of murdering a client. At trial, she testified that her client had sexually harassed and then assaulted her, at which point she killed him in self-defence. However, in a conversation with her pastor at the church she attended, Gruenke admitted that the Crown's theory that she and her boyfriend had planned the murder was correct. The Crown called the pastor as a witness, but Gruenke's lawyer objected, arguing that priest-penitent privilege made this evidence inadmissible.

The case made its way to the Supreme Court of Canada, which decided that, while there was no class privilege for priest-penitent communications, there might be circumstances in which it would recognize a privilege if the claimant could demonstrate that the communications in question met the four Wigmore criteria. Upon examining the circumstances, the court concluded there was no shared expectation of confidentiality between Gruenke and her pastor: the conversation did not happen in a confessional booth and there was no special statement on either person's part at the beginning of the conversation to the effect that "this is strictly confidential." The claim for privilege failed because it did not meet Wigmore criterion one, i.e., that "the communications must originate in a confidence that they will not be disclosed." In the words of Chief Justice Lamer:

> *Leaving aside the other components of the Wigmore test, it is absolutely crucial that the communications originate with an expectation of confidentiality . . . Without this expectation of confidentiality, the raison d'être of the privilege is missing.*

The lesson that lawyer Mary Marshall drew from this decision was that, in order to meet Wigmore criterion one, "You should begin your discussion with the statement, 'This must remain absolutely confidential.'"[10]

The implications of this legal opinion for the preservation of researcher-participant confidentiality were significant. It emphasized our concern about the SFU limited-confidentiality consent statement's proviso that "It is possible as a result of legal action, the researcher may be required to divulge information obtained in the course of this research to a court or other legal body." By imposing use of this statement, was the ethics committee effectively throwing research participants to the wolves by ensuring failure on Wigmore criterion one? Was it only because he guaranteed "absolute confidentiality" that Ogden had met the requirements of that criterion?

Law unto Itself argued that the VP-research's law-of-the-land rhetoric was based on a fundamental misunderstanding of some of the ethical and legal issues at stake:

> *Dr. Clayman seems to regard the law as a monolith, an*
> *inactive mass against which one must unquestioningly bow.*
> *Agreed, there is no statute in Canada recognizing researcher-*
> *participant privilege (i.e., there is no absolute protection),*
> *but there is more to law than statutes. And that is why*
> *the outcome of Mr. Ogden's case in Coroner's Court is so*
> *important to the defense of researcher-participant privilege*
> *and academic freedom. Why does Dr. Clayman persist in*
> *taking the position that law does not recognize researcher-*
> *participant privilege? Thanks to Mr. Ogden and no thanks*
> *to Drs. Clayman and Stubbs the "law of the land" is that the*
> *Wigmore test does apply to social science research, as will be*
> *determined on a case by case basis. Is it not in the interests*
> *of SFU to ensure that the test is applied vigorously when*
> *the research enterprise and the rights of participants (which*
> *according to Dr. Clayman's testimony in Small Claims Court,*
> *are the two main responsibilities of the Ethics Committee) are*
> *at stake?*
>
> *. . . Dr. Clayman believes that researchers should obey the*
> *law. He seems to have lost sight of the fact that Mr. Ogden*
> *maintained the confidentiality of his research participants* and
> *he obeyed the law.*[11]

Given the way the VP-research was digging in, an increasingly confrontational approach seemed warranted.

Temperature Rising

In its next issue, the *Simon Fraser News* followed Ogden and Clayman's articles by one of ours entitled "A Law unto Itself,"[12] which summarized the points we made in our two briefs to President Blaney. Shortly thereafter journalist Charlie Smith published an article on the SFU ethics debacle in the *Georgia Straight*.[13] Smith's article, "SFU Criminologists Want Research Confidentiality Back,"[14] reviewed the Ogden story and the numerous problems with the ethics committee's imposition of limited confidentiality.

In a reply to Palys and Lowman, President Blaney declared that his decision to refer the Ogden re-consideration to Dr. Clayman was "appropriate" and that he was not prepared to overturn that decision. Regarding the concerns we had voiced about the ethics committee's imposition of limited confidentiality, Blaney confirmed that, while the ethics policy would soon come under Senate review, "Until then, Policy R20.01, as approved by the SFU Board of Governors remains in effect." This statement resolved little, given our argument that the ethics committee's imposition of limited confidentiality had substantively changed the SFU research-ethics policy. Blaney noted that a meeting had been scheduled for us to meet with the ethics committee. He stated, "I am confident that the members of the committee will give careful consideration to your views and take whatever action is appropriate."

As the administration was digging in, we approached the SFU Faculty Association (SFUFA) for assistance, and asked to have a SFUFA observer present at any subsequent meetings we attended with the SFU administration or ethics committee. When SFUFA President Rick Coe and Executive Director David Bell became involved, one of their first steps was to apprise the Canadian Association of University Teachers (CAUT) of the situation unfolding at SFU.

Documents and emails flew back and forth in anticipation of our meeting with the ethics committee. The agenda itself was contentious. Apparently, the VP-research never gave ethics committee members an opportunity to express their views about the Ogden case. We were interested in what they, as researchers, would have to say about the administration's decision to abandon Ogden in Coroner's Court. Accordingly, we sought to have discussion of the university's treatment of Ogden included. Clayman insisted that the ethics committee's view was not relevant to the university's decision about how to respond to the subpoena. Ultimately, the various parties agreed to let the committee determine the meeting agenda.

We reiterated our view that it was inappropriate for the VP-research to remain as chair of the ethics committee in view of his institutional conflict of interest. While the ethics policy in effect at that time empowered the VP-research to chair the committee, it also allowed him to delegate that responsibility to someone else. We suggested that, as an interim measure, he might consider doing just that in recognition of his institutional conflict. Clayman refused to step down, but agreed to bring the issue forward at the meeting.

After several unsuccessful attempts to schedule the meeting, and because of some misunderstanding about document distribution, the meeting was delayed until December 18, 1997. One positive outcome was that several committee members wrote memos explaining their respective positions on the issues we were raising.

CHAPTER X

Meeting with the Ethics Committee

The First Meeting

Present at the meeting were Dr. Clayman (chair); committee members Dr. Steve McShane (business administration), Dr. Arthur Chapman (kinesiology), Dr. Robert Menzies (criminology), and Dr. Adam Horvath (education, attending by conference call); guests Lowman, Palys, and faculty association Executive Director David Bell; and two staff members from the VP-research's Office of Research Services. Absent were committee members Hanson and Ogloff — who had submitted written statements, both of which the committee considered at the meeting — and the university's occupational health and safety officer.

We began by requesting that "Dr. Clayman step down as Chair of this meeting for reasons of conflict of interest; [and] that the agenda of this meeting focus on the issues raised in the referenced documents." A member of the committee made a motion to that effect, which passed. At that point, Steve McShane became the chair. The committee then considered whether it should discuss the Ogden case, or whether the discussion would be limited to the limited-confidentiality policy. Clayman, who had elected to stay as a committee member, moved that "The agenda be restricted to discussion of the change which was made to the consent form template for R. 20.01." The motion passed by one. Clayman cast the deciding vote.

A lengthy discussion ensued focusing on the documents circulated prior to the meeting. As we have already described our position, the following discussion examines the three ethics committee member statements circulated prior to the meeting.

Hanson on a Dynamic View of Law

The first document in the package was by Dr. Philip Hanson of the Philosophy Department.[1] Of particular interest was its description of the meeting at which the committee adopted the limited-confidentiality protocol, and how Hanson — a philosopher, not a social science researcher — saw his role. In addition to distinguishing research ethics in the abstract and in practice (which we quoted at p. 62), Hanson also commented on our understanding of the law and how this related for him to one's perspective of the university as an institution:

> Bruce Clayman and Adam Horvath . . . have argued from a rather narrow construal of the law of the land: roughly, the law as extant code. If one also views the university simply as a "corporation" that provides facilities or infrastructure to its research "clients" (a.k.a. faculty and graduate students), whose interests are distinct from its own, then it is this narrow "reactive" view of the law that may well seem like the appropriate one – the one carrying the least risk to the university – to serve as a constraint on university policies. But one can, as John Lowman and Ted Palys do, think of the law more broadly and dynamically as encompassing not only code but also common law and precedents. And one can also have a different vision of the university, as an institution that embraces its faculty and graduate students as integral and essential constituents, societies in their wisdom having seen the value of an institution that proactively promotes and facilitates the pursuit of knowledge and understanding by its members.
>
> I myself think of the law and of the university in the latter way. And this has consequences for what morals I draw from the Russel Ogden case. His winning his case in Coroner's Court obviously establishes an important legal precedent here in Canada for researcher-participant confidentiality. Such precedents are very much in the interests of the research constituency at the university, and therefore, given my conception of the university,

ought to be proactively pursued by the university itself. The
university does not set itself above the law by upholding strict
confidentiality. Rather, it constructively contributes to, helps to
shape the law. That is how the law works. Nor does doing so
require a policy that would expect researchers to break the law
or stonewall the courts. Rather it requires a policy that upholds
the value of research, even research into illegal activity, and is
prepared to be persuasive about these values in a court of law.

When it came to institutional conflict of interest, Hanson suggested that even if the VP-research were to vacate his membership, his appointing a delegate would nonetheless involve an appearance of conflict because that individual still would be acting on the VP's behalf. The point was well taken, even prescient.

Ogloff on the Dignity of Persons

The second written statement was by Dr. James Ogloff.[2] His credentials made him an authoritative source in several fields of expertise: He had a law degree from the United States (although he clarified that he did not practice law); he was then chair of the Canadian Psychological Association's Committee on Ethics; and his forensic psychology research involved obtaining sensitive information from clients and research participants.

When it came to the principles that guided him, Ogloff stated, "My first obligation — as stated in the *Canadian Code of Ethics for Psychologists* — is to the respect for dignity of persons." For Ogloff, this meant,

> . . . *respect for the individual autonomy of our participants.*
> *As a result, the position I take is really quite simple: We must*
> *provide prospective participants with the necessary information*
> *in the informed consent process to ensure that they can make a*
> *reasonable decision of whether to participate in our studies.*

What information might this be? For Ogloff, it was his belief that a researcher could do nothing to protect research confidences from a legal authority who wanted them:

> *My sense of the law in Canada is that there is no widely*
> *recognized statutory or common law researcher/participant*
> *privilege. Veering a bit afield, the Supreme Court of Canada*
> *has failed to recognize a therapist/client privilege or a*
> *physician/client privilege. While we all agree that Mr. Ogden's*
> *"victory" with the Coroner was welcomed, the fact is that such*
> *a decision really has very little, if any, precedential value. It*
> *binds no court.*

This passage raised several issues. First, although everyone applauded Ogden's victory in Coroner's Court, Ogloff dismissed it as having no precedential value. He failed to recognize it exemplified a precedent that had already been set by the Supreme Court of Canada by showing the Wigmore criteria was an appropriate mechanism for examining research-based claims of privilege, and that an ethics-based claim could in fact pass that test. He similarly failed to appreciate that the case identified the best legal mechanism researchers have to protect researcher-participant communications, and how to prepare to do so. While one should not give a Coroner's Court more weight than it is due, neither should one write it off as having no value. The case points to the grounds on which researchers could begin to build the foundation for their ethical defence of research confidentiality in court.

It is also instructive to recall that, notwithstanding the thousands of research projects that are undertaken in Canadian universities every year, and the hundreds of thousands of research projects that have been under-taken in Canadian universities since their inception, Ogden's was the first Canadian case where a legal authority challenged a research confidence. Not only that, but he also fended off the challenge. There was not one instance in Canada of a legal authority ordering a researcher to violate a research confidence, and yet here was Ogloff waving the white flag of sur-render. At least his position was clear:

> *As it now stands, the error, to the extent there is one, in the*
> *wording of R20.01 PROTECTS prospective participants. Were*
> *we to revert back to the previous language, we would run*

> *the very real risk that research records pertaining to a future*
> *participant would be somehow seized by the courts.*[3]

This argument had three problems: First, what Ogloff was proclaiming as "R20.01" was actually the illicit policy created by the ethics committee that had never received Senate review or approval. Second, a risk that has never occurred is hardly "very real." Third, the wording may not protect research participants; if anything, as Ogden had pointed out in his interchange with Clayman in *Simon Fraser News*,[4] it invites police and other state authorities to subpoena researchers.

Ogloff concluded by urging the committee to "seek independent legal counsel on this matter." Although we agreed, we worried the administration would commission an opinion designed to serve as an *ex post facto* rationalization of limited confidentiality. When the VP-research and ethics committee finally did seek a legal opinion, we realized our concerns were justified.

Horvath's Recollections of Ogden's Research

We appreciated Dr. Adam Horvath's undated memo, which was distributed just prior to the December 18, 1997, meeting, as it documented his recollections of Ogden's ethics application, and particularly his alleged "waiver letter," a discussion Clayman had fought to avoid.

On several key issues, the Horvath and Harmon accounts agreed. In Horvath's view, the letter began with Ogden's statement he would not ask prospective participants for identifying information, and that he would not record it should it come to his attention. Ogden's pledge of "absolute confidentiality" made sense to Horvath in relation to that statement, i.e., it would effectively be done under conditions of anonymity, in which case there would be no information to subpoena:

> *Mr. Ogden's letter of 1992 assuming FULL*
> *RESPONSIBILITY FOR CONFIDENTIALITY was not at*
> *all ambiguous; it was clearly understood to mean that a)*
> *conditions noted above would be met, b) he realized the legal*
> *risks both to himself and his informants, c) he would inform*
> *his participants of these risks which they may choose or refuse*

101

> to accept, d) that he will act prudently to minimize these risks
> and assume full responsibility of the consequences if he fails to
> do so. Under these conditions we believed that the safety and
> privacy of all involved was assured, and the Committee gave
> its approval for the research. (Dr. Clayman was not present
> at any of these deliberations.). Contrary to the innuendoes
> contained in the documents [circulated by Palys and
> Lowman], at no time, to my knowledge, was the legal liability
> of SFU or the possible impact of controversy on the University
> was ever considered or discussed during this process.[5]

In our response to Horvath,[6] we agreed that Ogden's undertaking to "accept full responsibility for any decision I make with respect to the sharing of information" was not ambiguous; Ogden followed that protocol. Horvath did not appreciate that, even if one does not ask for identifying information, a participant may give it anyway, the researcher may discover it serendipitously, or might know an interviewee's identity in advance. This knowledge increases the researcher's responsibility to make sure no harm comes to research participants. Even when the researcher learns a participant's identity unwittingly, it would be unethical to say, "I told you not to tell me who you are, so now that you have, it's your problem."

These issues aside, Horvath understood that Ogden's taking full responsibility for confidentiality was an *ethical* pledge. Ogden took full responsibility even though some of his participants added to his burden by identifying themselves when they did not have to, and even though SFU added to that burden by abandoning him in court.

Did Ogden's letter have anything to do with SFU's liability? No. Like Harmon, Horvath held that liability considerations had nothing to do with the ethics approval process; indeed, he was offended by our mentioning it.[7] On what basis, then, could Clayman continue to insist that Ogden's ethical undertaking constituted a liability waiver?

Horvath Defends Limited Confidentiality

Horvath began his defense of the limited-confidentiality consent statement by noting that the coroner's subpoena had taken what was previously an abstract threat and made it real. Researchers should inform prospective research participants that it could happen again. We replied that the committee's limited-confidentiality doctrine

> would seem an example of a decision-making bias Kahneman
> & Tversky[8] refer to as the "availability heuristic," i.e., the
> tendency of decision-makers to give undue weight to one
> particularly salient event. Consideration of the broader picture
> reminds us that: (a) the Ogden experience is the only incident
> of its kind in the history of research in Canadian universities;
> and (b) no researcher, including Mr. Ogden, has ever been
> ordered by a Canadian court to violate confidentiality.

In response, Horvath intimated that we were proposing that researchers should act unethically by withholding information from prospective participants about which they should be informed:

> Drs. Lowman & Palys suggest that the interests of the research
> participants would be better served if this information was kept
> from them. I find this logic difficult to follow. Moreover the
> argument that many subjects would refuse to participate if they
> knew the limits of the legal safeguards seems self-serving. Do
> we want to increase the likelihood of an individual becoming
> a research subject by withholding information relevant to their
> decision? Participants are entitled to know all the pertinent
> factors relating to the confidentiality of the data.

Certainly, researchers should inform prospective participants about risks that have some probability greater than zero of occurring. However, a blanket requirement to utter a warning and impose limits on confidentiality whenever a researcher proposes to discuss criminal behaviour seemed alarmist and something that would cast a chill on criminological research. The committee threw out of the window the ability to make an unlimited pledge of confidentiality for a risk that had never materialized. In research like Ogden's, where the potential harms of disclosure to a participant are substantial, the risk of a court order for disclosure should be raised, along with a statement by the researcher about what he or she will do if that were to occur. The minimal standard for any researcher would be to protect research confidentiality "to the full extent permitted by law." Beyond that, the researcher would inform the participant whether he or she would continue to follow his or her ethical obligation and defy the order or follow the legal order and make the disclosure.

Another strand of Horvath's argument was to depict us as having an absolute commitment to confidentiality:

> The interests of science are dear to an academic community,
> but it is also easy to imagine situations where the greater
> societal good may not be served by an unequivocal bond of
> confidentiality. (For example, supposing that in the course of
> research inquiry, an impending homicide is discovered; or a
> pedophile discloses a credible intent to offend against a minor;
> or a person is likely to commit suicide.) In these instances
> a difficult ethical decision needs to be made on a case by
> case basis. It does not appear to me that there is a case for
> an absolute "sanctuary" for information obtained through
> legitimate research, although like Drs. Lowman & Palys, I
> would like to see the legal protection of research data extended.

This was the first of many "What if?" arguments that ultimately would be advanced, often with an ascending scale of seriousness, designed to show that, at some point there must be an ethical limit to confidentiality. We agreed that there were situations where we could imagine violating confidentiality to prevent harm from occurring. However, we disagreed that an *a priori* limitation to confidentiality satisfactorily addressed the conflicting ethical issues involved.

Again, we raised the matter of the degree of risk involved in a particular research project. In our collective sixty-plus years of social research experience — with police officers, judges, lawyers, prostitutes, pimps, sex buyers, drug dealers, former gang members, drug addicts, social activists, and the general citizenry — not one occasion has arisen where violating confidentiality would have prevented serious harm. No one we know in the School of Criminology has faced such a situation. This collective experience suggests that such situations are extremely rare. The better way to approach them is not to dispense with confidentiality on the presumption that our next respondent will tell us about his or her plans to blow up the world, but to trust our respondents and deal with the rare exceptions case by case. We consider Horvath's "What if?" scenario in later chapters, as it would arise repeatedly. In response, we asked Horvath[9] if there were any situations where his commitment to law would not be absolute, and where a researcher of conscience like Ogden might stand tall in defence of a privilege. Horvath suggested he would need to consider such situations case by case. Consequently, we did not understand why he would defend the ethics committee's consent statement, which categorically excluded that option.

Horvath's submission went on to make a statement that contradicted his claim that, "As a public institution, it would be morally and ethically wrong to assume that our research activities are above the law of the land":

> *The sentences added are DESCRIPTIVE/INFORMATIVE.*
> *There is no inference [sic] in the revised document (and none*
> *was intended) suggesting a specific action a researcher should*
> *take in case information obtained in the course of research was*
> *subpoenaed. Indeed for the ethics committee to direct or even*
> *counsel researchers to behave contrary to criminal law would*
> *be improper and WRONG. Having said this, there is nothing*
> *in the document to compel researchers to cooperate with any*
> *legal body, nor is there a suggestion that they ought to do so.*

And later:

> *This does NOT preclude a covenant by the researcher to*
> *protect the identity or information in the face of legal action*
> *beyond what is permitted by law. However, if such promise is*
> *made, the participant needs to know that she/he is dependent*
> *on the strength of the individual's promise as opposed to a*
> *legal contract enforceable in law. This is not a directive to*
> *"rat" or "squeal"; this is openness and transparency.*

We were puzzled. If the university were to accept a researcher making the sort of covenant that Horvath alluded to, confidentiality would *not* be limited. Why, then, did the ethics committee want to force a researcher to tell the participant that it is limited? Was Horvath indicating a way out of our disagreement?

Horvath's Questions

We met with the committee again on February 3, 1998. Shortly after that meeting, Horvath emailed us two further questions:

> *If you were to conduct a study such as Mr. Ogden's research to-day (knowing what you do know now): Would you provide any information to participants with respect to potential legal action to obtain information to you given in strict confidence by the participants? If the answer is yes, what form (content and method of communication) would you prefer?*

We responded:
> [W]e would conduct the research with the knowledge that, in the extremely unlikely event we were subpoenaed, we could refuse to testify. If charged with contempt, we would expect the university to stand beside us in court to defend the "highest ethical principles" policy R60.01 both affirms and requires. If Dr. Clayman's slogan "SFU Research Matters" has any substance, we would expect the University to fight vigorously, to the Supreme Court if necessary, to protect the rights of research participants and the integrity of the research enterprise . . . If found guilty of contempt, we would be willing to be incarcerated for it, because being convicted and sentenced would not change our minds about the ethics of our position. We agree that researchers are not above the law, which is why we would be prepared to go to prison to defend the ethical principles we espouse.[10]

Our response also commented on the "ethics of convenience" argument that Horvath had imputed to us:

*Some members of the Ethics Committee have interpreted our
criticism of the informed consent template as indicating an ethics
of convenience, i.e., that, in the interests of successfully soliciting
research participants, we would not want to tell them the "full"
story of what might possibly await them and us. On the contrary,
we believe that when the university tries to impose "limited
confidentiality" on the entire SFU research community, it is setting
too low a standard. Requiring us to use that lower standard is a
violation of our personal and disciplinary ethics. Obviously the
university cannot require researchers to break the law, but nor
should it absolutely preclude them from doing so.*

Further, we explained what we believed SFU's integrity in research policy
meant in this context:

*Policy R60.01 (on Research Integrity) starts with the words:
"Simon Fraser University supports and encourages the maintenance
of the highest ethical standards in research and scholarship.
Primary responsibility for high standards of conduct in research and
scholarship rests with the individuals carrying out these activities."
If the "primary" responsibility for maintaining the highest ethical
standards is with the researcher, then there must be a "secondary"
responsibility too, which we suggest lies with the university. If the
researcher is prepared to offer his/her liberty, then the least the
university can do is defend that liberty, along with the rights of
research participants, and the university's research ethics policy . . .*

*Because of the way it abandoned Russel Ogden and his
research participants, we believe the university has violated both
R20.01 and R60.01. By prioritizing liability over ethics, the
university has violated its own policy, and is unethical.*

At least this interaction had clarified our respective positions on the ethics and
law of research confidentiality. It helped us realize that the institutional conflict
of interest playing out at SFU was leading to a regime of *caveat emptor* (un)ethics.

CHAPTER XI
Caveat Emptor Ethics

Limited Confidentiality and Liability

We had two concerns about SFU's regime of limited confidentiality. First was the way the wording seemed likely to undermine researchers' ability to defend research-participant privilege by invoking the Wigmore criteria. The second was how the law-of-the-land doctrine undermined research and violated the academic freedom of researchers to follow an ethics-first philosophy. The ethics committee was imposing a resolution to potential conflicts between ethics and law that, in our view, is unethical: Criminologists should not go into the field limiting confidentiality in a way that could turn them into informers. Because we refused to limit confidentiality, the ethics committee was preventing us from meeting our contractual obligations as faculty members. However, it was doing much more than that. While researchers should have the academic freedom to adhere to either a law-first or ethics-first ethos according to their conscience, the law-of-the-land position set the ethical bar far too low by allowing researchers simply to throw in the towel when a subpoena arrives. The only proviso was that, in the name of informed consent, researchers should warn research participants that they would spill the beans: *caveat emptor*.

Against this liability-driven view, we argued that all researchers are ethically obliged to protect confidentiality to at least the full extent law permits. Ethics-first researchers must make every effort to work within the law until that very rare last instant when law and ethics diverge. Similarly, law-of-the-land researchers have a responsibility to fulfill ethical principles, which means protecting research-participant confidentiality until they have no legal options left and a court or other legal authority forces them to reveal confidential information. The question is, when exactly does one reach that point?

To protect confidentiality to the full extent law permits, the researcher and university are ethically bound to contest the subpoena to the highest court that will hear the case. While Clayman, Horvath, and Ogloff were prepared to stand in the way of our approach to protecting research confidentiality, they offered no clue about how they would respond in the event of a legal threat to confidentiality. The limited-confidentiality consent statement suggested that information would be "kept confidential to the full extent permitted by law" as if that had a clear meaning; but what did the committee think "the full extent permitted by law" involved and how would they go about protecting confidentiality to that extent? It appeared from the Ogden case that the university administration took mere receipt of a subpoena as the limit of law, and the challenging of a subpoena to be a challenge to the rule of law.[1] Given the priority that ethics committee members were placing on informed consent, why did the limited-confidentiality consent statement not inform participants how far SFU would go to defend research confidentiality in court?

None of the champions of limited confidentiality at SFU had a plan should a subpoena arrive. They offered no advice about how a researcher might defend confidentiality using common law and design research to enhance the defence. Ogloff, the only one holding a law degree, announced that he would simply surrender confidential records at the point a court so ordered:

> *The fact is that as a researcher and as a member of the Committee on Ethics I simply do not believe that I would be upholding my duty to prospective participants were I to lead them to believe that somehow their confidentiality could be protected — or that the University could somehow fight to protect their confidentiality should the research records be demanded by court order.*

The fact that he said this after Ogden had shown researchers how to use the Wigmore test to defend research participants, and that he endorsed a limited-confidentiality consent statement that potentially sabotaged that defence, suggested that Ogloff was prepared to abandon research confidentiality far sooner than "the full extent permitted by law." Instead of vigorously asserting research-participant rights, the limited-confidentiality consent statement effectively institutionalized a *caveat emptor* downloading of ethical responsibility and liability to research participants. Limited confidentiality thereby fostered a culture of disclosure rather than a culture of protection. In this perversion of ethics, limited confidentiality allowed researchers to violate research confidentiality as long as they warned prospective participants of their intentions. Under the guise of "respecting their autonomy," researchers would leave participants to make their own choices about what risks to take. They would download to research participants the responsibility for figuring out what "confidentiality to the full extent permitted by law" might mean — participants who would be likely to know even less about the laws of privilege than most researchers.

If push came to shove and a court were to order confidential research information the researcher could simply hand it over saying, "Sorry, but I told you that might happen," leaving their participants to mop up the mess.

The liability twist to the strategy resided in the *caveat emptor*: If researchers warned participants about the risk of court-ordered disclosure, neither the university nor the researcher would have to spend time or money protecting those participants in court.

Caveat emptor is hardly conducive to the foundation of trust necessary when the researcher knows the identity of the participant. Because this state of affairs more commonly exists in some areas of study than others, particularly for field researchers whose methodology emphasizes target sampling and long-term interaction with known participants, limited confidentiality infringed academic freedom, and with a high price. As the ethics committee had anticipated, limited confidentiality would have a marked impact on social science research at SFU. Sociologists, criminologists, and others — particularly graduate students working with time restrictions — began to avoid field and interview research. Some researchers chose not to do field research rather than follow the ethics committee's limited-confidentiality protocol, because it fell far short of the "highest ethical standard."

A Smoking Gun

At about this time, the School of Criminology chair appointed the two of us as the criminology ad hoc ethics liaison committee in order to facilitate our dialogue with the ethics committee. Acting as a liaison between the school and the committee gave us ongoing access to information about how the ethics committee was processing criminology applications and, in those instances where applicants invited our intervention, correspond with the Office of Research Services personnel involved in the review process. An example of the problems that limited confidentiality was creating came to our attention early in 1998. We draw the information below from our memorandum to the ethics committee delivered at the February 3, 1998, meeting.

Ethics committee members had insisted that our concerns over the way liability considerations were contaminating the ethics review process were misplaced. In response, we began our February 3 meeting with the ethics committee by drawing attention to a proposal that a criminology graduate student had submitted, which involved interviewing incarcerated youth about their prior illegal activity. As was usual at that time, a member of the VP-research's staff who had no formal research ethics training processed the application. The ethics committee as a whole never considered the application. The only way the staff member could have had authority to process applications under the extant university research ethics policy was if the VP-research had appointed her chair of the ethics committee. Because that is what she effectively had become, we began referring to her as the ethics committee chair's proxy.

In the process of vetting the student's application, there was an email interchange between the student's thesis supervisor and the chair's proxy about the appropriateness of the limited-confidentiality clause. In an attempt to find a compromise, the proxy proposed that the student "only ask questions about the activities for which you [the participant] have already been caught/punished," and tell the participants that, "it is important that you do not talk about illegal activities or activities for which you or your friends have not been caught." Ultimately, the ethics committee chair approved this wording in lieu of a statement about limited confidentiality.

However, when the student initially proposed the use of this wording, the proxy emailed her supervisor, saying:

> *I see that you try to get the point across to your youth subjects that you will ask questions about activities for which they have already been caught and punished. You clearly explain this in your statement to them. BUT you also state that, "It is important that you do not talk about illegal activities . . ." Why not? This is why the [limited-confidentiality] statement that I copied to you is very important here. What if, through no solicitation of your own, they volunteer information for which you are obligated to relay to the authorities or are asked to at a later date by the courts? You promised these youths complete confidentiality, so what do you do? You may not be wanting or asking them this particular information, but the fact they are detained and are youths who have been charged with an offence, puts you in a situation where you must "cover" yourself legally.*
>
> *You should add the sentence, in your statement to youths: "It is possible that, as a result of legal action the researcher may be required to divulge information in the course of this research to a court or other legal body. Therefore, it is imperative that you only answer the questions put to you and reveal nothing else." This way you have warned them and have legally followed your "promise" to confidentiality as far as you are legally bound.[2]*

Ethics application review should focus on the protection of research participants. However, according to the proxy, the purpose of adding the "limited confidentiality" statement was to "cover" the supervisor and the researcher "legally." Far from protecting them, this strategy was a way of displacing responsibility onto the shoulders of the youths if they did not comply. Here was tangible evidence that one purpose of ethics review was to protect the researcher and the university from research participants.

In response to the suggestion that the limited-confidentiality clause be added to the informed-consent statement, the supervisor expressed reservations about the effects the growing list of legal prophylactics would have on the integrity of interviews, suggesting that, "the extra warning you want her to add to her informed consent could create unnecessary fear, anxiety, and mistrust on the part of the youths or their parents."

The supervisor reminded the proxy that because the graduate student was asking youths about their convictions, there was no need for the "court action" clause on the consent form. Given that neither the supervisor nor the student was prepared to shift the burden of responsibility from themselves to the participants, the proxy subsequently used the ethics application process to transfer liability from the university to the researchers and participants:

> I now have it on record that you guarantee there will be no information volunteered/gathered by/from subjects which will prove that the clause which was requested to be inserted [the limitation of confidentiality on the informed consent form] is not required. I also have it on record that you, (your student) understand the implications involved with the legal issue.[3]

This communication created a guarantee where the researcher was not offering one, and seemed to say, "We, the University, have covered ourselves, and we've given you the information that will allow you to cover yourselves, so now if it all blows up, you and the participants are on your own." If, as the chair had claimed, limited confidentiality protected research participants, how could he transfer liability to them this way? What if these youths did not understand the meaning of the law and volunteered sensitive information anyway? Although the chair anticipated this possibility, once his concerns about liability were satisfied, he was no longer concerned about what impact such a disclosure might have on research participants.

This case illustrates the way that the institutional conflict of interest built into SFU's research ethics policy — protecting the university and researcher as well as the research participant — began to compromise what should have been its sole purpose, i.e., protecting research participants. In the process of discussing how to obtain informed consent, the ethics committee chair treated research participants more as risks to mitigate than persons to afford the protections that the research ethics policy described. Limited confidentiality transformed informed consent into a series of all-inclusive risk-management clauses with the result that, in the event of a court action, the university could capitulate without a struggle, arguing that it had fully met its legal obligations. Ironically, in the name of ethics, the university could leave research participants high and dry.

Again, this case illustrated that administrative staff were making a variety of weighty decisions about ethics, liability, and confidentiality without ever referring the application to the ethics committee as a whole for discussion. In their representation of its work, the ethics committee was treating research "in which the researcher might hear about violations of criminal and/or civil law" as sufficiently risky to warrant special mention in informed-consent statements, and yet, when such proposals were submitted to the ethics committee for review the VP-research, a physicist, delegated their consideration to a staff member who, like him, had no experience whatsoever doing social science research. Did members of the ethics committee even know what the VP-research and the proxy were doing in their name?

Our memorandum concluded by suggesting that it was time for an independent review of the entire ethics application process. The committee never responded; instead, the chair asked us to leave the meeting so the committee could consider the issues we had raised. We have no idea what transpired after we left other than that the committee did not reach a resolution. When the committee met again later that month, the discussion of limited confidentiality continued *in camera*.

Advising President Blaney

As the ethics committee was no longer interested in discussing its limited confidentiality doctrine with us, and because it had pulled down the blinds on its deliberations, we wrote to President Blaney calling for his immediate intervention. The letter[4] began by describing how courts conceptualize "reasonable apprehension of bias":

> *Procedural fairness and absence of bias are the two*
> *requirements of natural justice. The absence of bias*

114

requirement arises out of the right to be heard by an impartial tribunal, and is based on the premise that justice should not only be done but should be seen to be done. For this reason it is not necessary that actual bias be established. It is sufficient that there exists a reasonable apprehension of bias.[5]

In case law, Mr. Justice Cory had set out the test for reasonable apprehension of bias:

The duty to act fairly includes the duty to provide procedural fairness to the parties. That simply cannot exist if an adjudicator is biased. It is, of course, impossible to determine the precise state of mind of an adjudicator who has made an administrative board decision. As a result, the courts have taken the position that an unbiased appearance is, in itself, an essential component of procedural fairness . . . The test is whether a reasonably informed bystander could reasonably perceive bias on the part of an adjudicator.[6]

For there to be impartiality, no one should sit as a judge in his or her own cause. Seen in relation to this standard, SFU's actions failed at every turn. All the issues related to Ogden and limited confidentiality involved persons sitting as judges in their own cause:

1. VP-research Clayman continued to act on his institutional conflict of interest in contrast to the standard outlined in the draft *Tri-Council Policy Statement*. Although Clayman had stood aside and allowed another member of the committee to occupy the chair when the committee met on December 18 and February 3, he remained at the meeting and cast the deciding vote on the key issue of whether the discussion that day should include the Ogden case. By voting on that issue — which involved the question of whether the committee would review a decision he had been a part of — there was a reasonable apprehension of bias.

2. Clayman had insisted at the February 3 meeting that "exposure to liability is not an issue for the [Ethics] Committee." However, the memo we submitted to the committee documented a case in which liability management, not concern for research participants, was clearly the primary consideration.

3. There was a reasonable apprehension of bias involved in Clayman's reconsideration of the Ogden decision. The memo encouraged President Blaney to heed the letter signed by criminology faculty calling for an independent review. To avoid apprehension of bias, administrators involved in the Ogden decision should not conduct the review.

4. There would be a reasonable apprehension of bias in the ethics committee reconsidering its limited confidentiality protocol and deciding whether it had exceeded its jurisdiction by making substantive changes to SFU policy.

Our memo concluded by recommending

1. lest further damage be done before procedural violations can be considered, arrange the postponement of Tuesday's Ethics Committee meeting;

2. because the closed session of the Ethics Committee is an affront to the principle of open governance, immediately terminate the Ethics Committee's deliberation of changes to the informed consent form;

3. in recognition of the conflict of interest inherent in an administrator sitting on the Ethics Committee, remove Dr. Clayman from the Committee immediately; and

4. in consultation with the Faculty Association, establish a blue ribbon panel to conduct an independent review of the Ogden case, the Ethics Committee's limitation of confidentiality, and the entire ethics review procedure.[7]

These various issues would come to a head when we submitted two research proposals to interview off-street sex workers and their managers.

CHAPTER XII
An Unusual Research Opportunity

Ethnographic Research on Prostitution

In late 1997 and early 1998, an unusual research opportunity arose on which we decided to collaborate. Since 1977, Lowman had done research on prostitution and prostitution law and its enforcement in British Columbia. When it came to the sellers of sex, most of the survey research had focused on the street trade. In the mid-1990s, his research shifted to the off-street trade and to sex buyers. In November 1997, two escort-service owners who had read Lowman's opinion editorial on prostitution law in the *Province*[1] newspaper phoned unsolicited and invited him to visit their office. When Lowman arrived, he realized the office was located in a massage parlour, a venue for in-call prostitution. The women who worked as masseuses also worked for the escort service. After several meetings, the owners offered Lowman a job as a driver for the women going to meet their clients in hotels and other locations. He had what turned out to be a once-in-a lifetime opportunity to conduct ethnographic research on escort-agency and in-massage-parlour prostitution.

The opportunity to gain this kind of access to off-street sex work was important for numerous reasons. Research on street prostitution not only revealed the high rates of victimization of street-connected women,[2] but also showed how a succession of changes in the law, court decisions, and nuisance injunctions were putting them at greater risk by gradually displacing them into industrial areas where they became much more vulnerable to assault, sexual assault, robbery, and murder. Many women had already gone missing from Vancouver's Downtown Eastside — as many as thirty by that time — and there were indications that a serial killer might be operating in Vancouver, as was later shown to be the case. Researching off-street venues could make a significant contribution to the literature by providing information about the lives of persons involved in the off-street sex trade, especially with respect to violence. The off-street access we were being given might also provide an opportunity to contact clients of sex workers; sex buyers had been notoriously absent from research on prostitution in Canada up to that point. Chris Atchison and Laura Fraser had already collaborated with Lowman on an exploratory study of clients;[3] being able to contact clients directly in order to solicit their participation presented an unusual opportunity to expand this research.

The proposed research had important law and policy implications. Prostitution law and policy had become controversial across Canada during the 1980s and 1990s. In Vancouver the efforts of various groups to address whatever they perceived "the prostitution problem" to be was exposing the inconsistent and hypocritical state of prostitution law whereby prostitution itself was legal, but almost everything about it — including prostitution establishments — was not. The sex trade was clearly an area where researchers could contribute empirical information to inform debate about policy and law reform in a country where there are deep divisions over the legal status of prostitution.[4] The fact that, in the late 1990s, Vancouver Downtown Eastside street-connected women were going missing in ever-increasing numbers merely heightened the sense of urgency for the information needed to formulate law and policy. Although we did not know it at the time, research of this sort would become a central component of the expert evidence submitted on behalf of several constitutional challenges to prostitution law the Supreme Court of Canada ultimately decided when it ruled that a series of prostitution laws[5] were unconstitutional.[6]

On December 1, 1997, Lowman submitted an application to the ethics committee for an interview study of "owners and managers of escort services, massage parlours, and body rubs." On February 24, 1998, Lowman and Palys submitted an application to the ethics committee for a related research project entitled "Sex Work in Off-Street Venues," which involved interviewing sex workers.

For both studies, the proposals sent for the ethics committee to review explained that confidentiality was a core consideration:[7]

Because confidentiality will be an over-riding concern, we anticipate that most participants will not agree to sign a consent form. Whether the informed consent statement is written or verbal, it will ensure prospective participants that:

1. *Their participation is voluntary,*
2. *Their anonymity will be guaranteed,*
3. *All research material will be kept strictly confidential,*
4. *They can terminate the interview at any time, and*
5. *They can decline to answer any question.*
6. *All interviews will be taped. Participants will be ensured that tapes will be destroyed immediately after they have been transcribed, and that information revealing their identity will not be transcribed.*

. . . Regardless of whether it be written or verbal, the informed consent statement will NOT include the statement,
"Any information that is obtained during this study will be kept confidential to the full extent permitted by law . . . However, it is possible that, as a result of legal action, the researcher may be required to divulge information obtained in the course of this research to a court or other legal body."

In the process of outlining our reasons for this approach, we reiterated our objections to limited confidentiality:

The doctrine of limited confidentiality is in violation of SFU Policy R20.01, which does not limit "confidentiality" in any way. The purpose of R20.01 is to protect research participants. Limited confidentiality endangers research participants, and thus violates the policy. SFU policy R60.01 requires that

> researchers adhere to the "highest ethical standards." Because
> the doctrine of limited confidentiality subordinates ethics to
> law, it sets a lower ethical standard than "confidentiality,"
> and thus violates R60.01 as well. Because limited
> confidentiality is a "doctrine" subordinating ethics to law, it is
> an infringement of academic freedom, and thus a violation of
> the SFUFA-SFU Framework Agreement.

We made it clear that both studies would be limited to persons nineteen years of age and over.

The Ethics Committee Responds

The next meeting of the ethics committee was early in March 1994. At that meeting, VP-research Clayman announced that he would vacate the chair and leave the Committee, apparently in recognition of his institutional conflict of interest. Dr. McShane would continue as committee chair until the end of the semester when his term expired, at which point the VP-research would appoint a new chair. Clayman introduced Dr. Marilyn Bowman of the Psychology Department as the person he had appointed to take his place on the committee, still not recognizing the appearance of institutional conflict of interest such an appointment entailed. At that point, the minutes note, Clayman left the meeting.

McShane continued as interim chair. Minutes of the committee meetings after we submitted our proposals show that its first consideration was to develop a set of principles to guide evaluation of applications. The first of the two principles adopted at the March 3, 1998, meeting stated:

> A) The University Research Ethics Review Committee has a
> role and overriding obligation to protect research participants'
> interests and rights whether or not these interests and rights
> conflict with the researcher's interests or ability to conduct her
> or his research.

This first clause of this principle was a motherhood statement merely reaffirming the objectives of the committee's mandate to protect research participants. The second clause about the researcher's ability to conduct research was notable for the way it framed critics of limited confidentiality. The debate was less about opposing sets of principles and more about the ethics committee's moral obligation to stop sneaky self-interested researchers trying to protect their research by not informing potential participants about the risks of participating.

The second principle, which the committee adopted at the same meeting on a motion from Bowman that Horvath seconded, stated:

> B) *The University Research Ethics Review Committee believes that research participants have a right to be clearly informed by the researcher of all reasonably foreseeable consequences of their (i.e. research participants') involvement in a research study. This includes the possibility and consequences of a researcher being ordered by an officer of the court to disclose knowledge or information obtained by the researcher with a promise of confidentiality offered in good faith to the participants.*[8]

This principle began with the committee requiring researchers to inform prospective participants about "all reasonably foreseeable consequences." The answer to the question "what might 'reasonably foreseeable' include?" is given in the second sentence, which asserted by fiat what previously had been a subject of debate. "Being asked by an officer of the court to disclose" confidential information was now a "reasonably foreseeable consequence." It did not matter that Ogden was the only person in the history of Canadian research who a legal authority had asked to do so, or that he had successfully defended confidentiality in the face of the challenge. If a possibility that has only occurred once, and with no negative consequence to the research participant, counts as being a reasonably foreseeable risk, what else might be included? Pandora's ethics box was now open, inviting the committee's selective attention. The committee could conjure up all manner of "What if?" scenarios with no reality check required, and then congratulate itself for preventing evil researchers from trying to slip one by in order to get their next self-serving publications.

The committee adopted a third principle at the March 24, 1998, meeting, which stated:

> *C) Researchers will use consent forms as provided as template samples in the Request for Ethical Approval of Research application package, but individually-devised consent procedures consistent with these principles will be considered.*

This sealed the deal on the committee's limited-confidentiality doctrine. The committee was no longer willing to debate whether its limited-confidentiality consent template involved a change of policy, or whether the expectation that researchers would obey a legal order imposed a doctrine that violates academic freedom. Limited confidentiality was now the law at SFU.

The role that committee members Horvath and Bowman played in the imposition of limited confidentiality is worth highlighting for the contradiction it entailed.

Horvath had been a member of the ethics committee that, in 1992, approved Russel Ogden's absolute confidentiality protocol. Bowman had been the chair of the committee that awarded Ogden the 1995 Nora and Ted Sterling Prize in Support of Controversy. Her letter informing Ogden that he was the recipient[9] also constituted her speech at the ceremony. It began by outlining the importance of his research:

> *Mr. Ogden gained national and then international attention for his research into euthanasia and "assisted suicide" particularly as it is being practiced among persons with HIV infection . . . His research is controversial as to topic, and daring and controversial as to method. His findings represent an important contribution of facts to the public debate on the matter of assisted death. As a result of his study he has been invited to present his findings in Canada, the United States, and the United Kingdom. He was called upon to testify before a Senate Committee studying euthanasia and assisted suicide, and his work was frequently cited in other testimony to that*

Committee. It also coincided with an important Supreme Court of Canada case in which access to an assisted death was argued as a Charter right. Mr. Ogden's work has been published as a book: Euthanasia, Assisted Suicide & AIDS *(1994).*

Her letter affirmed the appropriateness of Ogden's methods and the importance of confidentiality to them:

> *In order to answer the questions he had identified as important in "assisted suicide," which is an offense under the Criminal Code of Canada, he decided to go "underground" to meet people actively participating in the process rather than relying only on safer, easier, university-bounded research methods such as a literature review or a public opinion survey. In order to earn the trust and cooperation of his informants he had to promise confidentiality as to their identities. This way he uncovered much that would not otherwise have been known. For this he had to face a legal challenge in the British Columbia Coroner's Court. He was subpoenaed and asked to identify the persons participating in the deaths known to him. In response Mr. Ogden showed courage in resisting this challenge to break his promise to his subjects, risking a contempt of court ruling and possible time in jail. He argued that research has an important social value that on balance weighed more importantly than any benefit that could be gained from revealing individual identities in these cases. He showed a willingness to place academic integrity and the confidence of his sources above his own personal security. His argument was eventually upheld in a precedent-setting decision that found him to be protected by common law privilege. This ruling provides a powerful precedent for all researchers studying delicate topics affecting social policy.*

How ironic that Bowman and Horvath moved and seconded a motion that, by requiring limited confidentiality, would have made it impossible for Ogden to do that research.

The final item of business in the March 24, 1998, meeting concerned who to recommend to the VP-research as chair following the expiry of McShane's term. According to the minutes, Horvath was the only person to volunteer. A motion to recommend the VP-research appoint Horvath as chair carried unanimously.

Does All Research Matter?

In March 1998, there were two other significant events in the midst of all this discussion. The first was the resignation of Dr. Robert Menzies of the School of Criminology from the ethics committee. Menzies was a full professor who taught qualitative research methods courses and who had extensive experience in field-based qualitative methods and archival-based historical research. Menzies was the only person on the ethics committee at that time with qualitative research experience and knowledge of criminological research. One might have hoped committee members would have seen him as a potential mediator of our conflict.

We have no idea what was discussed in the *in camera* sessions on limited confidentiality, but Menzies's general frustration was evident. On March 13, 1998, he submitted his letter of resignation to President Blaney, apprising him of "troubling policy and procedural irregularities that have plagued the (Research and Eethics Review) Committee . . . and to request that action be taken to establish an open, fair, informed, accountable and representative . . . " forum. The School of Criminology thenceforth refused to send any representative to the ethics committee until the administration addressed institutional conflicts of interest and put measures in place to ensure the committee followed university policy.

The second development was a letter from the chair of the Canadian Association of University Teachers' (CAUT) Academic Freedom and Tenure Committee, which inquired whether there were any further developments in the Ogden civil case and if CAUT might help.[10] At that point, CAUT established a "watching brief" on the ethics review process at SFU. We copied CAUT on all of our subsequent interactions with the ethics committee.

Addressing the Ethics Committee's Concerns

The ethics committee chair's response to the concerns about limited confidentiality that we stated in our two sex-work research applications[11] quoted the committee's three guiding principles and identified two major concerns:

> 1. *Oral Statement of Informed Consent*
> *The Committee has agreed that you may use oral rather [than] written informed consent for your research. However, we need to receive a statement used for oral consent in which you discourage participants from revealing information that may cause undue harm in the future and in which you advise them of the potential risk of being asked by a public authority to reveal the information you receive. The Committee is allowing some latitude on the wording of this, but some participant awareness of this risk is necessary. At the same time, the statement can clearly point to factors that may minimize this risk, such as the anonymity of the data, etc.*
>
> 2. *Data From under-age Sex Workers*
> *The Committee would like to know how you intend to prevent minors from participating and from receiving information about under-age sex workers and, if such information is inadvertently collected, what levels of protection you will offer them. The Committee is concerned about the compulsory disclosure requirements in British Columbia regarding child abuse which would include under-age sex workers.*

The committee's missive was problematic in two respects. The first concerned the requirement that we "discourage participants from revealing information that may cause undue harm in the future," which appeared born from the "What if?" license the committee had given itself to identify "reasonably foreseeable" risks. Asking us to identify a threat to confidentiality that had never actually happened was one thing, but now we were being asked to warn participants not to talk about things they might do in

125

the future that were not the subject of the research. This was the first hint of the second form of limited confidentiality that the ethics committee would subsequently attempt to foist on researchers: the "heinous discovery"[12] or "public-safety exception" to confidential communications. What should the researcher do if a research participant reveals plans to injure or kill someone? We responded:

> We do not anticipate participants "revealing information that may cause undue harm in future." We cannot ask participants not to reveal that which we cannot anticipate. As this would appear to be a problem applying to all research with human participants, perhaps the Ethics Committee could supply us with the wording that it is presumably going to impose on all researchers in the future.[13]

The second substantive concern was the way the committee's limited-confidentiality consent statement potentially shot the researcher's legal defence of confidentiality in the foot. The committee had done nothing to assuage our concerns that its approach to confidentiality might undermine our ability to satisfy Wigmore criterion one. In the absence of any other legal opinion, the best advice we had found was (1) in lawyer Mary Marshall's article "When Is a Secret Not a Secret?,"[14] and (2) the decision in *Atlantic Sugar v. US* (1980),[15] both of which suggested the ethics committee's approach was legal folly. The Marshall article, reflecting on the *Gruenke* case, underlined the importance of ensuring researchers and participants had a clear mutual expectation of confidentiality. In *Atlantic Sugar*, the researchers' warning to participants that confidentiality would be maintained "except as required by law" — a phrase that echoed the ethics committee's limited-confidentiality consent statement — was treated as a waiver of privilege.

The *Atlantic Sugar* case was one of only three losses we could find at that time in the voluminous literature on legal challenges to research confidentiality, which made it even more disconcerting that the ethics committee seemed intent on guiding us down that same losing path. In the absence of any formal Canadian legal opinion, these articles and one case clearly supported our position in a situation where the ethics committee adduced no evidence to the contrary.

As a compromise, we agreed to mention the risk that a public authority might ask us to reveal confidential information. However, in the interests of achieving fully informed consent and with the Wigmore criteria in mind, we proposed also to inform participants about what action we would take if such a request were to arise:

> [W]e propose to inform them that R20.01 requires researchers to treat as confidential any information provided by research participants, and that we intend to do precisely that, regardless of what a "public authority" might order. We propose to advise research participants that the Ethics Committee will support us in this endeavour given that its "overriding obligation [is] to protect participants' interests and rights . . ." Furthermore, because the University "supports the highest ethical standards" (R.60.01), we propose to advise research participants that the University will fight relentlessly in court to prevent any public authority from obtaining confidential research information.[16]

As for the concern about youth participants, our application clarified that our research would only involve adults. By asking how we would deal with youths, the committee was either engaging in more "What if?" speculation, or asking us to forget our research role and become investigators for the Ministry of Child and Family Services. Researchers should not ignore trouble when they find it, but neither should they go looking for it. We responded:

> In one project our target population is sex workers aged 19 and over in off-street venues; in the other project it is persons who manage sex workers aged 19 and over in off-street venues. In each case we propose to describe to potential research participants the various criteria delimiting the target population, and then ask them if they meet all the criteria. If a contact responds that they do not meet all the criteria, we will

> *not interview them. In this way sex workers less than nineteen*
> *years of age, and persons managing sex workers less than*
> *nineteen years of age will be screened out without us knowing*
> *which of the criteria made them ineligible to participate.*
> *We will instruct participants not to name other people in the*
> *business, and not to name themselves. If names are disclosed,*
> *we will not keep a written record of them. If a participant*
> *mentions a name during an interview, a pseudonym will be*
> *entered in the transcript. Tapes will be destroyed immediately*
> *after they are transcribed.*

The ball was again in the ethics committee's court.

Ethics Tennis

By the middle of April, McShane's term had expired and Dr. Horvath was the ethics committee chair. The committee was satisfied with our response regarding the possibility that research participants might tell us horrendous things that had nothing to do with the research, and our protocol to ensure all participants were nineteen years of age and over. However, it was still having difficulty with how we proposed to deal with the threat of subpoena. In Horvath's words[17]:

> *It is our understanding that, notwithstanding the committee's*
> *offer of flexibility on the language used in providing*
> *this important information, and our agreement that the*
> *information to the participants provided may be placed in a*
> *proper context, you are not ready to include such statement*
> *in your protocol. We appreciate your arguments in support of*
> *this refusal, but do not concur with your point of view and we*
> *cannot approve your research proposal in its current form.*

Horvath's letter did not identify where exactly the committee's disagreement lay. Instead of outlining the elements we would include in a consent statement, our reply[18] offered specific wording:

> *R20.01 requires researchers to treat as confidential*
> *information provided by research participants. There is a very*
> *remote possibility that we will be asked by a public body to*
> *reveal confidential information. In the unlikely event that*
> *this does happen, our course of action would be as follows:*
> *Because our University research ethics policy does not limit*
> *confidentiality, and because our Ethics Committee has said*
> *that its "overriding obligation [is] to protect participants'*
> *interests and rights . . ." we will resist any attempt by a*
> *"public body" to obtain confidential information. Because*
> *its overriding responsibility is to "protect participants" the*
> *Ethics Committee will do its utmost to defend confidential*
> *information should a public body or court request access to it.*
> *Because the University "supports the highest ethical standards"*
> *(R.60.01), it too will staunchly defend confidentiality in*
> *court. In the event that these efforts fail, and we are ordered*
> *to reveal confidential information by a court or public body,*
> *we will make a personal decision not to do so.*

Horvath responded[19] that the committee's problem lay with the additional statements regarding what the ethics committee and the university would do in the event of a subpoena:

> *The Committee did not feel that it is mandated to "defend*
> *confidential information" in a court of law. Similarly, the next*
> *sentence implies that the Committee has the power to compel*
> *the University "[to] staunchly defend . . ." In our opinion, the*
> *Committee does not have the mandate or power to compel the*
> *University to follow any specific course of action. Accordingly,*
> *these two sentences would need to be removed or re-phrased.*

The opening sentence of SFU policy R60.01 states, "Simon Fraser University supports and encourages the maintenance of the highest ethical standards in research and scholarship." Did the proposed statement go too far in stating, "Because the University 'supports the highest ethical standards' (R.60.01), it too will staunchly defend confidentiality in court"? Unlike the ethics committee, the university administration does have a budget for dealing with legal issues; why would the administration not act in a manner consistent with its two research ethics policies? The most promising aspect of Horvath's letter was his undertaking to pursue exactly that question:

> Notwithstanding the above, the Committee felt that the question of the University's response to legal action, should a researcher (student or faculty) be taken to court and compelled to reveal information obtained via research approved by the committee, is an important issue. Accordingly, we will proceed to request clarification of this matter by the administration.

Our reply[20] asked who the committee was going to send that question to and when we might expect an answer. It was all very well after four years of deliberation for the Committee and the SFU administration to finally give some thought to what they would do in response to issues that had been, in their words, "a real threat," but it was our research that was hanging in the balance. Field research opportunities like ours would not last indefinitely.

While it was imposing specific requirements on researchers to articulate what they would do in response to various imagined threats, the committee had never considered what *it* might do in such situations. Why were committee members uncomfortable with us stating, "Because its overriding responsibility is to 'protect participants' the Ethics Committee will do its utmost to defend confidential information should a public body or court request access to it"? The proposed statement merely said the committee would "do its utmost." Was that too much to ask?

Given the prospect of the university administration and ethics committee spending some time contemplating their respective roles, we looked for other ways to word the consent statement. The committee had stated it was prepared to approve the proposed consent statement if we removed the two sentences that committed the university and the ethics committee to some sort of positive action, but doing so would leave the following:

> R20.01 requires researchers to treat as confidential
> information provided by research participants. There is a very
> remote possibility that we will be asked by a public body to
> reveal confidential information. In the unlikely event that
> this does happen, our course of action would be as follows:
> Because our University research ethics policy does not limit
> confidentiality, and because our Ethics Committee has said
> that its "overriding obligation [is] to protect participants'
> interests and rights . . ." we will resist any attempt by a
> "public body" to obtain confidential information. In the event
> that these efforts fail, and we are ordered to reveal confidential
> information by a court or public body, we will make a personal
> decision not to do so.

Why would the ethics committee approve such a statement if it did not provide sufficient information to facilitate informed consent? Was the committee trying to foist the entire responsibility for protecting research participants and the integrity of the SFU ethics policy onto researchers? Surely, it would be beneficial for participants to know the university would defend their confidences, with the university's previous abdication of that responsibility in the Ogden case giving all the more reason for including those reassurances now. However, if committee members were prepared to accept an informed-consent statement that left the particulars of the committee's and the university's behaviours unspecified, perhaps it would accept a statement that allowed the same for the researchers. In that spirit, we offered the following:

> SFU policy R20.01 requires researchers to treat as confidential
> information provided by research participants. There is a
> very remote possibility that we will be asked by a public body
> to reveal confidential information. In the event that we are
> ordered by a court or other public body to divulge information,
> the confidentiality and anonymity of research participants will
> be maintained.

This statement would have informed participants about the possibility, however remote, of a subpoena; it affirmed unambiguously that confidentiality would be maintained regardless of what efforts were made by a third party to secure information gained in confidence; and it affirmed what policy R20.01 said the university ethics policy stands for, without specifically delineating how researchers, the ethics committee, and the university would meet their obligations. We asked, "Will the ethics committee accept this informed-consent statement, and if not, why not?"

It turned out we were still far from receiving an answer.

CHAPTER XIII

SFU's Administrative Culture: "Up On Dat Mountain, Dey Is Stuck Real Good"[1]

Up to this point, our narrative has focused on the conflict over limited confidentiality at SFU and the administration's failure to defend research confidentiality to the extent permitted by law. Of course, these conflicts over interpretation and enforcement of SFU policies did not play out in a vacuum. Our campaign to persuade the SFU administration to institute an independent review of the "Ogden decision" benefitted from the more general turmoil at SFU during a period when the relationship between the administration and the faculty association was souring. The ensuing description of this turmoil at SFU also shows how administrators selectively defended or dismissed confidentiality depending on whether or not it served their self-interest. In the process, it reveals that there can be serious consequences for administrators who violate university policies.

During the period that a centralized regime of research ethics oversight was evolving in Canada other university policies, including discipline and social control policies, were evolving too. A few years before the introduction of the TCPS, the granting agencies announced that, to be eligible to receive funding, a university must have a research misconduct policy that allows the institution to take disciplinary action against researchers who violate ethics policies.[2] Universities put other codes of conduct in place to control student, faculty, and staff behaviour, including policies to deal with threatening behaviour and harassment. In 1994, the British Columbia government extended the scope of its access-to-information law, which it designed to make publicly funded institutions more accountable, to include universities.

The evolution of academic disciplinary policies meant the university administration's policing function was expanding at a time when it did not train administrators to assume it. At SFU, numerous problems accompanied this expansion of the administration's social control function.

Three controversies in particular spoke to the river of distrust that was swelling between the SFU administration and faculty. They show that the administration's violation of its own policies was not restricted to the research ethics realm. We need to place what happened in the ethics realm in the broader context of problems with the administrative culture at SFU.

The Use and Abuse of Confidentiality at SFU

One of the first signs that all was not well at SFU was the March 9, 1995, faculty association *Newsletter*, which published a series of memoranda between President Stubbs and the association's Executive Director Susan Taylor and President Malgorzata Dubiel concerning retroactive pay increases that the Board of Governor's Compensation Committee (BGCC) had authorized for three senior administrators. An unknown third party had sent the memos to SFUFA. The Board of Governors approved these increases just one week after an arbitrator had accepted the administration's position that SFUFA members should receive no pay increases beyond their career progress increments. The *Newsletter* then quoted a copy of the June 14, 1994, BGCC minutes to the effect that, while the committee felt the pay rises were justified by the increased responsibilities of the three administrators, it expressed concern

> *about the ramifications of approving such salary increases*
> *at this time when the University is currently in negotiations*
> *with employee groups who are being offered no salary*
> *increase. It is anticipated that settlements with the Faculty*
> *Association and with APSA [the Administrative and*
> *Professional Staff Association] will be reached by the end of*
> *August. The Committee concluded that it would be unwise,*
> *in light of the current political climate, to give immediate*
> *approval of the increases.*

Consequently, members of the committee agreed "to defer consideration until September 1994, with the expectation that any increases approved at that time will be retroactive."

When Stubbs wrote to SFUFA confirming the memos were authentic, he provided details of the pay increases and his justification for recommending them to the Board of Governors. However, the letter was written under the heading "CONFIDENTIAL." It was as though Stubbs expected the association to become complicit in the BGCC's subterfuge over the pay increases.

SFUFA President Malgorzata Dubiel challenged Stubbs's selective and self-serving invocation of confidentiality: "I expect that you can understand the utter cynicism with which the executive views the timing of these increases for senior administrators. [They] should have been brought . . . to an open session of the Board of Governors at the time [they] were made." She concluded, "The executive believes that this event, once again, demonstrates the need for greater openness in university governance."

Admitting that he made a mistake, Stubbs set the record straight and copied it to other campus employee groups. However, for faculty going about their daily business, Dubiel's suggestion that the retroactive pay increase *once again* demonstrated the need for greater openness at SFU must have raised a few eyebrows. What was going on behind the scenes that led to this public remonstration of the SFU president?

Stubbs Pleads Confidentiality Again

SFUFA's public conflict with the administration escalated when it moved from the *Newsletter* into the local media. In September 1995, the *Georgia Straight* published the first of a series of items describing a Committee of Inquiry into a dispute involving criminology faculty, an independent researcher, and the SFU administration.[3] SFUFA's engaging the administration publicly a second time indicates the extent to which their relationship had deteriorated.

The first *Straight* article declared, "Secrecy Shrouds SFU Discipline." It reported how an external review[4] of the School of Criminology had chastised the SFU administration for failing to act on the recommendations of a formal inquiry into a dispute that revolved around academic, financial, and personal matters of an undisclosed nature, and breaches of university rules.[5]

Three weeks after the article appeared, the *Straight* published a letter[6] which revealed that, in part, the inquiry concerned the mobilization of SFU Policy GP25: Emergency Response to Threatening Behaviour.[7] However, the story that unfolded in the *Straight* was not about the incident that led to mobilization of GP25, but the administration's mishandling of the GP25 investigation.[8] Because the dispute escalated as a result, Stubbs convened a Committee of Inquiry to investigate and make recommendations.

Although the inquiry examined the university's role in the dispute, Stubbs refused to deal with the administration's malfeasance; in his eye, the investigation involved a personal dispute and nothing more. To facilitate this spin, he refused to field the *Straight*'s questions about the administration's culpability because the confidentiality provisions of the inquiry bound him to silence.[9] However, Stubbs failed to mention the recommendation section of the report deliberately avoided naming any of the individuals involved in the dispute so that Stubbs could make it public.

On reading Stubbs' comments, SFUFA President Dubiel wrote to the *Straight* lambasting his description of the conflict as a dispute between individuals:

> *This characterization continues a pattern whereby various university administrators have trivialized potentially serious incidents and deflected attention away from the university's actions and inactions since February of 1994 . . .*[10]

How does one hold a university to account in such circumstances?

One of the primary purposes of the B.C. *Freedom of Information and Protection of Privacy Act* (FIPPA) is to make public institutions accountable. The government applied the *Act* to university records for the first time in 1994.[11] It turned out to be a game changer. Indeed, in this instance the game was up once the *Straight* made a *FIPPA* request for a copy of the inquiry report. Initially, SFU sent the *Straight* a heavily redacted copy of the inquiry report; SFU deleted twenty-three of thirty-eight pages, and blacked out numerous sections in the remaining fifteen. Stubbs was formally responsible for these excisions, justifying them under *FIPPA* section 15, which deals with information that could harm a "law enforcement" matter, and section 22, which protects privacy.

Because it was difficult to see how any information in the inquiry report pertained to law enforcement, the *Straight* appealed Stubbs' decision to the B.C. Information and Privacy Commissioner — and won. The commissioner ordered that, "the majority of the report must be released in order to comply with the accountability requirements for public bodies under the . . . Act."[12] This was the first time anyone had used the *Act* to hold the SFU administration accountable, and it would not be the last. Indeed, the *FIPPA* information access provisions played a key role in our fight against the ethics committee's regime of limited confidentiality.

When it came to administrative malfeasance, worse was yet to come, and it would cost Stubbs his job.

Administration by Fiat

The SFU case that finally ended up making international news concerned its harassment policy. Numerous issues were at stake, including the fairness of the policy for handling complaints, the degree to which the administration complied with the policy's procedures, the impartiality of the proceedings, the competence of faculty to conduct inquiries, and the appropriateness of the confidentiality blanket that SFU was trying to throw over harassment panel hearings.

The case began in 1996 when student Rachel Marsden alleged that SFU's swim coach, Liam Donnelly, had sexually harassed her between May 1994 and September 1995. Donnelly denied the allegations, which were made just as he was about to file a complaint against Marsden for sexually harassing and stalking him. At his lawyer's advice, Donnelly did not proceed with his harassment complaint, arguing that SFU did not have jurisdiction to deal with an allegation of sexual assault, which was a criminal matter. He declined to attend the SFU harassment hearing of Marsden's complaint against him, which a three-person panel was conducting under the provisions of the SFU harassment policy. Instead, Donnelly contacted the RCMP.

The harassment panel found Donnelly guilty *in absentia*, and recommended that Stubbs fire him. Although the hearing cast doubt on the credibility of Marsden's testimony, and although Donnelly subsequently provided Stubbs with evidence alleging that it was Marsden who had been harassing him, Stubbs reasoned that in order to "maintain the integrity of the process for handling complaints" he should not consider evidence that had not been available to the investigating panel.[13] Critics argued Stubbs should have considered the additional evidence because, under the policy, he was empowered to overrule the panel, an argument with which the head of the panel agreed.[14] Nevertheless, on May 22, 1997, Stubbs fired Donnelly.

With the advice of his lawyer and a public-relations consultant,[15] Donnelly advanced his case in the court of public opinion. He released to the press the evidence he had given Stubbs, including an email that Marsden sent to Donnelly after the alleged sexual assault, in which she offered to fellate Donnelly, and an envelope of photos of her posing provocatively that she had slid under his office door. The press pounced on these salacious details. The dispute began making headlines across Canada. SFU's claim that harassment panel hearings were confidential only added to the allure. If the administration was resorting to secrecy, there must be something to hide.

After several journalists submitted *FIPPA* requests for copies of the twenty-one-page investigation panel report, SFU released just nine paragraphs. The ensuing media criticism of SFU's "bunker mentality" was scathing:

> *The brain trust at SFU wants us to think that it is not in our interest to put the work of the tribunal up for public examination . . . There is not a shred of information in the release that helps us to understand how and why the tribunal reached its decision. There are, however, numerous defences of SFU's resolutely tight-lipped position . . . We all know the real reason for hiding away the tribunal's report: It would not serve the interests of SFU authorities who have badly bungled this affair. SFU says privacy matters are at stake. We say justice, and the right to know how public institutions dispense it, are at stake.[16]*

At the time the Marsden-Donnelly conflict was starting to make news, Stubbs was on a three-month research leave writing a book about the English newspaper the *Observer*. While Stubbs was away, his stand-in,

VP-academic Dr. David Gagan, announced that SFU had entered mediation with Donnelly. On July 25, 1997, SFU reinstated Donnelly, paid his salary back to the day Stubbs fired him, and reimbursed his legal fees.[17] Four days later the *Vancouver Sun* reported Stubbs had requested a medical leave until the end of 1997.[18] The Board of Governors appointed Jack Blaney as president *pro tem* on September 15, 1997.

Blaney announced that one of his first tasks was to make SFU more open and fair, and revise the harassment policy before the end of the year.[19] Six weeks later he announced that Stubbs and the harassment policy coordinator had so seriously mismanaged the policy that eleven harassment cases heard between 1993 and 1996 would have to be reopened.[20]

On December 12, 1997, Stubbs resigned. In January 1998, the Board of Governors appointed Blaney to the position of president for a three-year term.

To top off the administration's string of procedural blunders, SFUFA discovered that, when the Board of Governors appointed Blaney president, it, too, failed to follow normal procedure. The *University Act* empowers the board to appoint a new president, but only with the approval of Senate. In February 1998, Senate had to rescue the board by retroactively authorizing its decision, but with the proviso that procedures "will be followed to the letter when the next President is appointed." Of this fiasco, Coe observed:

> *This is a cautionary tale because it typifies what I have seen over and over again at various levels of SFU's administration. A small number of people, operating perhaps with good intentions but behind closed doors, with little consultation and limited information, often ignoring established procedures . . . make a decision about what is best for SFU. Sometimes administrators have even withheld relevant information that might have led outsiders . . . to question their decisions. Sometimes they have won with these tactics. Sometimes they forced faculty members to put aside their research and spend extraordinary amounts of time collecting the information needed to oppose a decision intelligently. And then they wonder why lack of trust is such a problem on this campus,*

> *why some faculty seem to see a plot behind every innocent*
> *administrative move. That's why a crucial priority for our new*
> *Board Chair and President must be to change the culture of*
> *administration at SFU . . .*[21]

Blaney thus arrived in office keenly aware of the high cost that an administrator can pay for not following university policy. It was in this milieu that we initiated our campaign for justice for criminology graduate student Russel Ogden. In that same 1998 edition of the faculty association *Newsletter*, we wrote:

> *President Jack Blaney should recognize the procedural flaws and*
> *conflicts of interest that pervade VP-Research Bruce Clayman's*
> *review of the Russel Ogden case and should convene an entirely*
> *independent review to determine whether the University's*
> *actions were consistent with University policies.*[22]

The article proceeded to lay out the appearance of conflict that occurred when President *pro tem* Blaney assigned VP-research Clayman to review the Ogden decision. We reiterated our view that, by limiting confidentiality, the research ethics committee had substantively changed the research-ethics policy without the approval of Senate and the Board of Governors.

Although we might like to think that any progress we were making was due to our carefully prepared arguments, given what else had been happening at SFU, perhaps it was little wonder that those arguments gained traction.

CHAPTER XIV

SFU's "Hollow and Timid" Defence of Academic Freedom

In early June 1998, President Blaney, perhaps realizing that openness and accountability was the best way to change the administrative culture at SFU, announced there would be an independent inquiry into the university's decision-making regarding Russel Ogden's research. In the words of the *Simon Fraser News*:

> *The review will consider the background to the Ogden decision including: the requirements of the university research ethics policy that was in force in 1992; the circumstances surrounding the ethics approval given for Ogden's thesis research; the circumstances surrounding the supervision of his thesis research; and the reasons behind the university's decisions not to provide formal support during Ogden's inquest appearance and to limit payment of his legal expenses (including consideration of the nature of the university's responsibilities to researchers and research participants).*[1]

The administration and faculty association agreed that Dr. Nicholas Blomley of the Department of Geography, and Dr. Steven Davis of the Department of Philosophy — two professors who had nothing to do with the decision, and who had no connection to the VP-research, the ethics committee, the School of Criminology, or Ogden — would undertake the review.

The review's timing could not have been better for Blaney and SFU. Soon after, following almost two years of deliberation, Judge Daniel Steinberg released his decision in *Ogden v. SFU*.[2] He did not pull his punches.

Judge Steinberg's Small Claims Court Decision

The legal issue at the crux of Ogden's lawsuit against SFU was that it had breached a contract with him. Because he had satisfied the criteria that SFU imposes to meet the requirements of an MA, when the coroner challenged his SFU-approved research confidentiality protocol, Ogden argued that SFU had an implicit contractual obligation to help him meet that challenge. Judge Steinberg dismissed this claim. In the absence of any specific agreement or policy about what would happen in the event of a legal challenge, because it was up to SFU to decide which legal avenues to pursue, it was not contractually obliged to assist Ogden.

Ordinarily, the decision would have ended there, but Judge Steinberg continued, "I cannot leave this case without making some comment on some of the arguments of the defendant." In an *obiter dictum* Steinberg used harsh words to describe the VP-research's and president's academic leadership. After lauding the value of Ogden's research, the judge continued:

> *The vague statements of personal support as expressed by*
> *the president of the University, Dr. Stubbs, and the dean of*
> *Graduate Studies, Dr. Clayman, sound hollow and timid*
> *when compared with the opportunity they had as leaders of*
> *the University, to promote the demonstrated value of academic*
> *freedom and academic privilege as evidenced in this case.*
> *To set aside this opportunity because of fear that if they were*
> *to financially support Ogden by paying his legal fees in this*
> *context, some people might misapprehend that they were in*
> *favour of euthanasia, demonstrates a surprising lack of courage.*

Judge Steinberg then commented on former President Stubbs's concern that "challenging the legal process" by seeking to quash the subpoenas might generate publicity that "doesn't necessarily do the university a lot of good." His comments on this issue also had relevance for the question of what it might mean to defend confidentiality "to the full extent permissible by law."

> It is self-evident that the rule of law includes the right to determine what the boundaries or the extent of academic privilege might be by way of a challenge in court. This can only be determined by challenging in a particular matter a request to obtain what a researcher considers privileged information. Only if the challenge has been lost in the highest court in which the challenge is being made, would the rule of law say that the boundary of privilege in the particular case has been set . . . It is hard to understand how an institution of higher learning, engaged in very important social research, would be thought less of because it undertook to determine the boundaries of academic privilege, when the existence of that privilege is what made the research possible in the first place. The questions of the coroner to Ogden were a direct challenge to the academic freedom and privilege that were so necessary for the research that had been approved by the University. When, because of the possibility of bad publicity, the University turned its back on the researcher who was trying to uphold the standards that the University itself had set, it risked much harm to the reputation of the University and its ability to conduct this type of sensitive research.

Steinberg also questioned the university's argument that, by supporting Ogden, the institution might assume "unlimited liabilities related to student research" that could lead it to restrict future student research:

> There is no question here of unlimited liability. All parties agree that the legal fees charged Ogden for his defence in front of the coroner were reasonable . . . To argue that requiring the university to pay Ogden's legal account would inhibit the university from permitting controversial research by a student, is a sad commentary on the institution. The principles of tenure

of faculty and academic freedom and privilege were developed specifically to foster and promote the sense of freedom to investigate and to do research even in areas that some people might find controversial. This duty to pursue original research is in fact set out in s. 46 (c) of the University Act. There is a requisite amount of courage that must exist within the university culture in order to foster this activity.

. . . The University ought to consider whether the assertion of the principles of academic freedom and privilege as they extend to the benefit of all persons doing research under the auspices of Simon Fraser University ought to be left to the financial means of a student, who was conforming as he was required to the guidelines set by the University, or whether that burden is more appropriately shouldered by the University.

Although Ogden lost the legal argument, Judge Steinberg's decision was a stinging rebuke to SFU's senior administrators. The *obiter* stood out for two reasons. First, how was it that a judge could so clearly value the university and understand the centrality of research to its mandate and, in turn, the importance of research to society when university administrators could not? Second, the judge recognized the distinction between ethics and law. There are times when an institution should do what is ethically right rather than restricting itself to what is legally required.

For Ogden's supporters, the decision was a measure of vindication. The VP-research was less impressed. In *Simon Fraser News*, Clayman observed:[3]

The judge's comments, presented in the final six pages of his text, are indeed critical of the university's prior actions in the Ogden case. They will no doubt be of interest to the persons currently reviewing those actions. It is important to note that the judge's comments are his own personal views and have no legal status whatsoever.

Clayman was right: a judge cannot force a university to act ethically. That impetus would have to come from elsewhere.

CHAPTER XV

Dialogue with the Ethics Committee Continues

However heartening Judge Steinberg's views might have been, we were still engaged in dialogue with the ethics committee in an effort to get our research underway before the opportunity vanished. The next letter from Ethics Committee Chair Horvath,[1] which arrived four months after we submitted the first application, started by saying that he would try to "expedite the long standing negotiations between yourselves and the Ethics Committee" by fully apprising us of the committee's thinking.

An Olive Branch of Sorts

The committee did offer an olive branch of sorts by passing a motion describing the support it would provide and telling us that we could include this information in our informed-consent statement; but on the olive branch, a lemon grew:

> *The Ethics Committee believes in supporting, within its means, researchers in the application of Policy R20.01 "University Research Ethics." We would attend court proceedings to defend the principals [sic] of confidentiality and support the Committee's decision to give ethical approval of the project. The Committee believes that any promise of confidentiality is naturally limited both on moral and legal grounds.*

The committee was still insisting our informed-consent statement must indicate that confidentiality had limitations, which in its view went far beyond court-ordered disclosure. When noting that even we had acknowledged that confidentiality is not absolute, the example Horvath gave related not to court-ordered disclosure, but to the public-safety exception to confidentiality — the idea that other ethical obligations, such as saving a life, might override a pledge of research confidentiality. As he explained:

> I think we have reached a degree of consensus with respect
> to the fact the "absolute" or "unconditional" confidentiality
> is not a viable option: During our meetings with you,
> several Committee members, as well as yourself, identified
> situations when a researcher would not be acting ethically if
> the appropriate resources were not called upon to protect the
> safety or well being of a person at risk. Obviously, deciding
> when such action is appropriate is a difficult and problematic
> issue. It seems to me that a lot of our apparent differences are
> due to the difficulty of defining the limits of such exceptions
> to our commitment of confidentiality. The expression "strict
> confidentiality" has been discussed, as well as the applicability
> of various professional standards. At this time, it does not
> appear that the attempts to find a perfect word that globally
> defines the extent and limits of the contract of confidentiality
> between the researcher and a participant in a research project
> have gotten us very much closer to resolving this complex issue.

The implication was that, in the name of informed consent, we should inform participants that we would violate confidentiality to save a life. The committee had engaged in another abstract "What if?" scenario without considering whether the risk of us hearing of a threat to life and limb was reasonably foreseeable in our particular research. As far as we knew, there was not — and still is not — an example anywhere in the world of a breach of confidentiality for the reason the committee cited.

The committee still was not responding to our core argument. While confidentiality is not absolute — who can promise that no one will steal the data, that he or she could withstand torture, or that it is inconceivable that a higher ethical consideration might warrant a violation of confidentiality — does that justify an ethics committee forcing researchers to include *a priori* limitations to research confidentiality in informed-consent statements? Take heinous discovery, for example, and the ethical issues it raises. Although Horvath's June 23 missive stated that such instances ought to be "wrestled with at a case-by-case level," the committee was now imposing it as a blanket policy. The committee also failed to recognize the perverse ethical conundrum this policy would create.

By way of illustration, imagine a study that involves interviewing adults about their relationships with their parents. Imagine further that one of the participants in the study is harbouring ill feelings about his mother and is intent on killing her. If the researcher were to limit confidentiality by saying, "The information you provide me is completely confidential unless you tell me you are going to kill your mother, in which case I will feel obliged to tell legal authorities," what would happen? Will this warning help the mother? The irony is that it likely would do the exact opposite: The participant would not reveal his hostility, in which case he would have the opportunity to go ahead and kill his mother.

Consider, too, what such a limitation conveys to research participants: "We may be interested in learning about adults' interactions with their parents but we are going to treat you all as potential mother-killers." Surely it is more ethical and more in keeping with the trust relationship that researchers are supposed to share with participants to begin with the assumption that none of their participants are mother-killers and to deal with the exceptions if and when they arise. In our sixty combined years of social research, neither of us has encountered a would-be mother-killer despite never having limited confidentiality; and of course, while a criminologist might well be interested in interviewing persons who murdered their mothers, there would be no need to limit confidentiality because the deed already would have been done.

Rather than creating an *a priori* limitation of confidentiality, an alternative ethical approach is to argue that guarantees of confidentiality should not protect acts of bad faith,[2] in which case the appropriate response of the researcher would be to violate confidentiality in order to save a life.

However, he or she might achieve this goal without informing police or another authority.

We also encouraged the committee to go beyond abstract worries about subpoenas and, in the context of our research, think through the question of who would challenge our pledge of research confidentiality and which competing interests they would advance:

> [A] balancing of considerations is embedded in Wigmore's fourth criterion, and is the essence of its case-by-case consideration of claims to privilege. What exactly does the Ethics Committee envision will happen if we were to be subpoenaed? That a court will value the successful prosecution of a sex worker or sex-work manager more than it does the research enterprise? The Committee, none of whom are practising lawyers, appears to disagree with two court officials[3] about the workings of the law. Also, the Committee appears to value the research enterprise less than these two officials do.[4]

As if these objections were not enough, we also were concerned about the way the ethics committee appeared to be acting as a liability-management filter for the administration.

Liability Management Resurfaces

According to Horvath, the ethics committee did not like our proposed wording "confidentiality will be maintained" because it "suggests misleadingly that there is some other power which might otherwise prevent a researcher from breaking his agreement with his subjects." In its place, the committee proposed wording that Horvath claimed was "not inconsistent with your statement of April 23, 1998":

> In the event that we are ordered by a court or other public body to divulge information, we, the researchers, intend to maintain the confidentiality and anonymity of research participants.[5]

We objected that this statement deleted all reference to the university and ethics committee's responsibility to defend research confidentiality, placing the entire onus on us as researchers to do so. Indeed, it looked very much like the statement that Clayman had chosen to interpret as a waiver of the university's liability in Ogden's case:

> . . . We are not prepared to make a statement under the guise of "informed consent" that could be interpreted by the University as a waiver of liability, as it has done in the past, should a researcher be subpoenaed. For the Ethics Committee to foster such a situation is a violation of its responsibility to protect research participants, and an abuse of its power over researchers.[6]

We found the committee's proposal particularly perplexing because VP-research Clayman had already confirmed that the answer to our question[7] about legal representation should a faculty member be subpoenaed "is contained in Article 17 of the framework agreement[8] with the Faculty Association,"[9] which indemnifies faculty if they encounter legal problems while carrying out their contractual responsibilities teaching or doing research.

With these considerations in mind, we offered two further possibilities for consent statement wording. The first was as follows:

> R20.01 requires researchers to treat as confidential information provided by research participants. There is a very remote possibility that we will be asked by a public body to reveal confidential information. In the unlikely event that this does happen, the Ethics Committee will do its utmost to defend confidential information should a public body or court request access to it. Because the University "supports the highest ethical standards" (R.60.01), it will staunchly defend confidentiality in court. In the event that these efforts fail, and we are ordered to reveal confidential information by a court or public body, we will make a principled decision not to do so.

From our perspective, this statement had several advantages:

1. It did not limit confidentiality.
2. It was consistent with the "cultural values and sense of propriety" of the persons who would be asked to participate in our research, as the policy also required.
3. It fulfilled two of the stated purposes of the ethics policy: the provision of information necessary for informed consent and protection of research participants.
4. It was consistent with our disciplinary standard, i.e., that we maintain confidentiality when there is no legal protection and legal force is applied.
5. While mentioning the possibility of a public body asking us to divulge information, it clarified that we would not do so, and hence did not undermine our ability to invoke the Wigmore criteria.

Given the committee's propensity for preferring its wording to ours, we also proposed a second consent statement, which we based on Hanson's suggested wording in his submission to the ethics committee the previous December, but with an additional sentence:

> Any information that is obtained in this study will be kept in the strictest confidence . . . It is possible that, as a result of legal action, the researcher will be summoned to divulge information obtained in the course of their research. The University is committed to the value of researcher-participant confidentiality and is prepared to vigorously defend it in the courts in connection with all research whose protocols have been approved by its Ethics Review Committee. In the event that these efforts fail, and we are ordered to reveal confidential information by a court or public body, we will make a personal decision not to do so.[10]

If the committee was not prepared to accept the proposed consent statement, we asked it to justify its reasons "as per the criteria laid out in R20.01, R60.01, A30.01 and the *Framework Agreement.*" We asked for a quick response, pointing out that the ethics committee was impeding our academic freedom to conduct research.

At this point, the ethics committee finally heeded our suggestion that it obtain an independent legal opinion. However, when we read it we realized that it was hardly independent, and it was not a legal opinion.

CHAPTER XVI
What the Dickens?

Since the beginning of the debate on limited confidentiality, we have drawn attention to the ethics committee's lack of due diligence because, in the process of imposing its doctrine on SFU researchers, it had not obtained a formal legal opinion on confidentiality and privilege. Researchers might have different ideas about how far the ethical duty of confidentiality extends, but all researchers have a duty to protect it to the "full extent permitted by law." What does that actually entail? Is it invoking privilege until one exhausts every legal mechanism, or is the bar set somewhere lower?

Stacking the Deck

By September 1998, the ethics committee secured a budget to acquire a legal opinion. The person it chose was Professor Bernard Dickens, a well-respected lawyer and bioethicist affiliated with the University of Toronto. Curiously, the ethics committee asked for a "legally informed opinion" rather than a formal legal opinion:

> *Dear Professor Dickens:*
> *The Ethics Committee at Simon Fraser University has been debating the question of what kinds of information research participants ought to be provided in order to enable them to make a fully informed decision about participating in a particular research project. As part of our deliberation,*

we are seeking a legally informed opinion with respect to the following:

SFU Policy R20.01 requires researchers to treat, as confidential, information provided by research subjects. Although unlikely, there may be a possibility that researchers who collect information from people who are engaging in illegal behaviour may be compelled by a court to disclose that information. For example, in one case, a researcher was studying assisted suicide among men with AIDS. A Coroner decided that the benefits to society derived from the research outweighed the need to compel the disclosure of the data which were collected in confidence. In consideration of the background information provided above, our primary question is as follows:

Whether researchers who are collecting data from prospective subjects whom they may learn are engaging in illegal behaviour should be required to inform prospective subjects that there is a risk that disclosure of the data may be compelled by a court. If so, what should prospective subjects be told.

Please consider (among other possibilities) the following circumstances.

1. In some cases, information about illegal behaviour may be solicited by the researcher (e.g. a criminologist may ask specific questions about practices that contravene the law), in other instances such behaviour may be only observed in a naturalistic setting (e.g. an anthropologist may be observing the behaviour of a group of people some of whom may occasionally be engaging in behaviours that are illegal in some respect). Does the above distinctions [sic] make a substantial difference in terms of what participants are told about the legal limits of confidentiality?

2. A researcher may wish to promise participants confidentiality even in the face of pressure from the courts. In such cases:

   a. Is it proper for the University (via its Ethics Committee)

> to tacitly accept such a promise (i.e. approve the form
> that will communicate such undertaking to the would-
> be participants).
>
> b. Does such a promise, made voluntarily by the
> researcher, obviate the need for informing the
> participant that there is a possibility, although unlikely,
> that a court may attempt to compel the disclosure of
> the participant's identity and any other information
> the researcher obtained? May a researcher simply state
> that the information will not be divulged, or must the
> researcher qualify the above by stating that it is merely
> their intention not to divulge the information even if
> compelled by the courts, but that the promise has no
> status in law?
>
> We are seeking a response in written form, followed by a
> brief telephone interview, if necessary, to clarify issues arising
> from the text.
>
> Would you consider rendering an opinion on this
> question? If so, what kind of time frame would be realistic,
> and how much would you charge for such consultation?
>
> If you require some clarification of what we are seeking,
> please do not hesitate to contact me . . .
>
> Thank you for considering our request.
>
> Yours sincerely,
>
> Dr. Adam O. Horvath, Chair
> University Research Ethics Review Committee

The committee presupposed the answer to the very question it was asking, i.e., "are there legal limits to confidentiality?" If the ethics committee had conferred with us about what questions to pose — after all, it was supposed to maintain a non-adversarial relationship with applicants — we would have asked: a) Are there legal limits to research confidentiality? b) If yes, what are the relevant laws and jurisprudence identifying these limits? c) What legal strategy would be most effective for protecting research confidentiality?

The letter refers to researchers making a confidentiality pledge that has "no status in law." Again, this wording presupposes the very thing it should have asked, i.e., what form of promise would, in law, be most effective for protecting research-participant confidentiality? In that regard, it failed to ask one of the questions at the heart of our refusal to use the committee's limited-confidentiality consent statement, i.e., does that statement undermine Wigmore criterion one?

The committee asked questions about the ethics of research confidentiality of a person whose expertise lay in bioethics, not social science; so much for the committee being sensitive to "disciplinary standards," as the SFU ethics policy required. Indeed, the ethics committee chair did not even provide Dickens with a copy of the policy; Dickens did not mention it in his "evaluation." However, it turned out that the evaluation was not what it seemed.

Dickens' Evaluation

In October 1998 the chair sent us what he described as Dickens's "independent legal evaluation."[1] Shortly thereafter, the granting agencies released the final draft of the *Tri-Council Policy Statement: Ethical Conduct for Research Involving Humans*.

Horvath interpreted these two documents as vindicating his law-of-the-land advocacy. When he sent us Dickens's evaluation, his tone was triumphal:

> Over the past year, you have raised a number of interesting
> issues and we have corresponded extensively concerning
> these matters. Some of our original differences have been
> successfully resolved, others remain outstanding. In light of the
> fact that the independent legal evaluation and the Tri-Council
> Policy Statement on Ethical Conduct for Research Involving
> Humans are both so clearly supporting the position the
> University Research Ethics Review Committee has taken, we
> see little profit in continuing the debate about the wording of
> the informed consent document. You have, however, recourse
> to take this cause up with Dr. Gee's committee[2] whose task it
> is to develop new policies and procedures for ethical review.[3]

Horvath also attached an article that he intended to submit to *Simon Fraser News*[4] focusing on two aspects of Dickens's evaluation: (1) his assertion that any claim of researcher-participant privilege using the Wigmore test was bound to fail, and (2) the implications of this assertion for Dickens's views on the ethical requirements of informed consent with respect to the legal limits of confidentiality. Horvath claimed that Dickens's "analysis of the [ethics committee's] responsibilities with respect to inform- ing subjects of the possibility of legal action is very similar to the stance the [ethics committee] has taken in this debate." As Dickens put it:

> *Because research committees cannot permit investigators to promise more than they can deliver, or indeed to promise to commit contempt of court, they must ensure that subjects are appropriately informed of the limitations of the promise of confidentiality . . .*
>
> *It is common that research ethics committees require the law to be observed, and that they will not condone its violation by investigators . . . Obligations to the law set limits to the confidentiality that can properly be offered. Investigators and research ethics committees must address explanation to research subjects of confidentiality that can properly be offered them and that is available in law, recognizing that it is always less than absolute.*

Horvath's confidence in these conclusions would be short-lived for vari- ous reasons, not the least being that Dickens subsequently announced that he did not give his evaluation the same weight that Horvath gave it. This revelation came about serendipitously when we contacted Dickens to voice our surprise at many aspects of his evaluation, especially its omission of an analysis of case law on evidentiary privilege. We also questioned its status as an ethical opinion because it did not consider the requirements of the SFU ethics policy, such as its admonition that the ethics committee respect disciplinary standards. In an email response, Dickens told us he did not wish to be drawn into the debate at SFU and:

> Dr. Horvath requested a professional legal opinion, for a
> professional fee. I told him I could not deliver this within his
> time frame, but would send a non-researched opinion on the
> state of the law.

Subsequently, when the SFUFA asked if the ethics committee had spent the budget allotted for the legal opinion, the VP-research said that it had not. Because his was not a professional legal opinion, Dickens did not accept remuneration.

If the ethics committee ever tried to live up to the SFU ethics policy's admonition that "The proceedings of the Committee shall be non-adversarial in nature,"[5] that spirit had evaporated by the time it sought Dickens' involvement. While most people seek an expert opinion to guide decision-making, the ethics committee made a decision and then sought an opinion. Given that we were accusing the committee of violating the SFU research-ethics policy, it should have ensured that any request for a legal opinion reflected the concerns of both sides of the debate.

The Ethics of the Evaluation

Was Dickens truly independent, or did he already have a pony in the race? The pony took the form of doctoral student James Lavery. Dickens was a member of Lavery's supervisory committee and had co-authored at least one paper with him. Lavery's dissertation concerned AIDS patients and euthanasia, and examined propositions emanating directly from Ogden's research.

A comparison of the Dickens/Lavery approach — operating within the biomedical tradition of the University of Toronto's Institute of Medical Science/Joint Centre for Bioethics Collaborative Program in Bioethics — and the qualitative tradition that Ogden practised is illuminating. For Dickens and Lavery, the way to deal with confidentiality was to de-personalize the research interaction, make the research a one-shot study, and give repeated warnings to the participant that, if a court should order disclosure of confidential research information, the researcher would disclose it.

Their protocol created something of a cloak-and-dagger encounter in which researchers informed patients with HIV/AIDS about the study and asked anyone interested in participating to call a designated number to arrange an interview. Lavery told participants not to identify themselves or provide any identifying information. When the researcher met the participants for the interviews, again he told them not to identify themselves. As Lavery explained:

> Because of the nature of the proposed study, some of the
> participants may have had previous involvement in acts of
> assisted suicide or euthanasia. These are currently criminal acts
> under Canadian law. Although the audio tapes of interviews
> will be destroyed, and no names will appear anywhere
> on the transcripts, it may still be possible to recognize the
> participant, or someone else involved in the criminal activity,
> from information in the transcript. The transcripts would be
> turned over to authorities only under a formal court order, e.g.
> as part of a coroner's or criminal investigation. Under those
> circumstances, the study investigators have no legal privilege
> that allows them to withhold transcripts from the authorities,
> This is the main risk of participating in the proposed study.
> There is no way of determining how likely it is that this would
> occur. If you have not been involved in any of these activities,
> this risk does not apply to you.[6]

The research protocol developed under Dickens's supervision self-consciously differs from Ogden's undertaking of absolute confidentiality. Lavery's statement claims there is no legal way of protecting confidential information from court-ordered disclosure. That is not true. Ogden used the Wigmore test to protect confidential research information.

Lavery's informed-consent statement potentially exposed participants to harm by surrendering the researcher's ability to claim privilege on their behalf. Saying that the researchers "have no legal privilege" could void the expectation of confidentiality that the first Wigmore criterion requires. Rather than protecting research participants, it paves the way for the researcher to turn them in to the authorities without a fight. This was exactly the *caveat emptor* approach that Ogloff promoted at SFU, which, in the name of informed consent, sacrifices the participant's right to confidentiality by releasing the researcher and university from the obligation to fight for it. Researchers can gather their data and get their publications and, if trouble ever arises, the "ethical" researcher can walk away saying, "Sorry, but I warned you that might happen." *Caveat emptor.* By concealing the long history in North America of researchers successfully resisting subpoenas, the researcher does not provide the information necessary to achieve informed consent.

The ethics-first doctrine treats the researcher's ethical responsibilities differently. Codes of ethics expect researchers to respect the human dignity of their participants and protect them from harm.[7] It would be exploitative to ask people for information that could harm them if it could be linked directly to them, and then disclose their identities or their personal information to a court or other third party. Even a law-of-the-land researcher should aspire to a higher standard, the minimum being the effort to maintain confidentiality to the *full* extent that law permits.

Part of the logic of the ethics-first doctrine is epistemological. The Lavery/Dickens protocol is a stark reminder not only of how the ethics-first and law-of-the-land doctrines differ, but also how qualitative-field-research traditions differ from those of the more positivistic health sciences. The qualitative-research tradition is not satisfied with isolated and decontextualized fragments of information about a person's life that the researcher harvests for quantitative analysis. Qualitative researchers would like to know — epistemologically they need to know — participants as whole persons. To understand social action — the meaning that a phenomenon has for the people involved — one has to understand the context in which it occurs. This means spending time *in situ* trying to understand how they feel about the prospect of assisted suicide among persons with HIV/AIDS in the context of beliefs and attitudes about other people and the world. Research emanating from that epistemological perspective is often longitudinal; it involves developing long-term networks of key participants; anonymity is rarely an option.[8] Although qualitative researchers may well have private opinions that involve positive or negative value judgments about the activities in which their participants engage, they see their jobs as one of understanding why and how participants' beliefs and actions make sense to them in the context of their lives. Some researchers may be interested in the identities of participants in order to track them through time and in different information sources in the process of triangulating research methods.

These empirical aspirations would lead some researchers to dismiss Lavery's one-shot study of a small sample of people as a relatively superficial glimpse into their lives. His limited confidentiality protocol hardly inspires confidence that his research participants bared their souls. However, it constitutes respectable research at the Institute of Medical Science/Joint Centre for Bioethics/Collaborative Program in Bioethics at the University of Toronto, which awarded Lavery a doctorate for his work. Such is the nature of disciplinary diversity. There is no royal road to truth. In the name of academic freedom, one might expect researchers to defend the right of others to make different epistemological choices and be prepared to debate the status of the ensuing claims to knowledge.

While we lamented the narrow epistemological model that Dickens brought to the questions the ethics committee posed him, we wondered why the ethics committee did not apprise him of the SFU ethics policy requirement that "There is a professional responsibility of researchers to adhere to the ethical norms and codes of conduct appropriate to their respective disciplines."[9] Dickens's opinion failed to speak to criminological field researchers who have an ethical responsibility not to allow the state to turn them into informers.

Dickens on Wigmore

Dickens recognized the Wigmore test as being the appropriate vehicle for asserting privilege, but suggested that researcher-participant privilege was bound to fail on two grounds. First was his assessment of the relative social value of research compared to medicine. Dickens speculated that if courts did not think physicians' communications with patients were worthy of privilege, then research would come up short as well:

> The meaning of [the Wigmore] criteria for investigators can
> be understood through analogies with physicians and lawyers.
> Physicians undertaking therapy do not enjoy immunity from
> subpoena of medical records under these criteria. This suggests

160

*that investigators would not enjoy privilege either, on the basis
that the promotion of scientific research is not of greater social
significance than patients' recourse to therapy.*[10]

Second, even if a research project were to pass the first three criteria,
it would nonetheless fail on the fourth, where the court weighs research
needs against its need for evidence:

*The four Wigmore principles of privilege are not generally
considered satisfied in research studies. Investigators may
offer the assurance of non-disclosure (principle 1) and
consider confidentiality essential to their relation with subjects
(principle 2). They may also be persuaded, as indeed are
universities, that their research relations in the opinion of the
community ought to be fostered (principle 3). However, the
assessment that the injury to the relation with research subjects
by disclosure is greater than the benefit of disclosure to the
correct disposal of litigation (principle 4) is to be made by
the judicial officer confronted with the particular litigation in
which the documents are requested, not by the investigator or
the research ethics committee.*

*Wigmore himself considered that physician-patient
communications failed both the second and the fourth
conditions of privilege from subpoena. This is the basis of the
conclusion that research data are not gathered in circumstances
that satisfy all four of the principles of privilege.*[11]

Dickens's analysis is problematic on two grounds. First, his assertion
that the Wigmore criteria "are not generally considered satisfied in research
studies" is purely speculative; it comes with no supportive evidence, and,
as we show in Chapter 19, is contradicted in dozens of US cases where the
courts engage in a Wigmore-type of balancing exercise. Time and again, US
courts have protected research participants.

Second is Dickens's belief that, if the physician-patient relationship is not
worthy of privilege, then research also will come up short. His reasoning

misconstrues the basis on which courts adjudicate claims of privilege.

Although the social value attached to the relationship in question is an important consideration — criterion three requires that the relation is one the community sedulously fosters — their relative importance is not the question that Wigmore's criteria address. Certainly, the relationship in question must be socially valued, as both the physician-patient and the researcher-participant relationships are, but more than the social signifi-cance of the relationship is at issue. Also important is whether confiden-tiality is integral to the functioning of that socially valued relationship. In Wigmore's words, the purpose of recognizing privilege ". . . is to protect the perfect working of a special relation, wherever confidence is a necessary feature of that perfect working."[12] Thus, the lawyer-client relationship is privileged not because of its relative importance to society, although that is an important prerequisite, but because the legal profession could not func-tion and clients could not realize their constitutionally-based right to a fair trial if they constantly had to wonder whether their lawyers would divulge information they had disclosed in confidence in order for a prosecutor or litigant to use as evidence against them.

The physician-patient relationship falls short on several counts. Criterion one requires a mutual expectation of confidentiality. While the physician's examination of a patient normally occurs in a private room, relatively little about most patients' visits to their doctors is confidential. They tell their families they are going to an appointment and share the results of their check-ups; they sit in waiting rooms with dozens of other patients and are not concerned whether anyone will recognize them; they talk to their friends about their aches and pains; they compare notes about who is get-ting the most effective treatment for their arthritis.

In contrast, we teach researchers that their default position should be to ensure that research participant identities are either never obtained in the first place or to redact them at the first opportunity. There are several reasons for this practice. In some cases confidentiality is provided as a matter of polite-ness and/or because people's names are irrelevant — typically, researchers are less interested in the fact someone is named Fred than they are in the fact that he has had certain life experiences, for example, that make him an appropriate person to include in a purposive sample. Maintaining participant privacy is standard practice for those occasions where research confidentiality is crucial because of the deleterious impact that disclosure could have for a participant. Codes of ethics direct researchers to preserve research confidences unless the participant waives confidentiality, and to inform participants exactly how they will protect their confidentiality. Accordingly, there is a mutual expectation of confidentiality in the research context, except when the participant waives it, or when confidentiality is specifically limited — in which case the conditions associated with the limitation would define the extent of confidentiality the researcher provides.

The second Wigmore criterion asks whether confidentiality is essential to the existence of the relationship. In Wigmore's analysis, the physician-patient relationship rarely meets the test:

> *In only a few instances, out of the thousands daily occurring,*
> *is the fact communicated to a physician confidential in any*
> *real sense. Barring the facts of venereal disease and criminal*
> *abortion, there is hardly a fact in the categories of pathology in*
> *which the patient himself attempts to preserve any real secrecy.*
> *Most of one's ailments are immediately disclosed; the few that*
> *are not openly ascertainable are at least explained to intimates.*
> *No statistical reckoning is needed; these facts are well enough*
> *known.*[13]

Wigmore's reference to information concerning venereal disease and criminal abortion suggests there are specific instances in which recognition of a physician-client privilege might be appropriate because of the social stigma associated with a particular disease or practice.

Another way Wigmore analyzed the physician-client relationship was to ask, "Would people stop going to their doctors if they could not be assured of confidentiality?"

> *Even where the disclosure is actually confidential, it would*
> *none the less be made though no privilege existed. People*
> *would not be deterred from seeking medical help because*
> *of the possibility of disclosure in court. If they would, how*

> *did they fare in the generations before the privilege came? Is it noted in medical chronicles that, after the privilege was established in New York, the floodgates of patronage were let open upon the medical profession, and long-concealed ailments were then for the first time brought forth to receive the blessings of cure? And how is it today in those jurisdictions where no privilege exists, — does the medical profession in one half of the Union enjoy, in a marked way, an afflux of confidence contrasting with the scanty revelations vouchsafed in that other half where no privilege protects? If no difference appears, then this reason for the privilege falls away; for it is undoubted that the rule of privilege is intended not to subserve the party's wish for secrecy as an end in itself, but merely to provide secrecy as a means of preserving the relation in question, whenever without the guarantee of secrecy the party would probably abstain from fulfilling the requirements of the relation.[14]*

We extrapolate Wigmore's analysis of the doctor-patient relationship to suggest that the researcher-participant relationship has a stronger case for privilege. Although confidentiality is *not* important in many research areas — for example, in marketing research that asks whether you would rather travel to New York or Paris — in many other areas it is crucial for the acquisition of valid and reliable data. That is why in the United States there are now numerous research shield laws,[15] such as the "certificates of confidentiality" that are available through the National Institutes of Health (NIH) for health research.

The importance of confidentiality to Ogden's research participants highlights a unique aspect of the researcher-participant relationship that distinguishes it from other confidential relationships. In most of the cases where a party claims that a communication is privileged, the person divulging personal information in confidence has something to gain: the patient seeks a cure; the lawyer's client hopes to beat the rap; the penitent seeks the priest's absolution. In contrast, the research participant disclosing information about criminal activity or other sensitive information usually has little to gain — but much to lose — by the disclosure. The researcher is the person who asks for the information rather than the participant seeking to disclose it. If any risks arise from participating in research, it is because a researcher came into a person's life and asked him or her to participate. This feature of the researcher-participant relationship heightens the researcher's ethical burden.

Many researchers would refuse to do research if they did not feel that they could guarantee participant confidentiality. In our case, the battle over limited confidentiality was literally a battle over whether to continue criminological field research. If the choice came down to doing research with SFU-style limited confidentiality or not doing it at all, we would not do it. Asking for sensitive information under a pledge of confidentiality that the researcher might not keep — depending on a roll of the dice in court — would be unethical. Several criminology graduate students felt the same way; when the ethics committee started insisting on limited confidentiality if a researcher might learn about criminal activity in an interview, some graduate students began avoiding the more interactive forms of research, preferring statistical analysis of anonymized secondary data sets and document archives. One irony of this state of affairs is that the co-opting of research to aid the correct disposal of litigation will mean that the sought-after information is less likely to be created in the first place. It would not be available to the courts, and would leave policy makers and legislators with less information for evidence-based policy and law-reform analysis.

In sum, although confidentiality is not essential to all research, it is integral to the perfect working of the researcher-participant relationship when participants disclose sensitive information. Indeed, it is a prerequisite to that relationship occurring in the first place.

These various features of the researcher-participant relationship are not the only reasons to doubt Dickens's analysis. His most conspicuous omission is an analysis of the many US cases where researchers successfully defended confidential research information or research-participant identities. In Chapter 19, we describe these cases. In Chapter 20, we suggest that researchers should design their research with the Wigmore test in mind. In Canada, if researchers do not do this, they have not defended research confidentiality to the extent that law permits.

CHAPTER XVII
The TCPS Is Released

The Tri-Council Policy Statement

A second pivotal event in the fall of 1998 was the delivery of the much-anticipated final version of the federal *Tri-Council Policy Statement: Ethical Conduct for Research Involving Humans* TCPS).[1] The ninety-page document had been substantially revised from the version submitted by the Tri-Council Working Group the previous year, much to the chagrin of some of its members who expected their draft to be adopted much as submitted.[2] It was a momentous occasion in the history of Canadian research as it marked the time when the federal government seized the reins of research ethics oversight. To be eligible for federal granting council funding universities, colleges, research hospitals, and any other research organization would henceforth be required to sign a Memorandum of Understanding assuring that their institutional ethics policy and review procedures are consistent with the TCPS. Institutions were given a year to bring their procedures into compliance. SFU, which already had established an Ethics Policy Task Force, was among those institutions expected to create a new policy, because aspects of its extant policy — such as the appearance of institutional conflict of interest when an administrator chairs the ethics committee and appoints its members — clearly contravened the TCPS.

Horvath's October 8, 1998, letter to us declaring there would be little profit continuing the debate about the wording of the consent statement made only passing reference to the TCPS, saying it was "so clearly supporting the position the University Research Ethics Review Committee has taken." However, beyond that one line, his letter focused on Dickens's evaluation. It was left for VP-research Clayman to claim that the TCPS vindicated the ethics committee's limited-confidentiality doctrine, which he did in a letter published in *Simon Fraser News*:

> *Proposed new policy should strike balance*
> I was delighted to learn from their "rejoinder" published in the Sept. 10 edition of SF News that Drs. Lowman and Palys address the possibility of court-ordered disclosure of confidential information in their proposed informed consent statement. Since I am not a member of the committee, whose proceedings are confidential, I of course was not aware of that and based my earlier statements on their previous opposition to inclusion of such a statement. I hope that the manner that the issue is addressed by them is adequate for them to receive approval of their research.
>
> It is worth noting that the concept of confidentiality that is limited by the law — addressed by both Drs. Lowman and Palys and by Russel Ogden in the same issue of SF News — is also included in the new "Tri-Council Policy Statement: Ethical Conduct for Research Involving Humans." It can be found at: www.pre.ethics.gc.ca/eng/archives/tcps-eptc/Default/. There, it states that:
>
> 1. *"The researcher is honour-bound to protect the confidentiality that was undertaken in the free and informed consent process, to the extent possible within the law."*
> 2. *"The institution should normally support the researcher in this regard, in part because it needs to protect the integrity of its own REB [Research Ethics Board]."*
> 3. *"In the free and informed consent process, researchers should indicate to research subjects the extent of the confidentiality that can be promised, and hence should be aware of the relevant law."*

I am confident that the review of our ethics policy, now underway, will take into account all of these requirements of the Tri-Council Policy Statement.

It should produce a proposed new policy that permits the maximum degree of academic freedom that is consistent with our ethical obligations to potential subjects. Striking this balance has always been my goal and that of the Ethics Committee in the administration of the present ethics policy.

In the specific case of Mr. Ogden, it should be noted once again that the university supported him both financially and with a statement of support. There remains a difference of opinion about the appropriateness of the degree of support, which was influenced by his own explicit acceptance of full responsibility for the consequences of his decisions.

It should also be noted that there are differences of legal opinion about the extent to which the decision in coroner's court in Mr. Ogden's case establishes any legal precedent and the degree to which privilege exists under Canadian law . . . although it remains clear that there is no such privilege between researcher and subject.

Bruce Clayman
Vice President, Research[3]

The implications of the TCPS for research in general and research confidentiality in particular would be a topic of discussion for some time to come, both at SFU and at other research institutions across Canada. As might be expected in an area as complex and context-dependent as ethics, the document resembled an inkblot, with different commentators reading different interpretations into the ink. Clayman's interpretation of the quoted phrases was a reflection of the law-of-the-land lens through which he viewed research ethics. In contrast, we read the TCPS as a rebuke of just about everything SFU and the VP-research had done from the day Ogden received the coroner's subpoena up to that point.

The sentence "The researcher is honor-bound to protect the confidentiality that was undertaken in the free and informed consent process, to the extent possible within the law" made sense because, by setting the lowest standard for the protection of confidentiality, it ruled out the *caveat emptor* approach that many law-of-the-land advocates endorsed. The problem with the approach that the SFU ethics committee had implemented was that it did not protect confidentiality "to the extent possible within the law." That was possible only by challenging any subpoena and asserting privilege, which is precisely what the VP-research and SFU administration had failed to do in Ogden's case.

We read the second sentence that Clayman quoted — "The institution should normally support the researcher in this regard, in part because it needs to protect the integrity of its own REB [Research Ethics Board]" — as an indictment of SFU's failure to protect Ogden's research participants and its ethics committee's decisions. We resolved to hold SFU accountable to the injunction that research confidentiality should be protected "to the extent possible within the law," a principle that set the bar for the lowest level of protection.

The third sentence Clayman quoted — "In the free and informed consent process, researchers should indicate to research subjects the extent of the confidentiality that can be promised, and hence should be aware of the relevant law" — also made sense. One ought to be aware of the relevant law, which is why we were seeking a legal opinion on privilege, and doing our best to understand the requirements of the Wigmore test in order to protect research confidentiality "to the extent possible within the law."

Missing from Clayman's collection of TCPS quotes was the axiomatic statement that "legal and ethical approaches to issues may lead to different conclusions":

> *The law tends to compel obedience to behavioural norms. Ethics aim to promote high standards of behaviour through an awareness of values, which may develop with practice and which may have to accommodate choice and liability to err. Further, though ethical approaches cannot preempt the application of the law, they may well affect its future development or deal with situations beyond the scope of the law.*[4]

We read this as an agnostic statement that left the door open for both ethics-first and law-first positions, i.e., that while all researchers should do everything possible to protect research confidentiality "to the extent possible within law," law and ethics might "lead to different conclusions." In that final instant, a researcher should have the academic freedom to prioritize law or ethics according to his or her conscience. While choosing to be ethical in that final instant could not "preempt the application of law" — researchers are not above the law and can suffer consequences for disobeying it — researchers can attempt to influence the development of law to make it consistent with ethical principles.

Being open with prospective research participants about "the extent of confidentiality that can be promised" would require researchers to consider in advance whether their ultimate allegiance is to ethics or law, and to fashion their pledge accordingly. In either case, the obligation nonetheless would be to protect confidentiality "to the extent possible within law." Nowhere in the material Clayman quoted was there an injunction that, in the final instant, researchers must always subordinate ethics to law.

These questions about interpretation aside, the least satisfactory aspect of the TCPS was that it appeared to give license to epistemological and ethical imperialism in the ethics review process. At SFU, Horvath and Clayman were still the people in power and able to impose their will. A full eleven months after submitting our first research ethics application, and eight months after submitting the second, the ethics committee was continuing to block our research, and the chair had informed us that further dialogue would be fruitless.

When Horvath imposed closure, we formally appealed the ethics committee's decision. As we began that process, Professors Blomley and Davis were completing their independent review of the university's decision-making regarding Ogden.

CHAPTER XVIII
The Russel Ogden Decision Review

Mandate and Methods of the Ogden Decision Review

Professor Nicholas Blomley of SFU's Department of Geography and Professor Steven Davis of the Department of Philosophy[1] conducted the Russel Ogden Decision Review.[2] Their terms of reference stated:

> *The R. Ogden decision had two aspects:*
> 1. *Not to provide formal support during R. Ogden's appearance at a Coroner's Inquest*
> 2. *To limit payment of R. Ogden's legal expenses (which totalled approximately $10,000) to $2,000, intended to assist in his preparation for his appearance at the inquest.*

Blomley and Davis's mandate was to "consider the background to this decision including, but not limited to, the following matters":

> 1. *The requirements of the University Research Ethics Policy (Policy R 20.01) in force in 1992*
> 2. *The circumstances surrounding the ethics approval given for R. Ogden's thesis research.*
> 3. *The circumstances surrounding the supervision of R. Ogden's thesis research by various faculty members in the School of Criminology*

> 4. *The bases for the two decisions referred to [above] (including*
>   *consideration of the nature of the University's responsibilities*
>   *to researchers and to research participants) and the process*
>   *by which these decisions were made.*
>
> *The review shall recommend to the President concerning*
> *the need for further action, if any, by the University.*

To fulfill this mandate, Blomley and Davis constructed a chronology of events and documents, conducted interviews with relevant university administrators, School of Criminology faculty, and Ogden, and made a general call to the university community for anyone who had any other relevant information to come forward.

The Framing of the Ogden Decision

Blomley and Davis's analysis of the Ogden decision began by describing the way the administration framed the issues confronting it:

> *The question that the University appeared to pose centered*
> *on whether it had any legal obligations to assist Ogden.*
> *Moreover, the issue seems to have been framed somewhat*
> *negatively — that is, as a potentially burdensome obligation.*
>
> *Viewed as a negative issue, the concern seemed to be that*
> *of limiting any legal obligation to Ogden and by extension to*
> *anyone in the future in a similar position . . .*
>
> *It appears that there was no point at which the issues*
> *involved in the decision were framed positively as, for example,*
> *an opportunity for the University to explore through the courts*
> *the extent and the limits of academic freedom, to go to the*
> *defense of one of its researchers whose academic freedom*
> *was being put at risk or to protect the rights and interests of*
> *research participants in University approved research. In fact*
> *there is evidence that the University did not consider academic*
> *freedom or the protection of the rights and interests of research*
> *subjects as a central issues in the decision and that for this*
> *reason there was very little discussion of them in the VPs*

> *meetings at which the Ogden decision was considered or in*
> *the emails that circulated among the administrators about the*
> *decision . . . We find it remarkable that such issues were not*
> *raised, especially the issues of the protection of the rights and*
> *interests of research participants and of academic freedom.*

The university's concern about liability and adverse publicity over-whelmed any consideration of research ethics.

Contradictions Regarding Publicity

Blomley and Davis criticized the university's concern about negative pub-licity if it were to assist Ogden's defense. For them the issue at stake was academic freedom, not whether journalists would see SFU as supporting euthanasia. If the university perceived Ogden's views about euthanasia as the obstacle, why did no administrator bother to find out what his views were? Blomley and Davis found it "contradictory" for SFU Media and Public Relations to promote Ogden's research across North America and then for the administration to be concerned about publicity when legal complications arose. At no point did SFU consider the possibility that defending Ogden might produce favourable publicity:

> *Since research, one of the central missions of the University,*
> *and the principle of academic freedom that protects it are both*
> *poorly understood among the general public, the advantages*
> *that would flow to the University in being seen to defend these*
> *would seem, if not obvious, then, at least, worth exploring . . .*
> *The very fact that Ogden's thesis was controversial and receiving*
> *international media attention would seem to make the principles*
> *of academic freedom that made it possible worth promoting.*

Blomley and Davis pointed out that if SFU was concerned about Ogden's position on assisted suicide, it could have applied to act as an intervener in the coroner's inquest without having to commit to Ogden's views, whatever they might be.

173

Obligations to Students versus Faculty

The university suggested that its response to Ogden might have been different had he been a faculty member rather than a student. The SFU *Framework Agreement* legal indemnification clause would have meant the university had to support a faculty researcher contesting a subpoena. However, Blomley and Davis pointed out that SFU's own policies defining academic freedom apply to graduate students and faculty alike, including the research-ethics policy. The university's legal obligations to its employees and students might differ, but the ethical and legal issues at stake when the coroner subpoenaed Ogden were equally applicable to faculty and students. As to the extent of these obligations, the university argued that supporting Ogden might dig it into a bottomless liability pit. In reflecting on this argument, Blomley and Davis wondered why there was no evidence that the university had ever asked anyone about what the legal defence of academic freedom and research confidentiality might cost if the case were to go to the Supreme Court, let alone what the cost might be if the case ended in the Coroner's Court.

Supporting Researchers Who Challenge Subpoenas

Blomley and Davis were similarly critical of the university's view that challenging the coroner's subpoena would have placed university researchers above the law:

> One way in which the limits of academic freedom can
> be determined is by the courts. Given its legally unsettled
> nature, the issue requires legal dispute. Ogden's actions at the
> Coroner's Inquest, we would contend, were an attempt on his
> part to determine through the courts the extent and limits of
> academic freedom and by doing so to defend the principle of
> academic freedom.

They concluded the university was wrong to argue that there were no legal protections for research confidences:

> It is incorrect to suppose that there is no legal protection
> relating to academic freedom and the confidentiality of

> *information obtained from human participants in doing*
> *research. The Wigmore criteria provide some basis for such*
> *protection. These proved decisive in Ogden's defense before the*
> *Coroner's Inquest. For these criteria to be operative, it should*
> *be noted, an undertaking of confidentiality must be in effect.*

Even with respect to the prospect of defying a court order, Blomley and Davis thought that the university's concern about researchers being above the law was misplaced. Despite the differences between journalists and researchers, they noted:

> *When journalists are subpoenaed to appear in court to*
> *reveal their sources, publishers retain lawyers to defend the*
> *confidentiality of the journalists' sources. This occurs, even*
> *though the courts invariably find against journalists and hold*
> *them in contempt of court, when they do not reveal their*
> *sources. Despite this, publishers continue to defend journalists.*
> *One of their reasons is to uphold freedom of the press. It*
> *would be difficult, we believe, to argue that the publishers by*
> *continuing to defend the journalists are placing newspapers*
> *and the activities of journalists above the law.*

Indeed, when the coroner subpoenaed Ogden he also issued subpoenas to three journalists. Their publisher did support them in court. Although it turned out the coroner did not have the power to do so, he ruled that the journalists were in contempt of court. His ruling did not stop the publisher from continuing to defend the journalists in question.

The "Waiver" Letter

Blomley and Davis's final consideration involved the so-called waiver letter, in which Ogden said, "I take full responsibility for any decision I make with respect to the sharing of information." Having considered Ogden and Clayman's explanations of that key sentence, they concluded Ogden's was the more plausible. The university's interpretation failed to recognize that Ogden was applying for an ethics review, not a liability review, in which case the sentence was an ethical undertaking. If the letter was about liability, the ethics committee should have refused to accept it, as it potentially undermined research participant rights and interests; the committee could not trade ethical approval for the researcher's assumption of liability.

If Not Universities, Then Who?

Having dismissed SFU's justification for abandoning Ogden, Blomley and Davis turned to the reasons why the university should have fully supported Ogden in Coroner's Court. First, academic freedom was at stake:

> We have no doubt that the actions of the Coroner constituted
> a challenge to academic freedom as defined by the University
> itself. In so doing, more than Ogden's project was at stake.
> Central freedoms that determine the nature of a university were
> also at issue. For the University to have distanced itself from a
> court challenge to those very freedoms seems to us to have put
> in danger not only the research function at the centre of the
> University's mandate, but the very principles that distinguish the
> University from all other institutions.
>
> Challenges to academic freedom can come both from within
> and without the university. A university can guarantee to protect
> academic freedom against actions inside the institution that are
> within its legal and moral jurisdiction. It can, of course, give no
> such guarantee about threats to academic freedom that come
> from outside the university. But a university has the obligation
> to try to protect this freedom from such external threats and
> challenges. If universities do not take on this obligation to
> protect such a basic institutional right, who will?

Second, the university had a duty to protect Ogden's research participants regardless of what Ogden did:

> It would be very strange, indeed, for the University to lay
> out a policy in which its researchers have certain ethical
> obligations to research participants, but for it to argue that
> as an institution it did not have correlative obligations to

176

*them . . . [T]he University has a duty to assist researchers in
carrying out their obligations to protect the rights and interests
of research participants. In doing so it is not acting primarily
to provide aid to the researcher, but to fulfill its obligation to
protect the rights and interests of research participants . . . The
University had this obligation, even if Ogden's letter were to
be interpreted as a waiver letter. The reason is that even on
this interpretation Ogden would have only been able to waive
the responsibility the University had to him, but he would have
been in no position to waive the University's responsibilities to
the research participants in his research project.*

*. . . Luckily for the University, Ogden showed uncommon
moral courage in refusing to reveal his confidential sources at
the Coroner's Inquest.*

The bottom line for Blomley and Davis was that "the university made
the wrong decision."

The Review Recommendations

Blomley and Davis concluded with three recommendations for the
president's consideration:

1. *The University should give Ogden the amount of money
   for which he sued the University in Small Claims Court
   as a reimbursement for the balance of his legal fees and
   for his lost wages arising from his absence from work prior
   to his appearance at the Coroner's Inquest. This absence
   was due to an illness caused by the University's decision.*
2. *The University should write a letter to Ogden in which it
   apologizes to him for its decision and for any consequences
   that he suffered because of it. Moreover, it should
   acknowledge that Ogden's stand in the Coroner's Court
   was appropriate and principled.*
3. *The University should extend to graduate students
   engaged in University supervised and approved research*

> *the same legal support and protection that is now*
> *guaranteed to faculty members doing research.*

The SFU President Responds

On October 15, 1998, when SFU President Jack Blaney held his annual meeting with the university community, he announced he would reimburse Ogden for his lost wages and the balance of his legal fees, send him a letter of apology, and forward the recommendation concerning legal indemnification of graduate students doing research to the VP-academic for consideration. During the discussion period, chemistry professor Paul Percival congratulated the president on his decision. The audience gave Blaney a standing ovation for finally setting things right. President Blaney's October 21, 1998, letter of apology read:

> *Dear Mr. Ogden,*
>
> *I am writing this letter of apology on behalf of the University in response to the recommendation of Professors Blomley and Davis that you receive an apology for the decision made in 1994 concerning moral and financial support during your involvement with the Coroner and for the consequences of this decision for you.*
>
> *I am now persuaded that the University was wrong to deny you its support during your efforts to protect the integrity of your undertakings to those who provided confidential information for your M.A. thesis. Your actions were in the tradition of defending freedom for academic inquiry while the University's were motivated by narrower legal and procedural concerns.*
>
> *This has been a difficult period for you and I am very sorry that the University's decision led us into conflict with someone whose courage and initiative we would better have supported. It is my hope that my acceptance of the recommendation in the Blomley-Davis Report regarding your financial situation will at least deal with this aspect of your difficulties, and I hope that by formally recognizing that you*

*were in the right will help with the intangible effects of this
dispute.*

*Please accept the University's sincere apologies for our
earlier decision and its effects on you.*

Sincerely,

Jack P. Blaney

President

On November 9, 1998, Dean of Graduate Studies Bruce Clayman announced that, henceforth "where [a faculty or graduate student researcher's] academic freedom is challenged or compromised by an external body, the University has an obligation to provide legal advice, representation, and/or indemnification to him/her in defending against those actions."

Though the wording has changed slightly, this protection of graduate-student research participants remains SFU policy to this day. With its introduction, SFU went from being a university that lets its graduate students swing in the wind to one that offers what is probably as good a level of protection for graduate-student research participants as any university in the world. Blaney took a situation that had festered for years, resolved it, and turned it into a positive.

Whether everyone at SFU lived up to Blaney's hope "that all involved in this controversy have learned from it"[3] is another matter. In the student newspaper the *Peak*, Erin Fitzpatrick reported:

> *[P]erhaps the new policy statement should be greeted with
> more caution than optimism. Despite his statement in support
> of academic freedom, Dr. Clayman still stands by SFU's
> earlier decision not to support Russ Ogden and says he "simply
> didn't agree" with the Blomley and Davis report. "I don't
> agree with the decision that we should pay his legal bills and I
> don't agree that we owe him an apology."[4]*

If that were the case, the proper course of action would have been for Clayman to resign. He did not. Instead, he made himself available to influence national research ethics policy even though he had never conducted any research on human subjects. Although the appearance of conflict meant that he could not serve on SFU's ethics committee, the three granting agencies nonetheless appointed him to the Interagency Panel on Research, the body responsible for interpreting the *Tri-Council Policy Statement*. We, too, would become involved at the national level, but first, we had to deal with limited confidentiality at SFU.

CHAPTER XIX
"Researchers Should Be Aware of the Relevant Law"

In order to anticipate lawful threats to confidentiality the TCPS admonishes researchers to "be aware of the relevant law."[1] Given that the ethics committee and administration still had not obtained a formal legal opinion on protecting research confidentiality, we sought one instead. Further, we became familiar with every case involving a threat to research confidentiality we could find and corresponded with scholars who had written about those cases, most of whom were in the US, in order to get a sense of the issues that researchers face and how to address them.

Becoming Aware of the Relevant Law

In the process, we were amazed at the doors developing Internet technology was opening for researchers. In the late 1990s, the Internet was still in its infancy. AltaVista was the search engine of choice, Netscape was the browser of choice, and a couple of Stanford graduate students operating out of a garage in Menlo Park, California, were creating Google, which they incorporated in 1998. Email allowed short turnaround times for correspondence with experts around the world. By 1999, it had become possible to read about a case in the morning paper and, using Quicklaw, to access the decision that afternoon.

We began with three general questions with an eye to figuring out what it would take to protect research confidentiality to the full extent that law permits:

1. What, if any, statutes define evidentiary privilege?
2. How would a researcher claim privilege using common law?
3. What is the optimal way to design research to make it as resistant to legal challenge as possible?

Where to Look?

It is not possible to ascertain the full meaning of law by reading statutes. In the British common law tradition, a particular statute's meaning is refined as the courts apply it in concrete cases. In some instances, the courts formulate general principles of law without direct reference to a statute. "Common law" refers to the body of precedent made by judges as they interpret the law. In Canada, the ultimate source of precedent is the Supreme Court of Canada. When we embarked on this investigation, there was no Canadian jurisprudence dealing with researcher-participant privilege. There was just Ogden's case in Coroner's Court, a venue that cannot set precedent for other courts, as it is the lowest rung on the ladder.[2]

Given the absence of challenges to research confidentiality in Canadian courts, there are two other logical places to look. The first is other Canadian cases in which claims of privilege were involved, such as between priests and penitents, physicians and their patients, therapists and their patients, lawyers and their clients, accountants and their clients, police and informers, etc. Although not directly addressing the researcher-participant relationship, such cases could at least help us understand the logic the Supreme Court used, and the principles it invoked, in the assessment of such claims, which would aid in the consideration of how these might play out in the research context.

The second possibility is to look at cases involving research confidentiality in other common law jurisdictions. Although these decisions do not bind Canadian courts, Supreme Court of Canada decisions sometimes refer to US and British case law, particularly when there is little or no relevant case law in Canada. We discovered many instances of subpoenas seeking confidential research information in the United States,[3] in both criminal and civil proceedings. In other English-speaking jurisdictions, we have found only two lawful threats to research confidentiality.[4] Although one has to consider differences between Canada and these other jurisdictions

— for example, several of the US subpoenas were issued by grand juries, which Canada does not have — it is nonetheless useful to know the outcomes of cases that have come before US courts.

How Do Challenges to Research Confidentiality Arise?[5]

There are at least three areas of potential conflict between the law and the ethical requirement of confidentiality:

1. When researchers learn about a crime that a statute obliges citizens to report (mandatory reporting laws vary by jurisdiction, and may include elder abuse, child abuse, spousal assault, and terrorist activity).
2. When researchers learn about threats that research participants pose to third parties, a court might hold them liable for any harm they could have prevented.
3. When third parties such as litigants in civil trials or prosecutors, grand juries, congressional committees and various public bodies in the criminal context subpoena researchers to disclose identifiable information research participants may have revealed to the researcher. Coroners also can subpoena researchers who they think might have information relevant to an inquest.

Social scientists could find themselves confronting dilemmas in any of these areas. The first two involve situations where the researcher's violation of confidentiality would be a matter of their own initiative. In contrast, subpoenas create the threat of compelled revelation after the fact. Historically in the US, the threat of subpoena and court-ordered disclosure has represented the greatest threat to research participants. We consider these cases first.

Subpoenas and Court Orders for Disclosure: A Brief History

The general duty that all citizens have to testify when called upon constitutes the principal legal threat to research confidentiality. In the United States since the 1960s, legal authorities have subpoenaed dozens of researchers[6] and asked — and on four occasions ordered — them to violate research confidences.

The principal threats to research confidentiality in the US have come from congressional committees, grand juries, and private parties — usually corporations — using the discovery process in civil litigation. Since 1970, an extensive secondary literature describes these threats. One of the first recorded instances involved the FBI's threat to subpoena some of the sex research records of the Kinsey Institute at Indiana University. It seems that Hoover's FBI thought some individuals' sexual revelations might help the FBI recruit informants to aid prosecution of political activists and other "undesirables." The FBI backed down when members of the institute made it clear that, regardless of the legal consequences, they would not release confidential research information.

Conflicts between research ethics and law proliferated during Richard Nixon's presidency when politicians, law enforcement officials, prosecutors, and grand juries began trying to co-opt research for law-enforcement purposes. For example:

- A local county prosecutor subpoenaed a researcher studying a federally sponsored income maintenance program in New Jersey. The prosecutor was interested in determining if any participants had illegally collected welfare while receiving income maintenance. The researcher refused to reveal the names of his participants because he had guaranteed them anonymity.[7]
- Samuel Popkin, a Harvard political scientist, spent eight days in jail for refusing to reveal to a grand jury the identities of persons he interviewed regarding the *Pentagon Papers*, a classified Vietnam War study conducted by the US Department of Defence.[8]
- As part of its investigation into criminal liability arising from the Attica prison riot, the New York State Attorney's Office subpoenaed the records of the State Governor's Commission on the riot. The court ruled that, because of the threat to research that a violation of confidentiality would cause, it was in the public interest that it quash the subpoena.[9]

By the mid-1970s, Caroll and Knerr[10] had identified some two dozen instances of Congressional Committees, law enforcement agencies, prosecutors, and grand juries harassing researchers for information to aid the investigation and prosecution of research participants. Although the threat of this source of subpoenas has declined over the past forty years, three of the most important cases from the perspective of criminologists have occurred since then:

- Mario Brajuha was conducting participant observation research on "The Sociology of the American Restaurant" when the restaurant where he was working in and observing burned down under suspicious circumstances. A grand jury subpoenaed Brajuha to testify and produce his field notes to help its investigation. Brajuha refused. In a compromise, the court permitted Brajuha to anonymize his field notes before submitting them to the grand jury, thereby protecting his participants' identities.[11]

- University of Washington graduate student Richard Scarce was engaged in research with animal-rights activists at the time someone vandalized a university animal care facility. When the grand jury investigating the case subpoenaed Scarce, he refused to reveal information that would violate the confidentiality of individual participants. His claim of privilege was denied at trial and on appeal. Scarce maintained confidentiality nonetheless, and spent 159 days in jail until the judge deemed that his incarceration was no longer "coercive" but "punitive," at which time the judge released him.[12]

- In the summer of 2011, the Police Service of Northern Ireland (PSNI), using the provisions of the British–US Mutual Legal Assistance Treaty, sought disclosure of certain oral history interviews with former members of the Irish Republican Army that were housed in the "Treasure Room" of the Burns Library at Boston College. It was the first time, to our knowledge, that any third party has resorted to an international treaty to obtain confidential research information housed in another country.

The agreement the research participants signed promised them confidentiality until their deaths, and the researchers vowed to go the distance in protecting their participants' confidentiality. Boston College held the data, however, and engaged in a legal defence only reluctantly. College officials stated that their intention was always to promise confidentiality only "to the extent the law allows."[13]

From the mid-1970s on, large corporations embroiled in high-stakes litigation posed the greatest threat to research confidentiality. These corporations became interested in research findings either to discredit them or enlist them to support the corporation's case. The following summary of select cases gives a sense of the wide range of research affected; we review their outcomes later when we consider the implications of US jurisprudence for protecting confidential research information:

- Marc Roberts, a Harvard public health professor, interviewed employees of Pacific Gas and Electric Company (PG&E) in a study of utility company decision-making regarding environmental issues. Subsequently, a company sued PG&E for breach of contract. The plaintiff subpoenaed Roberts's interview notes believing that they might have a bearing on the case. Roberts refused, arguing that compelled disclosure of confidential information would stifle research into public policy, the very subject in which the public interest is greatest.[14]
- Professor Richard Snyder, a civil engineer at the University of Michigan and internationally recognized expert on highway safety, published a study entitled "On Road Crash Experience of Utility Vehicles." Shortly thereafter, victims of several serious crashes involving the Jeep CJ-5 sued the manufacturer claiming that its propensity to roll over made it unsafe. The Jeep Corporation thought Professor Snyder's research might help it in the litigation, and subpoenaed every conceivable record related to his research on the crash experience of utility vehicles.[15] Snyder contested the subpoena.

- Dr. Arthur Herbst, chair of obstetrics and gynecology at the University of Chicago, had compiled a registry of over five hundred women with vaginal and cervical adenocarcinoma dating back to 1940, and had published several articles based on its data. In 1984, plaintiffs brought an action against several companies alleging a drug they manufactured caused cervical cancer. The plaintiffs cited Dr. Herbst's research in support of the claim. One of the companies subpoenaed Herbst, ordering that he produce every registry record. Herbst refused, stating that information in the registry was confidential; it would not be possible to conduct this form of research if the court were to violate confidentiality.[16]

- On two occasions, American Tobacco Company subpoenaed Irving Selikoff of the Mount Sinai School of Medicine, in order to challenge his research regarding links between smoking and cancer.[17] Selikoff fought the subpoena.

- University of Georgia Medical School's Dr. Paul Fischer surveyed three- and six-year old children to determine whether they were able to identify R. J. Reynolds Tobacco Company's "Joe Camel" character. They were. As part of a suit against them in California, RJR subpoenaed Fischer, initially demanding all documentation in relation to his study, including the names of all the children who had taken part.[18] Fischer challenged the subpoena.

- In 1992, there was a class-action suit against Exxon Shipping Co. for damages emanating from the Exxon Valdez oil-tanker disaster. Upon hearing of University of Alabama sociologist J. Steven Picou's research on stress in Alaskan coastal communities following the disaster, Exxon subpoenaed Picou's field notes in the hope the company could use what participants told Picou to diminish the company's liability. Picou challenged the subpoena.[19]

- Professors Michael Cusumano and David Yoffie of Harvard and MIT had interviewed forty Netscape employees regarding their "browser war" with Microsoft. Not long after Cusumano and

Yoffie conducted the interviews, Microsoft had to defend itself against anti-trust charges. With respect to the browser wars, Microsoft argued that the stunning increase in market share it enjoyed at Netscape's expense was not because of the predatory business practices of which Microsoft stood accused, but rather because of poor business decisions by their rivals at Netscape. Microsoft subpoenaed the two researchers and asked for all interview tapes, transcripts, data files, correspondence, and field notes pertaining to the browser wars. The researchers refused, claiming these materials were privileged.[20]

- Dr. Sheldon Zink, director of the Program for Transplant Policy and Ethics at the University of Pennsylvania's Center for Bioethics conducted anthropological research with patients undergoing heart transplants. One patient, James Quinn, came to regret his transplant decision. He believed that various parties did not adequately inform him about his quality of life after the transplant. He died nine months later. Mr. Quinn's widow sued the hospital, the artificial heart's manufacturer, and her husband's "patient advocate." The lawyers for the various defendants served Dr. Zink with five subpoenas, noting that she had "observed Mr. Quinn's care for a long time and what she knows could be of great relevance to the case."[21] Zink refused: "The field notes are very sacred to me . . . I promised my subjects that I would never let anyone else read my field notes. I would not betray a trust in that way."[22]

- Arizona's educational policies require English Language Learning (ELL) students to spend most of their day separated from other students so they can focus on learning English. They join regular programming once they pass an English proficiency test. The policy's advocates call this "quality education." Critics call it "segregation," with all the attendant social ramifications. Researchers from the UCLA Civil Rights Project and the University of Arizona completed an independent evaluation of the policy's effects, which involved interviewing students and teachers across the state. The researchers promised students, teachers, school board members, and district personnel confidentiality to ensure candid reporting and to protect participants from negative repercussions, such as firing of teachers or cutting of district budgets. A court challenge to the ELL policy cited the researchers' published evaluations in support of their position. Lawyers for the plaintiff called the researchers as expert witnesses. Not content with merely cross-examining the researchers, however, the superintendent of schools subpoenaed their data, saying he wanted individual-level information so that he could decide for himself whether the researchers' conclusions were warranted. The researchers refused, saying they promised confidentiality and were willing to appear in court, but would not give up the raw data.[23]

The broad range of disciplines involved in these cases — pharmacology, medicine, education, computing science, anthropology, business admin-istration, civil engineering, criminology, sociology, gynecology, public health, sexology, and political science — suggests the SFU ethics commit-tee's imposing limited confidentiality only on research on illegal behaviour was either an over-reaction to a single Canadian case, or a misunderstand-ing of the range of disciplines whose research might become entangled in a criminal or civil suit.

Sources of Privilege[24]

All of the researchers named in the cases above showed courage and com-mitment to principle when confronted with challenges to research confi-dentiality. They faced an uphill battle when they refused to violate research confidentiality because, generally speaking, all citizens are obliged to give any material evidence at their disposal to aid the correct disposal of litiga-tion. As Wigmore stated, "We start with the primary assumption that there is a general duty to give what testimony one is capable of giving, and that any exemptions which may exist are truly exceptional."[25] However, the courts rule that some relationships are so important that the court protects communications occurring in those relationships from disclosure, in which case they are "privileged."

The legal concept of privilege arises in respect to a witness who is competent and compellable, and who has information relevant to the case a court is adjudicating, but who objects to answering certain questions "on the ground that it involves subject matter that is protected from the scrutiny of the court."[26] A statute may define a privileged communication, or it can emerge in common law.

Statutory Privileges

There are a few statutory privileges in Canada. The *Canada Evidence Act* defines some of these, such as "communications during marriage" (s.4.3), and the Queen's Privy Council and Ministerial privilege (s.37–39).[27]

Of particular interest to researchers is the privilege the *Statistics Act*[28] delineates. Statistics Canada researchers are required to take an oath of secrecy. Section 17b of the *Statistics Act* makes it an offence to violate that oath by releasing information that would identify any individual who participates in Statistics Canada research. Section 18 protects Statistics Canada research from court-ordered disclosure:

> *Information is privileged*
>
>   18. (1) Except for the purposes of a prosecution under this Act, any return made to Statistics Canada pursuant to this Act and any copy of the return in the possession of the respondent is privileged and shall not be used as evidence in any proceedings whatever.
>
> *Idem*
>
>   (2) No person sworn under section 6 shall by an order of any court, tribunal or other body be required in any proceedings whatever to give oral testimony or to produce any return, document or record with respect to any information obtained in the course of administering this Act.

The *Statistics Act* is a strong affirmation of the importance parliament attaches to research confidentiality, at least at Statistics Canada. Although Statistics Canada researchers routinely use it as the basis to guarantee unlimited confidentiality to research participants — a confidence that, as far as we know, no one has breached — it is not absolute. Any blanket assertion that one set of rights can *prima facie* supersede all others is contrary to Supreme Court jurisprudence that requires the balancing of conflicting *Charter* rights.[29] Theoretically, the *Statistics Act* is subject to *Charter* challenge. In that event, the court would balance the importance of the privilege against whatever other *Charter* right(s) the litigants or defendants were advancing in the case at hand. It is unclear whether the *Statistics Act* would trump provincial mandatory reporting laws relating to child and elder abuse, which represent a consideration for some researchers. In an effort to make the data gathered by Statistics Canada more accessible for academic research while still protecting participants, Statistics Canada designed a mechanism that allowed researchers to be categorized as its "deemed employees" for the period of their research.[30] Deemed employees are required to affirm the *Statistics Act* oath, whereby the researcher agrees to

> . . . not disclose or knowingly cause to be disclosed, by any
> means, any information obtained under the Statistics Act in
> such a manner that it is possible from the disclosure to relate
> the particulars obtained from any individual return to any
> identifiable individual person, business or organization.[31]

Statistics Canada allows data access only in designated Research Data Centres (RDCs) using stand-alone computers that cannot be hacked, because they are never connected to the Internet. Personal electronic devices — laptops, cell phones, external drives of any sort — are prohibited in the RDC. As the guide explains:

> Statistics Canada considers it important not only to avoid
> disclosure of confidential information, but also to avoid the
> perception of disclosure. It is the trust of the respondents that
> makes it possible for Statistics Canada to provide valuable data
> on the socio-economic condition of Canadian society.[32]

Clearly, Statistics Canada understands the importance of confidentiality to its research and the value of privilege. Its vigilance allows its researchers to make unequivocal pledges to prospective participants. For example, a Survey of Financial Security in which one of us was invited to participate said:

> *Your information is kept strictly confidential. No one, not the courts, Revenue Canada, or even the RCMP can access your information. Your information cannot be made available under any other law such as the Access to Information Act.*
>
> *Statistics Canada is careful to protect the confidentiality of your information. All Statistics Canada employees are required by law to take an oath of secrecy, and there are legal repercussions if the employee breaks that oath. Only those employees who need to see the questionnaire have access to them. We never release any information that could identify a particular individual or family.*[33]

Many forms of research on sensitive topics require this form of rock-solid guarantee.

Privilege in Common Law

Although the ethical obligations of Statistics Canada and academic researchers are much the same, there is no comparable statutory protection of academic research participants. Accordingly, if some third party were to seek access to identifiable data, a researcher would have to demonstrate that his or her communications with participants warranted recognition of a privilege through the common law.

Common law distinguishes two types of privilege: "class" and "case by case." Location of the onus of proof distinguishes them. In the case of a *class* privilege, the courts have accepted the crucial importance of confidentiality to the functioning of a class of relationships, in which case the onus is on the party seeking the information to demonstrate why the privilege should be set aside in that particular instance. When the courts have not recognized a class privilege, the onus is upon the person claiming the privilege to establish why the court should recognize it in that particular case; witnesses have to assert the privilege *case by case*.

Class Privilege

The privilege attached to the lawyer-client relationship is the clearest example of a class privilege. As Cory J. stated for the majority in *Smith v. Jones*:

> *The solicitor-client privilege has long been regarded as*
> *fundamentally important to our judicial system . . .*
>   *The privilege is essential if sound legal advice is to be given*
> *in every field . . . Without this privilege clients could never be*
> *candid and furnish all the relevant information that must be*
> *provided to lawyers if they are to properly advise their clients*
> *. . . It is because of the fundamental importance of the privilege*
> *that the onus properly rests upon those seeking to set aside the*
> *privilege to justify taking such a significant step . . .* [34]
>   *The decision to exclude evidence that would be both*
> *relevant and of substantial probative value because it is*
> *protected by the solicitor-client privilege represents a policy*
> *decision. It is based upon the importance to our legal system in*
> *general of the solicitor-client privilege.* [35]

Class privilege is not absolute. Indeed, in *Smith v. Jones* it was set aside, owing to a public-safety exception that, in the opinion of the Supreme Court of Canada, made it permissible to violate the confidence. In that case, an accused person revealed a plan to murder street prostitutes.[36] That decision is relevant because it held that solicitor-client privilege is the highest privilege that courts recognize:

> *By implication, if a public safety exception applies to solicitor-*
> *client privilege, it applies to all classifications of privileges and*
> *duties of confidentiality.* [37]

Currently, there is no class privilege for the researcher-participant relationship. One reason is that, until recently, Canadian courts had never had the opportunity to consider the concept of "researcher-participant confidentiality privilege."[38] In a legal opinion commissioned by the SFU Ethics Policy Revision Task Force, Michael Jackson and Marilyn MacCrimmon believed that the coroner's privileging of Ogden's research communications would have withstood judicial review. However, they doubted that the researcher-participant relationship would be granted a class privilege because "The Supreme Court has suggested that new class privileges will only be created for relationships and communications which are inextricably linked with the justice system in the way that solicitor-client communications are."[39] As the Supreme Court put it (*R. v. Gruenke*):

> *Whether a prima facie privilege exists for religious*
> *communications is essentially a policy issue. As a general*
> *principle, all relevant evidence is admissible. The policy reasons*
> *supporting a class privilege for religious communications must*
> *be as compelling as the reason underlying the class privilege*
> *for solicitor-client communications: that the relationship*
> *and the communications between solicitor and client are*
> *essential to the effective operation of the legal system. Such*
> *communications are inextricably linked with the very system*
> *which desires the disclosure of the communication. Religious*
> *communications, notwithstanding their social importance, are*
> *not inextricably linked with the justice system in that way.*

According to Jackson and MacCrimmon, the courts will recognize a class privilege only for a relationship that is inextricably linked to the justice system. Canadian researchers will thus have to assert privilege case by case unless legislators extend the protections in the *Statistics Act* or create some other research shield law, such as the US confidentiality certification system, which we describe in Chapter 21.

Case-by-Case Privilege

As McLachlin explains,[40] until 1976 in Canada, the general approach to evidentiary privilege was "categorical." Certain categories of relationships were considered privileged; anything lying outside those categories was not. Privileged communications included those between lawyers and clients, husbands and wives, and those involving state secrets. Courts considered the list of privileged relationships closed, unless they could fit a proposed relationship into one of the recognized categories. This changed in 1975, because of the decision in *Slavutych v. Baker, Collier, Swift and the Board of Governors of the University of Alberta.*

Yar Slavutych was an associate professor in the Department of Slavic Languages at the University of Alberta. In 1971, Slavutych's departmental chair asked him to fill out a tenure review form on a colleague. He was reluctant to oblige. It was not until the chair asked Slavutych a second time — and assured him the evaluation would be completely confidential and he would destroy it after the conclusion of the colleague's tenure application — that Slavutych completed it. Instructions on the form gave a deadline for submission and encouraged the referee to express his opinion "frankly." The chair was to return the form in an envelope marked CONFIDENTIAL. Slavutych followed the instructions. His evaluation was highly critical of his colleague. However, instead of destroying it at the end of the tenure deliberations, the departmental chair used it as part of the justification for a charge of misconduct against Slavutych, for which he could be dismissed.

And he almost was. The Arbitration Board considering his misconduct case found Slavutych guilty. The university president sent him a twenty-one-day warning of his imminent dismissal, as University of Alberta policy required. Slavutych appealed the Arbitration Board's finding to the Supreme Court of Alberta, and eventually to the Supreme Court of Canada. One of several issues he raised involved the status of the confidential tenure form; was it a privileged communication that the chair should not have used against him?

When considering his claim, the Supreme Court looked not to what category the communication fell into, but to the principles embodied in the Wigmore criteria as a way to assess whether a court should privilege a communication. In Slavutych's case, the Supreme Court ruled that it should. The court criticized the University of Alberta for breaching confidentiality, and awarded Slavutych all his costs.[41] As McLachlin explained:

> The significance of the Slavutych decision with respect to the
> question of privilege lies in the fact that the Supreme Court
> of Canada, for the first time, submitted the more flexible
> principles advocated by Wigmore for the traditional "category"

> approach. As a result it concluded that privilege would protect
> a confidential communication made between a member of
> a university staff and the university, not members of any
> category formerly recognized.[42]

Years later in a retrospective analysis of the influence of the *Slavutych* case, Sim[43] quoted Chief Justice Bora Laskin to the effect that:

> What the Slavutych case established is that the categories
> of privilege are not closed . . . This Court, speaking through
> Spence J. in the Slavutych case, was of the opinion that
> the fourfold test propounded in Wigmore on Evidence . . .
> provided a satisfactory guide for the recognition of a claim of
> privilege.[44]

Formal legal opinions by Jones, and Jackson and MacCrimmon make the same point with respect to the significance of *Slavutych v. Baker*. They add that it was in *R. v. Gruenke* (1991) that the Supreme Court formally adopted the Wigmore principles as the test for adjudicating claims of privilege.

At the time of writing, the Wigmore test is thus the appropriate mechanism to protect the identity of research participants in court. However, being successful is another matter. As Jones explained:

> [T]he Supreme Court, indeed all Courts, have adopted a
> conservative approach in applying the Wigmore principles.
> The accepted judicial view is that the search for truth is best
> accomplished through the admission of all relevant evidence,
> and that any departure from this rule is an extraordinary
> exception. In reference to such exceptions, Chief Justice Burger
> of the United States Supreme Court stated in United States v
> Nixon, 94 S.Ct. 3090 (1974) at 3108 that:
>> "Whatever their origins these exceptions to the demand
>> for every man's evidence are not lightly created nor expansively
>> construed, for they are in derogation of the search for truth."[45]

These comments suggest that the onus is on the researcher and the university to ensure that, when the next case occurs, they have "good facts" on hand to substantiate their defence of research confidentiality. In US lawyer Michael Traynor's eyes, the process of generating good facts begins well before a challenge arises:

> The best defence against an excessive subpoena requires that
> the researcher be alert to the possibility of a subpoena from
> the earliest planning of the research, and that he remain
> alert throughout the process. Taking early precautions and
> maintaining awareness allows the researcher to take advantage
> of existing protections, and enables him to quickly mobilize his
> defence should he be served with a subpoena.[46]

Given that the Supreme Court of Canada has identified the Wigmore test as the appropriate mechanism for evaluating privilege claims, how can researchers best prepare to satisfy its criteria?

CHAPTER XX

Implementing Wigmore Part I: Prerequisites for Consideration[1, 2]

The Supreme Court of Canada has made it clear that anyone wanting to assert a claim for privilege must do so using the Wigmore test. Although there is nothing stopping researchers in the US from invoking the Wigmore test,[3] we have not found a US research case that explicitly did so.[4] Nevertheless, when evaluating claims for a researcher-participant privilege, US courts use Wigmore's logic to evaluate privilege claims. On those occasions when assertions of researcher-participant privilege have failed, the cases clearly did not meet the Wigmore criteria in one or more respects.

What exactly does preparing for Wigmore involve? What can researchers and REBs do to ensure that, when that next case occurs, the researcher is armed with "good facts" to make the best case possible for the court's recognition of a researcher-participant privilege? In this chapter, we consider the first three criteria. We do so by drawing on Ogden's successful application of the Wigmore test to assert researcher-participant privilege, the Supreme Court of Canada's decision, making on privilege claims in other contexts, and the outcomes of cases involving research confidentiality in US courts. Our analysis brings together material we compiled for three peer-reviewed articles[5] as well as formal legal opinions by Paul Jones,[6] Michael Jackson and Marilyn MacCrimmon,[7] and Deborah Lovett.[8] We approached the task as researchers who wanted to understand law well enough to fulfill our ethical commitments to participants and make every possible effort to fulfill legal requirements that do not transgress our ethical boundaries.

Criterion One: "The Moment Confidence Ceases, Privilege Ceases"

The first criterion asserts that the people involved in the relationship for which they assert privilege must share the understanding that they uttered the communication in question in confidence. For Wigmore, "The moment confidence ceases, privilege ceases."[9]

The Supreme Court of Canada has set a high standard for "an expectation of confidentiality," as expressed in its adjudication of a claim for priest-penitent privilege. In *R. v. Gruenke*,[10] the court concluded that the mere fact Ms. Gruenke communicated her premeditation in a murder to a counsellor and pastor — persons with whom one might normally expect to have confidential communications — was not sufficient in itself to satisfy the first criterion of the Wigmore test. The Court wanted clear evidence that the communication in question — a confession, but not one that she made in a confessional — had a shared unambiguous expectation of confidentiality. Reflecting on the Supreme Court's ruling, lawyer Mary Marshall advised:

> [I]f you are speaking with a priest or doctor and you want your statements to remain confidential even in the event of court proceedings, you should begin your discussion with the statement "This must remain absolutely confidential."[11]

This opinion suggested that the SFU limited-confidentiality consent statement warning that "it is possible that . . . the researcher may be required to divulge information obtained in this research to a court or other legal body" could kill the possibility of a successful Wigmore defence.[12]

But while *R. v. Gruenke* was the leading authority at the time the SFU ethics committee was crafting its limited-confidentiality consent statement in 1995, CAUT legal advisor Paul Jones[13] highlighted a more recent (1997) case, *M.(A.) v. Ryan*, which further clarified the requirements of the first Wigmore criterion.

The case involved "M," a seventeen-year-old girl. Dr. Ryan, a psychiatrist, had indecently assaulted M. After the assault, M went to a second psychiatrist, Dr. Kathleen Parfitt, for treatment. Parfitt explicitly discussed the possibility that a court might, at some point, order disclosure of her therapy records. M made it clear that confidentiality was very important to her, and that she did not want the records revealed at any point to anyone, including a court. Parfitt stated that she would do "everything possible" to ensure no information was disclosed. The girl subsequently sued Ryan for damages, at which time he subpoenaed Parfitt's records, but not her personal notes. At issue was whether Ryan's right to secure records potentially relevant to testing the plaintiff's case against him outweighed her expectation that communications with her psychiatrist would be kept in confidence.

A British Columbia trial court decided against M and Parfitt on the grounds that their discussions about the possibility of a court order to disclose implied recognition that confidentiality was limited, i.e., that their claim for privilege failed on criterion one. However, the B.C. Court of Appeal decided, and the Supreme Court agreed, that mere consideration of the possibility of court-ordered disclosure in itself did not undermine the expectation of confidentiality. Writing for the majority of the Supreme Court, Justice McLachlin stated:

> The communications were made in confidence. The
> appellant stipulated that they should remain confidential
> and Dr. Parfitt agreed that she would do everything possible
> to keep them confidential. The possibility that a court
> might order them disclosed at some future date over their
> objections does not change the fact that the communications
> were made in confidence . . . If the apprehended possibility
> of disclosure negated privilege, privilege seldom if ever
> would be found.[14]

According to this decision, a warning about the possibility of court-ordered disclosure in itself would not scuttle a legal defence employing the Wigmore test. The phrase "over their objections" provides crucial information about what it would mean to defend research confidentiality to the extent that law permits. To achieve this, it is crucial to avoid wording that a court could construe as a waiver of privilege.

Avoiding Waivers of Privilege

Notwithstanding the Supreme Court's recognition that two parties can discuss prospective limitations to confidentiality without necessarily foregoing an "expectation of confidentiality," researchers should carefully word the way they inform research participants of such possibilities. The Supreme Court refers to the concept of a waiver of privilege in several rulings. For example, in *M.(A.) v. Ryan*, the B.C. Court of Appeal disagreed with the trial court's reasons for rejecting privilege, but substituted its own: that M did not assert the claim immediately. The Supreme Court disagreed: "The appellant's alleged failure to assert privilege in the records before the Master does not deprive her of the right to claim it. If the appellant had privilege in the documents, it could be lost only by waiver, and the appellant's conduct does not support a finding of waiver."[15]

Part of maximizing the legal protection of research confidentiality thus involves ensuring that a court could not construe any aspect of one's informed-consent statement as a waiver of privilege. This is consistent with the TCPS, which states, "the consent of the participants shall not be conditional upon, or include any statement to the effect that, by consenting, subjects waive any legal rights."[16] Just as solicitor-client privilege lies not with the solicitor but with the client,[17] so researchers are the guardians of privilege, not its holder. Research participants can waive their privilege, but the researcher cannot make waiver a pre-condition of participation in the research. Seeking such a waiver would protect the researcher and the university from liability, but only by exposing research participants to greater risk. As Traynor observed:

> *Researchers frequently qualify their assurances by adding a proviso that confidential data will not be disclosed except as required by law. Such a proviso may alert the source to the possibility of compelled disclosure and may strengthen the researchers' defense against a claim of liability premised in contract, promissory estoppel, or tort in the event of such a disclosure. On the other hand, such a proviso could lead the party subpoenaing the data to contend that the possibility of compelled production was anticipated and that enforcement of a subpoena, therefore, is not inconsistent with the qualified assurance given.*[18]

This cautionary note is vital because the TCPS's admonition that research-ers should warn research participants about "the extent of the confidential-ity that can be promised"[19] could create a booby trap. Researchers created such a trap in research that became the subject of *Atlantic Sugar v. United States*. Corporate respondents to an International Trade Commission ques-tionnaire were informed that the information they provided would not be disclosed "except as required by law." When Atlantic Sugar subpoenaed the survey records of other companies thinking it might help its own case, one of the companies that had completed the survey objected because the researchers had promised it confidentiality. The court rejected the claim, arguing that the US Customs Court's "requirement" of the information that researchers warned participants might occur was now occurring:

> When various persons responded to the questionnaires (from which the information subject to disclosure was evidently extracted) they were informed that the information would not be disclosed "except as required by law." The requirement of disclosure for judicial review is such a requirement, even though it may not have been exactly foreseen at that time.[20]

A similar situation arose in the case of the two sets of subpoenas issued for interviews comprising Boston College's Belfast Project, the oral history with paramilitaries from both sides of the Troubles in Northern Ireland. One of the issues debated in that case is just what pledges of confidential-ity researchers made to the Republican and Loyalist paramilitaries who gave interviews.[21] From the outset, the researchers adopted an ethics-first approach, promising unlimited confidentiality. Subsequently, they did their utmost to deliver on that promise by battling the subpoenas using every legal strategy possible. In contrast, relying on a clause in its contract with the project director, Boston College argued that its intention from the start was to pledge confidentiality only "to the extent American law allows." In turn, the attorney general who issued the subpoenas seized on that phrase as evidence that Boston College recognized there were limits to confidentiality, in which case Boston College should hand over the inter-views in question.

The trial court and First Circuit Court of Appeals both accepted the attorney general's interpretation of that phrase. Both courts identified elements of the evidentiary record that, in their eyes, undermined the claim for privilege. The trial judge drew attention to an email Boston College librarian Robert O'Neill sent to the researchers indicating that he was unsure whether the College could successfully defend the interviews against a subpoena. The judge decided this email indicated those involved in the Belfast Project understood there were limits in the extent to which they could protect the interviews.[22] For its part, the First Circuit Court of Appeals pointed to Boston College's Agreement of Donation with interviewees, which stated:

> Access to the tapes and transcripts shall be restricted until after my death except in those cases where I have provided prior written approval for their use following consultation with the Burns Librarian, Boston College. Due to the sensitivity of content, the ultimate power of release shall rest with me. After my death the Burns Librarian of Boston College may exercise such power exclusively.

Although assertive in its claim that no transcript would see the light of day until the death of the participant — with no limitations noted — the justices observed that the word "confidentiality" never explicitly appeared in the agreement "and provides only that access will be restricted."[23]

The Atlantic Sugar and Boston College cases show researchers may create more problems than they solve when they or their institutions limit their pledges of confidentiality. Clearly, they should seek legal advice to ensure their consent statement wording does not undermine research participants' rights if they find themselves in court claiming researcher-participant privilege.

The Boston College case also provides a significant lesson about the importance of documenting research protocols. Everyone involved with the Belfast Project understood confidentiality was essential if the participants were going to share their histories frankly. Boston College representatives repeatedly and independently told the researchers that the provisions for confidentiality of the archive were rock-solid. However, they never put those assurances in writing. The only written evidence regarding who said what was librarian O'Neill's email expressing caution about whether the archive could withstand the threat of subpoena, which served only to undermine the motion to quash the subpoenas that did materialize.

Documenting the Confidentiality Pledge and Its Importance to the Research

Problems arose in another US case because the pledge of confidentiality employed was not clear. The case involved Mario Brajuha, who was then a graduate student at New York University at Stony Brook. Brajuha had worked as a waiter in the New York area for more than a decade when he decided to make "The Sociology of the American Restaurant" his dissertation topic, at which point he began a more systematic approach to gathering data.[24] Although his research focused on one particular restaurant, his experience and connections gave him access to owners and employees in many other restaurants as well.

All went well until a fire levelled the restaurant that was the focus of his research. The police suspected arson. In the course of their investigation, they discovered that Brajuha had made field notes recording his observations. Investigators wondered whether these notes could shed light on the suspected arson. Shortly thereafter Brajuha received a grand-jury subpoena. Although he challenged the subpoena, his assertion of privilege was problematic because of the lack of documentation regarding his confidentiality pledge. Although sympathetic to his situation, and ultimately permitting Brajuha to redact identifying information before sharing his field notes with the justices in chambers, the appeals court was critical of the lack of documentation regarding which participants were pledged confidentiality:

> It is axiomatic that the burden is on a party claiming the
> protection of a privilege to establish those facts that are the
> essential elements of the privileged relationship.[25] Brajuha's
> factual proffer in support of his claim of privilege hardly rises
> to the level of conclusory assertions. His attorney's affidavit
> states only that Mr. Brajuha is a doctoral candidate at SUNY,
> writing a dissertation entitled "The Sociology of the American
> Restaurant," and that, in the course of his employment as a
> "participant observer" at various Long Island restaurants, he

has gathered information "from a variety of sources, many of whom were promised confidentiality."[26]

Brajuha's experience suggests that researchers must carefully document whatever pledge of confidentiality they make and to whom, without, of course, creating records that would violate the confidence.

Walk Your Talk

It is clear from judicial decisions based on the Wigmore criteria in Canada and assertions of privilege in the United States that courts expect those who claim confidentiality is essential to their work to behave in a manner consistent with that claim. Precautions should include procedures commensurate with the sensitivity of the confidential material. For example, principal investigators might discuss the importance of maintaining confidentiality with research assistants and train them in appropriate procedures to protect information. No one but authorized members of the research team should have access to confidential materials. Researchers should anonymize transcripts at the earliest opportunity and destroy tapes once transcripts have been prepared and verified. Researchers should keep identifiable material in a locked cabinet or in encrypted electronic files. This is good advice even if a subpoena never arrives.

A positive example of walking one's talk was Dr. Parfitt's interaction with patient M. As Jones[27] explained, while Ryan argued the discussion between Parfitt and the patient regarding the possibility of a court-ordered disclosure meant the court should allow disclosure of M's therapy records, the court viewed Parfitt's conduct outside that discussion as consistently affirming the importance of confidentiality to their communications. The victim-complainant explicitly stated that she did not want her communications with Parfitt disclosed to a court or anyone else. At one point, Parfitt stopped taking her usual notes; if there were no notes, a court could not seize them. There was thus clear evidence that both Parfitt and M understood the importance of confidentiality to their communications regardless of the apprehended threat of court-ordered disclosure, and acted in a manner that maximized confidentiality. Parfitt never stopped asserting privilege on behalf of her client, demonstrating her resolve by taking the case to the

Supreme Court despite negative outcomes at both the trial and appeal court levels; i.e., she defended confidentiality "to the full extent the law allows."

The most important lesson from this case is that the actions of M and Parfitt were consistent with their expectations. Although they entertained the possibility of court-ordered disclosure, their acknowledgement of that possibility in itself did not constitute a waiver of privilege. Indeed, as Supreme Court Justice McLachlin put it, "Far from waiving privilege, the appellant has asserted it throughout the proceedings."[28]

A contrasting example comes from the case of Ric Scarce and his research on animal-rights activists. While Scarce was never a suspect in the vandalism of an animal care facility that police were investigating, the prime suspect was a friend who had been house- and cat-sitting for Scarce while he was on holiday with his family. That friend was also a participant in Scarce's research. The vandalism occurred while the family was away. The morning after they returned home, Scarce and his family shared breakfast with the suspect. According to Scarce, they "discussed the raid like any other group might have discussed the same story around the breakfast table."[29] The prosecutor used that description to argue that it was the only time Scarce and his confidant could have talked about the vandalism, and that confidential conversations do not happen when others — members of his family in this case — are present. Scarce tried to assure the court that he held in private any research-related conversations he had with the friend/suspect — after his child and wife left for the day — but the damage was done.

Qualitative researchers should be particularly attentive to this problem. The importance of building rapport as a foundation for valid data sometimes blurs boundaries. Researchers should be careful to separate their researcher role from any other interactions that involve the participant, perhaps by recording dates of research-related discussions in field notes.

Summary of Evidentiary Requirements for Criterion One

1. In order to satisfy the evidentiary requirements for Wigmore criterion one, researchers need to make it clear to research participants that their interactions are strictly confidential, and create evidence of the pledge that will satisfy a court. In particular, the proposal should declare unambiguously the

researcher's intention to do "everything possible" to maintain confidentiality. This is the phrasing that the Supreme Court of Canada accepted as clearly indicating both the confidentiality of the communications and the intention of Dr. Parfitt in *M.(A.) v. Ryan.*

2. Researchers should record[30] their pledge of confidentiality and the participant's agreement to its conditions. The proposal submitted to the Research Ethics Board should describe the promise, as should any information sheet handed to prospective participants.[31] The participant's recognition and acceptance of the promise should be included on each interview transcript or recorded in field notes.

3. Researchers' actions should be consistent with their pledge of confidentiality. Judges scrutinize every detail of how allegedly confidential information is treated; they will expect those who claim privilege to have acted in a manner fully consistent with their pledge. In the research context, a court might ask, "Did the researcher avoid creating a paper trail? Were data stored in a secure location? Did the researcher anonymize data at the earliest opportunity? Did only authorized research personnel access the data? Did the training of research assistants include specific mention of the importance of confidentiality to the research?"

If confidentiality is important, then the courts will expect researchers to have walked their talk.

Criterion 2: Confidentiality Must Be Essential

According to Wigmore the object of granting privilege is "to protect the perfect working of a special relation, wherever confidence is a necessary feature of that perfect working."[32] The second criterion states: "This element of *confidentiality must be essential* to the full and satisfactory maintenance of the relation between the parties."[33] The second criterion thus requires evidence that confidentiality is "essential to" the relationship for which privilege is claimed.

Codes of Ethics All Assert Confidentiality as a Core Principle

Every code of research ethics we have ever seen identifies confidentiality as a core principle of research ethics. The *Tri-Council Policy Statement* that the Government of Canada implemented through its granting agencies in 1998 expressed the same view:

> *Information that is disclosed in the context of a professional or research relationship must be held confidential. Thus, when a research subject confides personal information to a researcher, the researcher has a duty not to share the information with others without the subject's free and informed consent. Breaches of confidentiality may cause harm: to the trust relationship between the researcher and the research subject; to other individuals or groups; and/or to the reputation of the research community.*

There is abundant evidence of the fundamental importance of confidentiality to research.

Confidentiality Provides Access to Unique Information

Does the provision of confidentiality really make a difference to research with human subjects? Authors of textbooks in research methodology and research ethics think so. For example, in *Ethics in Social Research*, Bower and de Gasparis explained:

> *The guarantee of anonymity to subjects has long been taken for granted as an indispensable condition in social research; it is the commonly held assumption in the profession, just as it is in medicine, law, and journalism, that people will tell a truer tale and act with less inhibition if they believe that what they say or do will be held in the strictest confidence. This scientific rationale, combined with the ethical principle that one respects the privacy of research subjects, has created uniform agreement among social scientists that confidentiality should be preserved by every possible means to protect the interests of both social science and the subjects of its research.[34]*

The assumption that forced disclosure of confidential research informa-tion will have an adverse effect on subsequent project viability is pervasive. The more clearly anonymous or confidential the data, the greater their perceived validity, particularly when the information could have serious negative repercussions for the research participant. A clear example is crimi-nological research on law enforcement and law breaking, especially when it concerns undetected or unreported law violations. How many offenders would talk openly about undetected offences if they thought the researcher might divulge that information to a court or anyone else? How could an ethical researcher solicit sensitive information from a volunteer participant knowing that he or she would turn it over to a court, especially if the court were to use it against that volunteer? The same concern applies to research on many other sensitive topics where release of the information would create negative consequences for the participant, such as stigmatization, financial loss, embarrassment, loss of reputation, loss of employment, etc.

The threat of court-ordered disclosure undermines the viability of certain kinds of research. The Boston College subpoenas offer a recent concrete example. Many observers have speculated on the impact the subpoenas would have on the viability of other oral history projects. Jon Tonge — a professor of politics at the University of Liverpool and vice-president of the Political Studies Association of the UK — reported that he had put on hold his planned interviews with IRA dissidents. Prospective interviewees were no longer interested in participating.[35] *The Guardian* noted that researchers stopped a parallel project — this one dealing with police officers, soldiers, and spies who fought the IRA — when prospective participants pulled out.[35] A former IRA operative stated he has now begun to "refuse interviews with academics because of the actions of the Boston researchers."[36] The remains of the Belfast Project itself are crumbling; many of the interviewees whose interviews were not lost in the court case have asked for the return of their tapes and transcripts. Boston College has acceded to those requests.[37]

Third parties who see the opportunity to access information of interest in a confidential data archive trade a short-term gain for the longer-term damage it will do to research. The Boston College subpoenas sought infor-mation relating to the 1972 murder of Jean McConville, who the IRA sus-pected was an informer. While it is not clear that the sought-after interviews have any real value to a murder investigation that lay dormant for decades, the attempt to obtain material from the Belfast Project archive has closed the door for other researchers. While the McConville family may achieve some closure by finding out what happened to their mother, dozens if not hundreds of others will pay the price, because they now may never find out what happened to their loved ones.

Statute-Based Protections in the US and Canada Substantiate the Importance of Confidentiality to Research

In Canada, only the participants of research conducted by Statistics Canada enjoy statute-based protection for their research confidences. In the United States, statute-based protections for research participants are more broadly available. For example, certificates of confidentiality are available for health research in which sensitive, identifiable data are gathered. The National Institutes of Health administers the confidentiality certification system, although a researcher does not have to be engaged in NIH-sponsored research in order to be eligible for a certificate. As the NIH information kiosk explains:

> Certificates of Confidentiality are issued by the National
> Institutes of Health (NIH) to protect identifiable research
> information from forced disclosure. They allow the investigator
> and others who have access to research records to refuse to
> disclose identifying information on research participants
> in any civil, criminal, administrative, legislative, or other
> proceeding, whether at the federal, state, or local level.
> Certificates of Confidentiality may be granted for studies
> collecting information that, if disclosed, could have adverse
> consequences for subjects or damage their financial standing,
> employability, insurability, or reputation. By protecting
> researchers and institutions from being compelled to disclose
> information that would identify research subjects, Certificates
> of Confidentiality help achieve the research objectives and
> promote participation in studies by assuring confidentiality and
> privacy to participants.[38]

The mere fact that the US has developed confidentiality certificates and a veritable "armamentarium" of other research shield laws at the federal and state levels[39] is unequivocal evidence that the US government is aware that valid data on sensitive topics cannot be gathered without participants having confidence that the information they voluntarily provide will not then be disclosed to their detriment. NIH's confidentiality certificate information kiosk identifies numerous sensitive research areas as eligible for certification, including:

- research on HIV, AIDS, and other STIs;
- studies that collect information on sexual attitudes, preferences, or practices;
- studies on the use of alcohol, drugs, or other addictive products;
- studies that collect information on illegal conduct;
- studies that gather information that if released could be damaging to a participant's financial standing, employability, or reputation within the community;
- research involving information that might lead to social stigmatization or discrimination if it were disclosed;
- research on participants' psychological wellbeing or mental health;
- genetic studies, including those that collect and store biological samples for future use; and
- research on behavioural interventions and epidemiological studies.[40]

"Privacy certificates" offer another form of protection for criminological research funded through the US National Institute of Justice.[41]

One problem with these research shield laws concerns the locus of authority to issue them: In the US, the government reserves that power. Leaving that power to government opens the door to abuse by allowing the state to favour projects that support its policies and actions, potentially leaving those who might be critical of government without protection. For example, while the British government did not stand in the way of the Police Service of Northern Ireland obtaining the Belfast Project interviews of IRA operatives who fought against the British, it has quashed inquiries into criminal acts — including murder — in which British forces and Northern Ireland Loyalists are alleged to have been involved.[42]

The Onus Is on the Researcher

As well as documenting the importance of confidentiality to research in general, the onus will be on researchers to prove confidentiality was essential to the "perfect working" of the researcher-participant relationship in their specific research. The US Court of Appeals clarified this consideration when Brajuha claimed a "scholar's privilege"[43] for his field research notes:

> Surely the application of a scholar's privilege, if it exists, requires a threshold . . . consisting of a detailed description of the nature and seriousness of the scholarly study in question, of the methodology employed, of the need for assurances of confidentiality to various sources to conduct the study, and of the fact that the disclosure requested by the subpoena will seriously impinge upon that confidentiality. Brajuha has provided none of the above.
> . . . Brajuha has made no showing whatsoever that assurances of confidentiality are necessary to the study he is undertaking. Astonishingly, he has not even stated explicitly that confidentiality was necessary to his particular study.[44]

In a health research case, another US court was more flexible in this regard. Richard Farnsworth led a class-action suit against the Procter & Gamble Company (P&G) arguing that one of its tampon brands caused Toxic Shock Syndrome in the women who used it.[45] The suit based its allegation on a Center for Disease Control (CDC) study that included information about medical histories, sexual practices, contraceptive methods, pregnancy histories, menstrual activity, tampon usage, and douching habits of its research participants. The CDC had complied with P&G's initial requests for information about the research, but sought a protective order when P&G subpoenaed participants' names in order to contact them as part of its plan to establish that the study was biased. While acknowledging that CDC gave no explicit guarantee of confidentiality, it argued that disclosure of participants' names would undermine CDC's ability to do similar research in future. The court agreed, stating:

> [T]he Center's purpose is the protection of the public's health.
> Central to this purpose is the ability to conduct probing scientific
> and social research supported by a population willing to submit
> to in-depth questioning. Undisputed testimony in the record
> indicates that disclosure of the names and addresses of these
> research participants could seriously damage this voluntary
> reporting. Even without an express guarantee of confidentiality
> there is still an expectation, not unjustified, that when highly
> personal and potentially embarrassing information is given for
> the sake of medical research, it will remain private.

The court allowed the CDC to contact each of the women who participated in order to ask who would waive their right to privacy; out of approximately three hundred women contacted, thirty-two waived privilege.

Brajuha's experience suggests researchers should explicitly address confidentiality in their research proposals and while gathering data. As Traynor advised:

> Researchers should determine at the outset whether they
> can obtain the necessary data free from any guarantee of
> confidentiality. If not, they should document the reasons
> requiring confidentiality. In many cases, confidentiality may
> be essential to protect data sources from an invasion of privacy,
> from embarrassment or distress, or from criminal prosecution,
> tax audits, or other government investigations, as well as from
> litigation by others.
>   . . . The researcher who prepares a written memorandum
> at the inception of the research setting forth the reasons for
> confidentiality will be well-prepared to persuade a court that
> the project could not have proceeded without the assurance of
> confidentiality.[46]

Ogden's research protocol exemplified the way researchers should be aware of the relevant law. His careful preparation of his confidentiality protocol laid the grounds for his successful assertion of researcher-participant privilege.

Evidence demonstrating the importance of confidentiality to Ogden's research came from three sources. First, at the proposal stage, Ogden explained to the SFU ethics committee why an unqualified guarantee of confidentiality was essential. This evidence established that the provision of confidentiality was part of a considered research plan, not a *post hoc* justification. Second, Ogden asked participants directly whether confidentiality was essential for their participation; all those who had first-hand knowledge of an assisted suicide said "yes." Third, the expert testimony of a criminologist established the importance of confidentiality to criminological research, and the expert testimony of a health nurse explained why preserving confidentiality was particularly crucial to AIDS patients.

On considering Ogden's evidence at criterion two, Jackson and MacCrimmon concluded:

> *This evidence was not just compelling as that of a compassionate health care worker who has dedicated his life to working with those on the outer margins of our society, but was compelling also in its relevance to establishing why confidentiality was essential to the relationship of researcher and subject in the study of euthanasia and AIDS. Thus, in Russel Ogden's case, there was a trilogy of evidence from a distinguished criminologist who has himself conducted empirical research, an expert experienced in working in both a caring and research relationship with AIDS patients, and the evidence of the researcher himself as to why, for to these particular research subjects, he needed to give assurances of confidentiality as a prerequisite to carrying out the research project.*[47]

Ogden's preparation exemplified the way researchers should design their research protocols to satisfy the second criterion of the Wigmore test.

Summary of Evidentiary Requirements for Criterion Two

Researchers will need to supplement expert testimony regarding the general importance of confidentiality to research with evidence that the provision of confidentiality was necessary for that particular project. An independent scholar with experience in the particular area under scrutiny might provide such testimony. Researchers should ask participants at the time they volunteer how important the maintenance of confidentiality is to their participation, and record their responses in the interview transcript and/or field notes.

Criterion Three: The Relationship Must Be Valued by the Community[48]

Having demonstrated a mutual expectation of confidentiality was essential to the perfect working of the relationship, the third criterion asks whether the relationship in question is one that the community values and believes should be sedulously fostered, i.e., carefully safeguarded because of the social benefits it brings. Does the community value research? A variety of communities may be relevant here, including the research community, communities of interest in relation to the research project, and the community at large.

The Research Community

It is clear the research community believes its relation with research participants is worth fostering and safeguarding. All research-ethics codes recognize the integral importance of confidentiality to the researcher-participant relationship.

The nature of the relationship between researcher and participant varies to some extent by research tradition. For example, experimental psychologists typically have a limited relationship that entails a single programmed interaction that may be relatively brief, often under an hour. It often involves the participant reading or listening to a set of instructions, and then being exposed to certain stimuli and/or responding to a structured questionnaire about the experience. Courts are unlikely to pose any challenge to research confidentiality in such research because participants typically remain anonymous. It is not necessary for researchers to identify them, and they do not record names unless identifiers are required for longitudinal studies or to link to other databases.

Qualitative research traditions place the researcher in a different relation to the participant than in more experimental and/or quantitative paradigms. Confidentiality is valued because it allows one to understand people in a manner that is not threatening to them, and is the basic expression of trust that allows researchers access into people's lives. John Lofland, then chair of the American Sociological Association's Committee on Professional Ethics, stated it this way:

> *Ethically, social scientists have desired not to harm people who have been kind enough to make them privy to their lives. At the level of sheer civility, indeed, it is rankly ungracious to expose to public view personally identified and inconvenient facts on people who have trusted one enough to provide such facts! Strategically, fieldwork itself would become for all practical purposes impossible if fieldworkers routinely aired their raw data — their field notes — without protecting the people studied. Quite simply, no one would trust them.*

In general, when it comes to sensitive topics, the less experimental and quantitative the research, the more important confidentiality is likely to be.

The Broader Community

With respect to the broader community, there is abundant evidence of the value placed on social science research and the researcher-participant relationship. Journalists frequently ask university researchers to explain their research results and comment on law, policy, and social trends. Governments engage researchers to evaluate government programs and policies and contribute to governmental committees, inquiries, and commissions. Researchers regularly act as expert witnesses to inform courts about evidence requiring specialized knowledge.

The hundreds of millions of dollars that granting agencies spend annually on research is another indicator of its importance. If we believe formulating policies, procedures, treatments, and law is better when based on evidence rather than stereotypes and uninformed opinion, damage to the researcher-participant relationship damages society itself. The researcher's role involves critically analyzing all aspects of society, and asking why social arrangements, such as law, are the way they are. It is only by fostering the researcher-participant relationship that researchers can provide the knowledge that courts and governments require for society's long-term benefit. We should not require research participants to pay the price for those benefits. As the three councils affirm, "Part of our core moral objection would concern using another human solely as a means toward even legitimate ends."[49]

Other Communities

Particular communities of interest may have a special concern about a specific case in which a witness asserts privilege, especially when a controversial topic is involved and there is a dearth of first-hand knowledge. In Ogden's case, the nurse who had spent a decade working with persons with HIV/AIDS provided evidence about the deleterious effect if Ogden had disclosed the names of his research participants. Legislators and policy makers comprise other potential communities of interest; for example, a Senate committee that was examining assisted suicide and euthanasia legislation invited Ogden to discuss the results of his research. In other cases, interveners who are not members of the researched group may also have an interest. For example, in the US, the American Civil Liberties Union has intervened in research confidentiality cases in order to support academic freedom and freedom of speech.

Summary of Evidentiary Requirements for Criterion Three

For criterion three, researchers will generally need expert witnesses to provide evidence regarding the specific research in question. In addition, one would hope that university administrators — such as vice-presidents of research and chairs of ethics committees — would be willing to provide general evidence about the need to protect research participants, academic freedom, and the research enterprise. Officers of disciplinary associations could provide similar evidence.[50]

CHAPTER XXI

Implementing Wigmore Part II: When the Rubber Hits the Road

Criterion 4: The Scales of Justice

Because they speak to the eligibility of a communication for privilege, if the researcher and REB have done their respective jobs, research on sensitive topics should comfortably pass the first three Wigmore criteria. They should be relatively easy to meet because they focus only on the researcher-participant relationship, and evaluate whether the prerequisites are in place for the court to consider the broader question of privilege. Criterion four places the relation on the scales of justice where the court weighs two competing considerations:

1. The adverse impact on the researcher-participant relationship if confidentiality were to be violated; with
2. The deleterious impact that non-disclosure would have on the particular legal proceeding in which the privilege is at issue.

And there lies the rub. Although researchers can speculate about who might be interested in the identity of their sources and would have the resources to press the issue in court — for example, Ogden's proposal correctly identified the coroner as a potential threat — they can never know for sure what competing interest will be at issue until a concrete challenge confronts them. However, in the interests of informed consent, they have to tell prospective participants ahead of time what they are prepared to guarantee.

In order for researchers to make an informed decision about what kind of guarantee to make, a review of the interests that third parties have pitted against research confidentiality is in order.

Weighing Competing Interests

In the US, the research most likely to arouse the interest of a third party is that relating to corporations or business.[1] Typically, two adversaries involved in high-stakes litigation hear about research that might be relevant to the dispute. When one litigant cites the research, the other subpoenas the researcher in order to challenge his or her methodology and findings. In such instances, third parties can affect both researcher and research-participant interests. Distinguishing these two sets of interests helps to understand the jurisprudence relating to them:

1. Situations where the personal interests of the *researcher* are at stake, such as having to reveal information before it is published, or having to spend large amounts of time responding to a subpoena; and

2. Situations where the personal interests of *research participants* are at stake, such as the participant's rights to privacy, which depends on the researcher taking legal action to maintain confidentiality.

Although in most instances these interests coincide, they sometimes conflict.

The Researcher in US Common Law

Receipt of a subpoena or an order to disclose information has the potential of disrupting the normal flow of research and publication. A researcher may receive a subpoena prior to research being ready for publication, leaving that researcher vulnerable to potentially career-damaging critique.[2] Such was the case in *Dow Chemical v. Allen*. Relying in part on preliminary research by two faculty members at the University of Wisconsin, the US Environmental Protection Agency ordered emergency suspension of two herbicides that Dow manufactured, and scheduled hearings that might result in their prohibition. Dow wanted to challenge the research and subpoenaed the two researchers, asking them ". . . to disclose all of the notes, reports, working papers, and raw data relevant to ongoing, incomplete animal toxicity studies so that it may evaluate that information with a view toward possible use at the cancellation hearings."[3]

The researchers, the university and, in an *amicus curiae* brief, the State of Wisconsin argued that the subpoena was overly burdensome and premature, given that some of the studies for which data were sought were still in progress. They argued that interruption of the research at that point would force the researchers to release data and conclusions that had not yet been subject to peer review, thereby exposing them to potential career damage if data still to be gathered did not support their conclusions. The court agreed, arguing that research deserves protection:

> *Academic freedom, though not a specifically enumerated constitutional right, long has been viewed as a special concern of the First Amendment. Nearly a quarter-century ago, Chief Justice Earl Warren wrote:*
>
> *"The essentiality of freedom in the community of American universities is almost self-evident. No one should underestimate the vital role in a democracy that is played by those who guide and train our youth . . . Scholarship cannot flourish in an atmosphere of suspicion and distrust. Teachers and students must always remain free to inquire, to study and to evaluate, to gain new maturity and understanding; otherwise our civilization will stagnate and die."*
>
> *To be sure, "Our Nation is deeply committed to safeguarding academic freedom, which is of transcendent value to all of us not merely to the teachers concerned."[4]*

Although the court affirmed academic freedom is not absolute, any intrusion should not be undertaken lightly:

> *Case law considering the standard to be applied where the issue is academic freedom of the university to be free of*

*governmental interference, as opposed to academic freedom
of the individual teacher to be free of restraints from the
university administration, is surprisingly sparse. But what
precedent there is at the Supreme Court level suggests that
to prevail over academic freedom the interests of government
must be strong and the extent of intrusion carefully limited
. . . Applying a balancing test, which gave predominant weight
to the grave harm resulting from governmental intrusion into
the intellectual life of a university, Justice Frankfurter wrote:*

*"[Academic] inquiries . . . must be left as unfettered as
possible. Political power must abstain from intrusion into this
activity of freedom, pursued in the interest of wise government
and the people's well-being, except for reasons that are exigent
and obviously compelling."*[5]

The court concluded that academic freedom superseded Dow's interests and quashed the subpoena.

The sheer volume of information sought and its impact on research has played a more central role in other cases. For example, when R. J. Reynolds Tobacco subpoenaed Dr. Irving Selikoff at the Mount Sinai School of Medicine to acquire information regarding ongoing research plus documentation for three published studies that addressed the link between smoking and lung cancer among persons also exposed to asbestos,[6] Reynolds requested,

*. . . all documents related to the studies that describe,
constitute, comment upon, criticize, review, or concern
the research design, methodology, sampling protocol, and/
or conduct of any of the studies; copies of questionnaires,
answers to questionnaires, interview forms, responses to
interviews, death certificates, autopsy reports, and other
causes of death . . . and data sheets, computer tapes and/or
copies of computer discs containing all coded data . . . in as
"raw" a form as possible.*[7]

Similarly, when faced with six separate lawsuits regarding an intrauterine device (IUD) known as the Copper Seven, the manufacturer subpoenaed Dr. Malcolm Potts, president of a non-profit institute that had done research on the effects of various IUDs. In its subpoena, the manufacturer demanded Potts produce seventy-seven different categories of documents that covered all studies the institute had conducted regarding IUDs. Potts estimated the documentation would total 300,000 pages and take his complete staff several weeks of full-time work to compile and copy.[8]

The courts quashed both subpoenas — in R. J. Reynolds case, because it placed an "unreasonable burden" on the medical hospital,[9] and in Potts's case, because "the burden of producing the information outweighed the plaintiffs' need for it."[10]

A different fate awaited Professor Richard Snyder, a professor of civil engineering at the University of Michigan and internationally recognized expert on highway safety. Snyder published a study entitled "On Road Crash Experience of Utility Vehicles." Victims of several serious crashes while driving the Jeep CJ-5 sued the manufacturer claiming that its propensity to roll over made it inherently unsafe. Jeep Corporation thought that Snyder's research might help its defence and subpoenaed "any and all research data, memoranda, drafts, correspondence, lab notes, reports, calculations, moving pictures, photographs, slides, statements and the like pertaining to the on-road crash experience of utility vehicles." Snyder received over eighty subpoenas and spent a good portion of his retirement fending them off.[11]

US courts have been particularly protective when researchers are not party to the litigation, as their independence contributes to the credibility of their evidence. One example is the case of Arthur Herbst, which Judge Barbara Crabb held to be "paradigmatic."[12] In that case, women who contracted vaginal adenocarcinoma were suing E. R. Squibb and Sons, Inc., for damages. The women cited research by Dr. Herbst of the University of Chicago who compiled a database of all cases of vaginal adenocarcinoma contracted since 1940. The research showed a link between a mother's use of Squibb's drug diethylstilbestrol (DES) during pregnancy and subsequent vaginal adenocarcinoma among their daughters. Squibb subpoenaed Herbst for all data in the registry. The courts agreed that Herbst should supply documentation sufficient to assess the validity of his research and its conclusions, but ordered that he not disclose the identity of the women in the database. As Judge Crabb explained:

> *Deitchman was a high stakes case in terms of money. It was*
> *also a high stakes case in another respect: the risk of serious*
> *harm to a significant research study. Not only did the district*
> *court and the court of appeals agree that Herbst's concern*
> *for the confidentiality of the registry was well-founded, even*
> *Squibb appeared to concede that the loss of confidentiality*
> *would affect the registry adversely and that "all society*
> *would be poorer . . . [because] a unique and vital resource*
> *for learning about the incidence, causes[,] and treatment of*
> *adenocarcinoma would be lost."*[13]

The *Squibb* case exemplifies the way US courts craft orders that minimize their impact on research. Even when they order researchers to testify, US courts have generally ensured protection of research participants. US courts weigh the balance in the researcher's favour when:

1. the subpoena is overly broad and/or gives the appearance of being a "fishing expedition" or harassment;
2. the person/organization issuing the subpoena has not demonstrated the relevance of the requested information to the litigation;
3. the researcher is an independent third party with no interest in the dispute; and
4. the issue on which the information is sought can be addressed through alternative evidence or is of marginal use.[14]

Although US courts generally have respected academic freedom, researchers should not assume that a court will understand the deleterious effects of a subpoena or court order, and should not over-generalize its prospective impacts. The more concretely one can articulate prospective effects with direct reference to the research at hand, the more likely the court will take those effects into account.[15] As Judge Crabb explained:

> *Researchers cannot assume that the judge will know anything about the milieu in which researchers work, about their resources or lack thereof, about what disruption of a particular study might mean, or about alternative sources of the same information. Researchers must educate the judge about these matters if they want them taken into consideration."*[16]

In sum, although these decisions show that academics can be compelled to testify, they also show that the Courts have protected researchers from litigants with deep pockets who engage in fishing expeditions, or attempt to harass, bully, or intimidate them. Courts protect research because of its potential social value. Indeed, the courts would sometimes thwart their own search for truth if their decisions were to cause the end of the empirical evidence that, with increasing frequency, plays an important role in litigation. In the long term, protection of research confidentiality is a general prerequisite to the correct disposal of litigation.

The Research Participant in US Common Law

The US literature reveals that attempts to discover the identities of research participants are relatively rare. Although subpoenas have ranged from minor and specific to voluminous and comprehensive, very few ask for participant identities.[17] This may be because the US courts have protected research confidentiality even in cases where researchers did not explicitly guarantee confidentiality.[18]

In cases where a researcher sought an exemption from testifying by asserting "academic privilege" or "researcher privilege," but ended up being required to testify and/or disclose records, the courts protected research confidentiality nonetheless. In *Deitchman v. Squibb*,[19] for example, the case went through several levels of appeal. An appeal court referred the case back to a lower court with the instruction that the subpoena should stand, but that Herbst should be allowed to redact all identifying information about the participants so that confidentiality would be maintained.[20]

The same was true in the case of Dr. Irving Selikoff, who various tobacco companies subpoenaed many times to aid their defence against class-action suits related to their products. Selikoff was required to attend court and produce documents despite the considerable administrative burden this placed on him, but in every case, the courts allowed him to redact information identifying research participants.

Exxon subpoenaed Dr. Stephen Picou, who was engaged in research with Alaskan Indigenous communities when the Exxon Valdez oil spill occurred, in the hope of finding information to undermine the claims that members of those communities were making regarding the effects of the spill. The court required that Picou testify and provide copies of his notes but, to Exxon's chagrin, permitted him to redact any identifying information from the copies.

Another case in point is the Farnsworth versus Procter & Gamble (P&G) suit involving Toxic Shock Syndrome. Centres for Disease Control researchers testified and provided aggregate information that gave P&G the opportunity to dispute their findings, but the court ensured participants would have to consent to the release of their names.

The court took a similar approach with Mario Brajuha's research on "The Sociology of the American Restaurant." Although it criticized Brajuha for failing to record his pledges of confidentiality and with whom he made them, the court nonetheless allowed him to anonymize his field notes before submitting them to the prosecutor who sought them.

In another case, Harvard public health professor Marc Roberts had conducted interviews with employees of Pacific Gas and Electric (PG&E) regarding how public utility companies make decisions about environmental issues. Later, a construction company sued PG&E for breach of contract. The construction company subpoenaed Roberts in the hope that his interview transcripts would throw light on the corporate decision-making that led to the alleged breach. Roberts claimed that the transcripts were privileged. Although the court refrained from determining whether a general "researcher's privilege" exists, it quashed the subpoena, noting that, ". . . the societal interest in protecting the confidential relationships between academic researchers and their sources outweighed the interests of this litigant and the public in obtaining the research data."[21]

The case that best demonstrates the weight that US courts attach to the researcher-participant relationship is that which pitted Microsoft, then the world's wealthiest company, against researchers from Harvard and MIT, two of the world's most prestigious universities. The US government had charged Microsoft with violating anti-trust legislation. Prosecutors pointed to the changing fate of the company in the browser wars — where an 80/20 market split that favoured Netscape's Navigator browser relatively quickly turned into a 20/80 split that favoured Microsoft's Internet Explorer — as an example of Microsoft's predatory practices.

When Microsoft lawyers discovered that Professors Cusumano and Yoffie had interviewed forty Netscape employees and written a book on the browser wars, they subpoenaed the professors and all their original raw data in the hope that it would support their argument that the exchange of market share resulted from Netscape's poor management decisions and not Microsoft's predatory practices. Cusumano and Yoffie claimed the records were privileged. Although Microsoft had shown that billions of dollars were at stake, the US Court of Appeals quashed the Microsoft subpoena. Under the heading "Calibrating the Scales," the court carried out the balancing exercise that Wigmore criterion four requires, without referring explicitly to the test. After acknowledging Microsoft's need for the information and its relevance to its case, the justices evaluated the weight of the researchers' countervailing claims:

> *The opposite pan of the scale is brim-full. Scholars studying management practices depend upon the voluntary revelations of industry insiders to develop the factual infrastructure upon which theoretical conclusions and practical predictions may rest. These insiders often lack enthusiasm for divulging their management styles and business strategies to academics, who may in turn reveal that information to the public. Yet, path-breaking work in management science requires gathering data from those companies and individuals operating in the most highly competitive fields of industry, and it is in these cutting-edge areas that the respondents concentrate their efforts. Their time-tested interview protocol, including the execution of a nondisclosure agreement with the corporate entity being studied and the furnishing of personal assurances of confidentiality to the persons being interviewed, gives chary*

> *corporate executives a sense of security that greatly facilitates*
> *the achievement of agreements to cooperate. Thus . . . the*
> *interviews are "carefully bargained-for" communications which*
> *deserve significant protection . . .*
>
> *Considering these facts, it seems reasonable to conclude —*
> *as the respondents' affidavits assert — that allowing Microsoft*
> *to obtain the notes, tapes, and transcripts it covets would*
> *hamstring not only the respondents' future research efforts*
> *but also those of other similarly situated scholars. This loss*
> *of theoretical insight into the business world is of concern in*
> *and of itself. Even more important, compelling the disclosure*
> *of such research materials would infrigidate the free flow of*
> *information to the public, thus denigrating a fundamental*
> *First Amendment value.*[22]

The central message of these US decisions is that academics are not special, but research participants are. The trust participants place in researchers to ensure they come to no harm fuels the research that benefits society as a whole. Academic researchers are subject to subpoenas like any other witnesses. There is no academic privilege. However, one can infer US courts have consistently recognized researcher-participant privilege because of the social value of research, the voluntary nature of most research participation, and the need for an unyielding ethical commitment to confidentiality to secure it.

In their formal legal opinion, Jackson and MacCrimmon confirmed that, when US courts do order disclosure of research information, they generally issue partial disclosure orders that rarely involve disclosure of the identities of research participants. Their general conclusion is that only very rarely will ethics and law conflict. Given the relatively small number of cases in which third parties have sought confidential research information in the country they referred to as "the most litigious nation on earth,"[23] the ethics and law of research confidentiality are, for the most part, in harmony. With the exception of grand jury proceedings, attempts to use legal processes to force researchers to disclose names of research participants had at that point been unsuccessful in every case but one — *Atlantic Sugar* — where the court order for disclosure was justified by the researchers' limitation of confidentiality.

Having shown that courts generally protect research participants' identities, Jackson and MacCrimmon then identified the scenario where a claim of researcher-participant privilege most likely would fail. They suggested that, if a court weighed researcher-participant privilege against the right of an accused to receive a fair trial, the accused likely would win. They based their conclusion on an analysis of two cases — one Canadian and one American.

The US case involved University of California at Berkeley graduate student Richard Leo.[24] Although Leo's experience did not involve a formal court order to disclose confidential research information, it is worth examining because it is the only known case where a court weighed an assertion of academic privilege against the right of an accused to a fair trial.

Leo's research for his doctoral dissertation involved direct observation of police interrogations. Achieving access was no small feat. It took three months of negotiation to secure ethics approval, but before that, it took two years of negotiations before the Laconia[25] Police Department (LPD) granted Leo access, plus several more months gaining the trust of the officers conducting interrogations. The main worry of the detectives was that an exposé of police interrogation practices by a hostile observer could have negative repercussions for individual officers and the police department as a whole.

Both the LPD and the University of California at Berkeley's ethics committee made confidentiality the primary condition of Leo's access to the interrogation room. Leo's thesis and other publications would use pseudonyms to refer to individual police officers and the department as a whole.[26] Leo saw protection of confidentiality as a core ethical obligation:

> *The protection of research sources from the compulsion of courts*
> *(or any legal authorities, for that matter) is especially important*
> *in research settings such as this one where the betrayal of*
> *promises of confidentiality will likely provide already suspicious*
> *research subjects with good reasons to deny future researchers*
> *entry. More generally, one of our most fundamental obligations*
> *as field researchers is to protect our subjects from invasions*
> *of privacy, humiliation, unwarranted exposure, internal*
> *and external sanctions or any other personal, social legal or*

professional liability to which they may be subjected because we
have created a data base of their activities.[27]

After the research was complete, an accused person alleged that his interrogators had violated his Miranda rights. He subpoenaed Leo, asking him to produce the field notes he took during the interrogation and to appear in court to testify. The particular case came as a surprise, because it was not a contentious interrogation:

> *[M]ore than six months after I had left the field I was called*
> *to testify in court as a percipient witness . . . During his brief*
> *interrogation, the suspect in this case had provided detectives*
> *with a full confession to his role in the armed robbery of a*
> *local food chain store and the physical assault on one of its*
> *employees . . . his interrogation lasted less than thirty minutes.*
> *During pre-trial proceedings, however, the suspect maintained*
> *he confessed only because the detectives had first threatened*
> *him with other prosecutions if he did not confess, and then*
> *prevented him from invoking his Miranda rights. Both*
> *detectives denied these allegations.*[28]

Leo and his attorney believed Leo's testimony supported the police account of events, although in court they continued to argue that

> *the subpoena should be quashed because the public interest*
> *in my research — research that is uniquely predicated on*
> *maintaining the assurances of confidentiality that I provided*
> *to my subjects — should outweigh any due process right the*
> *criminal defendant may possess to the discovery of my research*
> *notes or to the compulsion of my testimony.*[29]

The judge did not agree. In Leo's words:

> *[T]he defendant's due process rights clearly outweighed any*
> *public interest in my research . . . Since the defendant and two*

> *LPD detectives had given diametrically opposed accounts of what*
> *occurred during the interrogation in question, the judge concluded*
> *that my testimony was essential for resolving a dispute that was*
> *necessary to provide the accused with a fair trial.*[30]

Ultimately, Leo decided to testify, explaining:

> *At this point I privately consulted with my attorney. The*
> *university would support whatever decision I chose, he assured*
> *me. However, since turning over my notes would not harm*
> *my research subjects but instead help the prosecutor — the*
> *detectives had not threatened the suspect or prevented him*
> *from invoking his Miranda rights — there was little reason*
> *for me to risk jail . . . Under threat of incarceration, under*
> *the mistaken impression that my research notes would do no*
> *harm to the interests of my research subjects, and believing*
> *that my failure to testify could damage the future interests of*
> *all academic field researchers, I decided to comply with the*
> *judge's order to testify at the preliminary hearing.*[31]

Leo's case is, indeed, worth scrutinizing in detail. There are several problems with his logic for testifying. First, the decision to disclose confidential
research information is not solely a matter of personal choice; the university should have insisted that he defend research confidentiality at least to
the full extent permitted by law. Although Leo felt testifying would help
his participants, the decision about whether to testify was not his to make.
If there was a privilege, it was not an "academic's" privilege. Researcher-
participant privilege lay with the police officers who participated in his
research under Leo's confidentiality pledge. Leo should have asked the officers in question whether they would prefer to waive confidentiality; only if
they did so should he have agreed to testify.

As it turned out, the hearing did not produce the anticipated ruling
favouring the interrogators. Although Leo's notes and testimony established that the interrogators did not threaten the accused, they led the trial
judge to conclude police had violated the accused's *Miranda* rights for other

reasons. Accordingly, the judge did not admit the confession into evidence. The court convicted the accused of armed robbery, but dismissed the other charges. Leo initially felt that a failure to testify might irreparably harm the research relationship with police, but then concluded that his decision to testify had done just that:

> I will always regret having chosen to turn over my research notes
> and testify, even though I was under threat of incarceration
> and even if my research subjects considered my actions morally
> appropriate. Not only had I betrayed my research subjects, but
> I had also probably spoiled the field for future police researchers
> in Laconia, perhaps elsewhere as well. As a result of my decision
> to testify, it is likely that my study will not only be the first but
> also the last participant observation study of American police
> interrogation practices for some time to come . . . the social
> science community has a vested interest in preventing such a
> mistake from happening again.[32]

Jackson and MacCrimmon placed great significance on the judge's indication that he would order disclosure nonetheless:

> Professor Leo's analysis . . . provides an opportunity to look at
> one of the strongest cases that could be mounted for academic
> privilege. His study into police interrogation practices was
> one in which there was a strong empirical foundation for his
> claim that without guarantees of confidentiality . . . police
> officers would never have shared their trade secrets regarding
> interrogation techniques. His research related directly to the
> administration of justice and therefore was directly related to
> the interests that the most protected form of privilege — that of
> solicitor-client — is designed to protect. He could make a strong
> and compelling case that if researchers like him were required
> to disclose their research and testify in criminal prosecutions,
> whether for the prosecution or the defence, the ability to carry
> on this kind of research would be greatly undermined and this

> *avenue of knowledge would therefore be foreclosed to law and*
> *policy makers. Yet, even in the face of this argument, it is our*
> *opinion that Canadian courts, like the American judge in the*
> *Leo case itself, would favour the interests of an accused person*
> *to have access to the testimony of an independent witness whose*
> *evidence is directly relevant to the accused's person's ability*
> *to have a fair trial, including access to evidence necessary to*
> *either establish his innocence or to invoke the protection of rules*
> *that go to the integrity of the administration of justice and the*
> *control of unlawful police activities.*[33]

We have a different interpretation of the significance of Leo's case. The US government already recognizes the need for special protections for research of the type Leo conducted in the form of privacy certificates administered by the National Institute of Justice (NIJ) — but only for research that it funds.[34] Researchers funded by the NIJ must state explicitly how they will meet the terms of 28CFR22.22,[35] which requires that identifiable information gathered under NIJ only be used for research and statistical purposes and cannot be disclosed without the research participant's permission.[36]

Should participants for a university research project enjoy fewer rights simply because the researcher, whose project was clearly within the NIJ mandate, did not receive his funding through NIJ? This creates the situation where a government can facilitate confidentiality for the criminal justice research it funds, but force others to limit confidentiality or undertake the research with an unlimited pledge and face the possibility of imprisonment for contempt in order to protect participants. Although it might not be its intention, research shield legislation is a convenient tool for a criminal justice system that would prefer to cover its tracks while exposing its critics to prosecution.

Jackson and MacCrimmon's analysis did not distinguish academic privilege and the rights and interests of research participants. In most cases, these two categories are synonymous — asserting researcher-participant privilege is the way researchers will protect research participants. However, research-ethics codes do not safeguard academic privilege as such. The academic does not hold the privilege; it belongs to the research participant. Researcher-participant privilege and academic privilege are distinct.

Leo's decision to testify perhaps best served his research subjects' interests because the police interrogators apparently believed that his observational record supported their account of the interrogation. According to this line of reasoning, Leo's decision to testify would not cause the interrogators any negative consequences, and would enhance their interests by enhancing the likelihood of a conviction.

Why, then, did Leo not ask the interrogators if they would waive privilege? As Traynor advised researchers faced with a subpoena:

> *Researchers should promptly notify confidential sources*
> *whenever their data is subpoenaed. Giving timely notice*
> *to them may help the researcher and facilitate a solution.*
> *The sources may waive confidentiality, thereby eliminating*
> *the problem. They may support the researcher in pursuing*
> *remedies that would limit the scope of the subpoena. Notice*
> *also amplifies the court's awareness of the researcher's concern*
> *for the privacy of confidential sources.*[37]

It is not clear from Leo's article whether he did ask the interrogators to waive privilege. Apparently, he did not, even though he seems to have been aware of this possibility.[38]

Canadian Jurisprudence on Privilege

However helpful it is to peruse US cases regarding researcher-participant privilege, they do not bind Canadian courts. In the absence of any Canadian jurisprudence on researcher-participant privilege beyond the Ogden case and prior to the decision in *Parent & Bruckert* v *The Queen & Magnotta*, a consideration of how the Supreme Court had adjudicated other privilege claims — such as the claims of therapist-client privilege in *R. v. O'Connor*,[39] *A.(L.L.) v. B.(A.)*,[40] *M.(A.) v. Ryan*,[41] and *R. v. Mills*[42] — helps to anticipate the conceptual legal filters through which a claim of researcher-participant privilege would have to pass.

The adjudication of privilege involves a balancing of the rights of all persons involved in a particular court proceeding. As Madame Justice McLachlin stated in *M.(A.) v. Ryan*:

> *While the traditional common law categories conceived*
> *privilege as an absolute, all-or-nothing proposition, more recent*
> *jurisprudence recognizes the appropriateness in many situations*
> *of partial privilege. The degree of protection conferred by the*
> *privilege may be absolute or partial, depending on what is*
> *required to strike the proper balance between the interest in*
> *protecting the communication from disclosure and the interest*
> *in proper disposition of the litigation.*[43]

In this regard, Canadian and US courts employ a similar balancing of competing interests. They usually achieve the balancing by ordering "partial disclosure," which is done in the context of the facts of each case and the rights in conflict. Partial disclosure involves keeping the door partly open — admitting evidence needed to assess a researcher's methodology and conclusions — and partly closed to protect research participants. US courts have almost always closed the door on the identity of individual research participants.

Jackson and MacCrimmon suggested that when courts balance competing interests, the most difficult challenge to researcher-participant privilege will arise when pitted against an accused person's right to a fair trial. Given the absence of Canadian jurisprudence on such a conflict, one can only speculate about what the courts would do if asked to weigh the researcher-participant's right to confidentiality against the right of an accused to a fair trial; much would depend on the facts of the particular case. The case they found most informative for this sort of claim is *R. v. O'Connor.*

R. v. O'Connor

Several Aboriginal women sought therapy as part of the process of healing from a series of sexual assaults they suffered at the hands of Bishop O'Connor in a residential school. When O'Connor was charged, he sought to have records of the women's therapy sessions entered as evidence. The Crown objected, stating that giving access to the therapy records violated the women's privacy and equality rights. After much agonizing, the court decided by a margin of four to three that O'Connor's right to make full answer and defence took priority over the women's privacy and equality rights. Jackson and MacCrimmon treated the case as a clear-cut victory for the right to a fair trial over privacy rights. However, some of the circumstances of the O'Connor case suggest that, should these rights clash again, the result could be different. Jackson and MacCrimmon did not appear to give much significance to the fact that the information the Crown sought to protect on behalf of the women was no longer truly confidential at the time the court was asked to agree that it should be considered privileged. The women had already shared their therapeutic records with the Crown to facilitate O'Connor's prosecution. They were patient-litigants.

This status as patient-litigant distinguishes *R. v. O'Connor* from, for example, *M.(A.)* v. *Ryan.* In the latter case, M was merely seeking therapy and her records had nothing to do with the case against Ryan; the court recognized patient-client privilege in that instance. However, in *R. v. O'Connor*, where the records themselves were the source of the charges, the court ruled that O'Connor had a right to see them as part of his defence. The patient-litigants had a clear appearance of conflict of interest: They wanted the records disclosed to some parties, but not to others, leading Justices Lamer and Sopinka to comment:

> *Fairness must require that if the complainant is willing to release this information in order to further the criminal prosecution, then the accused should be entitled to use the information in the preparation of his or her defence.*[44]

The *R. v. O'Connor* ruling thus did not turn on the issue of privilege. The majority held that considerations of privilege were irrelevant when the complainants themselves had already waived the confidentiality of their records — they failed to satisfy Wigmore criterion one. Nonetheless, Justices Lamer and Sopinka did comment on the competing interests at stake:

> *[I]t must be recognized that any form of privilege may be forced to yield where such a privilege would preclude the accused's right to make full answer and defence. As this Court held in Stinchcombe (at p. 340), a trial judge may*

> require disclosure "in spite of the law of privilege" where the
> recognition of the asserted privilege unduly limits the right of
> the accused to make full answer and defence.[45]

The "may" in the preceding passage reveals the court's acknowledgement that just as privilege is not absolute, the accused's right to full answer and defence is not absolute either. As Madame Justice McLachlin commented in her minority decision:

> The Charter guarantees not the fairest of all possible trials, but
> rather a trial which is fundamentally fair. What constitutes
> a fair trial takes into account not only the perspective of the
> accused, but the practical limits of the system of justice and
> the lawful interests of others involved in the process, like
> complainants and the agencies which assist them in dealing
> with the trauma they may have suffered. What the law
> demands is not perfect justice, but fundamentally fair justice.[46]

Jackson and MacCrimmon drew a somewhat different picture by taking another passage from Madame Justice McLachlin, this one from M.(A.) v. Ryan:

> . . . [T]he court considering an application for privilege must
> balance one alternative against the other. The exercise is
> essentially one of good sense and good judgement. This said,
> it is important to establish the outer limits of acceptability. I
> for one cannot accept the proposition that occasional injustice
> should be accepted as the price of privilege. It is true that the
> traditional categories of privilege, cast as they are in all-or-
> nothing terms, necessarily run the risk of occasional injustice.
> But that does not mean that the courts, in invoking new
> privileges, should lightly condone its extension.[47]

This passage suggests the right to full answer and defence will supersede a claim of privilege if it compromises a defence. However, McLachlin's comments in R. v. O'Connor suggest that balancing a defendant's right to a fair trial and the privacy interests of research participants must also be evaluated case by case. Indeed, Justice L'Heureux-Dubé implied as much in her *R. v. O'Connor* minority opinion:

> As important as the right to full answer and defence may be, it must co-exist with other constitutional rights, rather than trample them. Privacy and equality must not be sacrificed willy-nilly on the altar of trial fairness.[48]

If, like privilege, the right to make full answer and defence is not absolute, then the Supreme Court will engage in a balancing exercise that weighs the right of a research participant to privacy with the right of an accused to a fair trial. Jackson and MacCrimmon based their opinion that research-participant privacy will generally lose out to the defendant's right to full answer and defence on the Supreme Court of Canada's rulings in civil suits related to sexual assault (*M(A.) v. Ryan*; *A.(L.L.) v. B.(A.)*) and criminal cases involving sexual assault (*R. v. O'Connor*) and murder (*R. v. Gruenke*). Most of their hypothetical examples involved heinous discovery,[49] i.e., situations where the researcher serendipitously discovers some heinous circumstance, such as being told the identity of a murderer and realizing an innocent person has been convicted and is being sent to prison for life.

Instead of focusing on these worst-case scenarios, consider other cases that might arise in research on prostitution. One of Lowman's studies included observing police enforcing the communicating law (*Criminal Code* section 213). This statute prohibited any public communication for the purpose of engaging in prostitution or engaging the services of a prostitute. As this was a summary offence, the maximum sentence was six months in prison. In practice, clients rarely went to prison. Indeed, in Vancouver from 1991 to 1994, 87 per cent of clients found guilty of communicating received an absolute or conditional discharge, and thus did not end up with a criminal record. Since that time, most of them were not even charged, but diverted into British Columbia's Prostitution Offender Program, colloquially known as John School. In this research, Lowman assured police that he would not divulge their identities. Without this pledge, the officers would not have participated. Limited confidentiality would have fatally compromised research validity.

What if one of the men charged with communicating, realizing that a researcher had observed the defendant's interaction with police, sub-poenaed the researcher as a material witness? How would a court weigh the various factors in the face of a claim for privilege in this instance? The likelihood is that even if convicted, the offender would not go to jail. Indeed, if given a discharge, six months after the date of conviction he would not even have a criminal record. The harm caused by this hypothet-ical wrongful summary conviction is hardly on a par with the harm done to David Milgaard, Donald Marshal, or Guy Morin — three men wrongfully convicted of murder who spent many years in prison. Yet the harm done to police research could be considerable. Given that the Supreme Court has clarified that a defendant's right to a fair trial is not absolute, the ser-iousness of the offence may well play a part in a court's evaluation of the importance of the two rights should they conflict.

When it comes to implications of *R. v. O'Connor* for claims of researcher-participant privilege, Jackson and MacCrimmon's analysis did not discuss key differences in this therapeutic situation as compared to research. The complainants had alleged that the bishop sexually assaulted them. They wished to see him punished. Thwarting his ability to use whatever means he could to mount a defence has the appearance of conflict because it helps to achieve these objectives.[50] In such situations, the court's attempt to bal-ance competing interests takes into account the interest of a complainant who has something to gain by revealing information to one party, but not to another.[51]

Research participants usually do not have this appearance of conflict of interest. Prostitution research participants divulge information in confidence about their own criminal and sexual activities to a researcher with the full knowledge they are offering us data that we will compile, analyze, and publish. Participants divulge information on the condition that the researcher does not release their names. Research participants typically receive nothing direct or tangible for their participation other than, perhaps, a hope that someone will hear their voices. Occasionally the researcher pays them each a modest fee. Their primary motive is to provide information for the purpose of the greater good, and the only reason the information is available in the first place is because the researcher pledged confidentiality — a compelling reason to recognize researcher-participant privilege when the research concerns sensitive topics.

Writing for the majority, Justices Lamer and Sopinka described the considerations that would be involved in balancing the privacy interests in therapeutic records of an accuser relative to the right of the accused to access them. One element they note, which Jackson and MacCrimmon largely bypassed, concerned the probative value of the records in question. In her dissenting opinion, Madame Justice L'Heureux-Dubé made the following remarks about therapeutic records of the type considered in R. v. O'Connor:

> [T]he assumption that private therapeutic or counselling
> records are relevant to full answer and defence is often highly
> questionable, in that these records may very well have a greater
> potential to derail than to advance the truth-seeking process:
>   . . . medical records concerning statements made in
> the course of therapy are both hearsay and inherently
> problematic as regards reliability. A witness's concerns
> expressed in the course of therapy after the fact, even
> assuming they are correctly understood and reliably noted,
> cannot be equated with evidence given in the course of a
> trial. Both the context in which the statements are made and
> the expectations of the parties are entirely different. In a trial,
> a witness is sworn to testify as to the particular events in issue.
> By contrast, in therapy an entire spectrum of factors such as
> personal history, thoughts, emotions as well as particular acts
> may inform the dialogue between therapist and patient. Thus,
> there is serious risk that such statements could be taken
> piecemeal out of the context in which they were made to
> provide a foundation for entirely unwarranted inferences
> by the trier of fact.[52] [Emphasis in original]

We could make many of the same comments with respect to research records, although different issues arise also in the research context. Scientific and legal standards of validity overlap, but differ in important respects. How would the court treat interview data? Does an interview transcript have greater probative value than hearsay? Does information from a taped interview have greater probative value than a set of notes taken during an interview? In the case of observational field notes, would it make a difference if the researcher generated the notes *in situ* or at the end of the observational period, or later that day? Are there any circumstances under which data are completely safe from probing by the courts? For example, are completely anonymized field notes and interview transcripts of any use to a court? What if the researcher conducted the interviews years ago — is his or her memory reliable?

A related issue involves destruction of data. Jackson and MacCrimmon offered a cautionary tale arising from *R. v. Carosella*,[53] a Supreme Court of Canada decision that dealt with destruction of documents created during the confidential interactions of a therapist and a patient who was also a complainant in a sexual assault case. In that case, a woman who had been sexually assaulted first visited a Sexual Assault Crisis Centre (the centre), where she was interviewed for more than an hour. As Jackson and MacCrimmon explained:

> *During the interview she was informed that whatever she said could be subpoenaed and introduced into court. The complainant said that was all right. The interviewer took about 10 pages of notes. After the interview, the complainant contacted the police and charges were laid.*

Carosella, the accused, made an application for the notes two years later. However, six months prior to his application, the Board of Directors of the centre passed a motion authorizing the destruction of several hundred files, which included the notes from the Carosella case. Carosella argued that the destruction of the notes violated his right to a fair trial. The case went all the way to the Supreme Court, which agreed with Carosella and stayed his charges. Although Jackson and MacCrimmon distinguished the therapeutic and research contexts, including their note that anonymizing interview records is considered ethical research practice (but not consistent with good therapeutic practice), they suggested any destruction or anonymization of identifiable data should be part of a clear plan, and should occur prior to any legal interest that might make the data interesting as evidence. After a third party expresses interest in research data, destruction of that material could lead to problems:

> . . . *researchers who destroy records once the records are*
> *subpoenaed or ordered to be produced in court may be subject*
> *to legal sanction. Section 127 of the Criminal Code makes it*
> *an offence to disobey a court order and section 139 makes it*
> *an offence to obstruct justice. In addition, a court retains the*
> *power to punish for contempt. Section 127 of the Criminal*
> *Code makes it an offence to disobey a court order and section*
> *139 makes it an offence to obstruct justice. In addition, a*
> *court retains the power to punish for contempt.*

Jackson and MacCrimmon's analysis of *R. v. Carosella* suggests that researchers who deal with sensitive information would be wise to:

1. include in their ethics applications their plans to anonymize data and destroy any original tapes, in order to make clear that their destruction is standard practice for the protection of research participants; and
2. destroy tapes and anonymize transcripts as soon as practicable.

Another factor the court considers is whether the case is criminal or civil. In *M.(A.) v. Ryan*, Madame Justice McLachlin wrote:

> *[T]he interest in disclosure of a defendant in a civil suit may*
> *be less compelling than the parallel interest of an accused*
> *charged with a crime. The defendant in a civil suit stands to*
> *lose money and repute; the accused in a criminal proceeding*
> *stands to lose his or her very liberty. As a consequence,*
> *the balance between the interest in disclosure and the*
> *complainant's interest in privacy may be struck at a different*
> *level in the civil and criminal case; documents produced in*
> *a criminal case may not always be producible in a civil case,*

> *where the privacy interest of the complainant may more easily*
> *outweigh the defendant's interest in production.*

In criminological research, participants' greatest concern is usually that a third party might use the information they supply to prosecute them, discipline them, or terminate their employment. Until recently, there was no recorded case of an attempt to obtain confidential research information to aid a prosecution. That changed in 2012 when detectives from the Service de Police de la Ville de Montréal (SPVM) executed a search warrant to obtain an audio tape and transcribed interview from Drs. Chris Bruckert and Colette Parent of the University of Ottawa. We return to this pivotal case in our penultimate chapter.

Summary of the Wigmore Strategy

The likelihood of a researcher receiving a subpoena and a court asking her/ him to reveal confidential research information is remote. In Canada, only Ogden, Bruckert, and Parent have had to defend research confidentiality in court. The importance of Ogden's case was that it established the Wigmore test as the only mechanism available in law to assert researcher-participant privilege. That it took nineteen years for a second case to arise, the one involving Bruckert and Parent, indicates just how rare this threat is in Canada.

If past US experience is anything to go by, even if a researcher receives a subpoena, the likelihood of there being an order to disclose identifying information is minuscule. The odds are probably greater that a research participant will be involved in a road accident on his or her way to an interview appointment. Because the risk has occasionally materialized, some research administrations require researchers to limit confidentiality "to the extent law allows" without defining that standard or advising researchers how to achieve it.[54]

Given that the common law is all they have to fend off challenges to research confidentiality, Canadian researchers and universities have an ethical responsibility to Wigmorize their research projects so that they really can protect confidentiality to full extent that law permits. Generally, to enhance a researcher's ability to assert privilege using common law, a research design should include four core elements:

1. Researchers should secure institutional ethics approval as part of demonstrating that their research is consistent with the ethics of their discipline and the TCPS, and that it is an authorized research project.

2. The application to a Research Ethics Board should include a discussion of why confidentiality is essential to undertaking the proposed research project, or why it is not. The application should provide clear evidence that any confidentiality guarantee is part of a well-considered research plan. Researchers should ask prospective participants if they would participate in the research if they knew that the researcher might disclose their name. A record should be made of the response as long as the record itself does not jeopardize confidentiality.[55] Such a record would provide further evidence that confidentiality was, and is, essential to this particular researcher-participant relationship.

3. On the basis of the researcher's experience, colleagues' experiences, and the extant literature, the researcher should consider the range of challenges to confidentiality that might reasonably be anticipated, and consider whether the benefits of doing the research outweigh the interests that might be represented in any reasonably foreseeable challenge to confidentiality.

4. If the researcher is convinced that the research is worth doing and that they could not do it without a guarantee of confidentiality, ensure that they make an unambiguous promise to that effect, and keep it.

In light of the existing North American jurisprudence, it appears courts will maintain confidentiality of participant identities in most cases.

CHAPTER XXII
Kangaroo Court

It had been more than ten months since we submitted our application to conduct research on escort service and massage-parlour managers to the SFU ethics committee, and eight months since the application to conduct research on off-street sex workers. It was beginning to look more and more like any approval at this point would make for a pyrrhic victory. The escort-service and brothel manager who had approached Lowman a year earlier with an invitation to conduct research was on the verge of leaving town. A once-in-a-lifetime research opportunity to examine Vancouver's off-street prostitution trade, especially safety issues, was crumbling at a time when more and more street sex workers were going missing in addition to dozens of known murders.[1]

Ethics Committee Chair Horvath's rejection of our proposals in the wake of the Dickens's opinion and the publication of the *Tri-Council Policy Statement* meant our launching a formal appeal. Because Clayman had been chair at the point we submitted our research applications, President Blaney directed VP-Academic Dr. David Gagan to hear the appeal.

The Appeal
Our appeal[2] outlined fifteen grounds, beginning with the ethics committee's imposition of its limited-confidentiality doctrine, which constituted an unauthorized substantive change to SFU's research-ethics policy, followed by an enumeration of the many problems this change created, with which by now the reader is no doubt familiar.[3]

Gagan's response was all too familiar. His March 5, 1999, decision simply reaffirmed the law-of-the-land position Clayman continued to promote. After some interaction with the ethics committee, on April 1, 1999, he commanded that we use the following consent statement:

> The researchers will use their best effort to maintain the confidentiality of information obtained during this study and the anonymity of its sources. Notwithstanding the above, you need to be aware that the confidentiality of the information obtained as part of a research project and the identity of its sources do not have full protection of the law in Canada. Courts can order researchers to surrender information or to reveal the identities of their sources.
>
> If such an order is made by a court, the University is committed to the promotion and protection of the academic freedom of its researchers and therefore will use its best effort to assist the researcher to maintain the confidentiality of the information and the anonymity of its sources. However, the University cannot and will not solicit or counsel its researchers to disobey a legal disclosure order and will not support researchers in their efforts to do so once all legal protections have been exhausted.
>
> At such time as all legal protections have been exhausted, you should be aware that the University, its governors, and its officers cannot and will not take further steps to prevent court-ordered disclosure. In these circumstances, information obtained during this study and/or the identity of its sources may be disclosed.

The statement was interesting in several respects, not least being that it was misleading. It's assertion that "the confidentiality of the information obtained as part of a research project and the identity of its sources do not have full protection of the law in Canada" failed to mention that it might have, and did, in the only case ever adjudicated in Canada. The admonition that we tell prospective participants that courts "can order researchers to surrender information or reveal . . . sources" implied that they had done so in the past.

Nowhere was there any mention that the researchers would be willing to defy a court order if law and ethics part company. Instead, Gagan asserted, "the University cannot and will not solicit or counsel its researchers to disobey a legal disclosure order and will not support researchers in their efforts to do so once all legal protections have been exhausted." While we held that a university should support the academic freedom of a researcher to make such a decision, Gagan would not entertain anything but the law-of-the-land position.

The final paragraph, which had no parallel in the ethics committee's proposed statement, clarified that the university would throw its researchers to the wolves — and by implication the research participants as well — in the event all legal processes were exhausted. Did this signal the university's intentions to disclose information over the researcher's objections using policies that gave the university the right to access all email that passes through its servers,[4] or hand over to the courts information stored in filing cabinets on university property?

It was a reminder that researchers who want to maintain control over confidential research information should review their university's policies about access to a researcher's physical equipment (filing cabinets, desks, and computers), email, and other records. We would never store any sensitive information — physical or digital — in any location over which we did not have care and control.

The appeal had eaten up another four months of our time and solved nothing. Once again, the administration was ordering us to behave in a manner that we believed to be unethical. SFU was clearly violating our academic freedom to conduct research and preventing us from performing our contractual employment duties. Given that we had exhausted the remedies the ethics policy made available, it was time to initiate the *Framework Agreement* "disagreement procedure."

The "Disagreement Procedure"

SFU's process for the "resolution of disagreements" involves four steps, the first of which involves informal efforts by the parties to attempt to resolve their disagreement. Accordingly, our first step was to inform Dr. Gagan that we had a disagreement and to request a meeting under step one of the procedure.

Step One

As usual, the meeting began with us pointing out the appearance of institutional conflict in Gagan's involvement in the appeal. We informed him that he had exceeded the purview of an appeal — i.e., to uphold or overturn a decision — when he retained and then exercised the right to censor any consent statement the ethics committee proposed, and substitute one of his own. Part of the irony surrounding our case was that Ethics Committee Chair Horvath had already acknowledged that the only remaining obstacle to a workable consent statement was our insistence that we inform prospective participants what the university and we would do in the event of a subpoena. By censoring information about what the researcher would do, Gagan made a bad situation worse.

It appeared that Gagan did not understand our position. We were endeavouring to follow the university ethics policy, which did not limit confidentiality in any way, required us to "consider the cultural values and sense of propriety" of our prospective participants, to follow our disciplinary standards, to maintain "strict confidentiality," and to leave it to the participant to determine whether, when, and where any identifiable information would be disclosed. Indeed, it was remarkable to see how much resistance we encountered for wanting to follow the existing policy. It was thus with some sense of irony that, while awaiting Gagan's appeal decision, we read VP-research Clayman's memo to deans, chairs, and Graduate Program chairs reminding them that disciplinary action could be taken against researchers who did not follow that policy:

> All projects undertaken by a faculty member or other SFU
> employee, graduate student or undergraduate student (outside
> a regular undergraduate course) requires the explicit prior
> approval of the University Research Ethics Review Committee
> (URERC) . . . Any faculty member or other SFU employee,
> graduate student or undergraduate student who undertakes

> *research without such prior approval is in violation of SFU*
> *Policy R20.01 . . . and this constitutes misconduct in research*
> *as described in SFU Policy R60.01.*[5]

Policy R60.01 pertains to "Integrity in Research and Misconduct in Research." Depending on the severity of the misconduct, the offender is "subject to a range of disciplinary measures up to and including dismissal or expulsion."

We sent Clayman an email asking what consequences SFU administrators faced if they did not follow the ethics policy. He did not reply.

Step Two

After Gagan's rejection of our overtures, we proceeded to step two of the disagreement procedure, "Problem Solving." At this stage, the complainant submits his or her grievance "in writing to the administrator immediately above the person whose act or omission is the basis of the complaint." Given that the VP-academic answers to the president, we submitted our complaint to President Blaney. However, in recognition of the appearance of institutional conflict of interest involved in SFU administrators being involved in the research-ethics review process, SFU proposed that we move directly to step three, "Conciliation." This was a key development insofar as it meant the creation of a conciliation committee to hear our disagreement. At last, an independent panel would consider our arguments.

Step Three

The conciliation committee comprised three members drawn from a conciliation panel that the university administration and the faculty association had established to hear grievances. The role of the conciliation committee was to

> . . . *assist the parties in their effort to resolve the grievance*
> *using mediation, conciliation or other procedures to encourage*
> *settlement. If a settlement is reached, it shall be committed to*
> *writing and signed by the parties.*[6]

Three developments around this time promised to help bring about a resolution. First, the American Sociological Association clarified its position on researchers violating court orders to disclose confidential research information. Second was the experience of two graduate students who submitted proposals to the ethics committee. Third was a memo from Ethics Committee Chair Adam Horvath, acknowledging that the committee had been using the unauthorized draft of its proposed revisions to the research ethics policy to adjudicate ethics applications.

The ASA Clarifies Its Code

The SFU research ethics policy admonished researchers and the ethics committee to respect disciplinary standards. Throughout our debates with the SFU ethics committee and various administrators regarding limited confidentiality we identified the American Sociological Association (ASA) and the Academy of Criminal Justice Sciences (ACJS) ethics codes as providing the disciplinary standard that guided our research. These codes stated:

> *Confidential information provided by research participants*
> *should be treated as such by members of the Academy, even*
> *when this information enjoys no legal protection or privilege*
> *and legal force is applied.*[7]

However, in the 1998 *Code*, ASA deleted the phrase "and legal force is applied." The confidentiality clause then read:

> *Confidential information provided by research participants,*
> *students, employees, clients, or others is treated as such by*
> *sociologists even if there is no legal protection or privilege to do so.*[8]

The revised *Code* included a section entitled "Limits to Confidentiality," the first portion of which stated:

> *Sociologists inform themselves fully about all laws and rules*
> *which may limit or alter guarantees of confidentiality. They*
> *determine their ability to guarantee absolute confidentiality*

> *and, as appropriate, inform research participants, students,*
> *employees, clients, or others of any limitations to this*
> *guarantee at the outset, consistent with ethical standards set*
> *forth [elsewhere].*

Like the *Tri-Council Policy Statement*, one could interpret the new ASA wording as being consistent with the ethics committee's limited-confidentiality policy. Horvath proclaimed as much in an email he sent to us, copied to the numerous observers on the growing copy list:

> *It seems to me that the ASA approach is quite consistent with*
> *what the URERC has been advocating all along:*
>   1. *Full discloser [sic] of legal limits*
>   2. *Researchers are permitted to make additional*
>   *commitments, if they wish to do so.*[9]

Three aspects of Horvath's interpretation deserve comment.

First, although he claimed that the ASA *Code* is "consistent with what the ethics committee has been advocating all along," he did not notice that it also was consistent with what we had been advocating all along.

Second, Horvath had clarified what he believed the ethical standards should be. The SFU ethics policy and TCPS expected researchers to adhere to disciplinary standards, which in our case was the ASA *Code*. Why did Gagan overrule our disciplinary standards and impose the administration's law-of-the-land policy?

Third, Horvath's memo begged the question, why did ASA remove the phrase "and legal force is applied" from its ethics code? The SFU Ethics Task Force Chair Ellen Gee had also asked this question. We wrote to ASA's Committee on Professional Ethics (COPE) asking for clarification. COPE published our question and its response in *Footnotes*, ASA's monthly newsletter.[10] Gee also wrote to Dr. Joyce Iutcovich, chair of COPE, asking her to clarify ASA's *Code* section on confidentiality. Iutcovich replied:

> *In your e-mail of 3/6/99 you stated that your reading of the*
> *new ASA Code "requires researchers (a) to know the relevant*

law regarding their ability to guarantee absolute confidentiality and (b) to discuss confidentiality and its limits with their research subjects." You then raised these questions:

1. With regard to (a) — In Canada (and the US, as far as I understand), there are no legal guarantees regarding academic privilege. Does this then mean that researchers are NEVER in a position to guarantee unlimited confidentiality?

Answer: You are correct that there are no legal guarantees regarding academic privilege similar to what some other professional groups have (e.g., lawyers, doctors, priests . . . However, this is a separate issue from the willingness of an academic to promise unlimited confidentiality of information gathered from research subjects. If the academic researcher is willing to make this promise, regardless of any legal pressure that may be brought to bear (e.g., when the courts hold someone in contempt if they are unwilling to reveal such information), then the academic must be willing to accept the consequences (e.g., go to jail . . .). Academic privilege is something that some researchers have been willing to fight for and, as Palys and Lowman pointed out, there may be a sound legal basis for arguing for this privilege in court. Hence, if an academic is willing to back up his/her promise, then the promise of unlimited confidentiality can be made.

2. With regard to (b) — this appears to mean that the ASA Code requires researchers to tell their subjects that any data obtained from them COULD be disclosed. Does this not impede research that criminologists (especially, but not exclusively) engage in, given that research subjects will either not want to participate or will hide information from the researcher? Also, does this not preclude researchers from using the Wigmore criteria (re criteria #1) in a court of law in any attempt to protect research-research subject confidentiality/academic privilege?

Answer: The ASA Code requires that researchers fully inform themselves of any laws that might require mandatory

>*reporting or place limits on confidentiality (e.g., many states require reports of child abuse and even those professionals that have "privilege" are obligated to report their knowledge of future criminal behavior or life-threatening situations). Once researchers are fully informed, it is then that they decide if there are circumstances (i.e., certain types of information) in which they are unwilling to promise absolute confidentiality. If there are, then the researchers are obligated to inform their subjects of such circumstances. If they are willing to promise absolute confidentiality regardless of circumstances, then the researcher can make this promise (as stated in the answer to #1 above).*
>
>*The essence of the 1997 Code is this: researchers are obligated to be fully informed, only make promises they are willing to back up, and be up front with the research subjects about what they are promising. It may be that a researcher is willing to promise confidentiality except in health- or life-threatening situations. If that is the case, then that is what can be promised.*[11]

ASA's response was consistent with the TCPS recognition that "ethics and law can lead to different conclusions." While researchers should be aware of the relevant law, it is up to them to decide which limitations, if any, they would place on their pledge of confidentiality.

Two Graduate Students

Limited confidentiality had become a core issue for the School of Criminology. To support our initiative successive Chairs Margaret Jackson and Rob Gordon appointed the two of us as the school's ad hoc ethics liaison committee, which became our main committee responsibility for several years. Part of our role involved assisting graduate students to prepare their applications for submission to the ethics committee. In the process, we realized that some graduate students were shifting their research focus to secondary data archives or conducting anonymous surveys in order to avoid ethics-committee review. In the case of those students who were undeterred, our role was to help formulate consent statements that might pass ethics committee muster without sacrificing strict confidentiality. While the appeal and grievance process was sidelining our research, the ethics committee approved two graduate students' applications that used consent statements we would have been happy to adopt.

The first was Victor Janoff's interviews with queer-bashing victims.[12] His consent statement read:

> Any information that is obtained during this study will be kept confidential to the full extent permitted by law. Knowledge of your identity is not required. You will not be required to write your name or any other identifying information on the research materials. Materials will be held in a secure location and will be destroyed after the completion of the study. There is a very remote possibility that I will be asked by a public body to reveal confidential information. In the unlikely event that this does happen, when a researcher's academic freedom is challenged or compromised by a court or other public body, the University is obliged to provide legal advice, representation, and/or indemnification to a researcher in defending against such actions. In the unlikely event that these efforts fail, and I am ordered to reveal confidential information by a court or other public body, I will make an ethical decision not to do so.

The second was Jay Jones's interviews with persons involved in the case of a controversial man's ongoing battle with a municipal council over the designation of his property, which he argued was a "museum," but which the council deemed to be an eyesore, and ordered him to clean up. The well-known man was not concerned about confidentiality because local media often reported his ongoing conflict with the municipality. However, the student wanted to guarantee confidentiality to other people involved in the case, including the mayor, city councillors, police officers, and demonstrators. Interviews could include discussions of civil and criminal offences. In February 1999, as we awaited Gagan's appeal decision, the ethics committee approved the following consent statement:

> *There is a very remote possibility that the researcher will be*
> *ordered by a court or other public body to reveal confidential*
> *information. In the unlikely event that this does happen, the*
> *University is obliged to provide legal advice, representation, and/*
> *or indemnification to the researcher in defending against such a*
> *challenge to academic freedom.*[13] *In the unlikely event that these*
> *efforts fail, and the researcher is ordered to reveal confidential*
> *information by a court or other public body, said researcher (Jay*
> *Jones) will make an ethical decision not to do so.*[14]

We included these examples in the documentation we prepared for the conciliation committee and indicated that we would be willing to utilize either.

Whoops: Administration by Fiat Exposed

In our ongoing role as criminology's ad hoc ethics liaison committee, we reviewed all ethics committee minutes. The January 4, 1999, minutes contained a curious reference to correspondence between Clayman and Horvath:

> *The Chair gave a brief overview of the development of Policy*
> *R20.01 referencing his memorandum of November 30, 1998,*
> *and January 4, 1999 and Dr. Clayman's e-mail response of*
> *January 4, 1999 bringing closure to the review.*

We submitted a request for these documents under the access provisions of the B.C. *Freedom of Information and Protection of Privacy Act (FIPPA)* and received them just before we met with the conciliation committee. In Horvath's words:

> *In preparation for my meeting with Dr. Gee's task force on*
> *November 16, 1998, 1 reviewed the history and development*
> *of Policy 20.01. During my review, it became evident that the*
> *terms of reference for R20.01 currently in circulation contain*
> *some unauthorized alterations.*

After more than a year of us arguing that the ethics committee had been implementing an unauthorized ethics policy in the process of stopping our research, Horvath realized that the policy posted on the ethics committee's web site was not the version Senate had authorized, but the draft containing the committee's proposed revisions. In his words:

> *I have investigated the history of the events leading up to these alterations and discovered the following:*
>
> 1. *The last revision of R20-01 was approved by the BOG on June 9, 1992.[15]*
> 2. *Beginning in January 11, 1994, the URERC developed proposals to revise the terms of reference document. The proposed revisions to the document were discussed at the URERC meeting of September 9, 1994 and some of the revisions were approved by the Committee at the URERC meeting of Dec. 2, 1994.*
> 3. *It appears that the original intent was to have these revisions approved by the Board of Governors (see URERC minutes of Jan 11, 1994, Action item p.4). However, the project to revise the terms of reference for 20.01 was abandoned when news of the Tri-Council's effort to develop a coordinated research review policy reached the Committee.*
> 4. *Sometime after these events, the "revised" (but not yet approved) terms of reference for the R20.01 document was reprinted instead of the original, and circulated to the academic community and to members of the URERC.*
> 5. *It appears that no one has noticed these changes until Nov 14, 1998.*
>
> *light of the above [sic], I have taken the following actions:*
>
> 1. *Withdrew the "unauthorized" version of R20.01 from the web and substituted the original R20.01.*
> 2. *Redistributed the original versions to members of the URERC.*
> 3. *Recalled all readily available copies of the "revised"*

> *R20.01 in circulation and reprinted the correct (old)*
> *version of the document.*
> *I would like the Committee to consider the above and*
> *recommend any further/other action it deems advisable.*
> *Sincerely,*
> *Adam O. Horvath, Chair*
> *University Research Ethics Review Committee*[16]

"It appears no one had noticed these changes until Nov 14, 1998." We were bemused (to put it mildly). We had been telling the ethics committee for more than a year it was implementing a policy that Senate and the Board of Governors had not approved. Did committee members respond to Horvath's request that they "consider the above and recommend any further/ other action it deems advisable"? Did any of them think an apology might have been in order given that they used an unauthorized policy to justify stalling our research for more than a year? No apology was forthcoming.

Ever defiant, and oblivious to the appearance of conflict of interest, Clayman responded:

> *Adam,*
> *In response to your memorandum of this date, I am*
> *pleased to confirm that R20.01, as presently posted, is the*
> *legitimate and authorized version of the policy relevant to*
> *the operation of the URERC. The additional changes that*
> *you identified are entirely reasonable and do not in any way*
> *violate the spirit of the original policy. If it were not for the*
> *impending major revisions of the policy, I would take these*
> *minor changes and the others previously proposed through the*
> *system and ultimately to the BoG for formal approval.*
> *From Bruce Clayman*
> *SFU Research Matters*[17]

The matter would have remained concealed were it not for our *FIPPA* request. Instead of informing us of the error and using the authorized policy to review our proposal, the ethics committee delayed our research for a further six months as we worked our way through the appeal and the grievance procedure. We included Horvath's memorandum about the committee's use of the wrong policy in an addendum to our submission to the conciliation committee.

The Conciliation

When we met with the conciliation committee, representatives of the faculty association accompanied us. The first surprise of the day was that Dr. Gagan, the university administrator against whom we had launched the disagreement, was not present. We discovered later that he had left the university administration, with no explanation ever given.[18] Instead of Gagan, Dr. Jock Munro represented SFU. The SFU Board of Governors had appointed Munro as VP-academic *pro tem* the day before the conciliation meeting.[19]

The conciliation meeting went surprisingly quickly given the eighteen months and mound of documentation it had taken to reach that point. We discussed just two issues: the content of the consent statement we would use, and compensation for the eighteen months SFU had delayed our research. Negotiations over the consent statement moved quickly when it became clear that the university had abandoned Gagan's law-of-the-land doctrine. The agreed-on statement read:

> *The researchers will do everything possible to maintain the*
> *confidentiality of information obtained during this study and*
> *the anonymity of its sources. If an order is made by a court*
> *that the researchers provide information or reveal the identities*
> *of their sources, the University will provide legal representation*
> *until all available court processes have been exhausted to assist*
> *the researchers to maintain confidentiality of information*
> *and sources. Even then, the researchers will not reveal any*
> *confidential information and will never do so unless they*
> *believe it is ethically proper, considering the circumstances, to*
> *reveal that information.*

As compensation for the eighteen-month delay, we each received a one-and-a-half semester teaching release.

We amended our application to the ethics committee, which now had Dr. James Ogloff as its chair, and received the following decision:

> In response to your request dated September 17, 1999, I am pleased to approve, on behalf of the University Research Ethics Review Committee, the minor revision in the research protocol of the above referenced Request for Ethical Approval of Research originally approved on June 28, 1999.
> Best wishes for success in this research.
> Sincerely,
> Dr. James R. P. Ogloff, Chair
> University Research Ethics Review Committee

We could now proceed with the research — or could we?

Dénouement

The eighteen months we devoted to fighting for the right to do our research yielded a positive outcome. However, it was a pyrrhic victory. In field research, opportunities come and go. It may not be possible to delay them as one could a lab-based study utilizing Introductory Psychology students as research participants. By the time we won the right to do our research, the opportunity to conduct it no longer existed; the escort service/brothel had closed.

We have yet to see a Canadian ethnography of an escort service or brothel of the sort we proposed, and it would take another nine years before a researcher would complete a targeted interview study with off-street sex workers in Vancouver. In a *Charter* challenge that went to the Supreme Court of Canada, the court cited that interview research, which master's student Tamara O'Doherty completed under our supervision.[20] In that challenge, the three sex worker applicants argued that the *Criminal Code* sections pertaining to bawdyhouse, living on the avails, and communicating were creating dangerous conditions for sex workers, thereby violating their right to life, liberty, and security of the person.[21] O'Doherty's research helped to demonstrate that there are substantial differences in the frequency of violence experienced by street and off-street sex workers. It was not the only study entered into evidence, but it was one of the most important, because it directly addressed a key and contentious point. The Supreme Court of Canada ended up striking down the impugned laws.[22]

Between December 1997, when the ethics committee refused to approve our research, application, and 2006, when O'Doherty conducted hers, more than forty sex workers went missing from the streets of Downtown Eastside Vancouver.

Research matters.

CHAPTER XXIII

Limited Confidentiality 2.0: The SFU Ethics Committee's "Duty to Report"

Déjà Vu All Over Again

President Blaney's letter outlining the resolution of our grievance was presented to the ethics committee at its July 1999 meeting. At that meeting Horvath announced that he would resign from the committee on September 1. Dr. James Ogloff, another Clayman appointee and limited-confidentiality advocate, would take the chair when Horvath resigned.

Following the controversy surrounding the SFU's ethics committee, the National Council on Ethics in Human Research (NCEHR) offered to conduct a site visit in order to

> review SFU's policy and processes in respect to the protection of
> human subjects in research, and to assist SFU administration,
> committee members and faculty researchers in interpreting
> and implementing the ethical guidelines provided through the
> Tri-Council Policy Statement: Ethical Conduct for Research
> Involving Humans.[1]

One of the structural changes that occurred in the wake of NCEHR's visit was that the VP-research no longer delegated the ethics approval process to his secretary. In her place, SFU created the position of ethics consultant. Although the VP-research still appointed the consultant, the person appointed was supposed to have some human-research experience. The first person to occupy the role was Dr. Ezzat Fattah, a professor emeritus from the School of Criminology. After a year, Dr. Hal Weinberg, a professor emeritus from the Department of Kinesiology and associate member of the Department of Psychology, replaced Fattah.

Weinberg first met the ethics committee at its July 2000 meeting. The minutes record him asking for "clear guidelines" to distinguish projects on which he could perform an expedited review from those that required full committee review. The minutes also record him as noting, "It is not clear what the researchers' obligations are regarding 'insidious discovery.'"

We had used the term "heinous discovery" to describe the situation where a researcher discovers that a research participant intends to do something so heinous that a higher ethic — the need to save a life, for example, or ensure that a court does not convict an innocent person — compels action, which may involve violating a pledge of confidentiality. In law, such circumstances warrant the public-safety exception to confidentiality.[2] The ethics committee had previously raised this issue when it asserted that research confidentiality is "naturally" limited.

Although SFU does not authorize the ethics committee to create policy, again it proceeded to do exactly that. This time the focus was on what to do in the event of a heinous discovery. In response to Weinberg:

> The Committee agreed that if the researcher receives
> information obtained from the subject [sic], which reveals that
> harm will be done to an individual, this information must be
> reported to the authorities immediately.[3]

Again, the ethics committee was proposing a solution to a complex issue without any knowledge of how disciplinary ethics codes deal with such a situation, or without the benefit of an analysis of relevant case law.

To reveal the folly of the ethics committee's spontaneous solution, consider the Supreme Court of Canada's position when it had to deal with the same issue one year earlier in the case that elaborated criteria for evaluating the public-safety exception to lawyer-client privilege.

Smith v. Jones

"Mr. Jones" (a pseudonym) stood accused of aggravated assault of a street prostitute in Vancouver. His attorney thought it would be useful to have a psychiatric assessment to help the preparation of his defense or, in the event of a conviction, consideration of his sentence. The attorney referred Jones to "Dr. Smith" (a pseudonym) for assessment. Because Jones's attorney referred him to Smith, solicitor-client privilege protected the communications between Smith and Jones.

Presumably because of his expectation that their communications would be confidential, Jones revealed to Smith that the assault was not an isolated incident, but rather part of a broader plan to kidnap, rape, and murder street prostitutes. He confided that this was more than an abstract plan; he had already prepared his basement apartment so that his victims would have no escape. He told people he was going on vacation so that no one would visit him. The assault with which he was charged was a trial run to see whether he had it in him to abduct a woman, rape her, shoot her in the face to impede identification, and dispose of her body in the bush somewhere outside Vancouver.

The discussion led psychiatrist Smith to conclude that Jones was a dangerous individual who likely would commit further offenses if not treated. He informed Jones's lawyer of this evaluation. Two months later, Smith phoned the lawyer for an update and discovered that Jones had decided to plead guilty to the assault. Jones's attorney did not intend to call Smith to give evidence at the sentencing hearing. Concerned about what might happen to street prostitutes if sentencing proceeded in the absence of his observations about the danger Jones posed, Smith sought legal help to intervene. Because solicitor-client privilege is a class privilege, the onus was on him to justify why the privilege should be set aside so that he could disclose to the court his communication with Jones. Smith brought a motion to do just that.

Although *Smith v. Jones* involves solicitor-client privilege, the case is relevant to researcher-participant privilege because:

> [Solicitor-client privilege] is the highest privilege recognized
> by the courts. By necessary implication, if a public safety

exception applies to solicitor-client privilege, it applies to all
classifications of privileges and duties of confidentiality.[4]

What circumstances would warrant a solicitor violating client confidentiality? The Supreme Court of Canada identified three criteria to determine
when violation would be permissible:

- **Clarity**: The threat must be to a clearly defined target. In this
  case, although Jones did not name a specific woman as a
  target, he was targeting a clearly identifiable group, i.e., street
  prostitutes working on the east side of Vancouver.
- **Seriousness**: This key issue concerns how high the bar should
  be set before a disclosure is permissible. The court noted that
  accused persons often have committed crimes before, and may
  well be planning future crimes. The court should not permit
  disclosure unless the threat involves a risk of serious bodily
  harm or death. Jones met that criterion given his plan to
  abduct, rape, and murder his targets.
- **Imminence**: Is the danger imminent? The imminence of the
  danger would make a difference to how a confidant responds
  to a particular situation. In this regard, Jones had admitted to
  Smith that he had begun to execute his plan by making his
  apartment escape proof. That, coupled with the practice assault,
  showed that the plan had gone beyond abstract consideration;
  Jones was in the process of implementing it. Because Jones was
  in custody, there was ample time to petition the court to set
  aside the privilege. However, if Jones had been free and was
  walking out of Smith's office with a gun in his hand, then the
  court recognized the confidant might have to make a decision
  more quickly, even immediately, about whether and how to
  intervene.

The key aspect of these criteria is that, if all three are satisfied, disclosure is permissible — but it is not required. The Court emphasized every
case needs to be considered on its own terms. While the Court's minority

opinion agreed that disclosure would be permissible in the case in question, such disclosures should be extremely rare. If lawyers anticipated them, they would be far less likely to refer their clients for psychiatric assessment, which mean that they would refer fewer individuals for treatment, with the result that more rather than fewer dangerous people will roam free:

> As the facts of this case illustrate, Mr. Jones was only
> diagnosed and made aware of the possibility of treatment
> because he felt secure in confiding to Dr. Smith. If that
> confidence is undermined, then these individuals will not
> disclose the danger they pose, they will not be identified, and
> public safety will suffer.[5]

The Supreme Court Justices all agreed that the clear, serious, and immediate danger to the women warranted a violation of solicitor-client privilege, but their six-to-three decision reflected their disagreement regarding how, to whom, and in what form the disclosure should take. The majority decided that the file containing the psychiatrist's report should be unsealed, that portions "which do not fall within the public-safety exception" should remain privileged, and that a ban on the publication of any other parts of it should be lifted. The three dissenting Justices viewed this as too broad a disclosure:

> The immediate concern for public safety is to ensure that
> the accused not harm anyone. This can be accomplished by
> permitting the psychiatrist to warn the relevant authorities
> that the accused poses a threat to prostitutes in a specific area.
> However, he should only disclose his opinion and the fact that
> it is based on a consultation with the accused. Specifically,
> he should not disclose any communication from the accused
> relating to the circumstances of the offence, nor should he be
> permitted to reveal any of the personal information which the
> trial judge excluded from his original order for disclosure.[6]

Writing for the minority, Justice Major explained that the disclosure should be more constrained to minimize the long-term impact the

violation of confidentiality might have on the likelihood of future offenders revealing such information:

> The chilling effect of completely breaching the privilege would
> have the undesired effect of discouraging those individuals in
> need of treatment for serious and dangerous conditions from
> consulting professional help . . .
>
> As appealing as it may be to ensure that Mr. Jones does
> not slip back into the community without treatment for his
> condition, completely lifting the privilege and allowing his
> confidential communications to his legal advisor to be used
> against him in the most detrimental ways will not promote
> public safety, only silence. For this doubtful gain, the Court
> will have imposed a veil of secrecy between criminal accused
> and their counsel which the solicitor-client privilege was
> developed to prevent. Sanctioning a breach of privilege too
> hastily erodes the workings of the system of law in exchange
> for an illusory gain in public safety.[7]

In contrast to the Supreme Court of Canada's nuanced analysis of the
public-safety exception, the SFU ethics committee approach to heinous
discovery was frought with problems.

The Ethics Committee's Duty to Report

Although the ethics committee had always emphasized the need to adhere
to the law, its "duty to report" policy violated the legal principles established in *Smith v. Jones* in numerous ways:

- Instead of taking a case-by case approach to heinous discovery, the
  committee formulated a blanket policy to apply to all threats of harm.
- Instead of using the criteria laid out in *Smith v. Jones*, the
  committee's new policy applied to harm in general, which
  presumably could cover anything from hurt feelings to a
  prospective murder.
- Instead of considering some of the alternative strategies

> researchers might employ to prevent the realization of a threat, the ethics-committee policy required researchers to report all threats of harm to "the authorities," whomever that might mean.

- Instead of understanding that different circumstances might allow different solutions depending on the imminence of the alleged threat, and recognizing that when a danger is not imminent, researchers might benefit from discussion with trusted colleagues, the ethics committee's new policy required researchers to contact authorities "immediately."

- Instead of making clear to researchers that, even in the event they decided to disclose confidential research information, their duty of confidentiality would still remain — in which case any disclosure must not exceed the minimum necessary to thwart the prospective harm — the ethics-committee policy required that "the information" be reported.

- Instead of indicating that hearing of a potential harm might justify disclosure in certain circumstances, the ethics-committee policy required it. It had turned "may" into "must."

The policy was ill advised in another respect. The committee required researchers to make judgments that, unless they were clinical psychologists or psychiatrists, they did not have the expertise to make. Who would be responsible for decisions that mistook bravado for dangerousness, or that confused fantasy and intention?

Two cases substantiated our concerns about the competence of researchers to assess dangerousness. The first, *Garner v. Stone*[8] in Georgia, involved a psychologist (Stone) who interviewed a police officer (Garner) as part of a routine fitness-for-duty assessment. In the course of the interview, Garner told Stone about fantasies he had of killing his captain and others. Stone took the descriptions as a serious threat and, believing he was obliged to report them, told Garner's superiors what he had heard. Garner's superiors demoted him to duty at the dog pound and eventually terminated him. Garner subsequently sued Stone for defamation, stating that his demotion and termination were due to Stone's violation of confidentiality, when he had talked about nothing more than a fantasy. The court awarded Garner $287,000 in damages when the jury agreed.[9]

The second case involved a similar scenario. Wanda Young was a student at Memorial University (Newfoundland) taking courses toward a social-work degree. Because of a missing footnote in a term paper, one of her professors mistook a case study that was included as an appendix as being a personal story. Believing the story was a cry-for-help confession for having sexually abused children, the professor sent a "suspected ill-treatment" report to Child Protection Services (CPS) without ever seeking any further clarification from Young. This led to various professors, the RCMP, and numerous social workers discussing Young's alleged abuse without her knowledge. After more than two years of Young finding doors closed to her for reasons she did not understand, a CPS worker finally interviewed Young and discussed the term paper. Young then showed the CPS worker the book from which she had taken the case study, at which point CPS realized the allegations were false. Young then sued the professor and university, alleging that their actions "combined to put in motion a series of events that would forever shape the course of [her] future by affecting her reputation in the community, her ability to complete her education and by reducing her income-earning capacity." Young won and was awarded $839,400 in damages.[10]

These two cases involve individuals — a psychologist in one case and a trained social worker in another — making erroneous judgments that adversely affected other people's lives. What opportunity for injustice was the ethics committee creating by requiring researchers with degrees in political science, communications, sociology, etc., to make such judgments about the mental state of research participants and report them "immediately" to "authorities"? Speculation on this issue took a dark turn when Lowman saw the ethics committee applying the policy to some research he was supervising in a directed-studies course.

The student was sociology doctoral student Gordon Roe, who proposed to conduct ethnographic research on injection-drug users in Vancouver's Downtown Eastside. Roe had already established a relationship with the Vancouver Area Network of Drug Users (VANDU) "who work to improve the lives of people who use illicit drugs through user-based support and education."[11] Roe had spoken to them about how his research protocols should respect their sub-cultural values, as the ethics policy of the day required.

Roe's ethics proposal outlined the importance of unlimited confidentiality, which he was prepared to guarantee. In keeping with the ethics committee's new heinous-discovery protocol, the research ethics officer asked him "to consider the situation where you may have to weigh your ethical responsibility to the subjects, with respect to absolute anonymity and confidentiality, against the possible consequences of that to the subject or to others."[12] Roe responded by considering the scenario of witnessing a knife fight. He suggested that his response — which could range from doing nothing to calling 9-1-1 for an ambulance — would depend on the circumstances.

Weinberg thanked Roe for his response, stating:

> My understanding of your response is that you acknowledge there are circumstances in which you may have to infringe on your guarantee of confidentiality and that you, as the researcher, are willing to accept the ethical responsibility for determining when the circumstances warrant infringement.
>
> If you do agree to accept responsibility for honourably determining the conditions or circumstances which may warrant and or determine the type of infringement, and your supervisor also agrees, I would recommend approval of the application.[13]

As Roe's supervisor, Lowman did not agree with this proposal. It resembled Ogden's undertaking, which the VP-research had insisted was a "liability waiver." The VP-research could similarly appropriate this statement as a waiver. Whether intended that way or not, Weinberg and the ethics committee chair were asking for a statement that would allow the university to download responsibility and liability for any errors of judgment to the student. Referring to it as a "responsibility contract," Lowman wrote to Weinberg and the ethics committee, objecting that

> [U]niversity authorities could interpret the agreement as
> a "contract" transferring all liability to researchers. This is
> exactly what the VP-Research did on the basis of a letter
> Ogden sent to the URERC saying that he would, "accept
> full responsibility for any decision I make with respect to
> the sharing of information." . . . During the Ogden v. SFU
> trial, Dr. Peter Harmon, a member of the URERC that
> approved Ogden's research, swore an affidavit saying that the
> VP-Research was misinterpreting Ogden's letter. But university
> lawyers successfully prevented the affidavit from being entered
> into evidence. The Ogden case showed that the student's and
> URERC's understanding of an agreement are not necessarily
> of concern to university officials and their lawyers when they
> control the interpretation presented to the court.

Creating a new duty to report and asking at least one field researcher to sign a responsibility contract were not the only ways that the ethics committee was again changing the ethics policy in its own image. We drew this incident to Ethics Committee Chair Jim Ogloff's attention, together with a longer list of infractions that we had encountered in our role as criminology's ad hoc research ethics liaison committee.

Ogloff did not reply.

It was time once again to apprise President Blaney of what the ethics committee was doing on his watch.

The President Intervenes a Second Time

On October 31, 2000, we sent an open letter to Blaney outlining different ways the ethics committee was continuing to violate or change the SFU research-ethics policy. The letter asked, "If the VP-Research and the URERC are exempt from the university research ethics policy, why should anyone else feel bound by it?" Invoking the SFU *Code of Faculty Ethics and Responsibilities* as our authority, we declared that, henceforth, we were refusing to undergo ethics review:

> University Policy A30.01 (Code of Faculty Ethics and
> Responsibilities) says that faculty, "have a responsibility to

> *abide by the rules and regulations established for the orderly conduct of the affairs of the University, provided that the rules and regulations do not infringe the academic freedom of faculty and students . . ." For several years the VP-Research and URERC have not abided by the rules and regulations specified in the university ethics policy, and have applied R20.01 in a way that infringes academic freedom and the URERC's duty to fairness. Because they continue to do so, we are invoking policy A30.01 and refusing to undergo ethics review until the University formally resolves the problems we outline below.*[14]

The letter concluded by noting that the SFU ethics policy stated, "Questions of interpretation or application of this policy or its procedures shall be referred to the President whose decision shall be final," and asked him to rule on the alleged violations we listed.[15]

On November 27, 2000, Dr. Blaney made his rulings under the research-ethics policy:[16]

- He ordered the ethics committee to cease imposing its duty-to-report requirement, because, as worded, it "creates the potential for an infringement of academic freedom."
- He ordered the ethics committee to cease imposing its duty-to-report requirement on researchers because, as worded, it "could expose participants and researchers to risk."
- While the ethics committee could continue to leave its limited-confidentiality consent statement on its website, the president ordered the committee to make researchers aware that this was not intended to violate their academic freedom and that alternative approaches to limited confidentiality were possible.[17]

The winds of change were blowing across SFU. A new ethics policy, re-jigged to make it consistent with the *Tri-Council Policy Statement*, was just around the corner.

CHAPTER XXIV
Making Ethics More Legal, or Law More Ethical?

SFU Creates a New Ethics Policy

One might think the resolution of our disagreement with the SFU administration would have been the end of our conflict with the ethics committee over limited confidentiality. Despite our ethical aversion to a law-of-the-land approach, we recognize that ethical people can view the world differently and that other disciplines may approach ethics issues in different ways than ours. There are no simple answers to some of life's questions about right and wrong. Having used the SFU disagreement procedure to establish the right of researchers to follow an ethics-first approach to research confidentiality, would it not make sense to ensure that there would be room for both law-of-the-land and ethics-first doctrines in the new ethics policy that the SFU Research Ethics Policy Revision Task Force (hereafter, the task force) was developing?

The task force's challenge was to develop a policy that would be consistent with the TCPS, and which would facilitate an inclusive perspective. For example, in its discussion of ethics review, the TCPS extolled the virtues of disciplinary and epistemological diversity and academic freedom:

> *For meaningful and effective application . . . ethical principles*
> *must operate neither in the abstract, nor in isolation from*
> *one another. Ethical principles are sometimes criticized as*

being applied in formulaic ways. To avoid this, they should
be applied in the context of the nature of the research and
of the ethical norms and practices of the relevant research
discipline . . . REBs should be aware that there are a variety of
philosophical approaches to ethical problems and that debate
between various schools of thought both informs ethical decisions
and ensures an evolving context for ethical approaches.[1]

The policy revision process did not live up to this vision of diversity. It soon became apparent some hard-liners sought to impose their law-of-the-land doctrine on all SFU researchers, with the result that the task force was unable to achieve consensus about the degree of confidentiality that the policy should permit researchers to guarantee. After producing three contentious drafts through 1999 and 2000 that occasioned rancorous debate in Senate, Blaney handed over the task of creating a new policy to a Senate committee chaired by Dr. Willie Davidson of the Department of Molecular Biology and Biochemistry.

Davidson sidestepped some of the core issues under dispute by modifying the draft policy the Senate committee had inherited from the task force. The revised draft, which became the new policy, dealt primarily with the administrative structure of SFU's new Research Ethics Board (REB). The committee designed the new policy to meet the TCPS's criteria for review while avoiding institutional conflicts of interest. The committee left research-ethics principles to the TCPS. This manoeuvre displaced the problem of limitations to confidentiality to the new REB. The only place the new policy alluded to privacy and confidentiality was in its preamble:

University researchers enjoy special freedoms and privileges,
which include freedom of inquiry and the right to disseminate
the results thereof, freedom to challenge conventional thoughts,
freedom from institutional censorship, and the privilege of
conducting research on human subjects with the trust and
support of the general public, often with public funding. With
these freedoms come responsibilities to ensure that research
involving human subjects meets high scholarly and ethical

> *standards, is honest and thoughtful inquiry, involves rigorous*
> *analysis and complies with professional and disciplinary*
> *standards for the protection of privacy and for methodological*
> *approaches. Review of research proposals by a Research Ethics*
> *Board takes into account these freedoms and responsibilities*
> *and provides accountability and quality assurance both to*
> *colleagues and to society.*[2]

One positive aspect of the new policy was its explicit reference to SFU's commitment to academic freedom and expectation that research protocols should comply "with professional and disciplinary standards for the protection of privacy and for methodological approaches." How would this abstract principle translate into practice? Much would depend on who was doing the review. Some submissions to the task force argued that SFU was large enough and its research sufficiently diverse to justify establishing two REBs — one for experimental and biomedical research and clinical trials, another for qualitative research — in order to ensure each committee had persons with appropriate expertise to provide effective ethics review.

The Davidson committee opted instead for a single board of eleven people. The REB's terms of appointment left us wondering whether there would be sufficient expertise in qualitative and field-based research represented among its members. To ensure that it was, Lowman put his name forward, and was elected to the new REB. This meant that the Board now had an advocate of the ethics-first perspective among its members. As the first ethics committee that would be responsible for ensuring that SFU researchers and the administration complied with the TCPS the new REB began to chart its way through various policy issues, including confidentiality. It undertook that task with several documents in hand, including various disciplinary ethics codes and the two existing legal opinions on research confidentiality. The REB also commissioned its own legal opinion on the same subject.[3]

Disciplinary Standards Regarding Ethics and Law

Much rested on the new policy's requirement that researchers should comply with disciplinary standards. We had invoked the American Sociological Association (ASA) and Academy of Criminal Justice Sciences (ACJS) as our disciplinary authorities. ASA had confirmed our view that, while researchers should be aware of the relevant law and should make every effort to comply with law, it should be left to the researcher's conscience to determine whether to comply with a court order to violate confidentiality.

The ASA and ACJS *Codes* were not alone in their view of the role of a researcher's conscience in making professional decisions. For example, the 1991 Canadian Psychological Association *Code of Ethics* stated in Principle IV.15 that psychologists should:

> Abide by the laws of the society in which they work. If those laws seriously conflict with the ethical principles contained herein, psychologists would do whatever they could to uphold the ethical principles. If upholding the ethical principles could result in serious personal consequences (e.g., jail or physical harm), decision for final action would be considered a matter of personal conscience.

The CPA released its revised *Code* (2000) at about the same time SFU was going through its policy development process. It said much the same thing when it advised that psychologists should

> [f]amiliarize themselves with the laws and regulations of the societies in which they work, especially those that are related to their activities as psychologists, and abide by them. If those laws or regulations seriously conflict with the ethical principles contained herein, psychologists would do whatever they could to uphold the ethical principles. If upholding the ethical principles could result in serious personal consequences (e.g., jail or physical harm), decision for final action would be considered a matter of personal conscience.[4]

Clearly, several disciplinary ethics codes admit the ethics-first approach to research confidentiality.

The Granting Agencies Clarify Their Position on Ethics and Law

Given that the TCPS encouraged respect for disciplinary standards and included specific recognition that "legal and ethical approaches to issues may lead to different conclusions"[6] one might have expected the controversy over limited confidentiality to be resolved: both the ethics-first and law-of-the-land perspectives are permissible, while *caveat emptor* (un)ethics is not. However, Horvath and Clayman's interpretation of the TCPS was very different from ours when it came to ethics and law. We read it as encouraging researchers to be both legal *and* ethical. For Horvath and Clayman, if the TCPS acknowledged those differences, it asserted that the way to avoid a conflict between ethics and law was never to make a promise that exceeded what a specific statute guaranteed. For them, common law appeared not to exist.

It was during the time that SFU was in the process of formulating its new ethics policy that an item appeared on the new TCPS website that would help to resolve the disagreement. As "stewards" of the new TCPS, the granting agencies were fielding questions from universities about how to make their research ethics policies TCPS compliant. To facilitate this process, the federal government set up a FAQ[6] page to archive answers to common questions. One of the questions and answers was as follows:

> Q: I wish to study street gangs, and with the approval of my local REB, plan to promise participants that their response to my questionnaire will be rigorously anonymous. Only I would have the key that could put names to the questionnaires.
> If I am subpoenaed by the local crown prosecutor who is demanding the personal response of each interviewee, should the university or REB defend me?
> A: Something to consider from the outset of your research is whether it is possible for you to construct a questionnaire in which neither you nor anybody else can retrieve the answers of particular individuals.
> Failing this, a first step in conducting your study would be to inquire about the policy of your own institution regarding legal assistance and the payment of fees for such assistance, in case individual response records are subpoenaed. If your REB has approved your proposal, the university should normally

> *defend you, although the question of costs may have to be*
> *negotiated if there is no clear university policy. Failure to do so*
> *could seriously undermine the credibility of the REB. Since you*
> *may win or lose your case, even if your university does provide*
> *legal counsel to argue that the subpoena is inappropriate, you*
> *should ensure that the gang members know in advance that*
> *the records may be subpoenaed and ultimately handed over to*
> *a third party.*

The single-mindedness of the response was striking. The suggestion that the hypothetical researcher construct the questionnaire so that responses were anonymous from the start — never gathering names in the first place if there was no need for them — was straightforward enough, a recommendation that one might expect to read in an introductory research methods text. However, beyond that point, the response was bizarre for its contextual naïveté. What court would allow a Crown prosecutor to engage in a fishing expedition of the sort envisaged in this scenario? Much more disconcerting was the respondent's presumption that, if the data were identifiable as to his or her source, the researcher would hand over the records if the court so ordered, in which case gang members should be warned at the outset that their responses might be disclosed. Clearly, whoever formulated the response had never done field research with gangs.

This FAQ provided an opportunity to query the granting agencies about the relation between ethics and law under the TCPS. We sent an email to the information officers at the three granting agencies and to NCEHR.[8] After an introductory preamble that identified the FAQ and response, our query continued:

> *We find the second paragraph of this response highly*
> *problematic both in what it assumes about law and in the*
> *"ethics" it appears to advocate.*
>
> *With respect to law, the proper response to this question*
> *would be that the scenario the questioner outlines – the Crown*
> *using a subpoena – is difficult to envisage. Any prosecutor*
> *familiar with the Canadian law of privilege would surely not*

*bother to subpoena the researcher, as they would know that no
judge would order disclosure of the information for a "fishing
expedition." The scenario envisaged did happen in the US
because of their grand jury system. But we do not have grand
juries here. In Canada, the Supreme Court has indicated it will
not tolerate "fishing expeditions" when a claim of privilege –
which we assume the researcher would invoke – is at stake.*

*With respect to ethics, the second paragraph of the response
appears to suggest that the Tri-Council Policy Statement
subjugates ethics to law, and that the researcher is expected to
hand the information over to a court if ordered. We cannot
believe this is the intention. For one thing, it would place the
Tri-Council Policy Statement in direct opposition to many
disciplinary ethics codes that encourage a primary allegiance to
ethics, not law, in those rare instance when the two conflict . . .*

*We have engaged in research on the ethics and law
of confidentiality and privilege for two years and recently
completed a paper outlining our ethical position (Palys
and Lowman, "Ethical and Legal Strategies for Protecting
Confidential Research Information;" a copy is attached).
You will see that our interpretation of the Tri-Council Policy
Statement is that it does not subjugate ethics to law. The paper
is actually a penultimate draft of an article we intend to submit
to the Canadian Journal of Law and Society. We invite you to
read it and welcome your comments. If we have interpreted the
Tri-Council incorrectly, please advise us as soon as possible, as
we would need to change the focus of the paper to publicize the
threat to academic freedom posed by the Tri-Council.*

It would take a few months, but a reply did arrive on April 27, 2000,
from NSERC's research ethics officer, writing on behalf of the three granting agencies:

*Thank you for your e-mail of 7 February 2000 regarding the
issue of confidentiality of research information in relation to*

the Tri-Council Policy Statement Ethical Conduct for Research Involving Humans. Please accept our apologies for not replying earlier.

First, let me stress that the Councils, as agents of the Canadian government, expect all Council-funded research to conform both to the ethical principles set out in the Tri-Council Policy Statement (TCPS) and the relevant laws. At the same time we also recognise that, in rare instances, ethical and legal approaches can conflict. The TCPS addresses this:

> *Norms for the ethics of research involving human subjects are developed and refined within an ever-evolving societal context, elements of which include the need for research and the research community, moral imperatives and ethical principles, and the law. (TCPS, page i.4)*
>
> *. . . Further, though ethical approaches cannot pre-empt the application of the law, they may well affect its future development or deal with situations beyond the scope of the law. (TCPS, page i.8)*

If there is a conflict, the researcher must decide on the most acceptable course of action. The principle of maintaining the confidentiality of research information is an important element of the TCPS. The onus is on the researcher to know the legal context of the research before starting his/her research activities, and to anticipate his/her options in the unlikely event of a court-ordered disclosure. It is also the researcher's responsibility, in consultation with the REB, to develop a free and informed consent process for recruiting research subjects, which takes into account that knowledge.

In reviewing the research protocol, the REB will take a subject-centred perspective to determine whether the consent process represents the risks accurately. In certain cases, it may be appropriate for the REB to request that the researcher inform participants of the risk of court-ordered disclosure, thus giving participants a qualified guarantee of

confidentiality. The REB could also suggest a methodological
solution to the problem by recommending that the research
be conducted anonymously.

> *A subject-centred approach should, however, also*
> *recognise that researcher and research subjects may not*
> *always see the harms and benefits of a research project in*
> *the same way. (TCPS, page i.7)*

> *In light of 2.4 (b) and 2.4 (c), REBs may require the*
> *researcher to provide additional information, including: .*
> *. . An indication as to who will have access to information*
> *collected on the identity of subjects, and descriptions of*
> *how confidentiality will be protected, and anticipated uses*
> *of data. (TCPS, Table 1, page 2.7)*

> *With respect to your comments on the study of street*
> *gangs, from an ethical perspective, we would continue to*
> *advocate a methodological approach that would guarantee*
> *the anonymity of the participants. Failing this, the researcher*
> *should be prepared to face a court order to disclose confidential*
> *research information and decide on his/her options, including*
> *the consequences of challenging this court order.*

We interpreted this response to mean the TCPS did *not* absolutely subjugate ethics to law; researchers have the right to follow their consciences in those rare instances when ethics and law part company.

A Research-Ethics or Research-Law Policy: Three Legal Opinions

The three legal opinions the new REB had at its disposal brought both overlapping and unique elements to the fore, depending in part on the context of their production. The Jones opinion arose in the context of our earliest debates with the SFU ethics committee. It focused on the question of whether the Wigmore criteria offered the most viable route for protecting research confidences in law, and whether the ethics committee's "except as required by law" requirement thwarted participant rights by creating a waiver of privilege. The Jackson and MacCrimmon opinion was a more comprehensive document that the Ethics Policy Revision Task

Force commissioned to help it draft a new ethics policy. The new REB commissioned the Lovett opinion to assess the legal probity of the forms and templates it was developing for use during the ethics review process.

Wigmore Is the Way

All three legal opinions agreed that invoking the Wigmore criteria is the best way to protect research confidentiality. All three commented that Ogden's success at Coroner's Court was a positive step on the path to courts recognizing researcher-participant privilege. Jones acknowledged the coroner was on a low rung in the justice system, while at the same time noting that significant change at the Supreme Court level usually begins in lower courts:

> [T]he decisions of the Honourable L.W. Campbell Coroner,
> in Inquest of Unknown Female (October 20, 1994 -
> 91-240-0838) and of the US Court of Appeals in Cusumano
> and Yoffie, in which researcher/participant privilege was
> recognized, are important signals. While neither decision
> would be binding on a Canadian Court their thoughtful
> consideration of the researcher/participant relationship carry
> considerable persuasive value. With respect to the Coroner's
> decision in particular, it is important to remember that
> advancements in the law, although eventually affirmed by
> the highest Courts, often commence at the most basic levels
> of the adjudicative process. Further, the Courts, in contrast
> to the situation even a decade ago increasingly utilize
> as evidence the very type of social science that would be
> protected and encouraged by the re-cognition of researcher/
> participant privilege. Such judicial familiarity would support
> arguments in favour of the expansion of privilege to capture
> the researcher/participant relationship.[8]

We have already quoted Jackson and MacCrimmon's conclusion that the Ogden decision would have withstood judicial review.[9] Lovett's opinion added that:

> *What this case demonstrates is that information obtained*
> *from a research subject by a researcher on a confidential basis*
> *may be protected from disclosure by case-by-case privilege*
> *in appropriate circumstances. Whether such privilege can*
> *be established will depend on the nature of the evidence put*
> *before the tribunal or the court in support of the privilege, the*
> *cogency and relevance of that information to the litigation and*
> *a balancing of the competing interests at stake.*[10]

The challenge, therefore, is for REBs and researchers to assess proposals in such a way that researchers will create "good facts" just in case theirs is the next project thrown into the legal crucible of privilege via the Wigmore test.

Protecting the University from Participants

Researchers begin with their professional ethical obligation to protect research participants in a situation where the balancing exercise at step four means that courts effectively make law after the fact. The goal should be to design a research-ethics policy that encourages researchers to do their utmost to respect law while not precluding a principled stand against any legal procedure that undermines research confidentiality.

The difference between law-first and ethics-first approaches is evident in the way diverse commentators conceptualize informed consent. Lovett held that contract law governs relationships between researchers and participants:

> *Neither the common law nor statute imposes a duty of*
> *confidentiality on a University researcher in respect of*
> *information obtained for research purposes. Thus the*
> *researcher's obligation to maintain confidentiality can be seen*
> *to be a contractual one arising from representations made by*
> *the researcher to the research subject, presently through the*
> *mechanism of "informed consent" forms.*[11]

Implicit in her perspective is that the university should offer no more than it legally is obliged to. With respect to confidentiality, for example:

> *A promise of confidentiality can be made a term of a*
> *contract, oral or written. In the event of disclosure of*
> *confidential information in violation of the contract term,*
> *the provider of the confidential information can sue for any*
> *damages suffered as a result of the contract breach.*[12]

In other words, promises incur liability, and incurring liability needlessly is not something that any lawyer would recommend. Jackson and MacCrimmon agreed that liability issues should be part of the policy formulation process:

> *In our opinion it is appropriate, and indeed necessary,*
> *in formulating an ethics policy to be concerned about*
> *liability issues. Privacy is a legally protected value and*
> *as we indicated in Part I of this Opinion, under certain*
> *circumstances a breach of privacy may ground a civil cause of*
> *action for damages under the BC Privacy Act.*[13]

In a similar vein, Lovett suggested that researchers not offer any pledge of confidentiality unless it is necessary to ensure that a confidential relationship is established:

> *It is my opinion that the trigger for a confidentiality assurance*
> *in an informed consent form should be the need to maintain a*
> *confidential relationship with the research subject.*[14]

With a perspective grounded in contract law, Lovett anticipated the worst-case scenario where the university challenges an order to divulge confidential research information and loses the case. The good news from her perspective is that a court can override a pledge of confidentiality without the university incurring liability. Lovett quoted McNairn & Scott's *Privacy Law in Canada* to explain that

> *[A] contractual obligation of confidentiality must yield*
> *generally to any legal requirements to disclose the subject*

information. The English Court of Appeal described this
general exception in Parry-Jones v. Law Society, in the
following terms:

> *. . . a [contractual] duty of confidence is subject to,*
> *and overridden by, the duty of any party to that contract*
> *to comply with the law of the land. If it is the duty of such*
> *a party to a contract, whether at common law or under*
> *statute, to disclose in defined circumstances confidential*
> *information, then he must do so, and any express contract to*
> *the contrary would be illegal and void.*[15]

According to Lovett, researchers should warn prospective research participants about this possibility as broadly as possible in order to cover the various forms of disclosure order:

> *If the general assurance is that the information will be kept*
> *confidential unless disclosure is "required or allowed by law"*
> *this would clearly encompass disclosure in circumstances where*
> *it is not required by court order or statutory provision but is*
> *warranted because of compelling and imminent public safety*
> *concerns. Having said that, it is my view that, even if the*
> *proviso was "except as required by law", a court would most*
> *likely construe it in such a way that disclosure for public safety*
> *concerns would not constitute a violation of the confidentiality*
> *agreement between the researcher and the research subject.*
> *In any event, if an application for court-ordered disclosure is*
> *successful, there would be no doubt that such disclosure would*
> *be required by law.*
>
> *It is therefore my opinion that, where it is necessary*
> *for a researcher to provide assurances of confidentiality to a*
> *research subject, it should be made clear that the information*
> *or communications at issue will be kept confidential unless and*
> *until disclosure is required under the law. The circumstances*
> *in which the law might require such disclosure need not be*
> *described unless the research subject asks for this information.*[16]

The legalism of Lovett's opinion explains her misunderstanding of our ethical position. For example, in regards to our concern, based on the *Gruenke* decision, that the "unless required by law" warning was problematic, Lovett stated, "Professors Lowman and Palys have described such a proviso as 'placing *a priori* limitations on confidentiality.' With respect, I cannot agree with such a characterization. The limitations exist. The limitations do not subsequently come into existence."[17]

We have never denied that there are legal limits to confidentiality. We were referring to *a priori* ethical, not legal, limitations.

At another point, Lovett argued that our unlimited pledge of confidentiality "misrepresents the limitations the law places on confidentiality agreements."[18] While she is correct regarding law, she does not evaluate the statement in terms of the ethical framework from which it emanates.

In sum, while we agree with these various lawyers that a university should be concerned about liability, that is not the role of a research-ethics policy. To avoid the appearance of institutional conflict of interest, a university should not build liability concerns into a policy that is supposed to protect research participants.

Managing Risk in the Researcher-Participant Relationship

Jackson and MacCrimmon took the issue of informed consent a step further than Lovett by suggesting that an informed consent statement should include three elements:

1. *Recognition of the necessity for confidentiality as the foundation of the researcher-subject relationship, together with an assurance of such confidentiality.*

2. *A realistic statement of the risks of disclosure generally, and any special risks associated with the specific research project.*

3. *A statement that the researcher and the University will do everything possible to protect confidentiality; that this will include challenging any subpoena or other legal process seeking disclosure, and where there is a meritorious case, exhausting all legal avenues of appeal. This statement should also include the University's*

commitment to cover reasonable legal costs associated with any such
challenge, including appeals.[19]

Problems arise in relation to the second element, as it is not clear what "a realistic statement of the risks of disclosure" might entail. In this regard, Jackson and MacCrimmon abandoned the *Tri-Council Policy Statement*'s ethical benchmark of "minimal risk" in favour of the legal concept of "material risk," which is employed when physicians are obliged to disclose material risks associated with medical procedures, such as operations. To explain material risk, they quoted Chief Justice Bora Laskin, who explained:

> *Even if a certain risk is a mere possibility which ordinarily*
> *need not to be disclosed, yet if its occurrence carries serious*
> *consequences, as for example, paralysis or even death, it*
> *should be regarded as a material risk requiring disclosure.*[20]

The risks of the medical procedures Laskin referred to include paralysis or death. However small that risk might be, if a patient were being given a choice of whether to have a certain operation, or participate in a bio-medical trial where death or paralysis are among the possible side effects, no doubt he or she would prefer to know about the risk. Jackson and MacCrimmon saw the consequences of the violation of confidentiality as being sufficiently serious as to be classified as a material risk. They suggested that the ongoing judicialization of society, the increasing incidence of large-scale lawsuits, and the growing collaboration between universities and the corporate sector mean that the risk of subpoena is rising across disciplines:

> *In light of these factors, we believe that it is reasonable to*
> *conclude that across the full spectrum of research activities there is*
> *a risk that research may become the subject of legal proceedings.*[21]

Is there a material risk across the "full spectrum of research activities"? Much research does not involve collecting identifiable data, in which case the possibility of a researcher violating a confidence is zero. There is also much research where researchers provide confidentiality because disciplinary ethics codes tell us it is the default unless the participant indicates otherwise. In much research, it is highly implausible that anyone would ever go to any significant lengths to attempt to acquire individual responses to researchers' questions.

Perhaps we will see more challenges to research confidentiality in the future, but experience does not support their projection. It took thirteen years after Jackson and MacCrimmon wrote their opinion, a period when tens of thousands more human research projects were conducted in Canada, for another challenge to research confidentiality to arise — the search warrant served on Bruckert and Parent's lawyer in relation to murder charges against Luka Magnotta, to which we return later. Meanwhile, Ogden remained the only researcher in Canada ever to have been subpoenaed and asked to divulge confidential research information, and he successfully defended it in Coroner's Court. The fact remains: There has *never* been a case of court-ordered disclosure of confidential research information in Canada. In the US, there have been four in the past fifty years where courts ordered researchers to disclose confidential information. Two of them — the orders to Popkin and Scarce — relate to grand-jury proceedings. Both researchers refused to comply. Canada does not have grand juries anyway. One of the other two cases — *Atlantic Sugar* — occurred precisely because the court viewed a limited-confidentiality statement as a waiver of privilege. In the other case, the limitation on confidentiality that the college claimed applied to Belfast Project interviews undermined arguments to quash the subpoenas. This is the record in what must now amount to hundreds of thousands, if not millions of research projects. Is this risk really the equivalent of the material risk of the medical procedures to which Bora Laskin referred?

Of course, subpoenas do happen, sometimes in the strangest of places. Although it would have been difficult to predict that a grand jury would subpoena Brajuha seeking confidential information from his "The Sociology of the American Restaurant" research for example, the conclusion that risks are everywhere and that researchers should routinely warn prospective participants about the possibility of court-ordered disclosure hardly seems reasonable. While dozens of US researchers have received subpoenas, courts have not repeatedly ordered researchers to violate research confidentiality. The reason is that researchers, often but not always with their university's support, have fought to preserve research confidentiality. Courts have understood that they cross an ethical and ultimately self-defeating line when the knowledge that litigants and prosecutors seek come at the expense of the volunteer research participants who shared that information only because of their understanding the researcher would maintain the confidentiality they promised. To continue to maintain this record, researchers collecting sensitive information non-anonymously should Wigmorize their research designs in anticipation of having to claim researcher-participant privilege.

Subjugating Ethics to Law

When it comes to what action universities should permit researchers to take to protect research confidentiality, Jackson and MacCrimmon took the law-of-the-land perspective when they said they would not allow researchers to state that they propose to defy a disclosure order. Their rationale for this doctrine begins in contract law:

> From a legal perspective, a promise to disobey the law may be
> misleading to the extent that a subject believes that it confers
> some legal recourse if the promise is broken. A promise to disobey
> the law is unenforceable as being contrary to public policy.[22]

True enough, but it is not an offence to make such a pledge. More importantly, it would be a mistake to conceptualize a research-ethics policy purely in legalistic terms, hence our writing this book. The conceptualization of the researcher-participant relationship as a "contract" may be appropriate for some biomedical research, but it makes much less sense in qualitative field research, particularly that which is community based, where the researcher-participant relationship depends on empathy and trust rather than the legal concept of contract.

Jackson and MacCrimmon argued that researchers cannot make a decision to exercise civil disobedience up front: "Whether ethics would require disobedience to the law depends on the facts and context of the particular case."[23] They argued that a blanket pledge to defy any court order to disclose would disrespect the rule of law, because it would not constitute a principled defiance of a particular law:

> *Careful balancing must be done in each case . . . As an*
> *example, if the Supreme Court of Canada having heard*
> *and considered all of the arguments in favor of extending*
> *privilege, and having acknowledged the significance of the*
> *harm that might be done to future research if confidentiality*
> *is not maintained, nevertheless determines that disclosure is*
> *necessary in order to avoid a serious miscarriage of justice,*
> *must not a researcher take the Court's reasons into account*
> *in making an ethical judgment about whether to obey that*
> *order? . . .*
>
>   *In our opinion while it may be ethical in limited*
> *cases to disobey an order to disclose, it is not ethical to*
> *promise unconditionally ahead of time to do so, since most*
> *commentators seem to agree that there are circumstances in*
> *which a researcher would be ethically obligated to obey a court*
> *order. An ethical decision to disobey the law ethically must*
> *be made in the context of the individual case and after the*
> *researcher has weighed all factors including the reasons of the*
> *court.*[24]

We have benefited greatly from Jackson and MacCrimmon's legal opinion because it helped refine our ethical position. However, we take issue with five elements of their analysis.

First, despite having pledged to maintain confidentiality even in the face of a court order to disclose, the ethics-first researcher might nonetheless make an *ethical* decision to violate confidentiality because of the specifics of a case. If, for example, the circumstances of a case exceeded the minimal criteria outlined in *Smith v. Jones* and, after due consideration, we felt the situation created a compelling ethical reason to violate confidentiality — for example, to save a life — we would not need a court to justify our decision to disclose confidential information. We would disclose it, probably long before a court would be involved. If we appealed a disclosure order all the way to the Supreme Court of Canada, we would have kept appealing because we believe maintaining the confidence is the ethical course of action. The court giving different weight to the interests at stake will not change our mind.

Second, while "careful balancing must be done in each case," in the research context where the requirement of informed consent requires that we must tell prospective participants ahead of time what we will do, our civil-disobedience ethic is based on the specific issues raised in the numerous court-ordered disclosure cases on record, to which there is a clear pattern. Having scrutinized every US case the secondary literature describes, having read most of the decisions relating to them, and having read every new decision as soon as we heard about it, *we have not found a single case where we believe violating a promise of strict confidentiality would have been ethically appropriate.* In other words, when claims of researcher-participant privilege themselves are analyzed as a "case" we have not found one in which violating confidentiality would have been justified. That contextual fact is the foundation of our belief that an *a priori* pledge to violate a court order to disclose confidential research information is ethical.

Third, we do not make the decision to engage in research in a societal vacuum; academe is not the island of *Lord of the Flies* (even if sometimes it may seem like it). Researchers make project-by-project decisions about what research they will do, often seek funding through peer-reviewed processes, and invariably involve justifying the ethics of what they do to REBs, who may or may not approve their projects. We would not engage in a project unless we believed the benefits to knowledge outweighed any reasonably foreseeable claims that might arise against research participants. For example, we would choose not to conduct research with active paramilitaries about future attacks because of the ethical conflict involved. However, we might well become involved in a project that involved interviews with former paramilitaries on attacks they had conducted previously. Lowman was willing to work as a driver for escorts as part of an ethnographic project regarding off-street prostitution. Palys has done observational research with police and witnessed some of them violating civil liberties. Ogden has done research that involved witnessing suicides. Researchers make case-by-case decisions about whether to get involved in a particular project.

Fourth, Jackson and MacCrimmon do not refer to the political context of our decision to pledge strict confidentiality. Researchers have to make the pledge of confidentiality at the outset of a situation where the Canadian state has not legislated protection for research participants. Should a third party attempt to access confidential research information, the courts will have to make a decision after the fact about whether a research communication is privileged. In the US, there are numerous research shield laws.[25] If Canada were to adopt such laws it would make a pledge to defy a disclosure order unnecessary. The US legislators who created confidentiality certificates helped make the law ethical. These shield laws codify our ethical position on research confidentiality. The debate should be about what kinds of research are eligible for protection, where those lines are drawn, and who should make those decisions, not whether there should be any lines in the first place.

The TCPS says that, "ethical approaches . . . may well affect [law's] future development . . ." The purpose of this book is to do exactly that. CAUT has lobbied, and we have encouraged, the three granting agencies to campaign for the creation of a research shield law in Canada.[26] It appears that, because there is no case of compelled disclosure, there is no perceived need. It is thus frustrating that, whenever we encounter arguments that Canadian researchers should warn prospective participants of the risk of court-ordered disclosure, the protagonists invariably cite US cases to justify their position. To deal with the contradiction, our ethical bottom line is straightforward: The absence of shield laws does not change the principle on which we base the ethics-first perspective on research confidentiality.

Fifth, the formulaic imposition of a warning to research participants that "confidentiality cannot be guaranteed,"[27] or that confidentiality will be guaranteed only to the extent permitted by law, has had a decidedly chilling effect on research.[28] In analysis of therapist-client privilege on appeal (*Jaffee v. Redmond*) the US Supreme Court recognized the potential cost of making promises of confidentiality on which a person cannot rely:

> *We part company with the Court of Appeals . . . We reject the balancing component of the privilege implemented by that*

> *court and a small number of States. Making the promise of*
> *confidentiality contingent upon a trial judge's later evaluation*
> *of the relative importance of the patient's interest in privacy*
> *and the evidentiary need for disclosure would eviscerate the*
> *effectiveness of the privilege. As we explained in Upjohn, if*
> *the purpose of the privilege is to be served, the participants*
> *in the confidential conversation "must be able to predict with*
> *some degree of certainty whether particular discussions will be*
> *protected. An uncertain privilege, or one which purports to be*
> *certain but results in widely varying applications by the courts,*
> *is little better than no privilege at all."*[29]

The ethics-first doctrine proposes civil disobedience in response to the evisceration of research confidentiality for fear of a threat that remains entirely theoretical in Canada.

Legally Sound, Ethically Wanting

Lovett's opinion confirmed our belief that universities should not leave research ethics entirely to lawyers. Lovett did not consider the implications of university or disciplinary ethics policies for the framing of ethical guarantees of confidentiality, or how case-by-case analyses of privilege claims create the ethical dilemmas for researchers that we set out to resolve. Nor did she discuss the TCPS proviso that:

> *Information that is disclosed in the context of a professional or*
> *research relationship must be held confidential. Thus, when a*
> *research subject confides personal information to a researcher,*
> *the researcher has a duty not to share the information with*
> *others without the subject's free and informed consent.*[30]

Lovett's opinion made no mention of protecting research participants, who she portrayed as persons from whom the university needs to protect itself. Informed-consent statements are nothing more than contracts that incur obligations, so avoid gratuitous clauses. While the university may decide to challenge third-party threats to research confidentiality, depending on whether it is in its interests to do so, it can protect itself by limiting confidentiality. If a subpoena arrives, the university can say, "Sorry, we told you that confidentiality is limited." *Caveat emptor.*

The Lovett opinion stood as the clearest example yet of how "legal and ethical approaches . . . may lead to different conclusions."[31] Nevertheless, Lovett's opinion helped to elaborate the legal context in which researchers operate; they need to understand law in order to fulfill their ethical obligations. It reinforced our view of the ethical bankruptcy of the *caveat emptor* approach to research confidentiality.

The Ethical Obligation of Law-First Approaches

One positive element of the Jackson-MacCrimmon opinion is that it did not let universities off the hook in the event that a court challenges research confidentiality. For Ogloff, Horvath, and Clayman, focusing only on statutes enabled them to assert that no defence was possible, thereby allowing them to surrender research confidentiality without a fight. In contrast, Jackson and MacCrimmon would commit the university to doing "everything possible" to assert researcher-participant privilege through the common-law Wigmore test, which would include "challenging any subpoena or other legal process seeking disclosure, and where there is a meritorious case, exhausting all legal avenues of appeal."[32] They added that an informed-consent statement "should also include the University's commitment to cover reasonable legal costs associated with any such challenge, including appeals."[33]

Back at the Ranch

With two legal opinions saying the university should not permit researchers to make an unlimited pledge of confidentiality, some members of the SFU REB continued to assert the law-of-the-land doctrine. Lowman continued to argue that such a doctrine violated the academic freedom of researchers to chart a different ethical course. Given the impasse, the REB sought advice from Professor Judith Osborne, the SFU associate vice-president responsible for policy, equity and legal issues, about the status of limited and strict confidentiality at SFU. Taking into account the interpretation we had received from the granting agencies over the "gangs" FAQ, she replied:

You have asked my advice on the wording of Form 2,
specifically the following text to be provided to participants in
a research project or experiment:

> *"Any information that is obtained during this study*
> *will be kept confidential to the full extent permitted by the*
> *law. Knowledge of your identity is not required. You will*
> *not be required to write your name or any other identifying*
> *information on research materials. Materials will be*
> *maintained in a secure location."*

. . . I recognize that the informed consent/confidentiality
issue is controversial within the University community.
There has been a lengthy debate about the extent to which
confidentiality assurances given by the researcher must
reference the legal constraints on such assurances. The REB
and the University have each sought legal advice on this
matter. The state of the law regarding case-by-case privilege
in the researcher/research subject relationship is unclear and
the higher courts in Canada have not to date recognized that
such privilege exists. The granting councils have acknowledged
that "legal and ethical approaches to issues may lead to
different conclusions" and that "though ethical approaches
cannot pre-empt the application of the law, they may well
affect its future development or deal with situations beyond
the scope of the law."

The debate at SFU has been around two different
approaches to research ethics approval for confidentiality
assurances to research subjects: the "law of the land" approach
(as reflected in the current wording of Form 2) and the "ethics
first approach." The University's position in this debate is
that, as a public body, it will not counsel a disregard for the
laws of the land. Nonetheless, it recognizes that there may
be situations in which a researcher would refuse on ethical
grounds to disclose confidential information despite a court
order to do so. University support for such a position would
have to be determined on a case-by-case basis using section

17 of the Framework Agreement where a faculty member is involved or using the analogous provision for graduate students where a graduate student is involved.

Regarding the Research Ethics approval process, there would seem to be room for two approaches:

1. *The researcher who adopts the "law of the land" approach will continue to use the wording in Form 2;*

2. *The researcher who opts for the so-called "ethics first approach" must be made aware of the University's position set out above and provide a signed understanding to that effect. S/he would have to provide information to the research participants along the following lines: "there is no obligation for you to provide any identifying information. Any identifying information provided to the researcher will be kept confidential to the fullest extent possible. Although it is unlikely that I would have to breach confidentiality, I might have to do so for ethical reasons and I encourage you to ask me about those reasons before agreeing to participate."*

I trust that this advice will be useful to the Research Ethics Board.[34]

It was an awkward solution and did not end the disagreements among REB members over the implementation of the TCPS and new SFU ethics policy, but it was the end of the debate over the imposition of confidentiality limited by law — at SFU, that is. With the debate over the approach to court-ordered disclosure resolved, the REB's attention turned to heinous discovery.

CHAPTER XXV
What If?

While it was easy to imagine situations where a higher ethical consideration, such as saving a life, might lead a researcher to violate a confidence, there is no known circumstance of such an event. Nevertheless, there was still no REB consensus on how to approach informed consent in the research context to address this theoretical possibility.

Three different sources would influence the course of the debate. The first was *Smith v. Jones*, which offered some general guidelines about the factors that might make a disclosure permissible, and the responsibilities that would accompany any decision to violate confidentiality. The second was a project in which researcher Ivan Zinger sought to study the effects of solitary confinement on prisoners, and could reasonably anticipate that he might hear about their plans to harm themselves or others. The third related to a drug trial at the University of Toronto affiliated Sick Children's Hospital. After medical researcher Nancy Olivieri had signed a confidentiality agreement with Apotex pharmaceuticals as part of her involvement in the drug trial, she felt ethically compelled to violate that agreement when the drug started showing serious side effects during the trial.

We have already described the case facts and decision in *Smith v. Jones* in Chapter 23. Below we extend the analysis to consider its implications for the ethics-first approach to research confidentiality. We then discuss Zinger's research, which led to our distinguishing anticipated and unanticipated heinous discovery. We leave consideration of the Nancy Olivieri case to Chapter 26, when we discuss the attempt of the Interagency Advisory Panel on Research Ethics (PRE), the overseer of the TCPS, to impose its own duty to report on Canadian researchers.

The significance of *Smith v. Jones*

The ethical and legal issues that *Smith v. Jones* raised have special significance for the public-safety exception when translated to the research arena. *Smith v. Jones* involved an incident in Vancouver, our home city. The case concerned violence against prostitutes, one of Lowman's primary research interests, and involved a prostitution stroll that has been the focus of some of his research. The women in his samples could have ended up being among Jones' victims. Indeed, sixty-three street-involved women went missing from Vancouver's Downtown Eastside, forty-nine of whom were likely murdered by serial killer Robert William Pickton. Although Lowman never knowingly interviewed someone like Jones, it is conceivable that he could have interviewed such a person in his research on men who buy sex.[1] Accordingly, the question of what to do if we realized we were interviewing a prospective serial killer provides a plausible scenario in which to compare various ethical and legal approaches in the research context.

If we were to conduct face-to-face interviews with men who buy sex and ask questions about crimes they plan to commit against prostitutes, we would have to choose between listening to their answers and not disclosing them, or not posing the questions in the first place. We would not ask those questions in the first place, because it would be unethical for us to conduct research knowing we would become informers. If Jones had been our research participant and started telling us what he told psychiatrist Smith, we would have encountered an instance of heinous discovery. Our ethical responsibility would be to take steps to ensure police protect street-connected women on the Downtown Eastside from Jones.

At the same time, Jones would not stop being our research participant to whom we would still have ethical obligations. The fact that a research participant has declared his murderous intent does not give a researcher license to throw him to the wolves. It is not possible in the abstract to decide what precisely we would do. Our objective would be to do our utmost to ensure the safety of the women while also encouraging Jones to seek help. Depending on the circumstances, we might refer Jones to mental health authorities. However, if the threat seemed imminent and there were no other options we would contact police.

While the three criteria the Supreme Court set out in law for deciding when a disclosure might be permissible are reasonable ethically, the majority decision concerning the scope of the disclosure is problematic. Our position is more in keeping with the minority opinion of Justices Lamer, Major, and Binnie, who agreed Smith could violate the privilege, but argued that the disclosure should be as limited as possible:

> While the danger in this case is sufficiently clear, serious and imminent to justify some warning to the relevant authorities, two principles should guide the analysis of the scope of the disclosure: (1) the breach of privilege must be as narrow as possible; and (2) an accused's right to consult counsel without fear of having his words used against him at trial is vital to our conception of justice . . . The immediate concern for public safety is to ensure that the accused not harm anyone. This can be accomplished by permitting the psychiatrist to warn the relevant authorities that the accused poses a threat to prostitutes in a specific area. However, he should only disclose his opinion and the fact that it is based on a consultation with the accused. Specifically, he should not disclose any communication from the accused relating to the circumstances of the offence, nor should he be permitted to reveal any of the personal information which the trial judge excluded from his original order for disclosure.[2]

The majority of the court went further, with the result that newspapers presented sufficient detail to identify the various parties. The irony of the publicity surrounding the case is that it may eventually endanger public safety, for, as the dissenting justices pointed out:

> As the facts of this case illustrate, the accused was only diagnosed and made aware of the possibility of treatment

because he felt secure in confiding to the psychiatrist. If that
confidence is undermined, then these individuals will not
disclose the danger they pose, they will not be identified, and
public safety will suffer.[3]

We refer to this as the heinous-discovery conundrum.[4] Some commentators, such as the SFU ethics committee and the REB that replaced it, argued that, in the name of informed consent, researchers should limit confidentiality to make prospective participants aware of the public-safety exception. The irony is that, if a researcher warned a man like Jones that the researcher would turn him in, Jones would be much less likely to disclose his plan to commit murder, in which case the researcher would not learn of the plan, and the murders would proceed. Is that an ethical outcome?

Jackson and MacCrimmon's View

Jackson and MacCrimmon suggested that, while the *Smith v. Jones* decision stopped short of creating a duty to disclose privileged information, when a threat meets the three public-safety exception criteria, the courts might, one day, impose such a duty:

The Supreme Court left open the question whether such
disclosure is mandatory. While the Court cited US cases which
had established a tort duty on doctors to disclose confidential
information when a public safety concern arises, the Court
refused to decide whether such a duty existed in Canada. At
the moment, a researcher or other person in a confidential
relationship may disclose confidential or private information in
order to protect the public safety. However, the possibility that
such a duty will be imposed in the future should be taken into
account by researchers in deciding whether to warn of a threat
to public safety.[5]

In terms of its implications for informed consent, Jackson and MacCrimmon argued that, in research that might trigger the public-safety exception, researchers should warn prospective participants about the possibility of the researcher intervening:

> . . . In the overwhelming majority of research situations it
> is extremely unlikely that a researcher would come across a
> scenario in which the public safety considerations of Smith
> v. Jones would be engaged. For the extraordinary case where
> this did come up, the Lowman and Palys analysis in which a
> researcher can justify violating confidentiality seems an ethical
> response. However, it is possible to envisage research projects
> where the possibility of heinous discovery or the public safety
> exception would be elevated to the level of a material risk
> requiring discussion as part of the informed consent process.
> Take, for example, a research project focussing on organized
> crime and the drug trade. If the research protocol envisages
> interviews with research subjects involved in the drug trade
> and could include disclosures of enforcement techniques for
> those who did not pay their debts or who otherwise breached
> their obligations, it is not at all far-fetched to anticipate that
> some informants, as a way to illustrate their enforcement
> strategies, might reveal the "next hit." Obviously, this is
> not something that would flow out of an informant on the
> first interview, but given a long and continuing research
> relationship founded upon mutual trust, highly sensitive and
> potentially incriminating evidence could be revealed. If a
> researcher is involved in this field of research and the risk of a
> public safety scenario being revealed is significantly enhanced,
> we believe that a researcher should explain to research subjects
> the existence of the public safety exception and the legal and
> ethical responsibilities that it will place upon the researcher.[6]

Like every other commentator with whom we have discussed the public-safety exception, Jackson and MacCrimmon did not address the heinous-discovery conundrum. Limiting confidentiality reduces the likelihood of a person disclosing a threat thereby making it more likely that they will carry it out. Because confidentiality is not absolute does not mean that it should be limited *a priori*.

Lovett's View

Lovett acknowledged that *Smith v. Jones* sets a high bar for the public-safety exception to solicitor-client privilege. She agreed that it established criteria to determine when it might be permissible to disclose confidential communications, but does not require disclosure in those circumstances. However, she cautioned:

> *Failure of a researcher to disclose information that would*
> *come within the public safety exception described in Smith*
> *(or within the common law duty to warn principles) could,*
> *in appropriate circumstances, lead to the imposition of such*
> *a duty in the event harm to a third party actually occurred*
> *subsequent to disclosure of information that it would occur.*
> *The most prudent course of action to be taken in such*
> *an extraordinary circumstance would therefore be for the*
> *researcher to seek a court declaration that disclosure is*
> *required, as was done by the psychiatrist in Smith v. Jones.*[7]

Yes, disclosures should occur only after careful case-specific consideration, with input from third parties. However, one can envisage a heinous-discovery situation that would require the researcher's immediate action, leaving no opportunity to seek a court order. Smith's advantage was that Jones was already in custody when he divulged his plans to murder sex workers.

Because Lovett wrote her opinion three years after Jackson and MacCrimmon's, she also provided commentary on *R. v. Brown.*[8] This allowed her to consider solicitor-client privilege against the right of an accused to full answer and defence in a situation where a potential wrongful conviction was at stake. "Innocence at stake" for a serious crime constitutes another instance of heinous discovery, as Lovett acknowledged:

> *Professors Lowman and Palys "regard the unanticipated*
> *revelation of wrongful conviction as a form of heinous*

discovery. If such a revelation occurs, researchers should
weigh the harm caused by a wrongful conviction against
the harm that violating a pledge of confidentiality would
do to the research enterprise when deciding to violate that
pledge:" Research Confidentiality and Researcher-Subject
Privilege, supra. *The Brown case makes it clear that, even*
in circumstances where the privileged communications may
support an accused person's wrongful conviction, the test for
disclosure is a very stringent one. Importantly, if confidential
information is ordered disclosed, and if relied on by the
defence, the provider of the information is given immunity.
The communication alone cannot be used to incriminate the
source of the information.[9]

The distinction between unanticipated and anticipated heinous discovery is important from an ethical perspective.

Unanticipated and Anticipated Heinous Discovery

Most researchers have a general inkling of what they will hear or see when they undertake research because of: (a) their experience in field settings; (b) their knowledge of the relevant literature; (c) what they learn from colleagues who have been in similar situations; and (d) how they explain the purpose of the research to potential participants.

Unanticipated heinous discovery refers to revelations that fall outside the agreement for confidentiality that the researcher established with the participant. For example, if a researcher were to interview the parents of Little League baseball players about the role of competitive sports in their children's lives and a parent declares his intention to murder his child's coach, that information is beyond the scope of the research. If a researcher interviews clients of sex workers about the process that led to their first experience buying sex and one of the clients starts revealing his plan to abduct and kill prostitutes, this, too, would be an instance of unanticipated heinous discovery. As Bok[10] argues, to ignore such serious unanticipated threats — assuming one believes them to be real — is to become complicit in the act.

301

Anticipated heinous discovery, however, is quite another matter ethically, as it would involve a researcher going into the field knowing full well that they might receive "heinous knowledge." What are the ethics and practical consequences of a researcher asking for information knowing full well they would report it? That is exactly the situation in which Ivan Zinger placed himself when investigating the effects of administrative segregation — a euphemism for solitary confinement — on prisoners.

Assessing the Effects of Solitary Confinement on Prisoners[11]

Zinger's research aspired to examine the effects of solitary confinement on prisoners. It was potentially an important study. Solitary confinement is widely used and controversial. One group of researchers[12] argues that there is no negative psychological effect to prisoners from solitary confinement *per se*, while others[13] argue that solitary confinement borders on "cruel and unusual punishment," and may lead prisoners to become more violent to themselves (suicidal, self-mutilating) and/or others (assaultive). There are numerous assaults, suicides, and murders in Canadian prisons; there had been forty-two major assaults on prisoners and staff, eight murders, and eleven suicides in the most recent year Zinger cited, and 731 attempted suicides recorded in a decade.[14] Did use of administrative segregation contribute to these, he wondered.

Zinger was an employee of Corrections Canada at the time he researched solitary confinement in three maximum-security prisons. The research design involved interviewing and assessing prisoners when authorities first placed them in segregation, repeating those procedures after thirty and sixty days, and comparing their responses to prisoners in the general population. Would prisoners in solitary confinement be more likely to show signs of aggression and violence toward themselves and others? However, in the process of securing their consent for participation, Zinger told them:

> Before we begin, I need to tell you that although the
> information you provide today will be confidential, there are
> limits. I have an obligation to disclose any information you
> may provide if it's in regards to your safety or that of the

institution. These areas include suicide plans, plans of escape,
injury to others and the general security of the institution.[15]

Although his dissertation reported the confidentiality limitation, the journal article based on it did not. Propensity for violence was exactly what the study sought to ascertain, and yet Zinger would report to the prison authorities any indication that a respondent was planning violence, suicide, or escape. What prisoner would volunteer such plans knowing the institutional consequences if they did?

Should the reader be surprised that Zinger found prisoners in solitary confinement to be no more likely than general-population prisoners to report a desire to harm themselves or others? Armed with that finding, he claimed that solitary confinement had no debilitating effects. Given that Zinger was a Corrections Canada employee at the time, and that his findings reaffirmed the appropriateness of Corrections Canada's policy on administrative segregation, there is an appearance of institutional conflict of interest.

If other researchers follow Zinger's lead and routinely limit confidentiality, what will be their credibility when institutions research themselves "with eyes wide shut?" Imagine wanting to study police interrogations in order to determine how frequently police violate the rights of accused, but with a limited confidentiality guarantee — the researcher will report any such violations to the interrogators' superiors. Imagine studying the ways forestry and mining companies circumvent environmental regulations and telling employees that, if a court ordered you to, you would hand over their names. Imagine the headlines describing the research findings: "Police Always Follow Procedure, Research Shows" or "Study Finds Resource Companies Always Respect Environmental Regulations."

These comments are not to minimize the ethical soul-searching that enters such situations. Rather, they suggest that, when proposing new studies, researchers need to consider their professional obligation to do the best they can to produce valid and reliable data, and the risks they pose research participants versus the potential value of the study. If the result is data of questionable validity, the researcher has put research participants at risk for nothing. The concern with Zinger's research is that, however important his research question and however thoughtful his research design may have been, his decision to limit confidentiality compromised the information he gathered and the conclusion he reached.

If a study puts people at risk by collecting "guilty knowledge,"[16] is it worth it? Zinger introduced his research by noting that nineteen prisoners died in custody in Canadian prisons from suicide or homicide in the preceding year. To what extent did solitary confinement contribute to that number? Could the termination of forced solitary confinement reduce that number? Do we really want answers to these questions?

By limiting confidentiality so the researcher effectively rules important and consequential findings out of bounds, Zinger likely reduced his chances of ever finding out. Is the long-term benefit of potentially saving nineteen lives per year worth doing research with an unqualified guarantee of confidentiality? Because strict confidentiality is a necessary condition of data validity, the researcher's choice is whether the research is sufficiently important to warrant unlimited confidentiality, finding a different way to answer his research question, or not doing the research.

In their response to these concerns, Zinger et al. argued they had no choice but to limit confidentiality:

> [T]o carry out its public safety mandate, CSC is required
> by law to provide information to victims, the police, and the
> National Parole Board "about escape threats, threats to other
> prisoners and the like" (CCRA 1992: ss. 25-26). Failure to
> inform the appropriate authorities of threats of serious harm
> may have severe consequences and may result in liability.[17]

In this regard, Zinger failed to distinguish his role as a researcher from his role as a CSC employee. The *Tri-Council Policy Statement* then in effect held that:

> To preserve and not abuse the trust on which many
> professional relations reside, researchers should separate their
> role as researcher from their roles as therapists, caregivers,
> teachers, advisors, consultants, supervisors, students or
> employers and the like. If a researcher is acting in dual roles,

*this fact must always be disclosed to the subject. Researchers
should disassociate their role as researcher from other roles, in
the recruitment process and throughout the project.*[18]

Zinger et al. cited sections of the Canadian Psychological Association
Code of Ethics that refer to confidentiality limitations to protect third parties
and allow researchers to comply with certain legal obligations. According
to the CPA *Code*, researchers should:

> *I.44 Clarify what measures will be taken to protect
> confidentiality, and what responsibilities family, group, and
> community members have for the protection of each other's
> confidentiality, when engaged in services to or research with
> individuals, families, or communities.*
>
> *I.45 Share confidential information with others only with
> the informed consent of those involved, or in a manner that
> the persons involved cannot be identified, except as required
> or justified by law, or in circumstances of actual or possible
> serious physical harm or death.*
>
> *II.39 Do everything reasonably possible to stop or offset
> the consequences of actions by others when these actions
> are likely to cause serious physical harm or death. This may
> include reporting to appropriate authorities (e.g., the police),
> an intended victim, or a family member or other support
> person who can intervene, and would be done even when a
> confidential relationship is involved.*[19]

Given this framework, Zinger et al. suggested that an unlimited pledge of
confidentiality would be unethical. Speaking of our critique, they asserted:

> *Rightly, the authors speak of honesty and trust, yet in essence
> suggest that researchers either:*
>
> 1. *deceive the participants by guaranteeing them full-
>   confidentiality and violate this confidentiality if they
>   divulge their intent to commit serious harm (an event that*

can be reasonably anticipated in correctional settings);[20]
or

2. *ignore, in the name of research, the participants'*
   threats to harm themselves or others, and thereby expose
   researchers and correctional authorities to the possibility of
   lawsuits.

This is why in accordance to legal and ethical
requirements, researchers in correctional settings, as well as
mental health service providers, routinely limit confidentiality
from the outset. This is more respectful of prisoners' right
to choose whether to take part in a study/treatment since
prisoners know up-front what will remain confidential and
what may be disclosed in specific circumstances. Informed
consent is all about this greater autonomy to choose.
Guaranteeing full confidentiality when there is a strong
possibility of being confronted with serious threats of violence
or self-injurious behaviour is professionally deceiving and
disrespectful to prisoners' dignity.[21]

Zinger et al.'s focus on informed consent and the research participant's right to refuse was reminiscent of the SFU ethics committee's justification for limited confidentiality: They used the prospective participants' right to choose to justify a *caveat emptor* approach that downloads responsibility to protect research participants onto those participants. Limited confidentiality of this sort tells research participants, "as long as you assume the risk, we will continue to collect data from you that could harm you if I divulge it."

Researchers do not inform participants about the liability bargain they are effectively making — in which case, how can the researchers claim to have given them enough information to achieve truly informed consent?

Mandatory Reporting Requirements

Zinger et al.'s "we had no choice" argument raises another issue researchers ought to consider when formulating research-confidentiality guarantees: mandatory reporting requirements.

In the preamble to its chapter on privacy and confidentiality, the TCPS added the caveat to the importance of confidentiality:

> *The values underlying the respect and protection of privacy and confidentiality are not absolute, however. Compelling and specifically identified public interests, for example, the protection of health, life and safety, may justify infringement of privacy and confidentiality. Laws compelling mandatory reporting of child abuse, sexually transmitted diseases or intent to murder are grounded on such reasoning.*[22]

When it comes to the public-safety exception, the *Tri-Council Policy Statement* used the word "may" rather than "must." A confidentiality violation to prevent a serious harm is discretionary: permission, not obligation. In contrast, laws compelling all citizens to report to authorities such acts as child abuse create legal obligations.

Legal reporting requirements vary considerably among countries, states, and provinces. Depending on their subject matter, researchers need to be aware of mandatory reporting requirements that may make unlimited guarantees of confidentiality impossible. Such laws raise the same kinds of issues as limitations of confidentiality in anticipation of heinous discovery. For example, speaking of mandatory child-abuse reporting laws, Glancy, Regehr, and Bryant explained:

> *Society has a responsibility to victims and to those who are unable to help themselves. As a result, it has been argued that the absence of reporting laws is a reflection of society's tolerance for abuse and neglect of vulnerable individuals. Mandatory reporting laws can, therefore, be seen as a means of supporting victimized women and relieving the burden of reporting currently placed on victims. Such societal recognition of assault and abuse could create pressure for increased funding to treatment programs and shelters. Arguments for mandatory reporting also point to the societal view that apprehending offenders overrides victim wishes for confidentiality.*[23]

But arguments against mandatory reporting laws are also compelling. As Glancy et al. note:

> There is also the issue of whether reporting a crime of violence without the victim's consent is an infringement on individual rights to autonomy. Victims may elect not to report an assault perpetrated against them for fear that it will lead to further abuse by the offender. They may also be aware of the secondary trauma experienced by many victimized individuals encountering the criminal justice system. Stripping victims of the right to decide whether or not to report a crime committed against them violates the ethic of self-determination.[24]

For researchers, mandatory reporting laws pose three concerns. First, absent exemptions for researchers, they create no-research zones because, arguably, it would be unethical for researchers to seek information they know they must report. This leaves researchers able to ask around, but not directly about some of society's most pressing and distressing social problems, where the need for accurate, valid information is often the greatest. Second, it creates validity issues. Why would anyone confess a crime to a researcher knowing the researcher would pass his or her identity along with his or her confession to police or other authority? Third, such reporting would seem to violate the principle that "Researchers should avoid being put in a position of becoming informants for authorities."[25] Researchers are supposed to spend their time trying to understand society's problems, not seek to become police informants.

The SFU Ethics Committee Tries Again

The first proposal the new SFU REB entertained to deal with heinous discovery was a new version of the "personal responsibility contract" that would require researchers to sign a document saying:

> I will ensure that, if I encounter data or circumstances that may be harmful to the subjects, participants, third

parties or the community, I will honourably determine
if that harm warrants a breach of confidentiality, and if
so, I will inform the subjects that [sic] the appropriate
persons or agencies of may [sic] observations.[26]

This second incarnation of the responsibility contract again drew fire for
its very broad definition of harm. Its requirement that the researcher inform
the research participant about the public-safety exception to confidentiality
created further problems. To begin with, the contract appeared to be more
about protecting the university from liability than protecting research participants from harm. Second, in the world of "what ifs?" that characterized
some REB deliberations[27] it is conceivable that informing the participant
might precipitate rather than prevent harm.

The chair suggested the REB should adopt the contract wording and
change it if it were to be determined that it was not consistent with the
TCPS. The REB authorized Lowman to write a letter to the Interagency
Panel on Research Ethics seeking an opinion on the wording, which he did
in June 2002.

This newest REB attempt to limit confidentiality rested not so much on
the conflict between a researcher's duty to research participants and his or
her general duty to public safety as with the fear that a researcher may have
a tort duty to prevent harm to third parties. Much of this fear rested with the
murder in California of student Tatiana Tarasoff, which brings us back to
developments in the administration of research ethics at the national level.

CHAPTER XXVI
The National Scene

The New Order

The creation of the TCPS brought with it a bureaucratization of the ethics regulation process both locally — in its rules for the composition of REBs — and nationally.

The granting agencies created two national bodies to interpret the TCPS for REBs and researchers, and to provide administrative support for developing it: the Secretariat on Research Ethics (hereafter "the Secretariat") and the Interagency Advisory Panel on Research Ethics (PRE). The first executive director of the Secretariat, Mr. Derek Jones, had previously taught health law at McGill.[1] Under the TCPS governance structure, the Secretariat "is mandated, among other things, to provide substantive, administrative and communication support to the [PRE]."[2] The Executive Director of the Secretariat sits as an *ex officio* member of PRE.[3]

PRE is "a body of external experts established in November 2001 by three Canadian research agencies . . . to support the development and evolution of their joint research ethics policy, the *Tri-Council Policy Statement: Ethical Conduct for Research Involving Humans*."[4] The three granting agency presidents appointed PRE's twelve volunteer members. One of the first twelve persons appointed was none other than Dr. Bruce Clayman, SFU's VP-research.

Clayman's appointment was curious in several respects: i) he is a physicist who, as far as we know, has never done any research with human participants; ii) his testimony in *Ogden v. SFU* indicated more concern about liability and image management than protecting research participants and academic freedom; and iii) the TCPS institutional conflict of interest guidelines forced Clayman from the SFU ethics committee, and yet here he was being appointed as a member of the group that would interpret the rules by which SFU's new REB would operate. His PRE website biography[5] cites his chairing of the SFU ethics committee as one of his contributions to ethics, even though the TCPS no longer permits such an arrangement because of the appearance of institutional conflict of interest.

In light of Clayman's record at SFU, it was with a wry smile that we read the announcement that Clayman would become the PRE chair after Dr. Howard Brunt of the University of Victoria finished his term. In the press release announcing the appointment, the funding agency presidents stated they "were impressed by Dr. Clayman's outstanding commitment to research ethics in Canada to date and felt that his leadership will be instrumental in serving their common goal to promote high ethical standards in human research."[6]

Were they really talking about the same Bruce Clayman, key member of the SFU administration that Judge Steinberg lambasted for its "hollow and timid" defense of academic freedom and "surprising lack of courage" in the Ogden case?

Reflecting on Clayman's appointment, one of our colleagues emailed us a terse comment: "Satire is dead."

Jones and the PRE

It would be more than four years before Jones and the PRE responded to the SFU ethics committee's queries regarding heinous discovery. They did so in an article in the *McGill Journal of Law and Health*. Jones invited us to comment on the opinion.[7] We base the following discussion of the public-safety exception on that exchange.

Recall that SFU's REB query to PRE arose because several REB members claimed that researchers have a "duty to inform" authorities to prevent a third party from being harmed, and a commensurate duty to inform prospective participants about this limitation to confidentiality. The claim that there is a duty to inform — sometimes referred to as a Tarasoff duty — originated in a 1976 California case.[8]

The case concerned a psychologist at the University of California at Berkeley whose patient, Prosenjit Poddar, told him he intended to kill Tatiana Tarasoff after she rejected his marriage proposal. After hearing this threat repeated in several sessions, the psychiatrist told Mr. Poddar he would take steps to restrain him if the threats continued, at which point Poddar stopped attending therapy sessions. The therapist informed campus security about his concerns. Security briefly detained and interviewed Poddar, who appeared to them to be rational, and released him after he promised to stay away from Tarasoff. However, soon thereafter when Tarasoff returned from a holiday, Poddar killed her. Tarasoff's parents sued the university and the therapist for negligence for failing to warn them or their daughter of the threat to her life. A lower court rejected the suit because there was no law requiring the psychiatrist to warn Tarasoff. The parents appealed to California Supreme Court, where the appeal court agreed four to three that:

> [O]nce a therapist does in fact determine, or under applicable
> professional standards reasonably should have determined, that
> a patient poses a serious danger of violence to others, he bears
> a duty to exercise reasonable care to protect the foreseeable
> victim of that danger.[9]

Although the California decision is not binding on other state courts, many states have since enacted Tarasoff-type laws, with wide variation in what they require.[10]

The three questions the SFU REB had posed to PRE were:

1. Does the TCPS bestow on researchers a "Tarasoff" duty to violate confidentiality when a research participant threatens to harm themselves or a third party?
2. If yes, is this Tarasoff duty triggered by a standard of preventing "significant harms" or by a higher standard of preventing "serious physical injury or death" (see, e.g., the

1999 Supreme Court of Canada case of *Smith* v *Jones*)?

3. Does the TCPS require researchers to immediately inform participants of an infringement of confidentiality when done to protect life and limb?[11]

Executive Director Jones fashioned the prologue to PRE's response to these questions. His framing of the response is instructive. Jones referred generically to "professional ethics norms" as if they are homogeneous, or have been evolving toward some common end. However, the only norm he cited was the code of ethics of the American Medical Association, which states that "physicians keep the confidences entrusted to them 'unless . . . required to do so by law or unless it becomes necessary in order to protect the welfare of the individual or of the community.'" Rather than canvassing a broad range of social and health-science ethics codes to illustrate their diversity, Jones made the AMA's law-of-the-land approach the standard-bearer for professional ethics norms.

PRE's portion of the response began straightforwardly enough by noting that the short answers to the SFU REB's three questions were: (1) "no, but a researcher may violate confidentiality in the circumstances outlined in the question;" (2) "no standard is articulated;" and (3) "no."[12]

PRE proceeded to discuss an array of circumstances in which researchers might reasonably disclose confidences, and then laid out a case for more inclusive *a priori* limitations to research confidentiality, most of which were based on putative professional duties to violate confidentiality in certain circumstances. With this response, Jones and PRE became the latest in a growing line of commentators to promulgate a culture of disclosure that focuses more on putative limits to research confidentiality than its importance. In the process, Jones and the PRE did exactly what many researchers complained from the start were the two main weaknesses of the TCPS's regulatory approach: (1) taking the medical profession's approach to ethics issues as the gold standard to be imposed on all other disciplines; and (2) seeing themselves as ethics gods — the font of right answers — instead of recognizing the diversity of ethics approaches that characterize the social and health sciences and humanities.[13]

The *Tarasoff* case involved a psychologist. The dilemma at the heart of that case sometimes does occur in therapeutic professions, such as psychology and psychiatry. Therapists often deal with people who are angry, depressed, possibly suicidal, and/or have hostile fantasies towards others. We expect (perhaps wrongly) the therapist to be able to determine when a patient is venting, fantasizing, or making a threat he or she intends to act out.[14] Even when the danger is real, it remains an open question whether the therapist best serves the interests of the patient, other prospective patients, and society by violating patient confidentiality. How many people will stop seeking treatment if they think the therapist with whom they share their innermost feelings may report them to police or appear as a witness for the prosecution?[15] The psychological and psychiatric literature contains extensive commentary about what circumstances, if any, warrant disclosure. Even therapists disagree about the wisdom of disclosure because of its potential long-term impact on the willingness of dangerous persons to seek treatment, the slippery slope it creates for the relationship between clinicians and law enforcers, and the confusion it creates between the supportive/healing role of the helping professions and the judgmental/enforcement role of the therapist once a culture of disclosure takes hold — not least because of the way the latter undermines the former.[16]

Compare the experience of psychotherapy with criminology. We have been involved in research with prisoners, non-convicted offenders, judges, lawyers, police officers, sex workers, pimps, sex buyers, porn distributors, civil servants, the general citizenry, assorted victims, correctional officers, and social activists of various stripes. We rarely complete a study without hearing about behaviour that is illegal, contrary to policy, a violation of civil rights, deviant, or corrupt, or that would be highly embarrassing to the persons divulging the information if we were to disclose their identities. Not once has a research participant told us they are going to commit suicide[17] or murder someone. We have never found a description of that scenario anywhere in the literature. The biggest threat for criminology is in ensuring our participants can talk to us about a whole range of criminal and marginal behaviour without fear that the information they provide will be used to prosecute, fire, discipline, or embarrass them. The commonplace problems psychiatrists face are not even on the map of most criminologists; similarly, what is commonplace for criminologists is rare for most other social scientists and humanities researchers.

The narrow perspective Jones and PRE brought to their analysis of the ethics of the public-safety exception saw them doing exactly what the advocates of limited confidentiality had done at SFU: emphasize a particular epistemological and ethical point of view and select only those parts of the TCPS and *Tarasoff* that support it. As van den Hoonaard argued in *The Seduction of Ethics,*[18] such imposed homogeneity impoverishes research, with society ending up the loser. However, despite its bioethical worldview, the TCPS holds that REBs and everyone else should respect disciplinary diversity.

According to PRE, the TCPS specifies criteria for evaluating and balancing competing duties; exceptional circumstances — such as the protection of health, life, and safety — may justify limited infringements of confidentiality. When these values conflict, what are the researcher's obligations?

> *On the one hand, society respects and values privacy and confidentiality. On the other hand, society cherishes and values other interests, like the protection of health, safety, or human life.*[19]

This phrasing portrays research and other cherished values as mutually exclusive: two different hands; but what if the purpose of research is to gain reliable information in order to enhance the protection of health, safety, and human life, or some other compelling public interest? It is precisely in research geared to these objectives that confidentiality is paramount.

In opposition to PRE's view, the ethics-first perspective issues from the belief that the public interest in the collection of accurate information about social phenomena is sufficiently great that the need to maintain confidentiality in certain kinds of research outweighs other foreseeable public interests. In a country that leaves decisions about researcher-participant privilege to be adjudicated after the fact, and where the legislature has never considered enacting research shield laws, the ethical rationale for the exercise of civil disobedience to defend research confidentiality against a court order to disclose is born.

We base the ethics-first approach on the law in action rather than an analysis of limitations in the abstract. A comment we made earlier bears repeating: After examining every civil and criminal legal case in Canada and the United States on record in which a third party challenged research confidentiality, we have yet to encounter one where we would have felt ethically compelled to violate a confidence. While instances of heinous discovery may have occurred in research, no researcher has reported one in the literature. Accordingly, as the Supreme Court argued in *Smith v. Jones*, when a person has a duty of confidentiality, they should violate it only in the most exceptional of circumstances. A researcher should consider whether to disclose, what to disclose, and to whom to disclose only on the basis of careful consideration of the unique circumstances of the case, time permitting. The idea of making a blanket warning of some categorical response is anathema to this view, cheapening confidentiality, and threatening research viability. A strict confidentiality approach is consistent with PRE's opinion that "the TCPS recognizes and accommodates ethical and legal duties to warn, but it does not impose them."[20] PRE never fully considered the implications of this statement. Indeed, the bulk of its opinion sounds quite to the contrary.

The Jones/PRE analysis also glosses over some of the key principles of the *Tarasoff* decision in the process of applying it to the research context. The decision begins with the default assertion that, for most of us, there is no duty to warn: "under the common law, as a general rule, one person owe[s] no duty to control the conduct of another, nor to warn those endangered by such conduct."[21] For Jones and PRE the *Tarasoff* decision created an exception to that rule for professionals — by which they apparently mean to include all researchers — when that is not in keeping with the principle that created the exception. The court clarified that the duty to protect was incurred by the therapist not because he was a professional *per se*, but because of the special relationship that he had with Poddar by virtue of his clinical skills as a psychologist — i.e., someone who is skilled "in diagnosing mental disorders and predicting whether a patient presents a serious danger of violence"[22] — and the extended time they spent together during Poddar's therapy. The psychotherapist's job includes assessing a patient's dangerousness, which is why psychiatrists, if they diagnose patients as posing a threat to themselves or others, have the power under civil commitment laws to lock them up. Researchers do not have that power. Significantly, the responsibility did not extend to the police who interviewed Poddar, because they did not have the same special relationship with him.[23]

The *Tarasoff* decision was not unanimous. The minority of justices in the four-three decision wrote a strong indictment of the duty the majority was creating:

> *Overwhelming policy considerations weigh against imposing a duty on psychotherapists to warn a potential victim against harm. While offering virtually no benefit to society, such a duty will frustrate psychiatric treatment, invade fundamental patient rights and increase violence.*
>
> *The importance of psychiatric treatment and its need for confidentiality have been recognized by this court. "It is clearly recognized that the very practice of psychiatry vitally depends upon the reputation in the community that the psychiatrist will not tell."*
>
> *. . . Given the importance of confidentiality to the practice of psychiatry, it becomes clear the duty to warn imposed by the majority will cripple the use and effectiveness of psychiatry. Many people, potentially violent — yet susceptible to treatment — will be deterred from seeking it; those seeking it will be inhibited from making revelations necessary to effective treatment; and, forcing the psychiatrist to violate the patient's trust will destroy the interpersonal relationship by which treatment is effected.*[24]

Because the court found the psychiatrist's role in the prediction and prevention of violence determinative in the Tarasoff case, Applebaum and Rosenbaum[25] argue that the duty to protect applies only in a clinical research setting; it would not apply to researchers as researchers, because they are not trained to assess the validity of any threat, nor would they normally spend the same amount of time or achieve the intimate understanding expected of psychiatrists when treating their patients. PRE cites Applebaum and Rosenbaum's article, but misses that key point.

PRE's imposition of what it sees as a ubiquitous acceptance of a duty to warn distorts the situation, even in psychiatry and psychotherapy. Critics argue the *Tarasoff* ruling changed psychiatrists from caregivers to "the new informants"[26] and agents of law enforcement.[27] In this light, the wholesale importation of the therapist's duty to protect into the research setting represents the conflict of roles the TCPS specifically warns researchers to avoid, another example of the problems created by bioethical imperialism.

SSHWC

Because the *Tri-Council Policy Statement* was conceptualized as a document that would evolve on the basis of experience and changing ethical values, it was not long after PRE and SRE came into existence that a web of committees was created to advise PRE, which in turn would advise the three granting agency presidents on the development of the TCPS.

One such committee was the Social Sciences and Humanities Research Ethics Special Working Committee (SSHWC), which met for the first time in 2003. Initial experience with the biomedically influenced TCPS indicated that many qualitative and community researchers in the social sciences and humanities were disenchanted with the way REBs were evaluating their ethics applications. SSHWC's mandate was to develop recommendations for a second edition of the *Tri-Council Policy Statement* (hereafter TCPS-2) that would better serve the social sciences and humanities. Palys was one of six appointees to SSHWC,[28] which also included four ex-officio members.[29]

SSHWC's first task was to undertake a national consultation of the social science and humanities research communities in Canada in order to ascertain their experience with the TCPS and identify priority areas for further attention. That consultation resulted in *Giving Voice to the Spectrum*[30] — a title that reflected the committee's aspiration to give voice to the full spectrum of social science research methods in TCPS-2.

SSHWC identified eight priority areas, one of which concerned "Privacy and Confidentiality," which, in turn, had two components: (1) how researchers and universities might respond in those rare instances where ethics and law conflict; and (2) dealing with heinous-discovery scenarios in research.[31] SSHWC held two further national consultations on privacy and confidentiality en route to preparing a set of recommendations to forward to PRE for its consideration.[32]

Ethics and Law

SSHWC's starting point was the TCPS recognition that "legal and ethical approaches may lead to different conclusions."[33] The challenge for TCPS-2 was to formulate policy that recognized those divergences, and elaborate ethical responses without becoming overly prescriptive.

Instead of focusing only on divergence, the committee also examined the ways law and ethics converge, including:

1. statutory protection for Statistics Canada researchers and university researchers whose projects make them eligible for recognition as "deemed employees" under the *Statistics Act* (see p. 147 above);
2. common-law protections available to researchers, such as the Wigmore criteria;
3. protections available to Canadian-based researchers doing research in the United States who are eligible for confidentiality certificates or some other kind of statutory confidentiality protection; and
4. protection that might exist in federal and provincial privacy legislation.

Regarding possible protections that might reside in privacy legislation, SSHWC could only say:

> *Another area of legislation that may provide some degree*
> *of protection for research participants is the Freedom of*
> *Information and Protection of Privacy legislation that now exists*
> *federally and in every Province.[34] But while the peer-reviewed*
> *literature now includes discussion on the prospective applicability*
> *of the Wigmore criteria and of the US confidentiality certificates*
> *and privacy certificates to research, we are unaware of any*
> *similar discussion in relation to privacy legislation.[35]*

319

Areas where ethics and law may diverge included: (a) criminal prosecutions and civil litigation; (b) unanticipated heinous discovery; and (c) mandatory reporting laws.

Criminal Prosecutions and Civil Litigation

Although SSHWC distinguished ethics-first and law-first approaches and asserted that both should be supported in research-ethics policy, it recommended that, as a minimum standard, all researchers, REBs, and research institutions should be obliged to protect research confidentiality to "the full extent permitted by law." It would only be in that rare instance when ethics and law produced different conclusions, that there would be any choice to make.

To guard against descent into *caveat emptor* ethics SSHWC recommended:

1. *in the consent process participants should be informed that researchers and their universities will do everything possible to protect confidentiality; they would disclose information only after exhausting every legal avenue to defend it;*
2. *ensure that nothing they say about limitations to confidentiality could be construed as a waiver of privilege; and*
3. *ensure that as little harm as possible could befall the participant by ". . . not gathering any information that could harm the participant if it were to be disclosed that they are not prepared to defend, or if they do gather it, to not record it in any identifiable form that can be accessed by a third party.*[36]

Unanticipated Heinous Discovery

SSHWC held that researchers have a fiduciary duty to research participants. With respect to heinous discovery in the research realm, SSHWC held that "the truth is rarely simple":

> *Although policies that speak of a "duty to report" make the decision seem relatively straightforward — one serendipitously comes across the information that some heinous event will occur unless the researcher intervenes and the researcher feels ethically compelled to do so — life's choices are rarely so clearly defined:*

1. *What happens when the source of the information is not the party who ostensibly will carry out the heinous deed? Is gossip and hearsay a reasonable basis on which to trigger a violation?*

2. *How is one to distinguish whether the information is real or whether the respondent is simply testing the researcher and/or pulling his/her leg?*

3. *Who is an appropriate person to judge whether the threat is real?*[37]

In discussing where the bar should be set for disclosure of a research-participant's plan to harm a third party, SSHWC adopted the three criteria from *Smith v. Jones*. SSHWC held that, even if a researcher decided to intervene to prevent a threatened harm, there were many possible interventions besides contacting police. The researcher's responsibility to the participant does not end at the point of disclosure; it should be as restricted as possible to prevent harm to the participant and should not adversely affect any of the participant's rights, such as the right to a fair trial.

SSHWC gave five reasons against warning participants confidentiality would be limited in the event of unanticipated heinous discovery, since:

1. unanticipated discovery is, by definition, a revelation that arises outside the anticipated bounds of the research;

2. by definition, it cannot be anticipated, which makes it difficult to articulate generic boundaries;

3. in *Smith v. Jones* the Supreme Court of Canada held that violation of a duty of confidentiality under the public-safety exception should be considered case by case;

4. in many cases, suggesting that they might harm other people would undermine a researcher's relationship with participants; and

5. giving the warning may not prevent the heinous event, but make it more likely to happen, because the researcher would never learn of the threat in the first place.

Mandatory Reporting Laws

With respect to mandatory reporting laws, SSHWC gave its preliminary views on three situations:

1. Where researchers gather information that they know from the outset they would report.

SSHWC suggested that researchers should not conduct such research, because it would embrace a policing function, and would violate the TCPS principle that it is, ". . . unethical for researchers to engage in covert activities for intelligence, police or military purposes under the guise of university research. REBs must disallow any such research."[38] The TCPS says, "Researchers should avoid being put in a position of becoming informants for authorities or leaders of organizations."[39] An ethical way of doing research on some topics would be under conditions of complete anonymity, such that no one could ever connect any reportable behaviour to any specific individual.[40]

2. Where a researcher does not set out to examine behaviour that is the subject of mandatory reporting laws, but where there was a foreseeable possibility that a research participant might reveal such information.

For example, if interviewing parents about their child-rearing practices, it is quite conceivable that a researcher might discover some abusive practices. SSHWC suggested that, when research of this sort is undertaken, researchers should be clear about how they interpret reporting requirements. It also encouraged analyses that could help illuminate how researchers can walk the ethical/legal tightrope that mandatory reporting laws create when they do not include exemptions for research.[41]

3. Where a research participant alleges that a third party is engaging in a behaviour that is subject to mandatory reporting.

SSHWC did not believe hearsay would trigger mandatory reporting requirements. The committee was not aware of any cases involving such a situation.[42]

The Research Community Responds

Many of the consultation submissions SSHWC received agreed that while protecting confidentiality was a collaborative task, with researchers and REBs already doing a good job, they felt university administrations needed reminding about their responsibilities in this regard.

Many commentators suggested Canada should create some kind of research shield legislation, such as the US system of confidentiality certification.

SSHWC's Recommendations

SSHWC conducted a second iteration of consultation after releasing *Continuing the Dialogue*, but circumstances precluded writing a further report summarizing its results. Instead, the granting agencies instructed SSHWC to conclude its work and present its recommendations by February 2008. By that time, Bruce Clayman had completed his term as chair of PRE, and Derek Jones's contract as executive director of SRE had expired. The agencies mandated their replacements — Dr. Norm Frohlich and Ms. Susan Zimmerman — to complete the advisory process and draft TCPS-2.

In addition to the recommendations noted above, SSHWC suggested wording that would address the ethics-and-law issue head on — leaving space for both ethics-first and law-first researchers — instead of leaving it to others to write. In formulating the recommended wording, SSHWC adapted the CPA *Code of Ethics*:

> *The law affects and regulates the standards and conduct of research involving human subjects in a variety of ways, such as privacy, confidentiality, intellectual property, competence, and in many other areas. Researchers are expected to familiarize themselves with the laws and regulations of the societies in which they work that are related to their activities as researchers. However, legal and ethical approaches to issues may lead to different conclusions.*

The law tends to compel obedience to behavioural norms; ethics aim to promote high standards of behaviour through an awareness of values. If the laws or regulations that are applied to one's research seriously conflict with the ethical principles contained in this policy statement, researchers will do whatever they can to uphold the ethical principles. Ethical approaches cannot preempt the application of the law, but they may well affect its future development or deal with situations beyond the scope of the law. Nonetheless, if upholding the ethical principles could result in serious personal consequences (e.g., jail or physical harm), decision for final action would be considered a matter of personal conscience. Researchers should consult with colleagues if faced with an apparent conflict between abiding by a law or regulation and following an ethical principle, unless in an emergency, and seek consensus as to the most ethical course of action and the most responsible, knowledgeable, effective, and respectful way to carry it out.[43]

Of course making promises to protect research confidentiality requires researchers and universities do exactly that, the minimal expectation being that they protect confidentiality to the extent possible within the law. Beyond this, SSHWC recommended that researchers:

1. *follow disciplinary standards and practices for the collection and protection of confidential information;*
2. *behave in a manner commensurate with the level of sensitivity of any identifiable information they hold (for example, in the case of very sensitive data, by anonymizing the data at the earliest convenience; by encrypting digital files, holding the raw data in a locked cabinet or secret location away from their office); and*
3. *incorporate any statute-based or common law legal protections (e.g., the Wigmore criteria) that are available to them when designing their research.*[44]

As for universities, SSHWC sought to ensure there would be "no more Ogdens," i.e., researchers should be able to count on universities to take seriously their obligation to defend research confidentiality to protect research participants, the integrity of their REB, and of course the academic freedom of researchers to pursue knowledge about all aspects of society. Toward this end, SSHWC recommended that universities and research institutes "create policies that give researchers and REBs easy access to qualified legal help that is independent of the university's own lawyers."[45]

The granting agencies disbanded SSHWC and all the other working groups in 2008, at which point PRE took the final sets of advisory committee recommendations and began drafting TCPS-2.

CHAPTER XXVII
Answer to a Riddle

By the time the granting agencies released TCPS-2 in December 2010, sixteen years had passed since the coroner subpoenaed Russel Ogden. After years of conflict, SFU recognized that, to protect academic freedom, it should not prevent ethics-first researchers from providing guarantees of strict confidentiality. TCPS-2 adopted and enhanced similar proposals that emphasized the fundamental importance of confidentiality to research. In this regard, it was a considerable improvement over the original TCPS, which gave more emphasis to the rare circumstances in which confidentiality might be limited.

TCPS-2 recognizes:

1. There is a "duty" of confidentiality.

> *When researchers obtain information with a promise of confidentiality, they assume an ethical duty that is central to respect for participants and the integrity of the research project. Breaches of confidentiality may harm the participant, the trust relationship between the researcher and the participant, other individuals or groups, and/or the reputation of the research community. Research that probes sensitive topics (e.g., illegal activities) generally depends on strong promises of confidentiality to establish trust with participants.*[1]

The strong and legally relevant term "duty" in TCPS-2 will make it an important reference point should a subpoena ever threaten research confidentiality in Canada again. As we will see in Chapter 29, it was put to just that use when police used a search warrant to seize Bruckert and Parent's "Jimmy" interview.

2. Researchers should separate their responsibility to protect research participants from any obligation they have to other authorities who might be interested in identifiable information about those participants. A role conflict may arise when gatekeepers, such as the Corrections Service of Canada in Zinger et al.'s case, can withhold access to prospective participants if researchers refuse to assume this reporting function. While the first TCPS dealt with this role conflict, TCPS-2 places it squarely in the section on confidentiality. It requires that researchers do not allow themselves to become informants:

> Researchers shall avoid being put in a position of becoming informants for authorities or leaders of organizations. For example, when records of prisoners, employees, students or others are used for research purposes, the researcher shall not provide authorities with results that could identify individuals unless the prior written consent of the participants has been given. Researchers may, however, provide administrative bodies with aggregated data that cannot be linked to individuals for purposes such as policy-making or program evaluation.[2]

3. We should leave a researcher's decision about whether to comply with a legal order to violate a pledge of confidentiality to his or her conscience.

> Researchers may face situations where they experience a tension between the requirements of the law and the guidance of the ethical principles in this Policy. In such situations, researchers should strive to comply with the law in the application of ethical principles. Researchers should consult

with colleagues, the REB or any relevant professional body,
and if necessary, seek independent legal advice to help resolve
any conflicts between law and ethics, and guide an appropriate
course of action.[3]

Researchers shall maintain their promise of confidentiality
to participants within the extent permitted by ethical principles
and/or law.[4]

4. Institutions are obliged to support researchers who are put in a position of defending research confidentiality:

Researchers shall safeguard information entrusted to them and
not misuse or wrongfully disclose it. Institutions shall support
their researchers in maintaining promises of confidentiality.[5]

After thirteen years of asking the three granting agencies and PRE the question, "Are research ethics absolutely subject to law, or is it possible for researchers to make a pledge of strict confidentiality?" we finally had an answer: Researchers shall uphold confidentiality to the extent permitted by ethical principles *and/or* law.

CHAPTER XXVIII
University Accountability on Trial

The police seizure of Bruckert and Parent's "Jimmy" interview in the belief that accused murderer Luka Rocco Magnotta was Jimmy had all the hallmarks of being a precedent-setting case. It was the first time the concept of researcher-participant privilege had arisen in a Canadian criminal proceeding.

At issue was whether police and prosecutors have the right to access any information they think might have material relevance to a criminal prosecution. The murder for which Magnotta stands accused was truly horrific. Magnotta had worked as an escort. Most sex workers give interviews on the proviso that researchers do not disclose their identities. The case pitched the value of the "Jimmy" interview for the prosecution against the damage that a violation of confidentiality would do to research. What was the potential probative value of the interview? Researchers conducted it five years prior to the murder, and at least three years before the victim and accused first met. If the accused were to plead not guilty by reason of insanity, how likely is it that an interview conducted five years prior to the offence could have a bearing on the accused's state of mind when committing it?

The case represented the perfect opportunity for the University of Ottawa (U of O) to do what SFU failed to do in 1994 when the coroner subpoenaed Ogden. It could live up to its ethical responsibility to protect research participant identities, protect the integrity of REB ethics review, show leadership on an issue of national importance, stand up for academic freedom, and use the occasion as an opportunity to educate the public about the value of research on sensitive topics and social issues.

Or it could run for cover.

Just like SFU, the U of O denied any liability and ignored its responsibilities to research participants. However, the ethics culture has changed since 1994. Now there is a mechanism for holding a university accountable to the principles elaborated in TCPS-2. Here was an opportunity to put it to the test.

When the U of O administration initially learned Montreal police wanted to obtain a copy of the "Jimmy" interview, they agreed to reimburse half of the fee the two researchers had paid for an initial consultation with their family lawyers — a few hundred dollars — and then did nothing despite the urgency of the threat to research confidentiality. At that point the Canadian Association of University Teachers (CAUT) stepped up to the plate. As the January 2013 *CAUT/ACPPU Bulletin* reported:

> *CAUT is funding [Bruckert and Parent's] legal case as*
> *the University of Ottawa has declined to do so. In a letter*
> *to CAUT executive director James Turk Dec. 19, 2012,*
> *university president Allan Rock said "The University of Ottawa*
> *recognizes its role . . . in safeguarding entrusted information.*
> *However, the University does not consider that its role extends*
> *to the payment of legal costs if researchers decide to challenge*
> *the seizure of research records in the context of criminal*
> *proceedings."*[1]

One significant change that occurred since the Ogden subpoena was that the TCPS (in both its first and current versions) now required university REBs to avoid the institutional conflict of interest that had plagued SFU. Unlike the situation that occurred years earlier at SFU where a VP-research-appointed committee watched in silence, members of the U of O's REBs argued pointedly that the university should provide legal support:

> *Twenty members of the University of Ottawa's research*
> *ethics boards have written to university president Allan*
> *Rock protesting the university's refusal to support two*

of its criminology professors' legal efforts to protect the confidentiality of their research records.

The REB members noted the research had been approved by the university on the explicit condition that the research participants' confidentiality would be protected.

The "inaction on the part of university officials entrusted with advancing intellectual inquiry is inexcusable," the letter said. "By failing to come forward in support of professors (Chris) Bruckert and (Colette) Parent, the university is setting a dangerous precedent."

The letter also warned of consequences from inaction: "a 'chill factor' placed on any research involving participants who require trust in the strength of confidentiality agreements they sign and that are co-signed by university researchers"; possible "censure by research funding agencies such as the Social Sciences and Humanities Research Council of Canada"; and "refusal of these same agencies to release research funds until the university's actions are brought into alignment with the Tri-Council Policy Statement on Research Involving Human Participants."[2]

In response, President Rock claimed the university had supported its researchers:

> *I would like to be clear that Professors Bruckert and Parent have the full support of the University of Ottawa in their proactive and responsible efforts to safeguard the confidentiality of this research.*
>
> . . .
>
> *With respect to payment of their legal fees, the University of Ottawa did in fact cover some of the initial legal costs related to this case.*[3]

The statement was reminiscent of VP-Research Clayman's claim that the university's token payment of $2,000 towards Ogden's legal fees constituted "support" — but Rock's claim was even more egregious. U of O had offered to pay a few hundred dollars at a time when CAUT had already spent more than $100,000 on legal fees. As CAUT Executive Director Jim Turk said in reply to Rock:

> The most charitable interpretation of your letter is that you were misinformed as, contrary to your claims, the University has utterly failed in its obligation to defend the confidentiality of Bruckert and Parent's confidential research records.
> Your letter states that: "The University of Ottawa places the utmost importance on the integrity of the research conducted by its professors and the critical role confidentiality plays in maintaining that integrity." Regrettably, your administration's actions belie that claim.[4]

Turk explained that CAUT had seen the significance of the case and, because of the need for immediate action, stepped in. CAUT kept the U of O informed of developments, waiting for President Rock to do the right thing:

> The two University vice-presidents promised a quick response at the June 20, 2012, meeting, acknowledging the urgency of the situation. But there was no timely response, meaning that CAUT either had to continue to make provision for Bruckert and Parent's legal support, oblige the two professors to assume costly financial responsibility for the defence of confidentiality, or leave them defenceless while waiting for the University to decide what it would do.
> The "quick response" from the University came almost three months later — on September 7th in an email from Vice-President Diane Davidson. Citing the fact that CAUT had covered the cost of legal counsel to defend Bruckert and Parent (amounting to over $100,000 at that point), Davidson said, "Je confirme par la présente que l'Université n'entend pas rembourser ces frais." [I hereby confirm that the University does not intend to pay these fees.][5]

Aside from its potential to set an important precedent for researcher-participant privilege, the U of O's dereliction of its duty to protect research confidentiality provided an opportunity to test the resolve of Canada's three funding councils to walk their talk when it comes to what TCPS-2 says about protecting research participants.

To be eligible for funding a university or research hospital must sign a Memorandum of Understanding (MOU) with the funding councils. The MOU commits the institution to providing a research infrastructure, including policies to control the conduct of research with humans and a mechanism to discipline researchers who do not comply with the expectations laid out in such documents as the *Tri-Council Policy Statement: Ethical Conduct for Research Involving Humans.*[6]

TCPS-2 bestows on researchers an "ethical duty of confidentiality."[7] While this ethical duty "must, at times, be balanced against competing ethical considerations or legal or professional requirements that call for disclosure of information obtained or created in a research context,"[8] researchers shall nonetheless, maintain their promises of confidentiality to participants to the extent permitted by ethical principles and/or law. This may involve resisting requests for access, such as opposing court applications seeking disclosure. Researchers' conduct in such situations should be assessed on a case-by-case basis and guided by consultation with colleagues, any relevant professional body, the REB and/or legal counsel. The researchers did exactly what the TCPS required of them, assessed the merits of their case, and set about opposing the warrant.

Surely, universities have a role to play in defending the research they approve against legal challenges. The desire to ensure that universities would never again abandon a researcher the way that SFU had initially abandoned Ogden motivated some of SSHWC's recommendations to PRE regarding privacy and confidentiality. It was because former SSHWC member Palys believed that U of O's response made a mockery of TCPS-2's Article 5.1 that, in April 2013, he laid a complaint against the University of Ottawa with the Secretariat on Responsible Conduct of Research. In June 2013, the *CAUT/ACPPU Bulletin* published a brief review of the complaint:

> The University of Ottawa has failed to meet its obligations
> under TCPS 2, and thereby has breached its obligations under
> its agreement with the granting agencies," said Palys in his
> letter to the secretariat. "At issue is whether TCPS 2 actually
> means anything and has any regulatory teeth, or does it
> regulate researchers while allowing university administrations
> to do whatever they please?
>
> Palys is asking that the university be required to apologize
> to the researchers for failing to support their principled defense
> of research confidentiality; to reimburse the cost of their legal
> defense of research confidentiality; and to establish policies for
> the legal indemnification of faculty and graduate students who
> might be faced with similar threats to research confidentiality
> in future.[9]

While we were waiting for the outcome of the complaint, the Quebec Superior Court released its decision on Bruckert and Parent's claim of researcher-participant privilege. Its decision promises to change the research confidentiality landscape in Canada.

CHAPTER XXIX
The "Jimmy" Interview: The Importance of "Good Facts"

Here was the case for which we had been preparing since 1997 when we first refused to use the SFU limited-confidentiality consent statement. Although such cases are extremely rare, if one did arise, we wanted to make sure researchers, REBs, universities, and granting agencies all know what it means to defend confidentiality to the extent permissible in law. Thanks in no small part to Chris Bruckert of the University of Ottawa and Jim Turk of CAUT, the "Jimmy" interview turned out to exemplify how to use common law to defend research confidentiality.

The Arguments

Bruckert and Parent's (the Petitioners') assertion of researcher-participant privilege was advanced before the Honourable Sophie Bourque J.S.C. of the Montreal Superior Court by Mr. Peter Jacobsen[1] and Ms. Tae Mee Park,[2] of Bersenas Jacobsen Chouest Thomson Blackburn LLP, a Toronto law firm.

Bruckert and Parent's claim of researcher-participant privilege for the "Jimmy" interview exemplifies the obstacle to anyone seeking an exception to the general rule:

> *If requested, all must testify before the courts about facts and events in the realm of their knowledge or expertise. In order that justice be rendered, the public and the judicial organization have the right to any and all information. That*

>*is the general rule: relevant information is presumptively
>admissible.*[3]

To be weighed against this interest was whether access to the interview should be restricted "to serve some overriding social concern or judicial policy," in this case the "researcher-participant privilege." The Petitioners used the Wigmore test to assert researcher-participant privilege.

In asserting its right to access the "Jimmy" interview, the Crown (the Respondent) agreed that the Wigmore test was the appropriate mechanism to evaluate the claim. As was expected given the case-by-case nature of the claim, Justice Bourque noted that the onus of proof was on the Petitioners to make their case. To meet this burden, the researchers presented evidence concerning their own qualifications, the details of the research project, the importance of the confidentiality agreement to their research, and the potential relevance of the "Jimmy" interview to an NCR[4] defence. The Crown did not introduce any evidence in its response.

The evidence that Parent and Bruckert's attorneys presented necessarily followed much the same strategy as Ogden's attorney, Mr. E. David Crossin QC (see Chapters 20 and 21 above) in the Vancouver Coroner's Court. However, the case also points to the importance of recent jurisprudence on journalist-source privilege for researchers, particularly *R. v. National Post*[5] and *Globe and Mail v. Canada (Attorney General)*.[6] The two cases were particularly relevant to Parent/Bruckert in several respects: (1) there were acknowledged parallels between the role of journalists and the role of researchers in the gathering and distribution of knowledge about society and the often crucial importance of confidentiality of sources in the production of that knowledge; (2) both cases involved case-by-case claims to privilege that the court agreed were best addressed by considering the claims in light of the Wigmore criteria; and (3) both cases involved, at criterion four, the weighing of competing interests in the context of a criminal trial. In a comment that speaks to all three of these issues, Judge Bourque quoted Justice Binnie from *R. v. National Post*:

The public has an interest in effective law enforcement. The public also has an interest in being informed about matters of importance that may only see the light of day through the cooperation of sources who will not speak except on condition of confidentiality . . . It is important, therefore, to strike the proper balance between two public interests — the public interest in the suppression of crime and the public interest in the free flow of accurate and pertinent information. Civil society requires the former. Democratic institutions and social justice will suffer without the latter.[7]

A particularly helpful aspect of the decision is that although the Crown conceded that the Petitioners had satisfied criteria one through three — but not criterion four — the court considered all four Wigmore criteria.

Applying the Wigmore Test

Criterion One: The communications must originate in a confidence that they will not be disclosed.

Justice Bourque concluded there was a clear expectation of confidentiality between Jimmy and the researchers because of the consistent manner in which it appeared in all documents related to the project — the SSHRC proposal, the ethics proposal to the REB, all recruitment information, training to research participants, etc. — which extended to all their research participants.

Noting the facts that Justice Bourque thought worthy of mention provides further clues to what future researchers who follow Wigmore can do to meet the requirements of the court. Justice Bourque noted that the U of O REB had approved the project,[8] and that the consent form clarified "Jimmy" had consented to the interview because the researcher promised confidentiality.[9] She further noted that the research assistant who informed the Montreal police of "Jimmy's" identity had been made aware of the importance of confidentiality on numerous occasions, and that he could not unilaterally revoke the confidentiality promise.[10] Under the weight of this evidence and the production of Magnotta's affidavit confirming that he was, indeed, "Jimmy," and still wished the court to respect his expectation of research confidentiality (i.e., he did not waive privilege), the Crown conceded that the Petitioners had satisfied criterion one: There had been a shared expectation of confidentiality.

Criterion Two: Confidentiality must be essential to the full and satisfactory maintenance of the relation between the parties.

The Petitioners' evidence affirmed confidentiality was essential to the relationship because of the numerous harms that a sex worker faces[11] should a researcher disclose their identity. The provision of confidentiality was a requirement of the SSHRC funding approval and the U of O REB. The Petitioners demonstrated that it took a considerable amount of time to build trust and rapport in order to be able to interview sex workers, because confidentiality is a prerequisite of their participation — they have to trust the researcher will abide by his or her promise. Lowman's expert testimony on prostitution research supported the Petitioners' position.

The abundance of evidence led Justice Bourque to conclude that Wigmore's second criterion "is clearly established in the case at bar."[12]

Criterion Three: The relation must be one that in the opinion of the community ought to be sedulously fostered.

At this stage of the test, the relationship is at issue, not the content of the communication. For Justice Bourque, the question was whether the relationship between academic researchers and their secret sources is one that the community thinks should be "sedulously fostered." The Petitioners argued unequivocally in the affirmative: Because of the general importance of academic research, the court should carefully safeguard the researcher-participant relationship. The court attached particular importance to protecting academic freedom:

> In McKinney v University of Guelph [1990] 3 SCR 229
> at page 282, Justice LaForest noted that academic freedom,
> necessary to allow "free and fearless search for knowledge and
> the propagation of ideas" is "essential to our continuance as
> a lively democracy." In her dissent in the same case, Justice
> Wilson wrote that the primary intent of academic freedom is

"the protection and encouragement of the free flow of ideas."

The Supreme Court of Canada has been very cautious over the years in intervening in university affairs, recognizing the importance of academic freedom in safeguarding the role of universities as self-governing centers of research, teaching and learning.

In other words, academic freedom and the importance of institutions of higher learning and academic research are key components of a democracy that values freedom of thought and expression.[13]

When it came to the importance of research generally, the court agreed. Justice Bourque drew extensively from the evidence the Petitioners provided, including nine paragraphs from the *Tri-Council Policy Statement* attesting to the vital role of academic freedom as well as privacy, confidentiality and anonymity to research. The court also agreed that the enactment of specific research shield laws — such as the Canadian *Statistics Act* and US "certificates of confidentiality," both of which protect the identities of health research participants from compelled disclosure in eligible research — are evidence of the importance of confidentiality to research on sensitive topics. The court concluded:

> *If investigative journalism (along with confidential sources) could help 'fill what has been described as a democratic deficit in the transparency and accountability of our public institutions,' the court agrees with the proposition that much academic research .... provides useful information on certain aspects of the human condition that are normally kept silent. This information is essential to understand and improve the social condition of vulnerable and marginalized communities.*[14]

Referring to research on sex work specifically, Justice Bourque concluded, "The evidence demonstrates that much of the research involving vulnerable people can only be conducted if human participants are given a guarantee that their identities and the information they share will remain confidential."[15] Confidentiality is not only necessary for research with marginalized populations, but also with police and clients of sex workers,[16] and is necessary for the accuracy and validity of information.[17] Justice Bourque also recognized that disclosure of confidential research information could have a chilling on research on all manner of sensitive topics.[18] She noted that sex-work research in particular has been presented to courts and legislators as "evidence based on social facts" and is "essential to the public in general, policy makers, academics, and sex workers."[19] More generally, she held that, "Academic freedom is even of greater importance when the work product of university researchers was obtained and/or created, and could have only been obtained and/or created, through a promise of confidentiality."[20]

Justice Bourque concluded that the Petitioners had satisfied the third criterion of the Wigmore test.

Criterion Four: The injury that would inure to the relation by the disclosure of the communications must be greater than the benefit thereby gained for the correct disposal of litigation.

The balancing exercise pits the importance of research confidentiality against the public interest in suppressing crime. Accordingly, the court weighed the potential probative value of the evidence and the seriousness of the crime against the public interest in respecting promises of confidentiality, an interest that had been established at criterion three.[21] Justice Bourque explained that the burden of proof still lay on the Petitioners to show that "the Jimmy–researchers relationship outweighs the public interest in investigating and prosecuting crime:"

> *Every claim to researcher-participant privilege is situation*
> *specific, with the public's interest in academic freedom,*
> *including the pursuit of knowledge and the free flow of ideas*
> *in our society, weighing heavily in the court's balancing*
> *exercise . . .*[22]

Although the public interest in academic freedom is of great importance, Justice Bourque continued, it is not absolute. Quoting Justice McLachlin, she was unable to accept the proposition that "'occasional injustice' should be accepted as the price of the privilege."[23] While public interest in the suppression of crime is considerable, it "is not sufficient to annihilate a case-by-case privilege claim."[24]

Justice Bourque declared: "One must exhaust possibilities of obtaining the information before requiring a researcher break his or her promise of confidentiality,"[25] a point to which she would return when evaluating the Respondent's need for information to achieve the correct disposal of litigation — in this instance, the criminal charges against Magnotta.

Probative Value of the Interview

The interview's probative value also played a role in the court's balancing of competing interests. The Crown argued that the interview was relevant evidence on two grounds:

1. "[T]he Jimmy interview contains information on Jimmy's prostitution activities, which are related to the first degree murder Magnotta allegedly committed because they both have a sexual dimension."[26]

However, the Crown did not present evidence that the murder was related to Magnotta's work as an escort, or that a sex worker is more likely than other people to commit a murder, and so the court dismissed this argument.

2. The interview would be relevant in the event that Magnotta advances a "not criminally responsible" (NCR) defence under section 16 of the Criminal Code,[27] because it "could provide valuable information on the accused's mental state and personality."[28]

To evaluate this argument, the Petitioners relied on the expert testimony of forensic psychiatrist Scott Woodside, head of The Sexual Behaviours

Clinic of the Centre for Addiction and Mental Health and a member of the Ontario Review Board, which reviews annually the status of every person in that province who was found not criminally responsible or unfit to stand trial for criminal offences on account of a mental disorder.[29] Woodside had been involved in somewhere between five hundred and six hundred NCR assessments since joining the University of Toronto Department of Psychiatry in 1998.

In Woodside's opinion, the information in the interview could have "some remote relevance" to assessing the presence or absence of a mental disorder,[30] but was extremely unlikely to have any relevance to the assessment of the accused's mental state at the time he is alleged to have committed the offences.[31] Consequently, the interview's value "as it would relate to a defence of NCR . . . is likely to be minimal."

Woodside held that the interview would be of limited value "assuming that the Crown and those assessing the accused possess a significant amount of information pertaining to Magnotta's prior social, physical and mental health history, and an extensive internet trail of his activities."[32] Consequently, the Court concluded, "there exists more useful contemporary material that could be used in an NCR assessment."[33]

It was now up to the court to weigh the competing interests at stake.

The Scales of Justice

The case pitted participant privacy and academic freedom against the need for information to achieve the correct disposal of litigation. In weighing each interest, the court could take into consideration the relevance of the information to the litigation, the availability of other sources of the sought-after information, and the seriousness of the offence.[34] In the process, the court made clear that it would not entertain a fishing expedition for evidence and would endeavor to respect academic freedom.

The combination of Magnotta's reasonable expectation of privacy — "Where research involves gathering information about research participants' very identities, the participant's reasonable expectation of privacy should be protected"[35] — Dr. Woodside's opinion that the interview would, at best be of minimal assistance to any NCR assessment, and that other more relevant material regarding his mental state is available, all favoured recognizing researcher-participant privilege. Nonetheless, the court reasoned, the interest in investigating serious crimes is very important. Consequently, in order to make a full and proper analysis of the privilege claim, Justice Bourque decided to examine the sealed interview transcript herself.

After examining the interview, the court concluded that none of its content had relevance to determining the presence or absence of mental illness at the time the interview was conducted in 2007, and none of it could help establish his state of mind when the offence was committed in 2012. The only potential relevance of the interview would be for cross-examination if Magnotta took the stand — but even then, it would relate to collateral matters. Consequently, the court concluded, "the potential relevancy of the Confidential interview is minimal at most and marginal."[36]

In the other pan of the scales of justice was a much greater weight. The court recognized the importance of the research project in shedding light on the indoor sex industry . . ."[37] SSHRC had considered the research important enough to fund it, which led to various publications and presentations. Further, the recent Supreme Court of Canada ruling in *Canada (Attorney General) v. Bedford* striking down three prostitution laws and Pivot Legal Society's Charter challenge together with B.C.'s Missing Women Inquiry illustrate the public importance of issues surrounding sex work. In addition, they illustrate the importance of research:

> *The Bedford case has taught us that the issues raised by such a constitutional challenge could be decided primarily because of the rich evidentiary record, comprising data derived from academic research on various prostitution aspects (safety, poverty, housing, morality, and economics), criminal law, ethics and public health.*
>
> *The Petitioners work contributes not only to the academic community's understanding of the sale and purchase of sexual services, but also to the broader public policy and society-wide discussions on this important, and controversial, aspect of Canadian life.*
>
> *Promises of confidentiality are integral to the Petitioners' work because it involves acquiring essential information*

> *from a marginalized population working in a stigmatized*
> *sector. Most participants like Jimmy would not agree to be*
> *interviewed in the absence of a promise of confidentiality and*
> *anonymity.*[38]

The court concluded, "both Petitioners' ability to undertake a similar research project in the future would be jeopardized if the promise of confidentiality is not upheld in this application."[39]

The court concluded its Wigmore criterion four analysis by recognizing the concept of researcher-participant privilege, and granting it in this instance:

> *Respondent argues that the search for truth and the*
> *investigation of Lin Jun's murder outweighs the public*
> *interest in respecting confidentiality in the case at bar.*
>
> *The evidence demonstrates that the public interest in*
> *respecting the promise of confidentiality is high.*
>
> *On the other hand, the interest in society of the*
> *investigation of serious crimes such as the one . . . in*
> *this case is high, but the probative value, if any, of the*
> *Confidential Interview in the pursuit of that truth is, at*
> *best minimal and marginal both theoretically and factually.*
>
> *Consequently, the Court concludes the Petitioners have*
> *met their burden on Wigmore fourth criterion and that*
> *the Confidential Interview is covered by the researcher-*
> *participant confidentiality privilege and that it should*
> *not be disclosed to the Respondent and return to the*
> *Petitioners.*[40]

Justice Bourque ordered the search warrant quashed and the sealed envelope containing the Jimmy interview returned to Bruckert and Parent once the delay to appeal had expired.

As the Crown elected not to appeal the decision, the court established the concept of researcher-participant privilege in Canadian common law, to be evaluated case by case. By being prepared with "good facts" whenever the next case comes to court, researchers and REBs can help that privilege achieve its fullest expression as its contours are embellished and refined. At the same time, this still leaves researchers in a state of considerable ambiguity, with the courts effectively making law after the fact. Justice Bourque's assertion of the legitimacy and importance of research should also revitalize discussion among policy makers regarding the prospective institutionalization of this privilege via statute-based protections that are akin to, but improve upon, those available in the United States.

CHAPTER XXX
Going the Distance

We began this book by recounting what happened when a legal authority ordered Russel Ogden to violate a research confidence or face a charge of contempt of court. Ogden was the first Canadian researcher ever to confront this threat to research confidentiality. In this concluding chapter we bring together the main themes of our examination of the ethics and law of research confidentiality by reflecting on how much things have changed — or not — since the Vancouver coroner subpoenaed Ogden two decades ago.

Defending Academic Freedom

The period of the limited confidentiality regime at SFU was an excellent illustration of how an REB should not exercise its power. Instead of asking whether a researcher's ethical protocol was consistent with the university's ethics policy, the ethics committee assumed there was only one right answer. That was the answer it preferred, and then enforced. The practice continued for a time at SFU, and still exists elsewhere, notwithstanding the advent of the TCPS. The experience suggests that one of the TCPS's greatest strengths can also be its curse. Both the current and former versions of the TCPS have done a reasonably good job of enjoining REBs to respect epistemological and disciplinary diversity. However, like all law and policy, through the process of implementation the TCPS became many things to many people. For SFU VP-Research Bruce Clayman and Ethics Committee Chair Adam Horvath, it supported their law-of-the-land doctrine. They did not recognize that one could read the policy as permitting the ethics-first approach to research confidentiality.

One of the main problems with the TCPS is that in enjoining REB members to do the right thing, it assumes they will; there are few checks and balances of REB power. Notwithstanding our criticism of drafts of TCPS-2 on that very point,[1] the final version provides no better safeguards than did the first TCPS. Like many policies, it is no better or worse than the people who implement it; the admonitions are there to defend academic freedom, but so, too, are the tools to violate it. Although SFU has recognized the problems with limited confidentiality, other universities still embrace the culture of disclosure, forcing researchers to limit confidentiality in a way that violates a researcher's academic freedom and spells the end of some important social research.

University of New Brunswick Professor Emeritus Will van den Hoonaard has documented the changing face of the research enterprise in Canada since the advent of the TCPS.[2] Although it is difficult to disentangle the impacts of the TCPS from other changes in the academy, interviews with researchers and REB members across Canada revealed widespread REB censorship and a growing propensity for researcher self-censorship in response to REB heavy-handedness. Through archival analysis of master's theses in anthropology and qualitative research presentations at conferences, van den Hoonaard shows that the number of participant-observer studies and ethnographies has dropped significantly since the advent of the TCPS, while the number of one-off interview studies has increased. Observers have noted the same in other countries with federal research-ethics codes.[3] All too often researchers acquiesce to REB doctrine instead of adhering to their own disciplinary standards and sense of principle.[4] Limiting confidentiality allows swift approval of applications instead of months of debate or withdrawal of a half-million-dollar grant because the researcher did not receive REB approval. Numerous universities, it seems, permit the *caveat emptor* approach.

Aside from studies like van den Hoonaard's, commentators have given little attention thus far to the impact of contemporary research-ethics regulation on knowledge production. While many US authors have recognized the way that ethics regulation often amounts to censorship,[5] relatively few have considered which voices contemporary ethics regulation silences. The most likely impact of limited confidentiality and *caveat emptor* ethics is on socially marginalized and vulnerable communities who will talk to social scientists only if their conversations are confidential. This includes not just law breakers, but also those who live on the margins of the law, various kinds of whistleblowers, persons who are harassed by legal authorities, or persons who suffer from health conditions that would affect their reputation, employability, or insurance benefits. British author Robert Dingwall[6] draws attention to the price a society will pay if researchers are turned into agents of the state:

> *In the contemporary world, citizens depend upon a great deal of expert knowledge in order to make good judgments about each other and about the social institutions that they encounter. The quality of that knowledge depends crucially on free competition between information providers. If what has traditionally been the most disinterested source of information, the universities, becomes systematically handicapped in that competition, then all citizens lose out. When we give up doing participant observation with vulnerable or socially marginal groups because of the regulatory obstacles, then a society becomes less well-informed about the condition of those who it excludes and more susceptible to their explosions of discontent. How helpful is it when the only ethnographers of Islamic youth in the UK are undercover police or security service agents?[7]*

Dingwall continued:

> *The great English sociologist, Herbert Spencer, drew an important contrast between industrial and militant societies. The latter type, which are well-exemplified by the former Soviet Union and its East European satellites, were, he argued, doomed to lose out in global competition because their authoritarian structures blocked diversity and innovation. Both socially and economically, they were frozen by their*

command systems. IRBs and other forms of pre-emptive ethical
regulation begin to look like the precursors of the surveillance
states that are being increasingly entrenched in the US and
the UK. Their incursions into liberty are justified in the name
of security, but may well have unanticipated consequences in
terms of prosperity. Wherever dissident voices are silenced,
innovation eventually dies.[8]

The result is a research enterprise relying more and more on existing public data sets prepared by institutional authorities from institutional perspectives to serve institutional ends, with the voice of people most affected by what those institutions do increasingly shut out. Ethics regulation is silencing critical voices, along with the accountability they sometimes generate. In the midst of a debate regarding the effect of what was then a relatively new ASA *Code of Ethics* section on covert research methods, Galliher stated:

Even after giving due weight to all the likely costs and risks
to the profession, the unavoidable question sociologists must
answer is whether a sociology that only poses approved
questions in an approved fashion is either empirically or
morally sound. Moreover, Erikson's warnings about risking
our freedom of inquiry by using clandestine research methods
may also be taken to suggest that freedom of inquiry exists
only so long as no attempt is made to employ this "freedom" by
conducting research outside of approved and safe boundaries.
Erikson's foreboding may well represent a correct assessment
of the situation, yet it seems wiser to recognize these problems
as constraints on our research which require thoughtful
consideration than to continue to believe in an academic
freedom that does not exist.[9]

He might just as well have been talking about limited confidentiality and the culture of disclosure that threatens research in Canada.

The Culture of Disclosure Undermines All Research on Sensitive Topics

An illustration of the consequence of limiting confidentiality because of the lack of statute-based protection is evident in the controversy surrounding the Boston College subpoenas described in our introduction. The purpose of the Belfast Project was

> . . . to gather and preserve for posterity recollections that would help historians and other academicians illuminate the intricacies of the Northern Ireland conflict in studies and books, and that would advance knowledge of the nature of societal violence in general, through a better understanding of the mindset of those who played a significant part in the events in Northern Ireland. In addition, if and when a truth and reconciliation process for Northern Ireland is launched by the British and Irish governments, following the model in South Africa following the end of apartheid, the trove of first-hand reports gathered and preserved by the Belfast Project may serve as a critical resource.[10]

It is a prime example of research that would not have been possible without guaranteeing the participants unlimited confidentiality — an ethics-first approach the researchers understood as the only way to proceed, and to which they subscribed. Neither the researchers nor the Boston College Agreement of Donation limited confidentiality in any way. The donor agreement promised interviewees that no one would release the tapes or transcripts of their interviews until they were deceased or they gave their permission.

The project convenors at Boston College who hired the coordinator and researcher understood the importance of confidentiality and told coordinator Moloney they would "run this by . . . university counsel," but never did. In the epitome of understatement, project convenor Robert K. O'Neill would later state, "In retrospect, that was my mistake . . . The contract unfortunately omitted the phrase 'to the extent American law allows.'"[11] However, if it had included that phrase and the law-first perspective it embodies, coordinator Moloney and researcher McIntyre say they never would have become involved in the project. Nonetheless, as ethics-first researchers, had the research records remained in their care and control, they would have been safe from third parties; instead, all research records were stored in the Burns Library at Boston College.

The Boston College case speaks volumes about the fundamental importance of confidentiality to research on sensitive topics, and the problems created when third parties want confidential research information that existing research shield laws do not cover. The US Attorney's arguments when Boston College brought a motion to quash the subpoenas illustrate the folly of limited confidentiality. Although the researchers understood that confidentiality was crucial and were prepared to defy a court order to protect it, the Attorney General was able to point to other researchers who limited confidentiality, and used them to undermine the claim the Belfast Project researchers were making:

> (E)ven many oral historians recognize that ensuring absolute protection [of research information] is not possible. See, e.g. Exhibit A (noting that Columbia University cautions participants that materials may be subject to subpoena). Notably, the contract between Boston College and the Belfast Project Director recognized that ensuring absolute protection was not possible:
>
>> Each interviewee is to be given a contract guaranteeing to the extent American law allows the conditions of the interview and conditions of its deposit at the Burns Library, including terms of an embargo period if this becomes necessary, as outlined herein. An appropriate user model, such as Columbia University's Oral History Research Office Guidelines statement, should be adopted.
>
> In a related letter from Boston College to Mr. Moloney, the Burns Librarian cautioned Mr. Moloney that, "I cannot guarantee, for example, that we would be in a position to refuse to turn over documents on a court order without being held in contempt" . . .
>
> Moreover, the standard forms from many other

universities do not include absolute confidentiality. See. e.g.
Exhibit 11 (sample forms). Thus, the notion that only absolute
secrecy is necessary to conduct sensitive oral history projects
is belied by authoritative experts in the field and by the
administrators of Boston College itself.[12]

These assertions are exactly what concerned us from the beginning: At worst, a court can interpret a limitation on confidentiality as a waiver of privilege; at best, such limitations suggest confidentiality is not as important as researcher lore might lead one to believe. Researchers pledge confidentiality in many types of research simply because participants' names are irrelevant, and it is ethical to acknowledge participants' rights to control their own information and who has access to it. However, there are many other types of research — like the Belfast Project — where it is crucial to provide confidentiality because disclosures could harm the volunteers who participate in the research, and going ahead with the research for society's gain would be exploitative and involve treating human participants as mere means to ends. The academy severely compromises academic freedom and research reliability when it places blanket limits on confidentiality.

The Belfast Project turned out to be an unmitigated disaster. The first disclosed interviews resulted in the arrest of two people in relation to the murder of Jean McConville — former IRA member Ivor Bell and Sinn Fein leader Gerry Adams,[13] sparking conspiracy theories and accusations that are destabilizing Northern Ireland's fragile peace. Researcher Anthony McIntyre is the subject of graffiti that describes him as a "Boston College tout."[14] He now lives in concern for his own life, the safety of his family,[15] and the safety of the interviewees who are still living.[16] Several participants are now suing Boston College for negligence in its failure to live up to the terms of the donor agreement.[17] In a last-ditch effort to retain some semblance of credibility, the College is in the process of dismantling the archive as it accedes to interviewee requests to return their tapes and transcripts.[18] As we write, the PSNI had submitted yet another subpoena for the remainder of the archive before it disappears,[19] while the NBC network has initiated its own case for access.[20] Boston College's credibility is in tatters, the venerable college now the prototypical example of how not to construct a research project, and the last institution one would want to trust with sensitive information. Because of the College's incompetence, its attempt to create a research treasure trove ended up in flames:

> Ricky O'Rawe picked up the package at his lawyer's office downtown the first week of May. It was a FedEx package, with a Chestnut Hill return address.
>
> When he got back to his house on the Glen Road in West Belfast, O'Rawe opened the package and stared at its contents: transcripts, CDs, tapes. It was his story, the oral history he had given to Boston College, about his life in the Irish Republican Army.
>
> The BC oral history project was envisioned as a treasure trove for historians to use in the future, as they seek to chronicle and comprehend the motivations of people who fought and killed and died here. But once hints about its controversial contents leaked out, it was police detectives, not academics, who began clamoring for the research.
>
> O'Rawe was trying to figure out what to do with the returned materials when the police in Northern Ireland made the decision for him. On May 22, after the police announced they were seeking the entire Boston College archive, 60-year-old Ricky O'Rawe walked into his study, the walls lined with sepia-tinged photos of old comrades who died in the three decades of war that the Irish, with their propensity for understatement, call The Troubles.
>
> He lit a fire and opened a bottle of Bordeaux. Then he threw his legacy, his story, his willingness to kill and be killed, onto the fire and watched it burn.[21]

The embers in O'Rawe's fireplace serve as a grim reminder that one of the biggest losers of this sorry saga is oral history — not just the history of the Troubles,[22] but also on researchers' ability more generally to ask questions about some of the most important and controversial issues of our time.[23]

We can only hope this debacle does not lead to further loss of life.

Research on Important Social Issues Is Avoided

The Boston College case shows that if research on sensitive issues goes ahead with only limited confidentiality, researchers who go ahead and ask for the information nonetheless place their participants — but not themselves, of course — in peril. A different example from the literature shows yet another cost: the loss of various kinds of research designed to inform public policy.

Judith Bernhard and Julie Young of Ryerson University in Toronto were proposing to study persons living in Canada under "precarious legal status."[24] This status includes those who entered the country illegally, people who entered legally but whose visas had expired, and people who were admitted under one status but became engaged in other activities once they had entered Canada, such as a person who had been admitted on a student visa but was now working illegally. The difficulties Bernhard and Young experienced did not involve a subpoena, but rather, the obstacles that the Ryerson Ethics Review Board (ERB) placed in their path.[25] Their experience epitomizes the potentially devastating impact of the culture of disclosure.

One role of social science is to provide information about niches of life that are important or controversial, and where little or no reliable information exists, so law reformers and policy makers do not operate in an informational void. Bernhard and Young were trying to illuminate one such void. No one even knows how many persons there are in Canada living under precarious legal status; estimates range from 40,000 to 600,000. Nor does anyone know the social costs associated with covert status, thereby making it difficult for service providers to develop meaningful policies. How many pregnant women do not receive medical treatment because they have no medical coverage and are afraid to see a doctor? How many abused women stay with their spouses because they fear disrupting a family will negatively affect their immigration eligibility? How many children do not begin school because their parents worry teachers will ask too many questions and, if they do, that some authority will apprehend their children?

Bernhard and Young's research was perceived to be important enough to receive SSHRC funding; only a minority of applicants receive such grants, having satisfied rigorous peer review. An interdisciplinary team developed the mixed-methods research proposal over a two-year period. Originally it called for 1,700 surveys and 250 interviews with persons living illegally and "institutional actors" — religious leaders, teachers, etc. — who have some sort of contact with persons living with precarious legal status.

The project constituted a rare example of research that clearly does face a plausible threat to confidentiality by an identifiable authority — the Canadian Border Services Agency (CBSA) — which had the means and motive to pursue Bernhard and Young's confidential research sources. As Bernhard explained:

> [G]iven the local context at the time, we felt we had reason to be wary. There had been publicized immigration raids in malls in the city and a non-status woman was detained and deported on Ryerson's campus during an international women's day event. Given this intensified focus on non-status issues, the uncertainty around confidentiality made us unwilling to take that risk.[26]

Media accounts of these events and others — where, for example, immigration officials held school-aged children as bait until their parents arrived to pick them up[27] — affirm Bernhard and Young's concerns were well placed.

The research was shaping up nicely until Bernhard and Young submitted their ethics application to the Ryerson ERB. Bernhard and Young had been concerned about how to build rapport, gain trust, and listen in a respectful way to highly vulnerable persons who they would ask to share their experiences, fears, and aspirations. The issue that sank the study was confidentiality and the impasse that arose when the ERB demanded the researchers limit confidentiality by law, something they were not prepared to do.

> Given the sensitive nature of our topic, no one contested that complete confidentiality was essential, or that our duty in conducting such research included the ability to provide research participants with such an assurance. The ERB insisted that we could not promise complete confidentiality, only confidentiality permitted by law. It appeared that if we went

> *ahead with multiple interviews, which would require that we*
> *collect and store contact information, there would be no way*
> *to unequivocally promise confidentiality to participants. Our*
> *proposal was the first to really push this question in the history*
> *of the university.*
>
> *. . . Finally, the ERB recommended that participants'*
> *consent forms be revised to include the following phrase:*
> *"Confidentiality will be provided to the fullest extent possible*
> *by law." We felt this coy turn of phrase would mislead study*
> *participants into a false sense of security. This "myth of*
> *confidentiality," a promise of confidentiality to the extent*
> *bound by law, meant, in effect, no real confidentiality at all.*[28]

In order to appease the committee and proceed without limiting confidentiality, Bernhard and Young had to abandon their original research
plan. The resolution was that they ended up conducting a superficial, cross-
sectional study that could not hope to answer the research questions they
originally posed.

> *The most significant compromise we made for both projects*
> *was not to collect or store participants' names or contact*
> *information so that these details would not appear in our files.*
> *This meant that we had to abandon the idea of multi-interview*
> *research. Because we could not record contact information,*
> *even if this was in code, we could only have one meeting with*
> *each participant. This was not ideal as it compromised the*
> *effectiveness of the research. We would not be able to build trust*
> *with participants over time, which would affect the extent to*
> *which they would be willing to share their experiences with us.*
> *As a result, we had to delve into challenging and confidential*
> *matters at our first meeting and were unable to clarify details or*
> *follow up about particular questions.*[29]

Instead of seeing Bernhard and Young's study as exactly the sort of
study universities should be standing behind as an example of the value

of social research that aims to contribute to the development of rational social policy, the ERB sought to limit confidentiality. Instead of embracing the law and requiring the researchers design their studies to anticipate the requirements of the Wigmore criteria, the Ryerson ERB sought to limit confidentiality, apparently without even considering the sort of scenario that might result in a legal challenge. How might the CBSA find out about the research? What occasion would lead to a subpoena? Would it be in the context of a deportation hearing, a show-cause hearing, or what?

It was yet another example of a philosophy of informed consent that attached little value to the research itself. It replaced Bernhard and Young's ethical concern for the safety of their participants with a *caveat emptor* logic that would have seen the ERB apparently having no qualms about throwing vulnerable research participants to the wolves. The researchers would have had to inform participants — persons from other countries who probably had no understanding of the law surrounding research confidentiality — about the limitations to confidentiality. As autonomous persons if they had chosen to accept that risk, Ryerson would be off the hook if any of them came to harm. Canada pays this kind of price for not having research shield laws. Ironically, the culture of disclosure would appear to be having a far more devastating impact on research than the problem it is supposed to solve.

Notwithstanding those concerns, recent events allow us to close this book on a more hopeful note, because of the Quebec Superior Court's decision in the Bruckert/Parent case and president of the granting agencies' interpretation of Article 5.1 of the TCPS in response to Palys's complaint against the University of Ottawa.

The Bruckert/Parent Decision Reaffirms the Need to Inform Researchers and REBs about Wigmore

Perhaps the most significant aspect of the Bruckert/Parent case is that it established, for the first time, a precedent in a Provincial Superior Court for the existence of a qualified researcher-participant privilege — "qualified" in the sense that it must continue to be asserted case by case. The decision establishes unequivocally that researchers can assert privilege by invoking the Wigmore criteria. Indeed, it is the only lawful mechanism to defend research confidentiality in court at their disposal.

The outcome of the Magnotta case should come as no surprise. Ogden showed the way in 1994 when he and his lawyers showed that his research satisfied the requirements of the Wigmore criteria.

As the two of us have argued,[30] researchers working on sensitive topics where confidentiality is a prerequisite for methodologically valid and ethical research should design their protocols to anticipate the Wigmore criteria. Patrick O'Neill made the same argument in a widely cited volume that discussed a broad array of field research issues,[31] as did the three formal legal opinions by Paul Jones, Michael Jackson and Marilyn MacCrimmon, and Deborah Lovett. All three opinions recognized that the Wigmore criteria represent the only mechanism available for protecting research confidentiality in Canada. How, then, can a researcher be said to protect research confidentiality "to the full extent law permits" if they do not first anticipate and then, if need be, invoke the Wigmore criteria? Advice to that effect has been in the literature since 2000.[32] SSHWC specifically recommended that reference to the Wigmore criteria be included in TCPS-2. Why, then, does TCPS-2 not mention the Wigmore criteria?[33]

Universities Are Obliged to Support Researchers in Defending Confidentiality to the Extent that Law Permits

Although the failure to inform researchers about the Wigmore criteria is a serious omission, TCPS-2 nonetheless does contain strong statements about the importance of confidentiality and academic freedom to research. Several times Judge Bourque's decision quoted TCPS-2 approvingly on both these issues when deploying the Wigmore test.

TCPS-2 affirms that researchers have "an *ethical* duty of confidentiality" [emphasis added]:

> *The ethical duty of confidentiality refers to the obligation of an individual or organization to safeguard entrusted information. The ethical duty of confidentiality includes obligations to protect information from unauthorized access, use, disclosure, modification, loss or theft. Fulfilling the ethical duty of confidentiality is essential to the trust relationship between researcher and participant, and to the integrity of the research project.*[34]

Making confidentiality a "duty" gives it considerable weight for the purposes of a Wigmore analysis.

With respect to legal challenges to research confidentiality, TCPS-2 clarifies that resistance is expected:

> *Researchers shall maintain their promise of confidentiality to*
> *participants within the extent permitted by ethical principles*
> *and/or law.*[35]

In addition to reaffirming the right of researchers to adopt either the ethics-first or law-first approaches, the phrasing asserts the minimum defence of confidentiality by all researchers is the extent permissible by law. REBs should ensure research on sensitive topics is designed to anticipate the Wigmore criteria, the basics of which are relatively easily accomplished (see Chapters 20 and 21).

If TCPS-2 obliges researchers to protect research confidentiality at least to the extent that law permits, then one would think the institutions that have signed MOUs obliging them to comply with the TCPS must provide the support necessary for researchers to achieve that level of protection. After all, Article 5.1 not only obliges researchers to safeguard information entrusted to them, but also declares, "Institutions *shall* support their researchers in maintaining promises of confidentiality." In response to Palys's complaint, the presidents of the granting agencies confirmed that the U of O had failed to live up to this responsibility when it did not fund Bruckert and Parent's legal defence of the "Jimmy" interview.

When informed of the complaint by the secretariat, the U of O argued, "Article 5.1 may state that institutions should [sic] support their researchers but it does not stipulate how this should be done. The article deals with the responsibility of researchers, not the responsibility of universities."[36] The U of O would go on to outline the many ways they felt they provided support: by repeatedly saying they supported the researchers in encouraging letters, by offering to pay a few hundred dollars of their initial visits to lawyers, by creating and funding an REB, and by never asking the REB to deny approval of research done on sensitive topics.

> *[Article 5.1 sets] out important principles and practices*
> *relating to the researchers' duties to maintain confidentiality.*
> *What they clearly do not do is to direct institutions to provide*
> *financial support to researchers who are faced with a request*
> *to release research data to the authorities.*[37]

The granting agency presidents' response was unequivocal: The U of O was wrong. Their letter to the University of Ottawa[38] and published interpretation[39] affirms that institutions must interpret Article 5.1 within the context of the entire TCPS, not decontextualized. According to the presidents, the larger picture is that:

> *The researcher conducts research under the auspices of the*
> *institution. The REB is appointed by the institution as its*
> *vehicle for reviewing research projects to ensure their ethical*
> *acceptability. In granting its approval for a study, the REB*
> *engages the responsibility of the institution to support the*
> *researchers in their commitment to protect participant*
> *confidentiality.*[40]

The letter sent to the U of O conveying the decision further asserted:

> *The Agencies' intent with respect to Article 5.1 is that*
> *institutions support researchers' ability to safeguard the*
> *information entrusted to them. In situations such as this,*
> *where safeguarding that information involves resisting*
> *an attempt to compel disclosure of confidential research*
> *information, support consists of providing researchers with the*
> *financial means to obtain the independent legal advice which*
> *makes that resistance possible.*
>
> *The agencies also note that the research in question*
> *was conducted with the approval of one of the University*
> *of Ottawa's research ethics boards. That too engages the*
> *responsibility of the institution to assist the researchers with*
> *their legal costs in this matter.*[41]

While the presidents did not penalize U of O — perhaps because this was the agencies' first opportunity to clarify the meaning of Article 5.1 — they affirmed that institutions should develop policies that explain how they intend to meet these obligations:

> Institutions under whose auspices or within whose jurisdiction such research is being conducted should establish a policy that explains how it will fulfill its responsibilities to support its researchers. The policy should include an explanation of the nature and the scope of the support, a mechanism to determine the level of support in individual cases, the source of funding (e.g., dedicated fund, insurance, agreement with professional association) and any other relevant criteria. The institution should establish such a policy in collaboration with its researchers.[42]

The letter from the agencies spoke approvingly of steps the U of O has taken to live up to its responsibilities under Article 5.1. Perhaps this was in reference to the independent settlement regarding legal fees U of O negotiated with CAUT. In a letter to President Rock dated October 17, 2013 — by which time legal costs had exceeded $300,000 — CAUT Executive Director Turk stated:

> On behalf of the Canadian Association of University Teachers, I want to thank you for your letter of October 2nd and the University's offer of $150,000 as an ex gratia payment toward the legal costs of protecting the confidentiality of the research records of University of Ottawa professors Chris Bruckert and Colette Parent. We are pleased to accept your offer. We understand that this is without prejudice to the views we have shared in previous correspondence. Nevertheless, we appreciate your support for the work we have undertaken on this important matter.
>
> We also want to thank you for your commitment to join CAUT in helping ensure support from Canadian universities

> *should there be an appeal from the decision of the judge of the*
> *Quebec Superior Court. Your willingness to write to members*
> *of AUCC and U15, alone or in partnership with us, will be*
> *important, given that the outcome of this case is of significance*
> *to all academics and universities in Canada.*[43]

The agencies' rebuke of the U of O and clarification of Article 5.1 is a sign that the granting agencies are walking some of their talk. However, it is important to recognize that Bruckert and Parent's experience could have been disastrous had CAUT not stepped up to the plate when the U of O abandoned them. At this point, it is important that the secretariat or PRE monitor universities to ensure they do indeed develop policies to support their researchers. The experience of a research participant invited to partake in a recent McGill REB-approved research project on End of Life Bioethics reveals just how important such monitoring will be.

How Will Universities Interpret Their Article 5.1 Responsibilities?

The McGill research in question was a Candian Institutes of Health Research (CIHR)–funded study of "perspectives on medicalized dying in Canada and how those perspectives should inform the development of an ethical end-of-life care policy."[44] The prospective research participant was Russel Ogden. On February 23, 2014, the researchers sought his participation as "the founder of the Farewell Foundation for the Right to Die." Their email concluded, "We look forward to speaking with you. Your participation is crucial for our study's success."

Ogden replied saying he was interested in participating, but that he had some questions relating "to the participation consent."[45] He pointed out he has received three subpoenas concerning confidential research information. He noted he was under investigation by various police forces and coroners services in relation to his having attended nine suicides and assisted suicides. Police had arrested him following his attendance at one of the suicides. Ogden also mentioned he was aware the University of Ottawa had failed to support Bruckert and Parent when police seized the "Jimmy" interview. In light of this background, he wanted to know the extent to which the researchers would protect research confidentiality, and what McGill would do to support them if a legal authority challenged the confidentiality guarantees the researchers were making.

Ogden felt the researchers had not clarified the extent to which they would be prepared to protect their raw data, and they were unable to explain what McGill would do. An extensive interchange occurred between Ogden and the researchers, the university's senior ethics administrator, and the university's research ethics officer, each of whom evaded the central question of what exactly McGill would do if research confidentiality were to be challenged in court.

Frustrated by the ongoing deflection of his questions, and because of his concern about the welfare of other research participants, on April 10, 2014, Ogden submitted a complaint to McGill's research ethics officer, Lynda McNeil, saying:

> I have repeatedly indicated my interest in participating in the research and the need to have the information necessary information for informed consent. I do not believe my dignity, rights, and welfare are being respected if I am denied answers to questions. As an invited participant in research, I do not understand why it is so difficult to get the information I need, particularly since this is about ethics.[46]

Just three days later, researchers Jennifer Fishman and Mary Ellen Macdonald emailed Ogden saying, "Unfortunately, we do not feel that we can confidently offer the protections you seek. Consequently, we will not be able to interview you for this study."[47]

Ogden was mystified. At no point did he specify what protections he was seeking. He sought information only about what protection McGill and the researchers were offering so he could make an informed decision about the scope of his participation.[48] Ogden replied, "Your decision to exclude me from the research appears to be retribution because I complained when my rights under the informed consent process were not being respected."[49] He then sent another complaint to the McGill research ethics officer to that effect.[50]

The interchange between Ogden and McGill began prior to the presidents of the granting agencies issuing their interpretation of Article 5.1.[51] However, the interpretation had been out for more than a month and had received significant attention at the annual meeting of the Canadian Association of Research Ethics Boards by the time Dr. Paul Brassard, the chair of McGill's Advisory Council on Human Research Ethics, responded to Ogden's complaint. Two components of Brassard's May 23, 2014, response spoke directly to the issue of university support to researchers when a lawful challenge to confidentiality occurs:

> 3. *Obligation of the University to support researchers if access to participants' data is sought by law enforcement authorities.* The University is well aware of its obligations pursuant to the Tri-Council Policy Statement: Ethical Conduct for Research Involving Humans and will fulfill them as stipulated. What would be done and how would depend on the particular circumstances of the case.
>
> 4. *Description of measures to be taken to oppose disclosure of participant data to law enforcement authorities as part of the consent form.* It is not required nor is it customary for the consent form to describe what measures would be taken as this will vary on a case by case basis.[52]

This statement reveals that, at the point Brassard responded to Ogden, McGill had failed to address the granting agency presidents' interpretation of Article 5.1 that requires universities to create policies outlining how they will support researchers. If their research-ethics oversight process functions properly, surely the default assumption should be that the institution will support any researcher who confronts a lawful threat to research confidentiality.

What Is A "Meritorious Case?"

According to the chair of its Advisory Council on Human Research Ethics, McGill's policy on support for researchers who confront a lawful challenge to research confidentiality is that it will figure it out as each case arises. This policy is inadequate in two respects: (a) it fails to provide informed consent because neither the researcher nor the research participant knows what support McGill will provide, and (b) it fails to address the granting agency presidents' requirement that universities have clear policies in place regarding how they will support researchers in their defense of research confidentiality. At the same time, we wonder whether this reflects an issue that Jackson and MacCrimmon raised when they suggested universities must support researchers in *meritorious cases*. Obviously, universities should not squander public funds, but given the crucial role confidentiality plays in research on sensitive topics, we would ask, "What is not a meritorious case?"

In this book, we have described dozens of researchers' experiences fending off lawful threats to research confidentiality. Which of these were not meritorious? There is not one where we believe the ethical outcome would have been to violate research confidentiality. Each one was worth fighting for, and there have been few losses.

We have argued the TCPS should advise researchers that the Wigmore test is the only option for resisting lawful threats to research confidentiality, in which case REBs and researchers should design their research in anticipation of its requirements. On the basis of concrete examples, we suggest that, if designed this way, research on sensitive topics should usually satisfy the first three criteria. At step four, the court would engage in a balancing of values; we cannot know the outcome in advance. However, if the researcher has prepared a proposal that anticipates the Wigmore criteria and the university REB approves it, then on what basis might it lack merit? The default assumption should thus be that the case is meritorious.

A Research Confidentiality Defence Fund

If universities do not defend research confidentiality and academic freedom, who will? The Bruckert/Parent case and the agencies' interpretation of Article 5.1 is a wake-up call for institutions, REBs, and researchers to understand that being prepared to protect research participants to the extent that law permits is part of the infrastructure cost of doing research. However, there is no good reason that whichever university next draws legal attention should have to foot the entire bill, given that the outcome potentially affects all universities.

If TCPS-2 Article 5.1 is to have consequence over the long term, the granting agencies should require institutions performing research to contribute to a research-confidentiality defence fund. A university would use that fund to pay for the defence of research confidentiality the next time a court comes calling. The mere existence of the fund would comprise a powerful indicator of the importance that universities attach to confidentiality in research on sensitive topics, and obviate any single university's temptation to fall short of the full support TCPS-2 and the granting agency presidents' interpretation commands.

Of course, these issues would be moot if the Canadian legislature were to enact some kind of research shield law.

Campaign for a Research Shield Law

Justice Bourque acknowledged in the Bruckert/Parent case that, in the US, research confidentiality is so important that federal and state legislatures have enacted numerous research shield laws to protect it. We have called for the development of similar statute-based protections in Canada:

> The Policy Statement recognises that ethical approaches
> may affect the future development of law. In this spirit,
> we encourage Canada's three granting Councils to initiate
> a campaign for legislation in Canada to create statutory
> protections along the lines of confidentiality certificates.
> And we urge all Canadian universities, faculty associations,
> disciplinary associations and the Canadian Association of
> University Teachers to support the three Councils in this
> endeavour.[53]

SSHWC urged PRE to inform itself about these protections:

> Because of the crucial importance of confidentiality for certain
> kinds of research, we recommend that PRE investigate legal
> mechanisms used in other jurisdictions (such as confidentiality
> certificates and privacy certificates) for resolving the theoretical
> disjunction between statutory legal protections and researchers'

*ethical obligation to protect participants by keeping identifiable
research information confidential.*[54]

CAUT took up the cause and offered its assistance to SRCR, PRE, and the
granting agencies. SSHWC provided a background paper to PRE on the US
protections. How have they responded?

Lobbying for Statute-Based Confidentiality Protections

Following SSHWC's recommendations and CAUT's offers of assistance, the
granting agencies responded in several constructive ways. First, they funded
four projects that would shed light on the research-confidentiality problem
and how other countries deal with it. Second, they contacted the presidents
of various scholarly associations across Canada to gauge the extent of support for the development of a research shield law. We were able to acquire
several responses through a freedom of information request to SSHRC,
which forwarded the responses of the associations that consented.[55]

The Canadian Psychological Association

The Canadian Psychological Association (CPA) emphasized the impact
the lack of guaranteed protection has had on research into important
social issues and noted the problems that arise when REBs follow the sort
of recommendations the PRE advocated[56]:

> *On behalf of the Canadian Psychological Association, I
> strongly support such a legislative initiative. As you point out,
> confidentiality certifications are available in US jurisdictions,
> but not, at present, in Canada.*
>
> *There are a number of areas of psychological research
> that involve socially sensitive topics. Some of these are in the
> area of forensic psychology, where researchers have similar
> problems to those faced by our colleagues in criminology
> and some researchers in sociology. You have identified some
> of these as examples in your memo (assisted suicide, drug
> use, prostitution). If research subjects are warned that their
> identity (or identified comments) will be reported they will*

protect themselves, fail to participate, and the research will be jeopardized.

The problem is not confined to those who study criminal activity. For example, psychologists who interview parents about problems in child-rearing often face similar problems. In 1997 as part of a province-wide survey by Santé Québec, a research group intended to conduct a telephone survey with parents to asked [sic] them about child-rearing practices. For various reasons, it was impossible to conduct the research anonymously; the researchers intended to keep identities confidential. The research was ultimately abandoned because of a ruling by the Ethics Committee of Santé Québec. The committee took the following position:

1. *If a parent responded in a way that could be construed as child abuse or neglect, the researcher would be compelled to report the matter.*
2. *Informed consent requires that research subjects be warned in advance of potential harms that might result from their participation.*
3. *Thus, as part of the informed consent procedure, the researchers would be obligated to warn all parents at the outset of the interview that confidentially could not be guaranteed.*

While this sounds reasonable, it is fraught with problems. Parents would have little idea what might constitute abuse or neglect in law, and a conservative view would lead them to refuse to be interviewed. The loss of data would give a misleading picture of child-rearing practices. It was thought preferable to abandon the project than to run the (high) risk of producing a distorted picture.

In this case, valuable information about social/health practices, which might have led to useful intervention to help parents and children, was lost because of the inability to guarantee confidentiality. Further, no useful purpose was served; no child in need of protection was identified or reported. This paradox was identified by Mr. Justice Clark in the mid 1970s in his dissent in the famous Tarasoff case. He predicted that if psychologists have to break confidentiality for what the courts perceive as the public good, they will adopt procedures to warn clients or research participants in advance. He was right; such warnings are now standard practice.

After noting researchers can use the Wigmore criteria to assert privilege case by case, CPA concluded:

It is important to conduct research on social and psychological problems to determine their nature, their causes, and their distribution in society. Such research is hampered, and in some cases made impossible, by the inability to guarantee confidentiality. Statutory confidentiality protection is necessary to overcome the reluctance of Research Ethics Boards, in the present circumstances, to sanction such research.

Here was clear support for the development of a research shield law.

The Canadian Law and Society Association

As with CPA, the Canadian Law and Society Association (CLSA)[57] brought attention to how lack of statute-based protection is compromising research on some of society's most pressing social issues:

The highly-publicized Russel Ogden case . . . graphically demonstrated the need for statutory confidentiality protection. While the coroner subsequently rescinded his subpoena . . . the repercussions of the case are still being felt. Certainly, unmistakable progress has occurred in the years since, largely through the coordinated, comprehensive work culminating in the Tri-Council Policy Statement on Ethical Conduct for Research Involving Humans, along with council-specific projects like the recently-formed Social Sciences and Humanities Research Ethics Special Working Committee.

Moreover, with REBs now in place across the country, some
university administrations are beginning to evince a more
rights-sensitive approach to the confidentiality question, and
to human participant research ethics issues more generally,
than prevailed in the not-so-distant past. Still, in the absence
of clearly articulated statutory guidelines and procedures,
Canadian researchers—and, in particular, young scholars with
the most to lose—continue to find themselves contending with
a multi-vocal, and often virtually incomprehensible, crossfire of
conflicting interpretations of general moral precepts, funding
agency standards, professional association policy statements,
university administrative criteria, and case law. While the
effects are often subtle, and difficult to document or quantify,
there is no doubt that disincentives continue to impede
the conduct of research on certain 'controversial' subjects,
especially those addressing "legally sensitive" topics. Such a
conclusion is certainly consistent with the personal and shared
experiences of many Canadian socio-legal scholars, and with
the volumes of available writing on the politics, ethics and
practice of social research.

The CLSA also encouraged lobbying for the development of statute-based
protections, such as confidentiality certificates, given appropriate structures
for granting them:

Our Association considers the confidentiality question to be
a critically important issue for our membership, as it is for
countless other scholars working in assorted institutional
and cultural contexts across the country. The enactment of
confidentiality protection is an especially high priority for
scholars in socio-legal disciplines, given the frequently sensitive
nature of our subject matter and our unconditional moral
obligation to ensure the safety and security of participants as
a sine qua non of human research. Our ethical responsibility
to participants (including their rights to privacy, and their

*security against legal repercussions stemming from their
research involvements) is sacrosanct. The incursion of any
form of legal compulsion to disclose research knowledge would
be catastrophic to the law and society community. Any such
erosion of absolute standards of privilege would irreparably
pollute research relations, turning researchers into potential
informers against their participants, and effectively closing off
all spheres of social inquiry where knowledge about criminality
and other forms of 'legally problematic' conduct or the
legal position of marginalized communities is being sought.
Accordingly, the encoding of protections through legislated
"certificates of confidentiality"—contingent, of course, on the
terms and conditions of these envisioned certificates, and on
how the granting process might be structured—is a potentially
progressive initiative. To the extent that it statutorily
entrenches the principle of absolute confidentiality, the
provision of certified privilege can help institute a stable and
enabling ethical and procedural environment for Canadian
university administrators and REBs, and a standardized set
of expectations for researchers. Shared principles regarding
the ethical conduct of human research, and the corresponding
rights and obligations of participants, researchers and third
parties, should be clearly reflected in law. For these reasons,
the CLSA would be very willing to involve itself in initiatives
aimed at realizing these goals, and to consider confidentiality
certificates as a potential means of so doing.*

Here again was unequivocal support for the development of a research
shield law.

The Council of the Canadian Historical Association

Sarah Carter, a Professor of History and council member from the
Canadian Historical Association (CHA) submitted a third response.[58]
She cautioned that her response was not formally representative of CHA,
because she had only contacted two other members of the governing

council and not formally polled the association's membership. The two CHA council members she quoted had opposing views. One, whose research involves the history of health care, was quite positive about the prospect of confidentiality certificates or their equivalent:

> It is clear to me that the protection offered by confidentiality certificates is relevant and important to historians . . .
> There is a dire need to protect research participants in this manner. Most obviously, this issue arises in the conduct of oral interviews but it is equally relevant for archival sources. Historians frequently discover details that, if fully disclosed, could harm individuals or groups of individuals.
>
> The eligibility criteria outlined by the US Dept. of Health and Human Services (and enshrined in the Public Health Act) are quite broad and cover several areas researched by historians. These include historical analyses of sexuality, alcohol and other drugs, violations of the law ("illegal activity"), and research about aspects of mental and physical health. Each of these areas is broad and I therefore believe that this is a serious issue for all historians but most especially those working on later 19th, 20th, or even 21st century documents or conducting oral interviews. My understanding is that certificates of confidentiality would provide a legal defense against a subpoena or court order, through which the researcher could resist disclosure.

The second offered a "be careful what you wish for" approach:

> . . . I do not want to go the legislation route. For one thing, once you start legislating in a field, one buys oneself a road out of common law and need all sorts of other legislation . . . Would I want statutory confidentiality for Canada? I'd have to say no. It would be addressing an American problem in a foreign legal climate . . . I don't see how such confidentiality certificates would hold up in court. I wouldn't want to argue

*that a scholar's interests are more important than the public
interest. There would be a hundred ways to "distinguish"
such certificates on the given facts and any committed judge
would look for such an opportunity. Also, being given such a
certificate would surely seize scholars with responsibilities to
society that they might not want: rights without responsibilities
flies in the face of the common law. In short, a statute may
offer a right but the court can read it a responsibility.*

The respondent's caution is well advised. As the CLSA said, much would depend on the conditions attached to the granting of confidentiality certificates. Should there be an application process, as with confidentiality certificates? Should Canada adopt the privacy certificate approach, which gives legal protection to whatever confidentiality guarantee the researcher makes? Should the protection be automatic, as is the case with the privilege that Statistics Canada researchers enjoy under the *Statistics Act*? All these protections would potentially be subject to legal challenges if a constitutional right was at stake, but each one would put the onus on whoever wanted the information to demonstrate why privilege should be set aside.

Going the Distance

This book began with the Ogden subpoena and described the experience we witnessed firsthand as the university administration first abandoned Ogden and his research participants, and then set out to ensure no one would ever make a pledge of confidentiality again that was not limited by law. SFU would eventually recognize the error of its ways, showing that redemption is possible.

The seeds of a similar process are also evident nationally. There has been a second case, and although the university administration involved would repeat SFU's early mistake, much has changed. TCPS-2 is clear in its affirmation of the integral importance of confidentiality to research and the ethical duty of researchers, universities, and research institutions to protect the integrity of the researcher-participant relationship, and the Quebec Superior Court has recognized the Wigmore criteria comprise the proper measure for assessing researchers' case-by-case claims for a research-participant privilege. The granting agency presidents chastised the University of Ottawa for abandoning its researchers, and issued a formal interpretation of TCPS-2 Article 5.1, which affirms universities must support the defence of research confidentiality in court and develop clear policies for how that support will be engaged.

We conclude by repeating our call for the granting agency presidents to lead the charge for the development of statute-based protections that will obviate future conflict between ethics and law.

In the interim, we encourage the presidents to explain to researchers and REBs in a revised TCPS-2 the need to design their research in anticipation of the Wigmore criteria. This strategy will ensure researchers present their strongest possible case, so courts respect research-participant protections and academic freedom. After all, if we in the academy do not make the strongest possible case for defending research-participant privilege and our academic freedom to conduct research, who will?

Acknowledgements

The events that culminated in this book took place over a twenty-year period. Many people have contributed in many ways, both to the journey, and to the book.

First, we extend our gratitude to friend and colleague Russel Ogden, without whose perseverance in adhering to policy and principle this book might tell a very different story.

At Simon Fraser University, during the period when the most vehement debates described in this book were taking place, we thank our colleagues in the School of Criminology who reminded us that we were not the only ones who understood the importance of research confidentiality to our discipline and research generally. We especially thank Chairs Margaret Jackson and Robert Gordon, who reassigned us to be the school's ad hoc ethics liaison committee, thereby freeing us from other administrative responsibilities and allowing us to monitor how the university administration was implementing its ethics policy beyond our specific case. Special thanks also to several graduate students who stuck their necks out for all the right reasons — Christie Barron, Victor Douglas Janoff, Jay Jones, Tamara O'Doherty, and Gordon Roe.

Beyond the School of Criminology, our thanks to David Bell, former Executive Director of the SFU Faculty Association (SFUFA) and Richard Coe, former SFUFA President, for their counsel and support; the late Ellen Gee, Chair of the SFU Ethics Policy Revision Task Force, for her attempt to design an ethics policy that respected disciplinary and epistemological diversity; and former Dean of Science Willie Davidson for achieving the ethics policy, at least on paper.

While university administrators do not come off particularly well in this story, we acknowledge former SFU President Jack Blaney for showing that redemption is possible; former Vice-President (Academic) Jock Monro, for showing that it is possible for a senior administrator to carry out his responsibilities without acrimony; and Vice President (Legal Affairs) Judith Osborne for affirming SFU's acceptance of both the "ethics-first" and "law-first" approaches to research confidentiality that we describe in this book.

Outside the university, we benefitted greatly from the advice of several American colleagues who had already walked that path — John Fanning, now retired from the Office of the Assistant Secretary for Planning and Evaluation in the U.S. Department of Health and Human Services; Michael Traynor of Cooley Godward LLP in San Francisco; Felice Levine, former Executive Director of the American Sociological Association; and Robert M. O'Neil, former Professor of Law, University of Virginia Law School and Director, The Jefferson Center for the Protection of Free Expression. We also benefitted from the input, encouragement, and exchanges of views with many other colleagues in Canada, the United States, and Australia, including Chris Bruckert, Thérèse De Groote, Lisa Given, Glenn Griener, Mark Israel, Michael Jackson, Richard Leo, Joseph Lévy, Michael McDonald, Michelle McGinn, John Mueller, Patrick O'Neill, Deborah Poff, Keren Rice, Zachary Schrag, and Susan Zimmerman.

Thanks to the Social Science and Humanities Research Council for funding "Protecting Privacy in Social Science and Humanities Research: An International Perspective." That grant allowed us to examine threats to research confidentiality in the UK, Australia and New Zealand in addition to the work we had already done examining the history of those threats in North America.

Special thanks are due to friends and colleagues who commented on drafts of this manuscript, including Howie Becker, Kirsten Bell, James Lorimer, Anthony McIntyre, Ed Moloney, Russel Ogden, John Russell, Jim Turk, and Will van den Hoonaard.

Thanks James Lorimer of Lorimer Press for his interest in our work and decision to publish this book, and to Jim Turk of CAUT. We are delighted to join the list of titles in the CAUT/Lorimer academic freedom series. Those at Lorimer and CAUT who became involved during the production process include Acquisitions Editor and Marketing Manager Morgan Tunzelmann, Copy Editor Solange Messier, and Production Manager Nicole Habib. We appreciate their desire to get it right.

Thanks to our partners Anne-Marie Lascelles and Laura Fraser for their patience and support during the seventeen years we struggled to convince university administrators and Canada's three funding agencies that they need to fight like hell to defend research confidentiality in court.

Finally, our thanks to Jim Turk, former Executive Director of the Canadian Association of University Teachers, and CAUT itself, for stepping into the breach on several occasions that we outline in this book. We and many others are forever in Jim's and CAUT's debt.

Select Bibliography

Books and Dissertations

Bok, Sissela. *Secrets: On the Ethics of Concealment and Revelation*. New York: Pantheon Books, 1983.

Bollas, Christopher, and David Sundelson. *The New Informants: The Betrayal of Confidentiality in Psychoanalysis and Psychotherapy*. Northvale, NJ: Jason Aronson, 1996.

Bower, Robert. T., and Priscilla de Gasparis. *Ethics in Social Research: Protecting the Interests of Human Subjects*. NY: Praeger 1978.

Jones, Jay S. *The Cleansing Time: Aesthetic Order, Social Control and the Dangers of Dave's World*. Simon Fraser University: Master's Thesis, 2000.

Lavery, James V. *Losing Yourself to AIDS: The Meaning of Euthanasia and Assisted Suicide*. University of Toronto: PhD dissertation, 1999.

McNairn, Colin H. H., and Alexander K. Scott. *Privacy Law in Canada*. Toronto: Butterworths, 2001.

O'Doherty, Tamara C. *Off-Street Commercial Sex: An Exploratory Study*. Simon Fraser University Master's Thesis, 2007.

Ogden, Russel. *Criminology M.A. Thesis Research Proposal for: Euthanasia and Assisted Suicide in Persons Who Have Acquired Immunodeficiency Syndrome (AIDS) or Human Immunodeficiency Virus (HIV)*. Burnaby, BC: SFU. September 24, 1992.

Ogden, Russel. *Euthanasia, Assisted Suicide and AIDS*. New Westminster, BC: Peroglyphics, 1994.

Palys, Ted. *Research Decisions: Quantitative and Qualitative Perspectives*. Toronto: Harcourt Brace, 1992.

Sopinka, John, Sidney N. Lederman, and Alan W. Bryant. *The Law of Evidence in Canada*. Toronto: Butterworths, 1992.

van den Hoonaard, Will. *The Seduction of Ethics: Transforming the Social Sciences*. Toronto: University of Toronto Press, 2011.

Wigmore, John Henry. *A Treatise on the System of Evidence in Trials at Common Law, Including the Statutes and Judicial Decisions of All Jurisdictions of the United States, England, and Canada*. Boston: Little, Brown and Company, 1905.

Zinger, Ivan. *The Psychological Effects of 60 Days in Administrative Segregation*. Carleton University: Doctoral Dissertation, 1999.

Academic Association Codes of Ethics and Commentaries Concerning Those Codes

Academy of Criminal Justice Sciences (ACJS). *Code of Ethics*. March 21, 2000. www.acjs.org/pubs/167_671_2922.cfm.

American Psychological Association (APA). *Ethical Principles in the Conduct of Research with Human Participants*. Washington, DC: APA, 1990.

American Sociological Association (ASA). *Code of Ethics*. Washington, DC: ASA, 1984.

Canadian Psychological Association (CPA). *Canadian Code of Ethics for Psychologists*. Ottawa: CPA, 1988.

Canadian Psychological Association (CPA). *Canadian Code of Ethics for Psychologists* (3rd

ed.). Ottawa: CPA, 2000. www.cpa.ca/cpasite/userfiles/Documents/Practice_Page/Ethics_
Code_Psych.pdf.

Iutcovich, Joyce, Sue Hoppe, John Kennedy, and Felice J. Levine. "Confidentiality and the
1997 ASA Code of Ethics: A Response from COPE," *Footnotes* 27, 2, 1999: 5. www.asanet.
org/footnotes/1999/ASA.02.1999.pdf.

Lowman, John and Ted Palys. "Confidentiality and the 1997 ASA Code of Ethics: A Query."
Footnotes 27, no.2 (1999): 5. www.asanet.org/footnotes/1999/ASA.02.1999.pdf.

Lowman, John and Ted Palys. "Going the Distance: Lessons for Researchers from
Jurisprudence on Privilege." Submission prepared for the SFU Research Ethics Policy
Revision Task Force. 1999. www.sfu.ca/~palys/Distance.pdf.

Medical Research Council, Natural Sciences and Engineering Research Council, and Social
Sciences and Humanities Research Council. *Tri-Council Policy Statement: Ethical Conduct
for Research Involving Humans* Ottawa: MRC/NSERC/SSHRC, 1998.

Palys, Ted. *The Ethics of Ethics: Comments Submitted to the Tri-Council Working Group Regarding
its March 1996 Draft Code of Conduct for Research Involving Humans.* Burnaby, BC: SFU,
1996. www.sfu.ca/~palys/codecomm.htm.

Palys, Ted. *Bulldozers in the Garden: Comments Regarding the Tri-Council Working Group's July
1997 Draft Code of Ethical Conduct for Research Involving Humans."* Burnaby, BC: SFU.
1997. www.sfu.ca/~palys/tcwg97.htm.

Palys, Ted and John Lowman. *When Roles Conflict: Research Ethics at SFU.* Brief prepared
for President Blaney in the wake of Dr. Clayman's reconsideration of the Ogden case.
November 17, 1997.

Palys, Ted and John Lowman. *Informed Consent, Confidentiality and the Law: Implications of
the Tri-Council Policy Statement.* Burnaby, BC: SFU. Report prepared for the SFU Research
Ethics Policy Revision Task Force, 1999. www.sfu.ca/~palys/Conf&Law.pdf.

Palys, Ted and John Lowman. *One Step Forward, Two Steps Back: Draft TCPS-2's Assault on
Academic Freedom.* Submission to the Interagency Advisory Panel on Research Ethics
regarding their December 2008 draft 2nd edition of the *Tri-Council Policy Statement:
Ethical Conduct for Research Involving Humans,* 2009. www.sfu.ca/~palys/Palys-
LowmanCommentsOnDraftTCPS2.pdf.

Palys, Ted and John Lowman. *TCPS-2's Enduring Challenge: How to Provide Ethics Governance
While Respecting Academic Freedom.* Burnaby, BC: SFU. Submission to the Interagency
Advisory Panel on Research Ethics regarding their December 2009 draft 2nd edition
of the *Tri-Council Policy Statement: Ethical Conduct for Research Involving Humans,* 2010.
www.sfu.ca/~palys/PalysLowmanCommentsReTCPS2Draft2-final.pdf.

Palys, Ted and John Lowman. "Defending Research Confidentiality 'To the Extent the Law
Allows': Lessons from the Boston College Subpoenas." *Journal of Academic Ethics* 10
(2012): 271–297.

Social Sciences and Humanities Research Ethics Special Working Committee (SSHWC).
Giving Voice to the Spectrum. Ottawa: SSHWC. June, 2004. www.sfu.ca/~palys/SSHWC-
GivingVoice-2004.pdf.

Social Sciences and Humanities Research Ethics Special Working Committee. *Reconsidering
Privacy and Confidentiality in the TCPS: A Discussion Paper.* Ottawa: SSHWC, 2005. www.
sfu.ca/~palys/SSHWC-2005-Report-ReconsideringP&C.pdf.

Social Sciences and Humanities Research Ethics Special Working Committee.
*Continuing the Dialogue on Privacy and Confidentiality: Feedback and Recommendations
Arising from SSHWC's Recent Consultation,* 2006. www.sfu.ca/~palys/

SSHWC-2006-Report-ContinuingTheDialogue.pdf.

Social Sciences and Humanities Research Ethics Special Working Committee. *Reconsidering "Reconsidering:" Issues Arising from SSHWC's Consultation on Privacy and Confidentiality.* Ottawa: SSHWC. Discussion paper, 2006.

Social Sciences and Humanities Research Ethics Special Working Committee. *SSHWC Recommendations Regarding Privacy and Confidentiality.* Ottawa: SSHWC, 2008. www.pre.ethics.gc.ca/eng/archives/policy-politique/reports-rapports/sshwc-ctsh/.

Magazine and Newspaper Articles

Austin, Ian. "'Fundamentals' SFU Chief's Focus." The *Province*, September 11, 1997, A11.

Bew, Paul. "The Closure of the Boston College Troubles Archive Is Historical Loss." *Independent.ie*, May 11, 2014. www.independent.ie/opinion/analysis/the-closure-of-the-boston-college-troubles-archive-is-historical-loss-30263223.html.

Blatchford, Christie. "The Web Can Enable Freedom in Dictatorships, But It Can Also Embolden Psychopaths," *National Post*, May 30, 2012. www.fullcomment.nationalpost.com/2012/05/30/luka-rocco-magnotta-1-lunatic-1-ice-pick/.

"Boston College Tapes: PSNI Bid to Obtain All Material," *BBC News Northern Ireland.* May 22, 2014. www.bbc.com/news/uk-northern-ireland-27527213.

Boychuk, Jason. "Magnotta Warrant." *CBC News.* June 1, 2012. www.documentcloud.org/documents/365767-magnotta-warrant.html.

Brewer, John D. "Inescapable Burden of 'Guilty Knowledge.'" *Times Higher Education*, January 26, 2012. www.timeshighereducation.co.uk/story.asp?storyCode=418834&sectioncode=262.

Clarke, Liam. "Boston College Tapes: Archive That Turned into a Can of Worms." *Belfast Telegraph*, May 13, 2014. www.belfasttelegraph.co.uk/news/local-national/northern-ireland/boston-college-tapes-archive-that-turned-into-a-can-of-worms-30267260.html.

Clayman, Bruce. "The Law of the Land." *Simon Fraser News.* October 30, 1997. www.sfu.ca/archive-sfunews/sfnews/1997/Oct30/opinion2.html.

Clayman, Bruce. "A Vice-President Responds." *Simon Fraser News.* July 16, 1998. www.sfu.ca/archive-sfunews/sfnews/1998/July16/opinion3.html.

Clayman, Bruce. "Proposed New Policy Should Strike Balance." *Simon Fraser News.* September 24, 1998, 2.

Cockburn, Lyn. "An Act of Courage." The *Vancouver Province*, May 12, 1991, 29.

Coe, Rick. "Senate Rescues Board." *Faculty Association Newsletter*, 1997/98 Issue No. 5, February 5, 1998, 1, www.sfufa.ca/documents/newsletters/9798/19980205.pdf.

"Complaint Targets uOttawa for Failure to Defend Confidentiality," *CAUT/ACPPU Bulletin* 60, no. 6 (2013). www.cautbulletin.ca/default.asp?SectionID=0&SectionName=&VolID=364&VolumeName=No%206&VolumeStartDate=June%2018,%202013&EditionID=38&EditionName=Vol%2060&EditionStartDate=January%2017,%202013&ArticleID=0.

Cullen, Kevin. "BC Exercise in Idealism Reopened Old Wounds." *The Boston Globe*, July 6, 2014. www.bostonglobe.com/news/world/2014/07/05/belfast-the-shadows-and-gunmen/D5yv4DdNIxaBXMl2Tlr6PL/story.html.

Daisley, Brad. "Clear Evidence Needed to Invoke Wigmore Rules." *The Lawyer's Weekly.* December 9, 1994, 28.

Dubiel, Malgorzata. "SFU Faculty Rep Criticizes President." *The Georgia Straight*, October 19-26, 1995, 4-5.

Farnsworth, Clyde. "Vancouver AIDS Suicides Botched." *New York Times*, June 14, 1994, C12.

Fitzpatrick, Erin. "SFU Promises to Protect Academic Freedom." The *Peak*, November 16, 1998. www.peak.sfu.ca/the-peak/98-3/issue11/freedom.html.

"Former IRA Prisoner Dubious About Re-opening Inquiries," *Tyrone Herald*, July 16, 2012. www.bostoncollegesubpoena.wordpress.com/2012/07/16/former-ira-prisoner-dubious-about-re-opening-inquiries/.

Fournier, Suzanne. "President Blamed in SFU Sex Case." The *Province*, July 3, 1997, A1, A4.

Fraser, Laura. "Fired SFU Researcher Replies." The *Georgia Straight*, October 12-19, 1995, 9.

Garr, Allen. "How a Spin Doctor Saved Donnelly's Reputation." The *Georgia Straight.* May 14–21, 1998, 13–14.

Geoghegan, Peter. "Links to Past under Attack," *The Scotsman.* July 11, 2012. www.scotsman.com/news/peter-geoghegan-links-to-past-under-attack-1-2403619.

Gillis, Wendy. "Luka Rocco Magnotta: Online Reaction to Video Reveals a Disturbing Appetite for Gore." *Toronto Star*, May, 31, 2012. www.thestar.com/news/canada/article/1204016--montreal-murder-case-online-reaction-to-video-reveals-a-disturbing-appetite-for-gore.

Gray, John MacLachlan. "Up on Dat Mountain, Dey is Stuck Real Good." The *Vancouver Sun*, November 1, 1997, C3.

Humphreys, Joe. "Historians Fear Boston Tapes Controversy Will Damage Research into the Troubles." *Irish Times*, May 10, 2014 www.bostoncollegesubpoena.wordpress.com/2014/05/10/

Jimenez, Marina. "SFU President Being Treated for Depression, Governors Told," The *Vancouver Sun*, July 29, 1997, A1.

Jimenez, Marina. "Former SFU Official Was Victim of Obsessive Behaviour, She Says," The *Vancouver Sun*, October 22, 1997, A1.

Jimenez, Marina. "SFU Harassment Rulings Invalid; 'Serious' Mismanagement Blamed." The *Vancouver Sun*, October 25, 1997, A1–A2.

Kaufman, Michael T. "Marvin E. Wolfgang, 73, Dies; Leading Figure in Criminology." *New York Times*, April 18, 1998. www.nytimes.com/1998/04/18/us/marvin-e-wolfgang-73-dies-leading-figure-in-criminology.html?src=pm.

Lee, Jeff . "Swim Coach Gets his Job Back in Settlement over SFU Sex Case." The *Vancouver Sun*, July 25, 1997, A1.

Lee, Jeff, and Jeremy Tobin. "SFU Admits it Was Wrong to Fire Donnelly." The *Vancouver Sun*, July 26, 1997, A1–A2.

Lowman, John. "The Hypocrisy of Canadian Prostitution Law." The *Province*, September 28, 1997, A47.

Lowman, John. "Pay Legal Fees, Urges Professor." *Simon Fraser News*, October 2, 1997. www.sfu.ca/archive-sfunews/sfnews/1997/Oct2/letters.html.

Lowman, John and Ted Palys. "A Law Unto Itself," *Simon Fraser News*, November 27, 1997. www.sfu.ca/archive-sfunews/sfnews/1997/Nov27/opinion2.html.

Lowman, John and Ted Palys. "The Liability of Ethics." *Simon Fraser News*, July 16, 1998. www.sfu.ca/archive-sfunews/sfnews/1998/July16/opinion2.html.

Martin, Andy. "Boston College Tapes: US Network NBC Launches Legal Bid." *BBC News Northern Ireland.* May 21, 2014. www.bbc.com/news/uk-northern-ireland-27505115.

Mason, Bruce. "SFU Research on Euthanasia and AIDS Attracts International Media Attention." *Simon Fraser Week.* February 17, 1994, 1, 3.

Matas, Robert. "SFU President Ignored New Harassment Information." *The Globe and Mail*, June 11, 1997, A5.

Mathews, David. "'Place-hacker' Prosecution 'Attack on Intellectual Freedom.'" *Times High Education*, May 23, 2014. www.timeshighereducation.co.uk/news/place-hacker-case-ends-with-two-conditional-discharges/2013527.article.

Matthews, David. "Gerry Adams Arrest: Police Access to Boston Tapes Has Dealt 'Blow' to Research." *Times Higher Education*, May 1, 2014. www.timeshighereducation.co.uk/news/gerry-adams-arrest-surrender-of-interview-tapes-has-dealt-blow-to-research/2013038.article.

McCartney, Jenny. "An American Oral History Project Makes Us Fear for Our Lives, Say Former IRA Members," The *Telegraph*, May 15, 2014. www.blogs.telegraph.co.uk/news/jennymccartney/100271584/an-american-oral-history-project-makes-us-fear-for-our-lives-say-former-ira-members/.

McDonald, Henry. "Hate Campaign Against Me Has Ratcheted Up Since Adams Arrest, Says IRA Historian." The *Observer* May 3, 2014. www.bostoncollegesubpoena.wordpress.com/2014/05/03/McDonald, Henry. "US Court Says IRA Member's Secret Testimony Can Be Handed over to Police." The *Guardian*, July 8, 2012, www.guardian.co.uk/uk/2012/jul/08/us-court-ira-secret-testimony.

McMurtrie, Beth. "Secrets from Belfast: How Boston College's Oral History of the Troubles Fell Victim to an International Murder Investigation. The *Chronicle of Higher Education*. January, 2014. www.chronicle.com/article/Secrets-From-Belfast/144059/

Moriarty, Gerry. "Boston College to Be Sued by Republicans over Troubles Tapes." *Irish Times*, May 13, 2014. www.irishtimes.com/news/politics/boston-college-to-be-sued-by-republicans-over-troubles-tapes-1.1793599.

Murray, Gemma. "Key Figures 'Upping the Ante' over Boston College Tapes." *News Letter* May 5, 2014. www.bostoncollegesubpoena.wordpress.com/2014/05/05/key-figures-upping-the-ante-over-boston-college-tapes/.

Ogden, Russel. "The Uncloseting of AIDS Euthanasia.," *Canadian HIV/AIDS Policy and Law Newsletter 1*, no. 1 (1994): 14–15.

Ogden, Russel. "An Insult to Free Inquiry." *Simon Fraser News*, October 30, 1997. www.sfu.ca/archive-sfunews/sfnews/1997/Oct30/opinion1.html.

"Ogden to Receive Apology, Compensation from SFU for Legal Expenses and Lost Wages," *Simon Fraser News*. October 22, 1998. www.sfu.ca/archive-sfunews/sfnews/1998/oct22/ogden.html.

O'Hagan, Patricia. "The Marsden/Donnelly Case and Me." The *Vancouver Sun*, October 18, 1997, 23.

Palys, Ted and John Lowman. "Research Ethics Update: Academic Freedom, Research Participant Rights undermined.," *Faculty Association Newsletter*, 1997/98 Issue No. 5, February 5, 1998, 3.

"REB Members Deplore uOttawa's Refusal to Defend Confidentiality," *CAUT/ACPPU Bulletin* 60, no. 4 (2013), www.cautbulletin.ca/default.asp?SectionID=0&SectionName=&VolID=360&VolumeName=No%204&VolumeStartDate=April%2016,%202013&EditionID=38&EditionName=Vol%2060&EditionStartDate=January%2017,%202013&ArticleID=0.

Renaud, T. "Ex-Cop Wins Rare Confidentiality Case: Jury Awards $287,000 for Psychologist Telling of Client's Lethal Fantasies." *Fulton County Daily Report*, January 5, 2000.

Shore, Valerie. "Universities Told to Develop Policies for Research Ethics." *Simon Fraser News*, January 12, 1995.

Smith, Charlie "Secrecy Shrouds SFU Discipline." The *Georgia Straight*, September 22-29, 1995, 8.

Smith, Charlie "SFU Boss Pleads Confidentiality." The *Georgia Straight*, October 12-19, 1995, 9.

Smith, Charlie. "Heavily Censored SFU Conflict Report Calls for Change." The *Georgia Straight*, November 2-9, 1995, 9.

Smith, Charlie "*Straight* Wins Info Decision but SFU Can Appeal Order to Release Report on Faculty-Staff Dispute." The *Georgia Straight*, May 2, 1996, 6.

Smith, Charlie. "SFU Criminologists Want Research Confidentiality Back," The *Georgia Straight*, December 4–11, 1997, 10.

"The Big Chill" (editorial). The *Province*. July 3, 1997, A24.

"The Returning of the Boston Tapes." *The Irish Times*. May 7, 2014. www.irishtimes.com/news/politics/the-returning-of-the-boston-tapes-1.1787071.

Todd, Douglas. "Mercy Killing Secret World Revealed." The *Vancouver Sun*, February 12, 1994, A1, A2.

"uOttawa Criminologists Go to Court to Protect Research Confidentiality," *CAUT/ACPPU Bulletin* 60, no. 1 (2013), www.cautbulletin.ca/default.asp?SectionID=0&SectionName=&VolID=354&VolumeName=No%201&VolumeStartDate=January%2017,%20 2013&EditionID=38&EditionName=Vol%2060&EditionStartDate=January%2017,%20 2013&ArticleID=0.

Wilson, Robin. "Penn Anthropologist Fights Subpoenas for Field Notes in Medical Case." *Chronicle of Higher Education* 49, no.28 (2003): A14.

Wilson, Robin. "When Should a Scholar's Notes be Confidential? An Anthropologist Involved in a Medical Lawsuit Says She'll Go to Jail Rather than Turn Hers Over." *Chronicle of Higher Education* 49, no.36 (2003): A10.

Zehr, Mary Ann. "Arizona Subpoena Seeks Researchers' ELL Data." *Education Week*. August 12, 2014. www.edweek.org/ew/articles/2010/08/12/01arizona.h30.html?tkn.

Academic Journal Articles and Book Chapters

Appelbaum, Paul S., and Alan Rosenbaum. "*Tarasoff* and the Researcher: Does the Duty to Protect Apply in the Research Setting?" *American Psychologist* 44, no. 6 (1989): 885–894.

Bernhard, Judith K., and Julie E.E. Young. "Gaining Institutional Permission: Researching Precarious Legal Status in Canada." *Journal of Academic Ethics* 7 (2009): 175–191.

Bond, Katherine. "Confidentiality and the Protection of Human Subjects in Social Science Research: A Report on Recent Developments." *American Sociologist* 13 (1986): 144–152.

Bonta, James and Paul Gendreau. "Re-Examining the Cruel and Unusual Punishment of Prison Life." *Law and Human Behaviour* 14, no.4, (1990): 347–372.

Brajuha, Mario, and Lyle Hallowell. "Legal intrusion and the politics of field work: The impact of the Brajuha case." *Urban Life* 14 (1986): 454–478.

Caroll, James D., and Charles R. Knerr. "A Report of the APSA Confidentiality in Social Science Research Data Project." *Political Science Quarterly* 8 (1975): 258–261.

Caroll, James D., and Charles R. Knerr. "Confidentiality of Social Science Research Sources and Data: The Popkin Case." *Political Science Quarterly* 6 (1973): 268–280.

Cecil, Joe S., and Wetherington, Gerald T. "Special Issue: Court-Ordered Disclosure of Academic Research: A Clash of Values of Science and Law," *Law and Contemporary Problems* 59, no. 3 (1996). www.law.duke.edu/shell/cite.pl?59+Law+&+Contemp.+Probs.+1+%28Summer+1996%29.

Crabb, Barbara B. "Judicially Compelled Disclosure of Researchers' Data: A Judge's View." *Law and Contemporary Problems* 59 (1996): 9–34.

Dingwall, Robert. "The Ethical Case Against Ethical Regulation in Humanities and Social Science Research." *21st Century Society* 3, no. 1 (2008): 1–12.

Dubiel, Malgorzata. "SFU Faculty Rep Criticizes President." The *Georgia Straight*, October 19–26, 1995, 4–5.

Farnsworth, Clyde. "Vancouver AIDS Suicides Botched." *New York Times*, June 14, 1994, C12.

Fischer, Paul M. "Science and Subpoenas: When Do the Courts Become Instruments of Manipulation?" *Law and Contemporary Problems* 59 (1996): 159–168.

Fitzgerald, Maureen H. "Punctuated Equilibrium, Moral Panics and the Ethics Review Process." *Journal of Academic Ethics* 2 (2005): 315–338.

Fitzpatrick, Erin. "SFU Promises to Protect Academic Freedom." The *Peak*, November 16, 1998. www.peak.sfu.ca/the-peak/98-3/issue11/freedom.html.

"Former IRA Prisoner Dubious About Re-opening Inquiries," *Tyrone Herald*, July 16, 2012. www.bostoncollegesubpoena.wordpress.com/2012/07/16/former-ira-prisoner-dubious-about-re-opening-inquiries/.

Fournier, Suzanne. "President Blamed in SFU Sex Case." The *Province*, July 3, 1997, A1, A4.

Fraser, Laura. "Fired SFU Researcher Replies." The *Georgia Straight*, October 12-19, 1995, 9.

Galliher, John F. "The Protection of Human Subjects: A Re-examination of the Professional Code of Ethics," The *American Sociologist* 8 (1973): 99.

Glancy, G.D., C. Regehr, and A.G. Bryant. "Confidentiality in Crisis: Part I – The Duty to Inform," *Canadian Journal of Psychiatry* 43 (1998): 1001–1005.

Hamburger, Philip. "The New Censorship: Institutional Review Boards." *The Supreme Court Review* (2005): 271–354.

Herbert, Paul B. "The Duty to Warn: A Reconsideration and Critique," *Journal of the American Academy of Psychiatry and Law* 30 (2002): 417–424.

Herbert, Paul B. "Psychotherapy as Law Enforcement." *Journal of the American Academy of Psychiatry and Law* 32 (2004): 91–95.

Herbert, Paul B. and Katherine A. Young, "Tarasoff at Twenty-Five." *Journal of the American Academy of Psychiatry and Law* 30 (2002): 275–281.

Joly, Jean. "Research Ethics Board: Summation." *Canadians for Health Research*, July 4, 2010. www.chrcrm.org/en/conference-proceedings/summation.

Jones, Derek J., and Interagency Panel on Research Ethics. "Interface of Law and Ethics in Canadian Research Ethics Standards: An Advisory Opinion on Confidentiality, its Limits & Duties to Others." *McGill Journal of Law and Health* 1 (2007): 101–105. www.mjlh.mcgill.ca/pdfs/vol1-1/jones-pre.pdf.

Katz, J. "Towards a Natural History of Ethical Censorship." *Law & Society Review* 41, no. 4 (2007): 797–810.

Lowman, John and Christine Louie. "Public Opinion on Prostitution Law Reform in Canada." *Canadian Journal of Criminology and Criminal Justice* 54, no. 2 (2012): 245–260.

Lowman, John and Ted Palys. "Limited Confidentiality, Academic Freedom, and Matters of Conscience: Where Does CPA Stand?" *Canadian Journal of Criminology* 43 (2001): 497–508.

Lowman, John and Ted Palys. "The Ethics and Law of Confidentiality in Criminal Justice Research: A Comparison of Canada and the United States. *International Criminal Justice Review* 11, no.1, (2001): 1–33.

Lowman, John and Ted Palys. "PRE's 'Interface of Law and Ethics in Canadian Research Ethics Standards: An Advisory Opinion on Confidentiality, its Limits & Duties to Others': The 'Law of the Land' Doctrine in All but Name." *McGill Journal of Law and Health* 1 (2007): 117–122. www.mjlh.mcgill.ca/pdfs/vol1-1/lowman-palys.pdf.

Lowman, John and Ted Palys. "Strict Confidentiality: An Alternative to PRE's 'Limited

Confidentiality' Doctrine." *Journal of Academic Ethics* 5 (2007): 163–177.

Lowman, John and Ted Palys. "The Betrayal of Research Confidentiality in British Sociology." *Research Ethics* 10 (2014): 97–118.

McDonald, Michael. "From Code to Policy Statement: Creating Canadian Policy for Ethical Research Involving Humans." *Health Law Review* 17, no.2-3, 2009: 12–25.

McLachlin, Beverly. "Confidential Communications and the Law of Privilege." *University of British Columbia Law Review*, 11 (1977): 266–284.

Moskoff, F., & Young, J. (1988). "The Roles of Coroner and Counsel in Coroner's Court." *Criminal Law Quarterly* 30 (1988): 190–209.

Menand, Louis. "The Limits of Academic Freedom." In *The Future of Academic Freedom*, edited by Louis Menand, 3–20. Chicago: University of Chicago Press, 1996.

Nejelski, Paul and Kurt Finsterbusch. "The Prosecutor and the Researcher: Present and Prospective Variations on the Supreme Court's Branzburg Decision." *Social Problems* 21 (1973): 3–21.

O'Doherty, Tamara . "Victimization in Off-Street Sex Industry Work." *Violence Against Women* 20, no. 10 (2011): 1–20.

Ogden, Russel. "Palliative Care and Euthanasia: A Continuum of Care?" *Journal of Palliative Care* 10, no. 2 (1994): 82–85.

Ogden, Russel. "The Right to Die: A Policy Proposal for Euthanasia and Aid in Dying." *Canadian Public Policy* 20, no. 1 (1994): 1–25.

O'Neil, Robert M. "A Researcher's Privilege: Does Any Hope Remain?" *Law and Contemporary Problems* 59 (1996): 35–50.

O'Neill, Patrick. "Good Intentions and Awkward Outcomes: Ethical Gatekeeping in Field Research." In *Walking the Tightrope: Ethical Issues for Qualitative Researchers*, edited by Will C. van den Hoonaard, 17–25. Toronto: University of Toronto Press, 2002.

Palys, Ted and John Lowman. "Ethical and Legal Strategies for Protecting Confidential Research Information." *Canadian Journal of Law and Society* 15 (2000): 39–80.

Palys, Ted and John Lowman. "Social Research with Eyes Wide Shut: The Limited Confidentiality Dilemma." *Canadian Journal of Criminology* 43 (2001): 255–267.

Palys, Ted and John Lowman. "Anticipating Law: Research Methods, Ethics and the Common Law of Privilege. *Sociological Methodology* 32 (2002): 1–17.

Palys, Ted and John Lowman. "Going Boldly Where No One Has Gone Before? How Confidentiality Risk Aversion Is Killing Research on Sensitive Topics." *Journal of Academic Ethics* 8, no. 4 (2010): 265–284.

Picou, J. Stephen. "Compelled disclosure of scholarly research: Some comments on "high stakes" litigation." *Law and Contemporary Problems* 59 (1996): 149–157.

Scarce, Richard. "(No) Trial (But) Tribulations: When Courts and Ethnography Conflict." *Journal of Contemporary Ethnography* 23 (1994): 123–149.

Scarce, Richard. "Good Faith, Bad Ethics: When Scholars Go the Distance and Scholarly Associations Do Not." *Law and Social Inquiry* 24 (1999): 977–986.

Traynor, Michael. "Countering the Excessive Subpoena for Scholarly Research." *Law and Contemporary Problems* 59 (1996): 119–148.

Tversky, Amos and Daniel Kahneman. "Availability: A Heuristic for Judging Frequency and Probability," *Cognitive Psychology* 5 (1973): 207–232.

Wiggins, Elizabeth C. and Judith A. McKenna. "Researchers' Reactions to Compelled Disclosure of Scientific Information." *Law and Contemporary Problems* 59 (1996): 67–94.

Wolfgang, Marvin. "Criminology: Confidentiality in Criminological Research and Other

Ethical Issues." *Journal of Criminal Law and Criminology* 72 (1981): 345–361.

Wolfgang, Marvin. "Ethical Issues of Research in Criminology." In *Social Research in Conflict with Ethics and the Law*, edited by P. Nejelski, 25–34. Cambridge, Mass.: Ballinger, 1976.

Wolfgang, Marvin. "Ethics and Research." In *Ethics, Public Policy, and Criminal Justice Research*, edited by F. Elliston and N. Bowie, 391–418. Cambridge, Mass.: Oelgeschlager, Gunn and Hain, 1982.

Zinger, Ivan, Cherami Wichmann, and Donald A. Andrews. "The Effects of Administrative Segregation," *Canadian Journal of Criminology* 43 (2001): 47–83.

Zinger, Ivan, Cherami Wichmann, and Paul Gendreau. "Legal and Ethical Obligations in Social Research: The Limited Confidentiality Requirement." *Canadian Journal of Criminology* 43 (2001): 269–274.

Legal Opinions on Research Confidentiality in Canada

Jackson, Michael and Marilyn MacCrimmon. *Research Confidentiality and Academic Privilege: A Legal Opinion*. Burnaby, BC: SFU. June 7, 1999, 33. www.sfu.ca/~palys/JackMacOpinion.pdf.

Jones, Paul. "Legal Opinion on Issues of Privilege." Reproduced as Appendix A in John Lowman and Ted Palys, *Going the Distance: Lessons for Researchers from Jurisprudence on Privilege*, 52–58. Burnaby, BC: SFU, 1999. www.sfu.ca/~palys/Distance.pdf.

Lovett, D. (2002). *Legal opinion for Research Ethics Board*. Legal opinion was commissioned by the 2002 SFU Research Ethics Board.

United States Research Confidentiality Best Practices

Fanning, John P. *Policies and Best Practices for Ensuring Statistical and Research Confidentiality*. Paper prepared for the Office of the Assistant Secretary for Planning and Evaluation. US Department of Health and Human Services, under contract PO HHSP 233200500320A.

Legal Cases

A.(L.L.) v. B.(A.) [1995] 4 S.C.R. 536.

Atlantic Sugar, Ltd. v. US, 85 Cust. Ct. 128 [1980].

Bedford v. Canada (Attorney General), [2010] O.J. No. 4057; 2010 ONSC 4264; 102 O.R. (3d) 321; Court File No. 07-CV-329807 PD1. Canada (Attorney General) v. Bedford, [2013] SCC 72.

Deitchman v. E. R. Squibb & Sons, Inc., 740 F.2d 556 (7th Cir. 1984).

Dow Chemical Co. v. Allen, 672 F.2d 1262 (7th Cir. 1982), at 1.

Dr. Colette Parent and Dr. Christine Bruckert v. Her Majesty the Queen and Luka Rocco Magnotta. Quebec Superior Court, No. 500-36-006329-125; 21 January 2014.

Garner v. Stone, No. 97A-320250-1 (Ga.,DeKalb County Super. Ct. Dec. 16, 1999).

Globe & Mail v. Canada (Attorney General) [2010] SCC 41.

Huerto v. Saskatchewan, [1995] 5 W.W.R. at 202.

In re American Tobacco Co., 866 F2.d 552 (2d. Cir. 1989).

In re American Tobacco Co., 880 F2.d 1520 (2d. Cir. 1989).

In re Bonanno, 344 F.2d 830, 833 (2d Cir. 1965).

In re Grand Jury Proceedings, James Richard Scarce, 1993.

In re Grand Jury Subpoena Dtd. January 4, 750 F.2d 223 (2nd Cir. 12/13/1984), 13.

In re Michael A. Cusumano and David B. Yoffie [*United States of America v. Microsoft*

Corporation], No. 98-2133, United States Court of Appeals For the First Circuit] (1998). www.law.emory.edu/1circuit/dec98/98-2133.01a.html.

In re R. J. Reynolds, 518 N.Y.S.2d 729 (Sup. Ct. 1987).

In re Request from the United Kingdom Pursuant to the Treaty Between the Government of the United States of America and the Government of the United Kingdom on Mutual Assistance in Criminal Matters in the Matter of Dolours Price. United States District Court, District of Massachusetts, M.B.D. No. 11-MC-91078. Motion of Trustees of Boston College to Quash Subpoenas. Filed June 7, 2011.

In re Request from the United Kingdom Pursuant to the Treaty Between the Government of the United States of America and the Government of the United Kingdom on Mutual Assistance in Criminal Matters in the Matter of Dolours Price. United States District Court, District of Massachusetts, M.B.D. No. 11-MC-91078. Government's Opposition to Motion to Quash and Motion for an Order to Compel. Filed July 1, 2011.

In re Snyder, 115 F.R.D. 211 (D. Ariz. 1987).

Inquest of Unknown Female. October 20, 1994. *Oral Reasons for Judgment of the Honourable L. W. Campbell.* 91-240-0838, Burnaby, B.C.

Jaffee v. Redmond (95-266), 518 US [1996].

M.(A.) v. Ryan [1997] 1 S.C.R. 157.

Miriam Flores et al v. State of Arizona et al. [2010] Order. Case 4:92-cv-00596-RCC Document 952.

Newfoundland Telephone Company v. Newfoundland (Board of Commissioners Public Utilities), [1992] 1 S.C.R. 6235 at 645, 89 D.L.R. (4th) 289, 304.

Pacific Press Ltd. v. Cain, [1997] B.C.J. No. 1061.

Parry-Jones v. Law Society, [1968] 1 All ER 177, [1969] 1 Ch 1.

R. v. Brown, (2002) S.C.J. No. 35 (Q.L.) 2002 SCC 32.

R. v. Carosella, [1997] 112 C.C.C.(3d) 289.

R. v. Gruenke, [1991] 3 S.C.R. 263.

R. v. Mills, [1999] 3 S.C.R. 668.

R. v. National Post [2010] S.C.J. No. 16, [2010] A.C.S. No. 16, 2010 SCC 16]. File no. 32601.

R. v. O'Connor, [1995] 4 S.C.R. 411.

Richard A. Farnsworth, et al (Plaintiffs) v. The Procter & Gamble Company, et al (Defendants/ Appellants) v. Center for Disease Control (Movant/Appellee) [1985] CA11-QL 259. No. 84-8330.

Richards of Rockford Inc. v. Pacific Gas and Electric Co., 71 F.R.D. 388 (N.D. Cal, 1976).

Riebl v. Hughes [1980] 2 S.C.R. 880.

R. J. Reynolds Tobacco Co., v. Fischer, 427 S.E.2d 810, 811 (Ga. Ct. App. 1993).

Rodriguez v. British Columbia (Attorney General), [1993] 3 S.C.R. 519.

Russel Ogden v. Simon Fraser University. Provincial Court of BC (Small Claims), No. 26780 (Transcript, June 21, 1996).

Russel Ogden v. Simon Fraser University. Provincial Court of BC (Small Claims), No. 26780. June 10, 1998. www.sfu.ca/~palys/steinbrg.htm.

Slavutych v. Baker [1975] S.C.J. No. 29.

Smith v. Jones [1999] 1 S.C.R. 455 at 45–46.

Solicitor General of Canada v. Royal Commission of Inquiry into Confidentiality of Health Records in Ontario [1981] 2 S.C.R. 494.

Tarasoff v. Regents of University of California, 17 Cal. 3d 425, 551 P.2d 334, 131 Cal. Rptr. 14

(Cal. 1976) [cited to Cal. 3d].

United States v. Ed Moloney and Anthony McIntyre, No. 11-2511. United States Court of Appeals for the First Circuit. www.bostoncollegesubpoena.wordpress.com/2012/07/06/first-circuit-court-of-appeals-ruling/.

United States v. Kovel, 296 F.2d 918, 923 (2d Cir. 1961)

United States v. Stern, 511 F.2d 1364, 1367 (2d Cir. 1975)

Upjohn Co. v. United States, [1981] SCT-QL 261.

Vancouver Coroner's Court, "Unknown Female" Case #91-240-0838.

Wright v. Jeep Corp., 547 F. Supp. 871 (E.D. Mich. 1982).

Young v. Bella, [2006] 1 S.C.R. 108.

Endnotes

Foreword

1. Adam Dodek, "Solicitor-Client Privilege in Canada." Discussion Paper for the Canadian Bar Association, February, 2011. www.cba.org/CBA/activities/pdf/Dodek-English.pdf.

2. *R. v.* National Post, [2010] 1 SCR 477, 2010 SCC 16. www.canlii.org/en/ca/scc/doc/2010/2010scc16/2010scc16.html.

3. "Article 5.1 Researchers shall safeguard information entrusted to them and not misuse or wrongfully disclose it. Institutions shall support their researchers in maintaining promises of confidentiality." *Tri-Council Policy Statement: Ethical Conduct for Research Involving Humans.* www.pre.ethics.gc.ca/pdf/eng/tcps2/TCPS_2_FINAL_Web.pdf.

4. Perhaps the most dramatic illustration of this was during the McCarthy period in the 1950s. See Ellen Schrecker, *No Ivory Tower: McCarthyism and the Universities.* Oxford: Oxford University Press, 1986. Also see James L. Turk and Allan Manson (eds.), *Free Speech in Fearful Time: After 9/11 in Canada, the U.S., and Australia & Europe.* Toronto: James Lorimer & Company Ltd., 2007.

5. See, for example, John Dewey and Horace M. Kallen (eds.), *The Bertrand Russell* Case. New York: Viking, 1941; Andrew G. Bone, "Bertrand Russell's Wartime Dismissal from Trinity College", pp. 19-41 in Turk and Manson, op cit.; Jon Thompson, Patricia Baird and Jocelyn Downie, *The Olivieri Report.* Toronto: James Lorimer & Co., 2001. For an example being played out currently, see Carl Elliott, "Dan Markingson Investigation." http://markingson.blogspot.ca/.

6. John Lowman and Ted Palys reviewed statutory and common law protections available to researchers and their participants in both the US and Canada, including "confidentiality certificates," which do not exist in Canada. See John Lowman and Ted Palys, "The Ethics and Law of Confidentiality in Criminal Justice Research: A Comparison of Canada and the United States", *International Criminal Justice Review* 11(1), 1-33 (2001).

7. After the case was resolved, University of Ottawa President Allan Rock did offer to cover half of CAUT's legal costs for the case — an offer CAUT accepted.

Chapter 1

1. "REB" stands for "Research Ethics Board," the label most commonly used in Canada to refer to a duly authorized research ethics review committee. In the United States, these committees are referred to as "Institutional Review Boards" (IRBs). We vary our use of the terms depending on context, but all refer to the institutional entity that scrutinizes the ethical probity of research proposals involving the use of human participants. At SFU until 2000, that entity was called the University Research Ethics Review Committee (URERC). When SFU revised its research ethics policy in 2000, the URERC was renamed the Research Ethics Board.

2. "Frequently Asked Questions (FAQs) on Certificates of Confidentiality," National

Institutes of Health, accessed December 6, 2012, www.grants.nih.gov/grants/policy/coc/faqs.htm#278.

3. John Lowman and Ted Palys, "The Betrayal of Research Confidentiality in British Sociology," *Research Ethics* 10 (2014): 97–118.

4. The Canadian Institutes of Health Research (CIHR), the Natural Sciences and Engineering Research Council (NSERC), and the Social Sciences and Humanities Research Council (SSHRC).

5. See Ted Palys and John Lowman, "Defending Research Confidentiality 'To the extent the law allows': Lessons from the Boston College Subpoenas," *Journal of Academic Ethics* 10 (2012): 271–297.

6. Henry McDonald, "US Court Says IRA Member's Secret Testimony Can Be Handed over to Police," *Guardian*, July 8, 2012, www.guardian.co.uk/uk/2012/jul/08/us-court-ira-secret-testimony.

7. Corey Boling, "Oral History and the Law: Boston College's Woes," *Witness Blog*, July 31, 2012, www.blog.witness.org/2012/07/oral-history-and-the-law-boston-colleges-woes/.

8. Christie Blatchford, "The Web Can Enable Freedom in Dictatorships, but It Can Also Embolden Psychopaths," *National Post*, May 30, 2012, www.fullcomment.nationalpost.com/2012/05/30/luka-rocco-magnotta-1-lunatic-1-ice-pick/; Wendy Gillis, "Luka Rocco Magnotta: Online Reaction to Video Reveals a Disturbing Appetite for Gore," *Toronto Star*, May, 31, 2012, www.thestar.com/news/canada/article/1204016--montreal-murder-case-online-reaction-to-video-reveals-a-disturbing-appetite-for-gore.

9. "Magnotta Warrant," *CBC News*, contributed by Jason Boychuk June 1, 2012, www.documentcloud.org/documents/365767-magnotta-warrant.html.

10. *Dr. Colette Parent and Dr. Christine Bruckert v. Her Majesty the Queen and Luka Rocco Magnotta.* Quebec Superior Court, No. 500-36-006329-125; 21 January 2014. [Hereafter Parent & Bruckert v The Queen & Magnotta] (Crown's factum at 14–15).

11. *Parent & Bruckert v. The Queen & Magnotta* (Affidavit of Dr. Scott Woodside).

12. *Parent & Bruckert v. The Queen & Magnotta* (Affidavit of Dr. John Lowman, 60–62.).

13. *Parent & Bruckert v. The Queen & Magnotta* (Crown Factum).

Chapter II

1. Ted Palys, *Research Decisions: Quantitative and Qualitative Perspectives* (Toronto: Harcourt Brace, 1992). The book was in production at the time and came out the following spring.

2. American Psychological Association (APA), *Ethical Principles in the Conduct of Research with Human Participants* (Washington, DC: APA, 1990). [Hereafter cited as "APA Ethical Principles – 1990."]; Canadian Psychological Association (CPA), *Canadian Code of Ethics for Psychologists* (Ottawa: CPA, 1988).

3. American Sociological Association (ASA), *Code of Ethics* (Washington, DC: ASA, 1984).

4. ASA, *Code of Ethics*, s.11.

5. American Political Science Association (APSA), *A Guide to Professional Ethics in Political*

Science, (Washington, DC: APSA, 1989).

6. Michael T. Kaufman, "Marvin E. Wolfgang, 73, Dies; Leading Figure in Criminology," *New York Times,* April 18, 1998. www.nytimes.com/1998/04/18/us/marvin-e-wolfgang-73-dies-leading-figure-in-criminology.html?src=pm.

7. Marvin Wolfgang, "Ethical issues of research in criminology." In P. Nejelski (ed.), *Social Research in Conflict with Ethics and the Law* (Cambridge, Mass.: Ballinger, 1976, pp. 25–34); Marvin Wolfgang, "Criminology: Confidentiality in criminological research and other ethical issues." *Journal of Criminal Law and Criminology,* 1981, 72, 345–361; Marvin Wolfgang, "Ethics and research." In F. Elliston and N. Bowie (eds.), *Ethics, Public Policy, and Criminal Justice Research* (Cambridge, Mass.: Oelgeschlager, Gunn and Hain, 1982, pp. 391–418).

8. Marvin Wolfgang, "Criminology: Confidentiality in criminological research and other ethical issues," 351.

9. Marvin Wolfgang, "Criminology: Confidentiality in criminological research and other ethical issues," 352–353.

10. "Code of Ethics," *Academy of Criminal Justice Sciences (ACJS),* March 21, 2000, s.B19. www.acjs.org/pubs/167_671_2922.cfm.

11. The policy formally incorporated only minor editorial changes during that period. The version here is the one in effect when Ogden submitted his proposal. A copy of the policy [hereafter *1992 Ethics Policy*] can be recovered from the Wayback Machine Internet Archive at https://web.archive.org/web/19990220051311/http://www.sfu.ca/policies/research/r20-01.htm.

12. 1992 Ethics Policy, 1.

13. URERC is the acronym for the University Research Ethics Review Committee, which we refer to as the ethics committee.

14. Nicholas Blomley and Steven Davis, "Russell Ogden Decision Review," SFU, October 1998, www.sfu.ca/~palys/ogden.htm.

15. *Russel Ogden v. Simon Fraser University.* [Hereafter *Ogden v. SFU.*] Provincial Court of BC (Small Claims), No. 26780 (Transcript, June 21, 1996, 45-46.

Chapter III

1. Lyn Cockburn, "An Act of Courage," the *Vancouver Province,* May 12, 1991, 29.

2. Franklin Moskoff and J. Young, "The Roles of Coroner and Counsel in Coroner's Court," *Criminal Law Quarterly* 30 (1988): 190–209.

3. Section 2 of the Charter states: "Everyone has the following fundamental freedoms: a) freedom of conscience and religion; b) freedom of thought, belief, opinion and expression, including freedom of the press and other media of communication; c) freedom of peaceful assembly; and d) freedom of association." To support their claim they cited *Regina v. Bubley,* [1976] 6 W.W.R. and CBC v. Lessard, [1991] 3 S.C.R.

4. *Rodriguez v. British Columbia* (Attorney General), [1993] 3 S.C.R. 519. Sue Rodriguez had amyotrophic lateral sclerosis (Lou Gehrig's disease) a degenerative neurological condition. While still healthy enough to do so, she campaigned to have the assisted

suicide law struck down on the grounds that it violated her *Charter* rights. In a 5–4 majority decision, the Supreme Court of Canada rejected her claim. In 1994 she took her own life with the help of an anonymous physician.

5.   Mr. Latimer is a Canadian farmer who euthanized his severely disabled twelve-year-old daughter who had suffered from a variety of painful conditions from birth onward. He was convicted and sentenced to life in prison. He was granted day parole in 2008 and full parole in 2010.

6.   Often referred to in the media as "Dr. Death," Dr. Kevorkian achieved notoriety by his publicly expressed support for the right of terminally ill patients to assisted suicide, and his willingness to preside over these events. A videotape of his administering a lethal injection was shown on national TV, which resulted in his being charged with first-degree murder. Kevorkian was convicted of second degree murder and served eight years of a ten-to-twenty-five year prison sentence.

7.   Clyde Farnsworth, "Vancouver AIDS Suicides Botched," *New York Times*, June 14, 1994, C12.

8.   Ibid.

9.   B. Mason, "SFU Research on Euthanasia and AIDS Attracts International Media Attention," *Simon Fraser Week*, February 17, 1994, 1, 3.

10. Ibid.

11. Douglas Todd, "Mercy Killing Secret World Revealed," *Vancouver Sun*, February 12, 1994, A1, A2.

12. Our chronicle of events at SFU after that point is taken from three key sources: (1) The briefs submitted by the defendant and complainant in *Russel Ogden v. Simon Fraser University*, a lawsuit filed by Ogden against the University in 1996 in British Columbia Provincial Court; (2) Judge Daniel Steinberg's 1998 decision in that case (Made available by permission of Judge Steinberg at www.sfu.ca/~palys/steinbrg.htm); and (3) An independent review of SFU's decision-making in the Ogden case conducted by SFU Professors Blomley and Davis in 1999 at the behest of SFU President Jack Blaney, www.sfu.ca/~palys/ogden.htm. The trial transcripts contain the sworn testimony of various key SFU administrators, including President John Stubbs and VP-research/Dean of Graduate Studies/Chair of the Ethics Committee Bruce Clayman. As Judge Steinberg's decision notes, "virtually none of the relevant facts are in dispute," i.e., for the most part, the events outlined here have been accepted as accurate by both sides.

13. *Ogden v. SFU*, "Memorandum of Argument of the Applicant," 3.

14. Ibid.

15. In a 1998 article in the *CAUT/ACPPU Bulletin*, the Association's monthly newspaper, and in a 2000 article in the *Canadian Journal of Law and Society*, we requested information about any cases readers might know about. The request was repeated again in various written and oral forums over the next decade. No other cases were forthcoming. At this point we presume that if there had been another such case, it would have been drawn to our attention.

16. Russel Ogden, "Criminology M.A. Thesis Research Proposal for: Euthanasia and Assisted Suicide in Persons Who Have Acquired Immunodeficiency Syndrome (AIDS)

or Human Immunodeficiency Virus (HIV)." University Ethics Committee approved September 24, 1992, 34.

17. Letter from Russel Ogden to Vice-President (Research) Bruce Clayman, faxed May 24, 1994.

18. The bill eventually came to $11,367.38.

19. Vancouver Coroner's Court, "Unknown Female" Case #91-240-0838. (Transcript for June 1, 1994, 9).

20. Ibid., 10.

21. www.smrlaw.ca/lawyers/edavidcrossin.

Chapter IV

1. Michael Jackson and Marilyn MacCrimmon, "Research Confidentiality and Academic Privilege: A Legal Opinion," SFU, June 7, 1999, 33. www.sfu.ca/~palys/JackMacOpinion.pdf.

2. Canada Evidence Act (R.S.C., 1985, c.C-5). www.laws.justice.gc.ca/en/C-5/index.html. See s.37–39.

3. Statistics Act (R.S.C., 1985, c. S-19). http://laws-lois.justice.gc.ca/eng/acts/S-19/FullText.html. See especially s.18.

4. R. v. Mills, [1999] 3 S.C.R. 668 at 83; Slavutych v. Baker, [1975] S.C.J. No. 29.

5. J. H. Wigmore, A Treatise on the System of Evidence in Trials at Common Law, Including the Statutes and Judicial Decisions of All Jurisdictions of the United States, England, and Canada (Boston: Little, Brown and Company, 1905), 3185 (emphases in original).

6. Michael Jackson and Marilyn MacCrimmon, "Research Confidentiality and Academic Privilege: A Legal Opinion," SFU, June 7, 1999, www.sfu.ca/~palys/JackMacOpinion.pdf. Our legal analysis of the Ogden case is based on the legal opinion prepared by Professors Michael Jackson, QC and Marilyn MacCrimmon of the UBC Faculty of Law for an SFU President's Task Force created in 1999 — chaired by Dr. Ellen Gee — to advise on the content of a new ethics policy in the wake of the controversy described in this book. Their analysis included detailed examination of Ogden's claim for privilege.

7. Vancouver Coroner's Court, "Unknown Female" Case #91-240-0838. Transcript of proceedings, August 19, 1994, 8.

8. Vancouver Coroner's Court, "Unknown Female." Transcript of proceedings, August 19, 1994, 22.

9. Vancouver Coroner's Court, "Unknown Female" Transcript of proceedings, August 19, 1994, 33–35.

10. For example, see Russel Ogden, Euthanasia, Assisted Suicide and AIDS (New Westminster, BC: Peroglyphics, 1994); Russel Ogden, "The Right to Die: A Policy Proposal for Euthanasia and Aid in Dying," Canadian Public Policy 20, no. 1 (1994): 1–25; Russel Ogden, "Palliative Care and Euthanasia: A Continuum of Care?" Journal of Palliative Care 10, no. 2 (1994): 82–85; Russel Ogden, "The Uncloseting of AIDS Euthanasia," Canadian HIV/AIDS Policy and Law Newsletter 1, no. 1 (1994): 14–15.

11. When Ogden submitted his research proposal in 1992 *no* Canadian researcher had *ever* been subpoenaed and ordered to divulge confidential information to a court under threat of contempt. The next legal challenge would not arrive until 2012.

12. "Inquest of Unknown Female," October 20, 1994. Oral reasons for judgment of the Honourable L. W. Campbell, 91-240-0838, Burnaby, B.C., 9.

13. Ibid., 10.

14. See, for example, *Slavutych v. Baker*, [1975] S.C.J. No. 29; *R. v. Gruenke*, [1991] 3 S.C.R. 263. *R. v. Mills*, [1999] 3 S.C.R. 668.

15. B. Daisley "Clear evidence needed to invoke Wigmore rules," *The Lawyer's Weekly*, December 9, 1994, 28.

16. Michael Jackson and Marilyn MacCrimmon, "Research Confidentiality and Academic Privilege: A Legal Opinion," *SFU*, June 7, 1999, www.sfu.ca/~palys/JackMacOpinion. pdf.

Chapter V

1. 1 Section 5(b) of the research ethics policy dictated that the Standing membership of the committee would include the Vice-President, Research or his/her delegate as Chair; the Director of University Medical Services; the University Safety Officer; and, six members of faculty appointed by the Vice-President, Research.

2. 1992 SFU *Ethics Policy*.

3. Memorandum by Nancy McNeil, SFU research grants officer, to Dr. [Name deleted], Department of Kinesiology, reporting the ethics committee's reactions to Dr. [Name deleted]'s preliminary proposal, July 15, 1993.

4. Of course, these ethical criteria are consistent with liability-driven concerns to the extent that a liability-driven analysis would treat the informed consent statement as a liability waiver, and an explicit statement of the voluntary nature of participation as a way to maximize participant culpability (i.e., "Nobody forced you to take part; you chose to do so"). But because informed consent and truly voluntary participation also are consistent with an ethics-driven analysis — and there was no clear evidence of non-ethical concepts being used in those discussions (using, instead, words like "safety") — a more generous interpretation is that the ethics committee was, at those times, behaving as an ethics committee should. Compare that, however, to the January 19, 1994 minutes which indicate that liability was the primary concern.

5. These minutes were secured through a *BC Freedom of Information and Protection of Privacy Act* (FIPPA) request. The name of the applicant and referents to him/her were deleted by the University's FIPPA Officer.

6. Minutes of the ethics committee, January 19, 1994, 2.

7. Minutes of the ethics committee, September 9, 1994.

8. Dr. Bruce Clayman, "The Law of the Land," *Simon Fraser News*, October 30, 1997, 5.

9. Minutes of the ethics committee, November 23, 1995.

10. According to the minutes' listing of which members attended the meeting, there was not a quorum. Indeed, at each of the meetings where limited confidentiality was

discussed, the VP-research and the committee were themselves in violation of the ethics policy.

Chapter VI

1. *Russel Ogden v. SFU*, Transcript for June 20, 1996, 1.

2. Ibid., 3, (our italics).

3. Ibid., 13–15.

4. *Russel Ogden v. SFU*, Transcript for June 21, 1996, 66–68.

5. Ibid., 73–75.

6. *Russel Ogden v. SFU*, Transcript for June 27, 1996, 11.

7. *Russel Ogden v. SFU*, Transcript for June 20, 1996, 85.

Chapter VII

1. The group comprised a dozen academics with affiliations in centres, institutes, and departments of anthropology, law, history, microbiology and immunology, medicine, applied ethics, medical genetics, philosophy, electrical engineering, education, and psychology.

2. In 2000, the Medical Research Council became the Canadian Institutes of Health Research (CIHR), but at the time we are discussing, it was still known as the MRC.

3. Michael McDonald, "From Code to Policy Statement: Creating Canadian Policy for Ethical Research Involving Humans," *Health Law Review*, 17(2–3), 2009: 12–25, at16.

4. Jean Joly, "Research Ethics Board: Summation," *Canadians for Health Research*, July 4, 2010. www.chrcrm.org/en/conference-proceedings/summation.

5. Tri-Council Working Group. 1996 draft code, section 2, 3.

6. Tri-Council Working Group. 1996 draft code, section 2, 12–13.

7. Tri-Council Working Group. 1996 draft code, section 6, 2.

8. Ted Palys, "The Ethics of Ethics: Comments submitted to the Tri-Council Working Group regarding its March 1996 Draft *Code of Conduct for Research Involving Humans.*" (1996). www.sfu.ca/~palys/codecomm.htm

9. Ibid.

10. Ibid.

11. Part 2 (Prescriptions, Procedures and Practices), Section III (Privacy, Confidentiality, Access to Personal Records, Secondary Use of Data, and Data Linkage), III-1.

12. Part 2 (Prescriptions, Procedures and Practices), Section IV (Conflict of Interest), Part B (Institutional Conflicts of Interest), IV-2.

13. Ted Palys, "Bulldozers in the Garden: Comments Regarding the Tri-Council Working Group's July 1997 Draft *Code of Ethical Conduct for Research Involving Humans*," *SFU*, 1997, www.sfu.ca/~palys/tcwg97.htm.

14. L. Menand, "The Limits of Academic Freedom," in *The Future of Academic Freedom*

(Chicago: University of Chicago Press, 1996), 3–20. McDonald, "From Code to Policy Statement."

Chapter VIII

1. Letter from Neil Boyd, Director of the School of Criminology, to Dean of Graduate Studies and VP-research Dr. Bruce Clayman, dated October 11, 1994.

2. Ibid.

3. Brian Burtch, Robert M. Gordon, Simon N. Verdun-Jones, Curt T. Griffiths, Charles Singer, Margaret A. Jackson, Robert Menzies, Karlene Faith, N. K. Banks, John Lowman, T. S. Palys, Ezzat A. Fattah, Mark Carter, Raymond R. Corrado, Dorothy Chunn, William Glackman.

4. John Lowman, "Pay Legal Fees, Urges Professor," *Simon Fraser News*, October 2, 1997, 10(3), www.sfu.ca/archive-sfunews/sfnews/1997/Oct2/letters.html.

5. Dr. Bruce Clayman, Vice-President, Research, to Dr. John Lowman, October 28, 1997.

6. Russel Ogden to SFU President *pro tem* Jack Blaney, November 11, 1997.

7. Liz Elliott, Simon N. Verdun-Jones, Robert Menzies, Dany Lacombe, Dorothy Chunn, Raymond Corrado, Ted Palys, Garth Davies, John Lowman, Karlene Faith, Mark Carter, Rob Gordon, Neil Boyd, Brian Burtch, William Glackman, Joan Brockman, Ehor Boyanowsky, Marie Krbavac, Curt Griffiths, Douglas Cousineau, and Margaret Jackson, Director.

Chapter IX

1. *Simon Fraser News* is for the most part a feel good weekly newsletter published by the university's media and public relations staff whose main purpose is to write positive articles about SFU and the achievements of members of the university community, although it also occasionally includes articles on controversial issues of concern to the campus community.

2. Russel Ogden, "An Insult to Free Inquiry," *Simon Fraser News*, October 30, 1997, 10(5), www.sfu.ca/archive-sfunews/sfnews/1997/Oct30/opinion1.html.

3. Bruce Clayman, "The Law of the Land," *Simon Fraser News*, October 30, 1997, 10(5), www.sfu.ca/archive-sfunews/sfnews/1997/Oct30/opinion2.html

4. Ted Palys and John Lowman, "When Roles Conflict: Research Ethics at SFU," November 17, 1997. Brief prepared for President Blaney in the wake of Dr. Clayman's reconsideration of the Ogden case.

5. *Russel Ogden v. SFU*, Transcript for June 21, 1996, 67.

6. Tri-Council Working Group, 1997 draft, p. IV-2.

7. John Lowman and Ted Palys, "SFU's Ethics Review Committee: A Law unto Itself," November 17, 1997. Brief prepared for President Blaney in the wake of Dr. Clayman's reconsideration of the Ogden case.

8. Mary Marshall, "When Is a Secret Not a Secret?" 1992. The article was published in the firm's newsletter and originally posted at www.cookdukecox.com/newsletters/issue6-1992/secret. htm but was no longer there when we checked in 2010. A copy is available on request.

9. *R. v. Gruenke*, [1991] 3 S.C.R. 263.

10. Marshall, "When Is a Secret Not a Secret?"

11. Lowman and Palys, "SFU's Ethics Review Committee."

12. John Lowman and Ted Palys, "A Law unto Itself," *Simon Fraser News*, November 27, 1997, 10(7), www.sfu.ca/archive-sfunews/sfnews/1997/Nov27/opinion2.html.

13. A weekly Vancouver news magazine devoted to promoting local entertainment that employs several columnists to write commentaries on local news.

14. Charlie Smith, "SFU Criminologists Want Research Confidentiality Back," the *Georgia Straight*, December 4–11, 1997, 10.

Chapter X

1. Memorandum by Phillip Hanson, December 10, 1997, to Dr. Bruce Clayman, Chair; Members of the ethics committee; and others who will be present at the December 18 meeting. Subject: Issues on and relating to agenda, December 18 meeting.

2. Emailed memorandum by James Ogloff to Dr. Clayman, members of the committee, Professors Lowman and Palys, December 18, 1997.

3. The seizing of records is not the only issue: Ogden was called on to testify, not produce records.

4. Ogden, "An Insult to Free Inquiry."

5. Emailed memorandum by Adam Horvath to Dr. Clayman, members of the committee, Professors Lowman and Palys, undated, circulated prior to meeting of December 18, 1997.

6. John Lowman and Ted Palys, "Response to Dr. Horvath," memorandum circulated to members of the ethics committee and other observers, January 6, 1998.

7. Our worries about liability considerations starting to contaminate the ethics review process were not in relation to the ethics committee's actions under Dr. Leiss's chairmanship in 1992; in fact it is in part because we are so convinced that liability was *not* on the ethics committee's agenda at that time that we are so sure that Ogden's undertaking was an ethical one, and not financial. The first indications of liability considerations entering the ethics review process come after Dr. Clayman's watch began, first with the ACE-Inhibitor proposal considered in early 1994, and then in the university's approach to the coroner's subpoena.

8. See Amos Tversky and Daniel Kahneman, "Availability: A Heuristic for Judging Frequency and Probability," *Cognitive Psychology* 5 (1973): 207–232. More generally, see Daniel Kahneman, Paul Slovic, and Amos Tversky, *Judgment Under Uncertainty: Heuristics and Biases* (New York: Cambridge University Press, 1982).

9. Lowman and Palys, "Response to Dr. Horvath."

10. Ted Palys and John Lowman, "The Highest Ethical Standards," memorandum to Dr. Horvath, members of the ethics committee, and others, February 8, 1998.

Chapter XI

1. However, it is interesting that the SFU administration did not see it the same way when it sought to quash Ogden's subpoena of SFU President Stubbs to testify in *Ogden v. SFU*.

2. Memorandum from John Lowman and Ted Palys to Ethics Committee and others. (February 3, 1998).

3. Ibid.

4. John Lowman and Ted Palys to SFU President Jack Blaney, February 23, 1998.

5. *Huerto v. Saskatchewan*, [1995] 5 W.W.R. at 202.

6. *Newfoundland Telephone Company v. Newfoundland* (Board of Commissioners Public Utilities), [1992] 1 S.C.R. 6235 at 645, 89 D.L.R. (4th) 289, 304.

7. John Lowman and Ted Palys to SFU President Jack Blaney, February 23, 1998.

Chapter XII

1. John Lowman, "The Hypocrisy of Canadian Prostitution Law," the *Province*, September 28, 1997, A47.

2. John Lowman and Laura Fraser (1996). *Violence against persons who prostitute: The experience in British Columbia*. (Technical Report No. TR1996-14e). Ottawa, ON: Department of Justice Canada.

3. Chris Atchison, Laura Fraser, and John Lowman, "Men Who Buy Sex," in *Prostitution: On Whores, Hustlers and Johns*, ed. Vern Bullough and James E. Elias (Amherst, NY: Prometheus Press, 1999) 172–203.

4. John Lowman and Christine Louie, "Public Opinion on Prostitution Law Reform in Canada," *Canadian Journal of Criminology and Criminal Justice* 54, no. 2 (2012): 245–260.

5. The SCC struck down the communicating, living on the avails, and bawdy house laws.

6. *Bedford v. Canada*, [2010] ONSC 4264; *Canada (Attorney General) v. Bedford*, [2012] ONCA 186; *Canada (Attorney General) v. Bedford*, [2013] SCC 72.

7. The information about how confidentiality would be protected was parallel on the two applications. The quote here is from the joint application for the "Sex Work in Off-Street Venues" application of February 24.

8. This is the wording as finalized by the ethics committee at its meeting of April 7, 1998.

9. Dr. Marilyn Bowman, Chair of the Sterling Prize Committee, to Russel Ogden, July 14, 1995. The letter informed him he had been chosen for the award.

10. Dr. Patrick O'Neill, Chairperson, CAUT Academic Freedom and Tenure Committee, to Palys and Lowman, March 19, 1998.

11. There were two letters dated March 26, 1998 relating to the two prostitution projects under review — Lowman's study of escort and massage parlour owners and managers and Lowman and Palys' study of off-street sex workers.

12. We began using this phrase to refer to the unanticipated discovery of a future event

so heinous that it invoked a higher ethic to address, regardless of whatever promises one might have made about the protection of confidentiality. Examples might include hearing about an imminent murder, or children about to be trafficked into sexual slavery.

13. Drs. Lowman and Palys to ethics committee, April 3, 1998.

14. Marshall, "When Is a Secret Not a Secret?"

15. *Atlantic Sugar, Ltd. v. US*, 85 Cust. Ct. 128 [1980]. We thank Professor Michael Traynor for supplying us with a copy of the decision in that case.

16. Drs. Lowman and Palys to ethics committee, April 3, 1998.

17. Dr. A. Horvath, Chair, University Research Ethics Review Committee, to Drs. Lowman and Palys, April 16, 1996.

18. Drs. Lowman and Palys to the SFU Ethics Committee, April 23, 1998.

19. Dr. A. Horvath, Chair, University Research Ethics Review Committee, to Drs. Lowman and Palys, May 6, 1998.

20. Drs. Lowman and Palys to SFU Ethics Committee, May 19, 1998.

Chapter XIII

1. We borrowed this title from John MacLachlan Gray, "Up on dat mountain, dey is stuck real good," *Vancouver Sun*, November 1, 1997, C3.

2. Valerie Shore, "Universities Told to Develop Policies for Research Ethics," *Simon Fraser News*, January 12, 1995.

3. Charlie Smith, "Secrecy Shrouds SFU Discipline," the *Georgia Straight*, September 22–29, 1995, 8; Laura Fraser, "Fired SFU Researcher Replies," the *Georgia Straight*, October 12–19, 1995, 9; Charlie Smith, "SFU Boss Pleads Confidentiality," the *Georgia Straight*, October 12–19, 1995, 9; Malgorzata Dubiel, "SFU Faculty Rep Criticizes President," *The Georgia Straight*, October 19–26, 1995, 4–5; Charlie Smith, "Heavily Censored SFU Conflict Report Calls for Change," the *Georgia Straight*, November 2–9, 1995, 9; Charlie Smith, "*Straight* Wins Info Decision but SFU Can Appeal Order to Release Report on Faculty-Staff Dispute," the *Georgia Straight*, May 2, 1996, 6.

4. 1995 Report of the Review Committee of the Simon Fraser School of Criminology.

5. Smith, "Secrecy Shrouds SFU Discipline," 8.

6. Fraser "Fired SFU Researcher Replies," 9.

7. GP25 called for a confidential investigation of any person accused of threatening behavior ("the respondent") on campus.

8. In this instance, SFU mobilized the policy in response to a complaint by the fired researcher about her employer. Ralph Yeomans, then head of SFU's Traffic and Security Department, conducted the investigation, which "turned up many references [to the respondent's] unacceptable verbal conduct and aggressive behaviour which certainly affects the well-being of other people." However, rather than addressing these problems, a serious violation of the GP25 investigation procedure then occurred,

throwing gasoline on the fire. An unknown party gave the respondent a copy of the confidential report, including the names of all the witnesses who had been interviewed. The respondent then proceeded to confront one of the witnesses.

9. Smith, "SFU Boss Pleads Confidentiality," 9.

10. Dubiel, "SFU Faculty Rep Criticizes President," 4–5.

11. www.universitycounsel.ubc.ca/access-and-privacy/useful-resources/

12. Smith, "*Straight* Wins Info Decision," 6.

13. Robert Matas, "SFU President Ignored New Harassment Information," the *Globe and Mail*, June 11, 1997, A5.

14. Suzanne Fournier, "President Blamed in SFU Sex Case," the *Province*, July 3, 1997, A1, A4.

15. Allen Garr, "How a Spin Doctor Saved Donnelly's Reputation," the *Georgia Straight*, May 14–21, 1998, 13–14.

16. "The Big Chill," editorial in the *Province*, July 3, 1997, A24.

17. Jeff Lee, "Swim Coach Gets his Job Back in Settlement over SFU Sex Case," July 25, 1997, A1; Jeff Lee and Jeremy Tobin, "SFU admits it Was Wrong to Fire Donnelly" the *Vancouver Sun*, July 26, 1997, A1-A2. Also see O'Hagan's response to media interest in her role in the harassment policy scandal: "The Marsden/Donnelly Case and Me," the *Vancouver Sun*, October 18, 1997, 23. O'Hagan subsequently claimed that she, too, had become the subject of Marsden's obsessive behavior; see Marina Jimenez, "Former SFU Official Was Victim of Obsessive Behaviour, She Says," the *Vancouver Sun*, October 22, 1997, A1.

18. Marina Jimenez, "SFU President Being Treated for Depression, Governors Told," the *Vancouver Sun*, July 29, 1997, A1.

19. Ian Austin, "'Fundamentals' SFU Chief's Focus," the *Province*, September 11, 1997, A11.

20. Marina Jimenez "SFU Harassment Rulings Invalid; 'Serious' Mismanagement Blamed," the *Vancouver Sun*, October 25, 1997, A1–A2.

21. Rick Coe, "Senate Rescues Board," Faculty Association Newsletter, 1997/98 Issue No. 5, February 5, 1998, 1, www.sfufa.ca/documents/newsletters/9798/19980205.pdf.

22. Ted Palys and John Lowman, "Research Ethics Update: Academic Freedom, Research Participant Rights undermined," Faculty Association Newsletter, 1997/98 Issue No. 5, February 5, 1998, 3.

Chapter XIV

1. "SFU to review decision in Ogden case." *Simon Fraser News*, June 18, 1998, *12*(4).

2. *Russel Ogden v. Simon Fraser University*. Provincial Court of BC (Small Claims), No. 26780, June 10, 1998. www.sfu.ca/~palys/steinbrg.htm

3. Bruce Clayman, "A Vice-President Responds," *Simon Fraser News*, July 16, 1998, www.sfu.ca/archive-sfunews/sfnews/1998/July16/opinion3.html.

Chapter XV

1. Dr. A. Horvath, Chair, University Research Ethics Review Committee, to Lowman and Palys, June 23, 1998.

2. Sissela Bok, *Secrets: On the Ethics of Concealment and Revelation* (New York: Pantheon Books, 1983).

3. This was a reference to Coroner Larry Campbell, who recognized Ogden's claim for a public interest privilege in the *Inquest of the Unknown Female*, and Judge Daniel Steinberg, who made the decision in *Ogden v. SFU*. Neither took the challenge of a subpoena to be a challenge to the rule of law. They both appeared to place a much higher value on research than members of the SFU ethics committee.

4. Lowman and Palys to SFU ethics committee, August 15, 1998, 5.

5. Dr. A. Horvath, Chair, University Research Ethics Review Committee, to Lowman and Palys, June 23, 1998.

6. Lowman and Palys to SFU ethics committee, August 15, 1998, 8.

7. John Lowman and Ted Palys, "The Liability of Ethics," *Simon Fraser News*, July 16, 1998, www.sfu.ca/archive-sfunews/sfnews/1998/July16/opinion2.html.

8. Article 17 reads, "The University recognizes the obligation not only to provide a harassment-free environment and conditions under which academic freedom can flourish, but also, to provide legal advice, representation and/or indemnification to members of the bargaining unit who encounter problems as a result of carrying out in good faith their responsibilities . . ."

9. Clayman, "A Vice-President Responds."

10. Lowman and Palys to SFU ethics committee, August 15, 1998, 11.

Chapter XVI

1. The evaluation was dated September 29, 1998.

2. The reference to "Dr. Gee's committee" refers to a task force that had been established by President Blaney to develop a new ethics policy, as would be required when the *Tri-Council Policy Statement* came into effect to ensure that the university was in compliance.

3. Dr. A. Horvath, Chair, University Ethics Review Committee, to Drs. Lowman and Palys, October 8, 1998.

4. A. Horvath, Response to Drs. Palys and Lowman's Communication: "Rejoinder to Bruce Clayman," October 6, 1998. The article was never published in *Simon Fraser News* but appeared for a time on the university research ethics review committee's website.

5. SFU Policy R20.01 (1992): University Research Ethics. Section 6(h).

6. James V. Lavery, "Losing Yourself to AIDS: The Meaning of Euthanasia and Assisted Suicide." PhD diss., University of Toronto, 1999.

7. An exception to this general principle is critical research which, by pointing out inequity, injustice, prejudice and discrimination and the like, may well produce results that the participants would consider "harmful" to their interests. Even in such

PROTECTING RESEARCH CONFIDENTIALITY

circumstances, however, it would not be ethically acceptable to deceive participants by collecting information on a promise of confidentiality with the intention of disclosing it. It is one thing to do covert research that anticipates criticizing the community it studies, but quite another to promise confidentiality in order to access information for research without intending to honour it.

8. For example, one way we would contact an escort agency would be to find out who the owners are, and approach them with a request to participate in our research.

9. SFU Policy R20.01 (1992): University Research Ethics, Section 2.

10. Bernard Dickens, PhD, LL.D., F.R.S.C., Professor Faculty of Law, Faculty of Medicine and Joint Centre for Bioethics, to Dr. A. O. Horvath, Chair, SFU University Research Ethics Review Committee, September 29, 1998, 2.

11. Ibid., 3.

12. J. H. Wigmore, *A Treatise on the System of Evidence in Trials at Common Law, Including the Statutes and Judicial Decisions of All Jurisdictions of the United States, England, and Canada* (Boston: Little, Brown and Company, 1905), 3211.

13. Wigmore, *Treatise on the System of Evidence*, 3350.

14. Ibid., 3350–1.

15. For a description, see J. P. Fanning, "Policies and Best Practices for Ensuring Statistical and Research Confidentiality." Paper prepared for the Office of the Assistant Secretary for Planning and Evaluation. US Department of Health and Human Services, under contract PO HHSP 233200500320A.

Chapter XVII

1. Medical Research Council, Natural Sciences and Engineering Research Council, and Social Sciences and Humanities Research Council, *Tri-Council Policy Statement: Ethical Conduct for Research Involving Humans* (Ottawa: MRC/NSERC/SSHRC, 1998). Hereafter TCPS.

2. For example, see McDonald, "From Code to Policy Statement."

3. Bruce Clayman, "Proposed New Policy Should Strike Balance," *Simon Fraser News*, September 24, 1998, 2.

4. TCPS, p.i.8.

Chapter XVIII

1. SFUFA nominated one of the reviewers; the administration nominated the other.

2. Nicholas Blomley and Steven Davis, "Russel Ogden Decision Review," *SFU*, 1998, www.sfu.ca/~palys/ogden.htm.

3. "Ogden to Receive Apology, Compensation from SFU for Legal Expenses and Lost Wages," *Simon Fraser News*, October 22, 1998, 13(4), www.sfu.ca/archive-sfunews/sfnews/1998/oct22/ogden.html.

4. Erin Fitzpatrick, "SFU Promises to Protect Academic Freedom," the *Peak*, November 16, 1998, 100(11), www.peak.sfu.ca/the-peak/98-3/issue11/freedom.html.

402

Chapter XIX

1. TCPS 1998, 3.2.

2. See *Pacific Press Ltd. v. Cain*, [1997] B.C.J. No. 1061. The coroner recognized that Ogden's research communications were privileged, but denied that the journalists' communications were. Pacific Press argued that the coroner exceeded his jurisdiction in threatening the journalists with a charge of contempt. Justice Downs in BC Supreme Court agreed, noting that a coroner's inquest is not a "court of law," and that the proper procedure would have been for the coroner to ask the Supreme Court of BC for a declaration that the witness was in contempt.

3. Joe S. Cecil and Gerald T. Wetherington, "Special Issue: Court-Ordered Disclosure of Academic Research: A Clash of Values of Science and Law," *Law and Contemporary Problems* 59, no. 3 (1996), www.law.duke.edu/shell/cite.pl?59+Law+&+Contemp.+Prob s.+1+%28Summer+1996%29. A particularly useful initial resource was the special issue of *Law and Contemporary Problems* devoted to court-ordered disclosure of confidential research information. The collection includes articles by researchers, lawyers, and judges and contains a wealth of information about US cases, the experiences of researchers who were subpoenaed, legal strategies to contain or quash third party subpoenas, and judicial perspectives on such cases.

4. An Australian case concerned the Hindmarsh Island bridge controversy, which pitted property rights against Aboriginal religious beliefs. The controversy concerned access to an anthropologist's documentation of claims that Aboriginal women were making about their religious traditions — which took the form of "secret women's business" — in their attempt to prevent the building of a bridge. See Iris Stevens. "Report of the Hindmarsh Island Bridge Royal Commission" (Adelaide: South Australian Government Printer, 1995). Just as we were going to press, a second case came to light involving geographer Bradley Garrett's doctoral research on "place hackers," people who trespass private places — such as sewers, the tops of bridges, and London underground tunnels — in order to photograph and experience the large parts of the modern world that are privatized and generally off limits to most citizens. While Garrett's case does not involve the use of subpoena power, it illustrates a different kind of threat to research confidentiality. London Transport Police arrested Garrett at Heathrow Airport. While he was in custody, police raided his home and seized his computer and his research records. In addition to Garrett, police arrested eight place hackers and charged them with conspiracy to commit criminal damage. In May 2014, the conspiracy charges against seven of the accused were stayed or dismissed. Garrett and one other person plead guilty to criminal damage. Garrett received a three-year conditional discharge and his co-accused an eighteen-month conditional discharge. The case has caused widespread concern about the academic freedom of researchers to examine life at society's margins, and about the police seizure of confidential research records (David Mathews, "'Place-hacker' Prosecution 'Attack on Intellectual Freedom,'" *Times Higher Education*, May 23, 2014, www.timeshighereducation.co.uk/news/place-hacker-case-ends-with-two-conditional-discharges/2013527.article.

5. Portions of this section appeared in John Lowman and Ted Palys, "The Ethics and Law of Confidentiality in Criminal Justice Research: A Comparison of Canada and the United States," *International Criminal Justice Review* 11 (2001): 1–33.

6.   For example, see K. Bond "Confidentiality and the Protection of Human Subjects in Social Science Research: a Report on Recent Developments," *American Sociologist* 13 (1986): 144-152; J. Caroll & C. Knerr, "A report of the APSA confidentiality in social science research data project," *Political Science Quarterly*, 8 (1975): 258–261; J. Cecil and G.T. Wetherington (eds.), "Court-Ordered Disclosure of Academic Research: A Clash of Values of Science and Law," *Law and Contemporary Problems* (Special Volume) 59 (1996); J. Lowman & T. Palys, "The Ethics and Law of Confidentiality in Criminal Justice Research: A Comparison of Canada and the United States." *International Criminal Justice Review* 11 (2000): 1–33.

7.   Bond, "Confidentiality and the Protection of Human Subjects in Social Science Research."

8.   J. Caroll and C. Knerr, "Confidentiality of social science research sources and data: The Popkin case." *Political Science Quarterly* 6 (1973):268–280; R. M. O'Neil, "A researcher's privilege: Does any hope remain?" *Law and Contemporary Problems* 59 (1996): 35–50.

9.   P. Nejelski & K. Finsterbusch "The prosecutor and the researcher: Present and prospective variations on the Supreme Court's Branzburg decision." *Social Problems*, 21 (1973): 3–21.

10. Caroll and Knerr, "A report of the APSA confidentiality in social science research data project."

11. *In re Grand Jury Subpoena Dated* January 4, 1984; M. Brajuha and L. Hallowell "Legal intrusion and the politics of field work: The impact of the Brajuha case." *Urban Life, 14* (1986): 454–478.

12. *In re Grand Jury Proceedings,* James Richard Scarce, 1993; Richard Scarce, "(No) trial (but) tribulations: When courts and ethnography conflict," *Journal of Contemporary Ethnography, 23,* (1994): 123–149; Richard Scarce, "Good faith, bad ethics: When scholars go the distance and scholarly associations do not." *Law and Social Inquiry* 24 (1999): 977–986.

13. See Ted Palys and John Lowman, "Defending Research Confidentiality 'To the extent the law allows': Lessons from the Boston College Subpoenas," *Journal of Academic Ethics* 10 (2012): 271–297.

14. *See Richards of Rockford Inc. v. Pacific Gas and Electric Co.,* 71 F.R.D. 388 (N.D. Cal, 1976).

15. *In re* Snyder, 115 F.R.D. 211 (D. Ariz. 1987); see also *Wright v. Jeep Corp.,* 547 F. Supp. 871 (E.D. Mich. 1982). Cited in B. B. Crabb "Judicially compelled disclosure of researchers' data: A judge's view," *Law and Contemporary Problems* 59 (1996): 9–34.

16. *Deitchman v. E. R. Squibb & Sons,* Inc., 740 F.2d 556 (7th Cir. 1984).

17. See *In re American Tobacco Co.,* 880 F2.d 1520 (2d. Cir. 1989); In re American Tobacco Co., 866 F2.d 552 (2d. Cir. 1989); see also E. C. Wiggins & J. A. McKenna. "Researchers' reactions to compelled disclosure of scientific information," *Law and Contemporary Problems* 59 (1996): 67–94.

18. *R. J. Reynolds Tobacco Co., v. Fischer,* 427 S.E.2d 810, 811 (Ga. Ct. App. 1993); P. M. Fischer, "Science and subpoenas: When do the courts become instruments of manipulation?" *Law and Contemporary Problems* 59 (1996): 159–168. J. S. Picou,

J.S. "Compelled disclosure of scholarly research: Some comments on "high stakes" litigation." *Law and Contemporary Problems* 59 (1996): 149–157.

19. See In re Michael A. Cusumano and David B. Yoffie [*United States of America v. Microsoft Corporation*], No. 98-2133, United States Court of Appeals For the First Circuit] (1998). www.law.emory.edu/1circuit/dec98/98-2133.01a.html.

20. R. Wilson, "Penn Anthropologist Fights Subpoenas for Field Notes in Medical Case," *Chronicle of Higher Education* 49, 28 (2003): A14.

21. R. Wilson, "When Should a Scholar's Notes be Confidential? An Anthropologist Involved in a Medical Lawsuit Says She'll Go to Jail Rather than Turn Hers Over," *Chronicle of Higher Education* 49, 36 (2003): A10.

22. See *Miriam Flores et al v. State of Arizona et al.* [2010] Order. Case 4:92-cv-00596-RCC Document 952; Zehr, M.A, "Arizona Subpoena Seeks Researchers' ELL Data," Education Week, August 12, 2014, www.edweek.org/ew/articles/2010/08/12/01arizona.h30. html?tkn.

23. Portions of this chapter are from John Lowman and Ted Palys, "Going the Distance: Lessons for Researchers from Jurisprudence on Privilege," *SFU*, 1999, www.sfu. ca/~palys/Distance.pdf. Submission prepared for the SFU Research Ethics Policy Revision Task Force; Ted Palys and John Lowman, "Ethical and Legal Strategies for Protecting Confidential Research Information," *Canadian Journal of Law and Society* 15 (2000): 39–80. The legal analysis benefitted from formal legal opinions prepared by Paul Jones (1999), Legal Advisor to the Canadian Association of University Teachers, who prepared his opinion at the request of the SFU Faculty Association; and another by Professors Michael Jackson and Marilyn MacCrimmon (1999) of UBC Faculty of Law, who prepared their opinion at the request of the SFU Research Ethics Policy Revision Task Force chaired by Dr. Ellen Gee.

24. John H. Wigmore, *Evidence in Trials at Common Law* 8 (Boston: Little Brown and Company, 1961), 70.

25. B. McLachlin, "Confidential Communications and the Law of Privilege," *University of British Columbia Law Review* 11 (1997): 266.

26. Canada Evidence Act (R.S.C., 1985, c.C-5). www.laws.justice.gc.ca/en/C-5/index.html.

27. Statistics Act (R.S.C., 1985, c. S-19). http://laws-lois.justice.gc.ca/eng/acts/S-19/FullText. html.

28. See e.g., *R. v. Mills*, [1999] 3 S.C.R. 668.

29. "Statistics Canada Research Data Centres (RDCs): Guide for Researchers under Agreement with Statistics Canada," Statistics Canada, 2005, www.statcan.gc.ca/rdc-cdr/ pdf/researcher-rechercheur-guide-eng.pdf.

30. Ibid., 9.

31. Ibid., 15 (emphasis in original).

32. Statistics Canada, Survey of Financial Security, 1999.

33. *Smith v. Jones* [1999] 1 S.C.R. 455 at 45–46.

34. Ibid., 51.

35. The court clarified this was because the prospective harm was serious (involving death), imminent (Jones had already mobilized the plan), and directed toward a clearly identified target (prostitutes on a specific Vancouver stroll).

36. *Smith v. Jones*, 15.

37. This changed in 2014, as we outline in Chapter 28.

38. Jackson and MacCrimmon, "Research Confidentiality and Academic Privilege," 29.

39. B. McLachlin, "Confidential Communications and the Law of Privilege," *University of British Columbia Law Review* 11 (1977): 266–284.

40. Professor Slavutych remained at the University of Alberta and enjoyed a long and productive career. He retired from the University in 1988 and passed away in July 2011. www.legacy.com/obituaries/edmontonjournal/obituary.aspx?n=yarslavutych&pid=152438316&fhid=7178#fbLoggedOut.

41. Beverly McLachlin, "Confidential Communications and the Law of Privilege," 277.

42. P. Sim, "Privilege and Confidentiality: The Impact of *Slavutych v. Baker* on the Canadian Law of Evidence," *Advocate's Quarterly* 5, 1984: 357–379.

43. Laskin CJC writing for the minority in *Solicitor General of Canada v. Royal Commission of Inquiry into Confidentiality of Health Records in Ontario* [1981] 2 S.C.R. 494. Cited in Sim, "Privilege and Confidentiality."

44. Paul Jones, *Legal Opinion on Issues of Privilege* (1999). See Appendix A of John Lowman and Ted Palys, "Going the Distance: Lessons for Researchers from Jurisprudence on Privilege."

45. Michael Traynor, "Countering the Excessive Subpoena for Scholarly Research," *Law and Contemporary Problems* 59 (1996): 120.

Chapter XX

1. Portions of this chapter are from John Lowman and Ted Palys, "Going the Distance: Lessons for Researchers from Jurisprudence on Privilege," *SFU*, 1999, www.sfu.ca/~palys/Distance.pdf. Submission prepared for the SFU Research Ethics Policy Revision Task Force; Ted Palys and John Lowman, "Ethical and Legal Strategies for Protecting Confidential Research Information," *Canadian Journal of Law and Society* 15 (2000): 39–80; and Ted Palys and John Lowman, "Anticipating Law: Research Methods, Ethics and the Common Law of Privilege," *Sociological Methodology* 32 (2002): 1–17. The legal analysis benefitted from discussion with and formal legal opinions prepared by Paul Jones (1999), Legal Advisor to the Canadian Association of University Teachers, who prepared his opinion at the request of the SFU Faculty Association; and another by Professors Michael Jackson and Marilyn MacCrimmon (1999) of UBC Faculty of Law, who prepared their opinion at the request of the SFU Research Ethics Policy Revision Task Force chaired by Dr. Ellen Gee.

2. As neither of the authors of this book are lawyers, we do not offer the specific legal advice that an attorney provides a client. Ours is a general discussion of the application of the Wigmore criteria to research. In the event of a specific challenge to research confidentiality, professional legal advice should be sought.

3. For example, see Ted Palys and John Lowman, "Anticipating Law: Research Methods, Ethics and the Common Law of Privilege," *Sociological Methodology* 32 (2002): 1–17; Traynor, "Countering the Excessive Subpoena for Scholarly Research."

4. In the US, challenges to research confidentiality have often been regarded as threats to the exercise of a scholar's First Amendment Constitutional right to freedom of expression — often referred to as "academic privilege" or "a scholar's privilege" as a variant of "journalistic privilege" — rather than a matter of research-participant rights. Academic research that is not protected by statute is subject to Federal Rule of Evidence 50, which states that, "the privilege of a witness . . . shall be governed by the principles of the common law as they may be interpreted by the courts of the United States in light of reason and experience." See, for example, *Upjohn Co. v. United States*, [1981] SCT-QL 261.

5. John Lowman and Ted Palys, "The Ethics and Law of Confidentiality in Criminal Justice Research: A Comparison of Canada and the United States,: *International Criminal Justice Review* 11(1) (2001): 1–33; Ted Palys and John Lowman, "Ethical and Legal Strategies for Protecting Confidential Research Information," *Canadian Journal of Law and Society* 15(1), (2000): 39–80; Ted Palys and John Lowman, "Anticipating Law: Research Methods, Ethics and the Common Law of Privilege," *Sociological Methodology*, 32, (2002): 1–17.

6. Jones, *Legal Opinion on Issues of Privilege* (1999) at 3.

7. The legal opinion by Professors Michael Jackson and Marilyn MacCrimmon (1999) of UBC Faculty of Law was prepared at the request of the SFU Research Ethics Policy Revision Task Force chaired by Dr. Ellen Gee. See footnote 50.

8. Deborah Lovett, "Legal Opinion for Research Ethics Board." This legal opinion was commissioned by the first SFU REB in the post-TCPS era. The putative purpose of the opinion was for Ms. Lovett to evaluate the legal probity various forms the REB had produced that were to be used by the REB in the ethics review process. We consider Ms. Lovett's opinion only briefly in this and the next chapter, but in greater detail in Chapter 24.

9. Lord Eldon, from an 1819 decision in *Parkhurst v. Lowten*, cited by Wigmore, *Treatise on the System of Evidence*, 3233.

10. For the details of this case, refer to p. 91.

11. Mary Marshall, "When Is a Secret Not a Secret?"

12. See Ted Palys and John Lowman, "Informed Consent, Confidentiality and the Law: Implications of the Tri-Council Policy Statement," section 3.1. (1999). Report prepared for the SFU Research Ethics Policy Revision Task Force. www.sfu.ca/~palys/Conf&Law.pdf.

13. Jones, *Legal Opinion on Issues of Privilege* (1999) at 3.

14. *M.(A.) v. Ryan* [1997] 1 S.C.R. 157, 11.

15. Ibid., 3.

16. CIHR *et al.* (1998), 2.6.

17. See J. Sopinka, S. N. Lederman, & A. W. Bryant. *The Law of Evidence in Canada.*

(Toronto: Butterworths, 1992).

18. Traynor, "Countering the Excessive Subpoena for Scholarly Research," 122.

19. CIHR *et al* (1998), 3.2.

20. 85 Cust. Ct. 128 (1980). The case is discussed by Michael Traynor at 122 of "Countering the excessive subpoena for scholarly research," and is all the more provocative because it goes against the grain of many other US court decisions that protect confidentiality. We thank Mr. Traynor for supplying us with a copy of the decision.

21. Palys and Lowman, "Defending Research Confidentiality."

22. In Re: Request from the United Kingdom pursuant to the Treaty between the Government of the United States of America and the Government of the United Kingdom on Mutual Assistance in Criminal Matters in the Matter of Dolours Price; *United States of America v. Trustees of Boston College.* Case 1:11-mc-91078-WGY. www.bostoncollegesubpoena.wordpress.com/court-documents/young-ruling/.

23. In Re: Request from the United Kingdom pursuant to the Treaty between the Government of the United States of America and the Government of the United Kingdom on Mutual Assistance in Criminal Matters in the Matter of Dolours Price; *United States v. Ed Moloney and Anthony McIntyre,* No. 11-2511. United States Court of Appeals for the First Circuit. www.bostoncollegesubpoena.wordpress.com/2012/07/06/first-circuit-court-of-appeals-ruling/.

24. Mario Brajuha and Lyle Hallowell, "Legal Intrusion and the Politics of Fieldwork: 'The Impact of the Brajuha Case,'" *Urban Life,* 14 (1986): 454–473.

25. *United States v. Stern,* 511 F.2d 1364, 1367 (2d Cir. 1975); *United States v. Kovel,* 296 F.2d 918, 923 (2d Cir. 1961), burden not "discharged by mere conclusory or ipse dixit assertions." In re Bonanno, 344 F.2d 830, 833 (2d Cir. 1965).

26. In re Grand Jury Subpoena Dtd. January 4, 750 F.2d 223 (2nd Cir. 12/13/1984), 13.

27. Chad Skelton, "Privacy Nightmare," the *Vancouver Sun,* March 8, 2006, 1. The articles detail how laptops containing sensitive information had been left in cars and stolen, how insecure data banks were hacked, and how equipment that was sold or discarded was never wiped clean of confidential data.

28. Jones, "Legal Opinion on Issues of Privilege."

29. *M(A) v. Ryan* at 14.

30. Scarce, "(No) trial (but) tribulations," 126.

31. This is not a recommendation for using signed informed consent statements, since the very existence of the statement may compromise confidentiality.

32. The information sheet is advisable in many circumstances as it can serve as the participant's reminder of any pledges the researcher has made, though there are also many situations where mere existence of such a sheet could pose a threat to the participant, e.g., when interviewing victims of abuse whose abusers might find the information sheet; when interviewing political activists under repressive regimes.

33. Wigmore, *Treatise on the System of Evidence,* 3211.

34. Ibid., 3186, (emphasis in original).

35. R. T. Bower and P. de Gasparis, *Ethics in Social Research: Protecting the Interests of Human Subjects.* NY: Praeger, 1978).

36. Professor Tonge made the statement as part of a discussion about the implications of the Belfast Project that was held on the *Prime Time* television show on the RTÉ One network on July 12, 2012. See transcript at www.bostoncollegesubpoena.wordpress. com/2012/07/13/transcript-rte-prime-time-looks-at-the-controversy-over-the-boston-college-interviews/.

37. Henry McDonald, "US Court Says IRA Member's Secret Testimony Can Be Handed over to Police," *The Guardian*, July 8, 2012, www.guardian.co.uk/uk/2012/jul/08/us-court-ira-secret-testimony.

38. "Former IRA prisoner dubious about re-opening inquiries," *Tyrone Herald*, July 16, 2012, www.bostoncollegesubpoena.wordpress.com/2012/07/16/former-ira-prisoner-dubious-about-re-opening-inquiries/.

39. "The Returning of the Boston Tapes," *The Irish Times*, May 7, 2014, www.irishtimes.com/news/politics/the-returning-of-the-boston-tapes-1.1787071.

40. www.grants2.nih.gov/grants/policy/coc/.

41. J.P. Fanning, "Policies and Best Practices for Ensuring Statistical and Research Confidentiality." Paper prepared for the Office of the Assistant Secretary for Planning and Evaluation. US Department of Health and Human Services, under contract PO HHSP 233200500320A.

42. www.grants2.nih.gov/grants/policy/coc/.

43. www.nij.gov/funding/humansubjects/privacy-certificate-guidance.htm.

44. Peter Geoghegan, "Links to Past under Attack," *The Scotsman*, July 11, 2012, www.scotsman.com/news/peter-geoghegan-links-to-past-under-attack-1-2403619.

45. Some US literature and jurisprudence refers to "a scholar's privilege." Just as lawyer-client privilege is the privilege of the client and not the lawyer, in our view the privilege emanating from the researcher-participant relationship belongs to the participant, not the researcher.

46. In re Grand Jury Subpoena dated January 4, 1986, paragraphs 14–17.

47. *Richard A. Farnsworth, et al. (Plaintiffs) v. The Procter & Gamble Company, et al (Defendants/Appellants) v. Center for Disease Control (Movant/Appellee)* [1985] CA11-QL 259. No. 84-8330.

48. Traynor, "Countering the Excessive Subpoena for Scholarly Research," 121.

49. Jackson and MacCrimmon, "Research Confidentiality and Academic Privilege," 105.

50. Portions of this section are from Palys and Lowman, "Informed Consent, Confidentiality and the Law"; Palys and Lowman, "Ethical and Legal Strategies for Protecting Confidential Research Information"; and Palys and Lowman, "Anticipating Law."

51. TCPS at i-4.

52. For example, in the United States, both the American Sociological Association and the American Psychological Association have submitted *amicus curiae* briefs in support of researchers whose pledges of confidentiality were challenged in court.

Chapter XXI

1. It is now quite rare for subpoenas to arise in the context of criminal trials in the US. When they do arise in relation to a criminal matter, it is more likely in the grand-jury context than in a trial.

2. See E. C. Wiggins and J. A. McKenna, "Researchers' Reactions to Compelled Disclosure of Scientific Information," *Law and Contemporary Problems* 59, 3 (1996): 87.

3. *Dow Chemical Co. v. Allen*, 672 F.2d 1262 (7th Cir. 1982), at 1.

4. Ibid., 47–49.

5. Ibid., 51–52.

6. In re R. J. Reynolds, 518 N.Y.S.2d 729 (Sup. Ct. 1987).

7. Wiggins and McKenna, "Researchers' Reactions," 69.

8. Ibid., 70, 76.

9. Ibid., 69.

10. Ibid., 76.

11. O'Neill, 40.

12. Barbara Crabb, "Judicially Compelled Disclosure of Researchers' Data: A Judge's View," in Cecil and Wetherington, 9.

13. See Crabb, "Judicially Compelled Disclosure," 14.

14. See, e.g., Crabb, "Judicially Compelled Disclosure"; Wiggins and McKenna, "Researchers' Reactions"; Fischer, "Science and Subpoenas".

15. See Crabb, "Judicially Compelled Disclosure." Wiggins and McKenna, "Researchers' Reactions."

16. Crabb, "Judicially Compelled Disclosure," 30.

17. Ibid., 79.

18. *Recall Farnsworth v. Proctor and Gamble, supra.*

19. *Deitchman v. E. R. Squibb & Sons, Inc.* 740 F.2d 556 (7th Cir. 1984).

20. Wiggins and McKenna, "Researchers' Reactions," 85. It should be noted that even though no confidences were violated, there was an impact on Dr. Herbst's research nonetheless. Wiggins and McKenna, who interviewed Dr. Herbst and other researchers who had been subpoenaed years after the fact in order to assess the subpoena's long term effects, stated: "Dr. Herbst reported that, as predicted in the affidavits he submitted, some physicians who became aware of the dispute over the DES Registry records stopped sending information to the Registry, even though identifying information has not been released."

21. Crabb, "Judicially Compelled Disclosure," 24.

22. *Cusumano and Yoffie v. Microsoft, supra,* at 9.

23. Jackson and MacCrimmon, "Research Confidentiality and Academic Privilege," 112.

24. Jackson and MacCrimmon, "Research Confidentiality and Academic Privilege," 85–93.

25. "Laconia" is a pseudonym protecting that police department's identity.

26. Pledges that, as far as we know, Leo has always maintained.

27. Leo, "Trial and Tribulations," 117.

28. Ibid., 125.

29. Ibid., 127.

30. Ibid., 128.

31. Ibid., 138.

32. Ibid., 130.

33. Jackson and MacCrimmon, "Research Confidentiality and Academic Privilege," 93.

34. This contrasts with National Institutes of Health–administered confidentiality certificates, which are available for a wide variety of health-related research topics regardless whether it is funded by NIH or not (see pp. 175 above).

35. Title 28 of the *Code of Federal Regulations,* Part 22, Section 22.

36. As the NIJ website explains, these regulations: i) protect the privacy of individuals by limiting the use of private, identifiable information for research or statistical purposes; ii) protect private information provided by individuals from use in any judicial, legal, or administrative process without the individual's prior consent; iii) improve the scientific quality of NIJ research programs by minimizing the subject's concerns over the use of the data; and iv) clarify for researchers the limitations on the use of privately identifiable information for only research or statistical purposes. See www.nij.gov/nij/funding/humansubjects/confidentiality.htm.

37. Traynor, "Countering the Excessive Subpoena," 134.

38. Leo, "Trial and Tribulations," 132.

39. *R. v. O'Connor,* [1995] 4 S.C.R. 411.

40. *A.(L.L.) v. B.(A.)* [1995] 4 S.C.R. 536.

41. *M.(A.) v. Ryan* [1997] 1 S.C.R. 157.

42. *R. v. Mills,* [1999] 3 S.C.R. 668

43. Ibid. 18.

44. *R. v. O'Connor,* 6.

45. Ibid., 17

46. Ibid., 10–11.

47. *M.(A.) v. Ryan,* 32.

48. *R. v. O'Connor,* 56.

49. Jackson and MacCrimmon, "Research Confidentiality and Academic Privilege," 129–31, 139–40.

50. We accept that the motive of the women was simply to assert their privacy and equality interests; we mention this only to point out that their behaviour is also consistent with this more adversarial interpretation.

51. Whether it makes sense in the context of other social objectives is a separate issue. The point here is that, in the adversarial court setting, the judge's role is to help ensure the battle is fought fairly.

52. *R. v. O'Connor,* 49.

53. *R. v. Carosella,* [1997] 112 C.C.C.(3d) 289.

54. For example, Bernhard and Young (2010) describe such a policy at Ryerson University in Toronto. We do not know at this time just how widespread the practice is.

55. We mean "record" broadly. For example, the researcher could note the response anonymously or with a pseudonym in contemporaneous field notes, or have a verbatim record in an anonymized interview transcript.

Chapter XXII

1. Lowman and Fraser, "Violence Against Persons Who Prostitute."

2. There were two appeal submissions. We sent the first "R20.01 Appeal: Summary of Grounds" to Gagan on November 3, 1998. The second submission entitled "R20.01 Appeal" explained the grounds for appeal in greater detail, and included numerous appendices.

3. The grievance documents are posted at www.sfu.ca/~palys/Grievance.pdf.

4. Policy GP24 — "Fair use of information and communications technology" — gave SFU that right.

5. Memorandum from Dr. Bruce Clayman, VP-research, to Deans, Chairs and Graduate Program Chairs, December 2, 1998.

6. SFU *Framework Agreement* , Article 12. www.sfufa.ca/index.php?option=com_content&task=view&id=26&Itemid=27.

7. Academy of Criminal Justice Sciences (ACJS) *Code of Ethics,* Article B-19. www.acjs.org/pubs/167_671_2922.cfm.

8. For a copy of the ASA *Code of Ethics,* see www.asanet.org/about/ethics.cfm.

9. Email from Adam Horvath to John Lowman, with an extensive cc list of twenty-six persons in such locations as the SFU administration, CAUT, members of the ethics committee, the NCEHR site visit team, and SFUFA, March 26, 1999. Subject heading: "American Sociological Association Code of Ethics and Unlimited/Limited Confidentiality."

10. See John Lowman and Ted Palys, "Confidentiality and the 1997 ASA Code of Ethics: A Query," *Footnotes* 27, 2 (1999): 5, www.asanet.org/footnotes/1999/ASA.02.1999.pdf; J. Iutcovich, S. Hoppe, J. Kenney, and F. Levine, "Confidentiality and the 1997 ASA Code of Ethics: A Response from COPE," *Footnotes* 27, 2, 1999: 5, www.asanet.org/

footnotes/1999/ASA.02.1999.pdf.

11. Email from Dr. J. Iutcovich, Chair of the ASA Committee on Professional Ethics, to Dr. Ellen Gee, Chair of the SFU Ethics Task Force, February 23,1999, Subject: Response to Ethics Query. The email was forwarded from Dr. Gee to other members of the Ethics Task Force with cc's to Drs. Palys and Lowman on March 23, 1999.

12. D. V. Janoff, "Pink Blood: Queer-Bashing in Canada" (master's thesis, SFU, 2000). A revised version was published as D.V. Janoff, *Pink Blood: Homophobic Violence in Canada* (Toronto: University of Toronto Press, 2005).

13. This clause reflected SFU's extension of the *Collective Agreement*'s legal indemnification for faculty to graduate students conducting research, as per Blomley and Davis's third recommendation following their review of the Ogden decision.

14. See Jay S. Jones, "The Cleansing Time: Aesthetic Order, Social Control and the Dangers of Dave's World" (master's thesis, SFU, 2000).

15. Dr. Horvath's memo listed the date as June 9, 1982, but we assume this was a typo.

16. Memorandum from Adam O. Horvath, Chair, University Research Ethics Review Committee, to ethics committee members, November 30, 1998, Re: Policy R20-01.

17. Email from Bruce Clayman to Adam O. Horvath, January 4, 1999.

18. Gagan retired in 2005 and became Professor Emeritus in SFU's Department of History.

19. "Munro Named VP-Academic, *pro tem*," *Simon Fraser News*, July 2, 1999, www.sfu.ca/archive-sfunews/sfnews/1999/July2/inbrief.html. Munro had previously served as VP-academic.

20. T. C. O'Doherty, "Off-Street Commercial Sex: An Exploratory Study" (master's thesis, SFU, 2007), www.ir.lib.sfu.ca/handle/1892/9250. Also see T.C. O'Doherty, "Victimization in Off-Street Sex Industry Work," *Violence Against Women* 20, no. 10 (2011): 1–20.

21. *Bedford v. Canada* (Attorney General), [2010] O.J. No. 4057; 2010 ONSC 4264; 102 O.R. (3d) 321; Court File No. 07-CV-329807 PD1. *Canada (Attorney General) v. Bedford*, [2013] SCC 72.

22. *Canada (Attorney General) v. Bedford*, [2013] SCC 72.

Chapter XXIII

1. *Formal NCEHR Site Visit Report* (October, 1998). Site visit team and authors of the report were Drs. Janet Storch, Glenn Griener, and Richard Carpentier.

2. *Smith v. Jones*, [1999].

3. Minutes of the ethics committee, July 4, 2000.

4. *Smith v. Jones* [1991], 44.

5. Ibid., 31.

6. Ibid., 4.

7. Ibid., 11.

8. *Garner v. Stone*, No. 97A-320250-1 (Ga.,DeKalb County Super. Ct. Dec. 16, 1999).

9.   T. Renaud, "Ex-Cop Wins Rare Confidentiality Case: Jury Awards $287,000 for Psychologist Telling of Client's Lethal Fantasies," *Fulton County Daily Report*, January 5, 2000.

10. *Young v. Bella*, [2006] 1 S.C.R. 108.

11. See www.vandu.org/.

12. Email from Hal Weinberg, SFU Director of Research Ethics, to Gordon Roe, October 8, 2000. Weinberg forwarded his email to Ogloff, Chair of the Ethics Committee, who indicated in an email dated October 31, 2000, that he agreed with Weinberg's recommendation and would approve the proposal if Roe agreed to make the responsibility contract part of his application.

13. Email from Hal Weinberg to Gordon Roe, October 17, 2000.

14. John Lowman and Ted Palys to SFU President Jack Blaney, October 31, 2000.

15. In addition to a lengthy section that outlined the problems associated with the ethics committee's new "duty to report" policy, we noted numerous other violations:
     • From 1994 on the ethics committee under Clayman's chairship had violated policy by delegating approval of faculty of business administration research ethics applications to that faculty when the ethics policy gave neither the chair nor the VP-research nor the ethics committee nor the faculty of business administration such power. The violation of policy meant that approximately seven years' worth of faculty of business administration research ethics proposals had never received ethics review according to the SFU ethics policy.
     • When the Ogloff-chaired ethics committee informed SFU researchers that research involving secondary databases would now be included among those projects requiring review, it was imposing a different definition of "research" than the one used in the policy.
     • Notwithstanding the resolution of our grievance against the university, the ethics committee continued to post its limited confidentiality consent statement — and only that statement — on the ethics committee website, thereby giving researchers who were unaware of the grievance the impression that limited confidentiality was the only university-approved policy. We asserted that the ethics committee violated their academic freedom in the process.
     • While the ethics policy stated that the responsibility of ethics review of research conducted in graduate courses lay with the department or faculty in which the courses were taught, the ethics committee had recently ordered that it must review all graduate student research.

16. SFU President Jack Blaney to John Lowman and Ted Palys, November 27, 2000, with cc to James Ogloff and Bruce Clayman.

17. The President also ordered the ethics committee to:
     • cease its practice of delegating responsibility for ethics review to the faculty of business administration.
     • stop using a different definition of research than the one used in the policy and to stop its practice of evaluating proposals that involved secondary data.
     • cease its new requirement that all graduate student research must be reviewed by the committee and return to the practices outlined in the policy that made thesis and dissertation research subject to committee review and course-related research subject to departmental or faculty review.

Chapter XXIV

1. TCPS, p. i9.

2. SFU Policy R20.01: Ethics Review of Research Involving Human Participants, revised July 31, 2006, www.sfu.ca/policies/gazette/research/r20-01.html.

3. The two existing documents were the legal opinions by Paul Jones (1999), legal advisor to CAUT, and Professors Michael Jackson and Marilyn MacCrimmon (1999) of the UBC faculty of law, both of which we have incorporated in previous chapters. The new opinion commissioned by the REB was by Deborah Lovett (2002) of Lovett & Westmacott, Barristers, Solicitors and Mediators, of Vancouver.

4 *Canadian Code of Ethics for Psychologists* (3rd edition). (2000). Ottawa: CPA. (Principle IV.17) www.cpa.ca/cpasite/userfiles/Documents/Practice_Page/Ethics_Code_Psych.pdf.

5. TCPS, i.8.

6. Frequently Asked Questions.

7. At this point the infrastructure for administering the TCPS was not yet in place, so the Interagency Advisory Panel (PRE), whose mandate would include issuing interpretations of the TCPS in response to questions such as ours, did not yet exist.

8. Jones, "Legal Opinion on Issues of Privilege," 56.

9. Jackson and MacCrimmon, "Research Confidentiality and Academic Privilege," 40.

10. Lovett, "Legal Opinion for Research Ethics Board," 33.

11. Ibid.

12. Ibid.

13. Jackson and MacCrimmon, "Research Confidentiality and Academic Privilege," 139.

14. Lovett, "Legal Opinion for Research Ethics Board," 36.

15. Ibid., 33. The full reference for McNairn & Scott is: Colin H. H. McNairn and Alexander K. Scott, *Privacy Law in Canada* (Toronto: Butterworths, 2001). The case from the English Court of Appeal mentioned is *Parry-Jones v. Law Society*, [1968] 1 All ER 177, [1969] 1 Ch 1.

16. Lovett, "Legal Opinion for Research Ethics Board," 37.

17. Ibid., 36.

18. Ibid., 37.

19. Jackson and MacCrimmon, "Research Confidentiality and Academic Privilege," 131.

20. *Riebl v. Hughes* [1980] 2 S.C.R. 880. Quoted in Jackson & MacCrimmon (1999), 16.

21. Jackson and MacCrimmon, "Research Confidentiality and Academic Privilege," 145.

22. Ibid., 135.

23. Ibid., 175.

24. Ibid., 179.

25. J.P. Fanning, "Policies and Best Practices for Ensuring Statistical and Research

Confidentiality," 2007. Paper prepared for the Office of the Assistant Secretary for Planning and Evaluation. US Department of Health and Human Services, under contract under PO HHSP 233200500320A.

26. We first made that argument in Palys and Lowman, "Ethical and Legal Strategies for Protecting Confidential Research Information."

27. J.D. Brewer, "Inescapable Burden of 'Guilty Knowledge,'" *Times Higher Education*, January 26, 2012, www.timeshighereducation.co.uk/story.asp?storyCode=418834&sectioncode=262.

28. Ted Palys and John Lowman, "TCPS-2's Enduring Challenge: How to Provide Ethics Governance While Respecting Academic Freedom. (2010). Submission to the Interagency Advisory Panel on Research Ethics regarding their December 2009 draft 2nd edition of the *Tri-Council Policy Statement: Ethical Conduct for Research Involving Humans*, www.sfu.ca/~palys/PalysLowmanCommentsReTCPS2Draft2-final.pdf; Social Sciences and Humanities Research Ethics Special Working Committee (SSHWC). "Reconsidering 'Reconsidering': Issues Arising from SSHWC's Consultation on Privacy and Confidentiality." (2006). Discussion paper prepared for SSHWC.

29. *Jaffee v. Redmond* (95-266), 518 US [1996].

30. TCPS (1998), 3.1.

31. Ibid.

32. Jackson and MacCrimmon, "Research Confidentiality and Academic Privilege," 131.

33. Ibid.

34. Memorandum from Judith Osborne, Associate Vice-President, Policy, Equity & Legal, to Dr. Bruce Whittlesea, Chair REB, January 2003. Subject: "Advice."

Chapter XXV

1. John Lowman, Chris Atchison, and Laura Fraser, "Men Who Buy Sex, Phase 2: The Client Survey," 1997. Study funded by the Ministry of Attorney General, Province of B.C.

2. *Smith v. Jones*, 4.

3. Ibid.

4. For example, see John Lowman and Ted Palys (2007) "Strict Confidentiality: An Alternative to PRE's 'Limited Confidentiality' Doctrine," *Journal of Academic Ethics*, 5 (2007): 163–177. ; Ted Palys and John Lowman, "Ethical and Legal Strategies for Protecting Confidential Research Information," *Canadian Journal of Law and Society*, 15 (2000): 39–80.

5. Jackson and MacCrimmon, "Research Confidentiality and Academic Privilege," 49.

6. Ibid., 168.

7. Lovett, "Legal Opinion for Research Ethics Board," 35.

8. *R. v. Brown*, (2002) S.C.J. No. 35 (Q.L.) 2002 SCC 32.

9. Lovett, "Legal Opinion for Research Ethics Board," 13.

10. Sissela Bok, *Secrets: On the Ethics of Concealment and Revelation* (New York: Pantheon Books, 1983).

11. The material in this section is based largely on our interchange with Zinger and his colleagues following publication of Zinger's research. See Ivan Zinger, Cherami Wichmann, and D. A. Andrews, "The Effects of Administrative Segregation," *Canadian Journal of Criminology* 43 (2001): 47–83; Ted Palys and John Lowman, "Social Research with Eyes Wide Shut: The Limited Confidentiality Dilemma," *Canadian Journal of Criminology* 43 (2001): 255–267; Ivan Zinger, Cherami Wichmann, and Paul Gendreau, "Legal and Ethical Obligations in Social Research: The Limited Confidentiality Requirement," *Canadian Journal of Criminology* 43 (2001): 269–274; John Lowman and Ted Palys, "Limited Confidentiality, Academic Freedom, and Matters of Conscience: Where Does CPA Stand?" *Canadian Journal of Criminology* 43 (2001): 497–508.

12. James Bonta and Paul Gendreau, "Re-Examining the Cruel and Unusual Punishment of Prison Life," in *Long-term Imprisonment: Policy, Science, and Correctional Practice*, ed. T. J. Flanagan (Thousand Oaks, CA: Sage, 1995).

13. Michael Jackson, *Prisoners of Isolation: Solitary Confinement in Canada* (Toronto: University of Toronto Press, 1983).

14. Zinger, Wichmann, and Gendreau, "Legal and Ethical Obligations," 270.

15. Interview schedule reproduced in I. Zinger, "The Psychological Effects of 60 Days in Administrative Segregation" (1999). Doctoral dissertation, Department of Psychology, Carleton University, Appendix 4: 107.

16. J. D. Brewer, "Inescapable Burden of 'Guilty Knowledge,'" *Times Higher Education*, January 26, 2012, www.timeshighereducation.co.uk/story.asp?storyCode=418834&sectioncode=262.

17. Zinger, Wichmann, and Gendreau, "Legal and Ethical Obligations," 271.

18. TCPS (1998), 2.8.

19. Zinger, Wichmann, and Gendreau, "Legal and Ethical Obligations," 271–272.

20. The authors insert a footnote here noting that one of their research assistants was in fact grabbed by a prisoner through a protective divider.

21. Zinger, Wichmann, and Gendreau, "Legal and Ethical Obligations," 272.

22. TCPS (1998), 3.1.

23. G.D. Glancy, C. Regehr, and A.G. Bryant, "Confidentiality in Crisis: Part I – The Duty to Inform," *Canadian Journal of Psychiatry* 43 (1998): 1001–1005.

24. Ibid.

25. TCPS (1998), 2.4.

26. SFU Research Ethics Board, *Minutes*, May 13, 2002.

27. See, for example, Maureen H. Fitzgerald, "Punctuated Equilibrium, Moral Panics and the Ethics Review Process." *Journal of Academic Ethics* 2 (2005): 315–338.

Chapter XXVI

1. His McGill biography described him as "a graduate of Harvard University Law School, [who] has devoted his career as a health lawyer, bioethics analyst and scholar to issues at the confluence of science, technology, ethics, and public law." www.mcgill.ca/files/healthlaw/Derek_J_Jones.pdf.

2. Secretariat *Terms of Reference*. www.pre.ethics.gc.ca/eng/secretariat/tor-cdr/.

3. The secretariat has more recently been renamed the Secretariat on Responsible Conduct of Research (SRCR). An organizational chart showing the relationship among PRE, SRCR, and the granting agencies can be found at www.pre.ethics.gc.ca/eng/secretariat/organizational_structure-structure_organisationelle/ along with information concerning their respective terms of reference, membership, and so on.

4. Interagency advisory Panel on Research Ethics — About Us. www.pre.ethics.gc.ca/eng/panel-group/about-apropos/.

5. Panel Members – Dr. Bruce Clayman. www.pre.ethics.gc.ca/eng/panel-group/about-apropos/members-membres/bruce/.

6. Press release from Michèle Bourgeois-Doyle, Communications Officer, Secretariat on Research Ethics, May 3, 2005.

7. See D. J. Jones and Interagency Panel on Research Ethics, "Interface of Law and Ethics in Canadian Research Ethics Standards: An Advisory Opinion on Confidentiality, its Limits & Duties to Others," *McGill Journal of Law and Health* 1 (2007): 101–105, www.mjlh.mcgill.ca/pdfs/vol1-1/jones-pre.pdf; See also John Lowman and Ted Palys, "PRE's 'Interface of Law and Ethics in Canadian Research Ethics Standards: An Advisory Opinion on Confidentiality, its Limits & Duties to Others': The 'Law of the Land' Doctrine in All but Name," *McGill Journal of Law and Health* 1 (2007): 117–122, www.mjlh.mcgill.ca/pdfs/vol1-1/lowman-palys.pdf; and John Lowman and Ted Palys, "Strict Confidentiality: An Alternative to PRE's 'Limited Confidentiality' Doctrine," *Journal of Academic Ethics* 5 (2007): 163–177.

8. *Tarasoff v. Regents of University of California* 17 Cal. 3d 425, 551 P.2d 334, 131 Cal. Rptr. 14 (Cal. 1976).

9. Tarasoff [1976], 31.

10. P. B. Herbert and K. A. Young, "Tarasoff at Twenty-Five," *Journal of the American Academy of Psychiatry and Law* 30 (2002): 275–281.

11. D. J. Jones and Interagency Panel on Research Ethics, "Interface of Law and Ethics in Canadian Research Ethics Standards," 106.

12. Ibid.

13. For examples, see Will C. van den Hoonaard, *The Seduction of Ethics* (Toronto: University of Toronto Press, 2011).

14. The accuracy of their judgement is another matter.

15. Incidentally, this is exactly what happened in Poddar's case; he was attending therapy and stopped when the psychiatrist said he would take steps to restrain him.

16. C. Bollas and D. Sundelson, *The New Informants: The Betrayal of Confidentiality in*

Psychoanalysis and Psychotherapy (New Jersey: Jason Aronson, 1995); P. Herbert, "The Duty to Warn: A Reconsideration and Critique," *Journal of the American Academy of Psychiatry and Law* 30 (2002): 417–424; P. Herbert, "Psychotherapy as Law Enforcement," *Journal of the American Academy of Psychiatry and Law* 32 (2004): 91–95.

17. We have, however, interviewed persons who have considered suicide at some point in their lives.

18. Will C. van den Hoonaard, *The Seduction of Ethics* (Toronto: University of Toronto Press, 2011).

19. Jones and PRE, "Law and Ethics," 107.

20. Ibid., 106.

21. *Tarasoff v. Regents of University of California*, 17 Cal. 3d 425, 551 P.2d 334, 131 Cal. Rptr. 14 (Cal. 1976) [cited to Cal. 3d].

22. Tarasoff [1976], 28.

23. Tarasoff [1976], 44.

24. Tarasoff [1976], 100–109. Citations of legal cases and sources in the literature within the quote have been removed to enhance readability.

25. P. S. Appelbaum and A. Rosenbaum, "*Tarasoff* and the Researcher: Does the Duty to Protect Apply in the Research Setting?" *American Psychologist* 44, no. 6 (1989): 885–894.

26. C. Bollas and D. Sundelson, *The New Informants: The Betrayal of Confidentiality in Psychoanalysis and Psychotherapy* (Northvale, NJ: Jason Aronson, 1996).

27. P. B. Herbert, "Psychotherapy as Law Enforcement," *Journal of the American Academy of Psychiatry Law* 32 (2004): 91–95.

28. The other five members were: Dr. Will van den Hoonaard, who was also a member of PRE and SSHWC's first chair; Dr. Lisa Given; Dr. Joseph Lévy; Dr. Michelle McGinn and Dr. Patrick O'Neill, who joined PRE and became its second chair after van den Hoonaard's term expired (though van den Hoonnaard would stay on as a member of SSHWC). The membership was expanded by one in 2005 to include Dr. Mary Blackstone.

29. The two who stayed for the life of SSHWC were Dr. Glenn Griener, who represented the National Committee on Ethics in Human Research, and Dr. Keren Rice, who represented the Social Sciences and Humanities Research Council. The Canadian Institutes for Health Research were first represented by Dr. Kathleen Oberle and then Dr. Bernard Keating. The Canadian Federation for the Humanities and Social Sciences's representatives were Dr. Michael Owen, Dr. Deborah Poff, and finally Dr. Maureen Muldoon. Ms. Thérèse de Groote, a Senior Policy Analyst with the Secretariat, also attended all SSHWC meetings, offering administrative support and serving an important liaison function between SSHWC, SRE, and other working groups.

30. Social Sciences and Humanities Research Ethics Special Working Committee, "Giving Voice to the Spectrum," *SFU*, June 2004, www.sfu.ca/~palys/SSHWC-GivingVoice-2004.pdf.

31. SSHWC, "Giving Voice to the Spectrum," 29–32.

32. The reports on privacy and confidentiality include: SSHWC "Reconsidering Privacy and Confidentiality in the TCPS: A Discussion Paper," *SFU*, 2005, www.sfu.ca/~palys/ SSHWC-2005-Report-ReconsideringP&C.pdf; SSHWC, "Continuing the Dialogue on Privacy and Confidentiality: Feedback and Recommendations Arising from SSHWC's Recent Consultation," *SFU*, 2006, www.sfu.ca/~palys/SSHWC-2006-Report-ContinuingTheDialogue.pdf; and SSHWC, "SSHWC Recommendations Regarding Privacy and Confidentiality," *SFU*, 2008, www.pre.ethics.gc.ca/eng/archives/policy-politique/reports-rapports/sshwc-ctsh/.

33. TCPS (1998), i-8.

34. We flag this area because, in the United States, both certificates of confidentiality and privacy certificates arose out of legislation mandating participant privacy in research funded or otherwise sponsored by the US federal government.

35. SSHWC, "Reconsidering Privacy and Confidentiality," 12–13.

36. Ibid., 19.

37. Ibid., 19–20.

38. TCPS, 1–12.

39. TCPS, 2–4.

40. SSHWC, "Reconsidering Privacy and Confidentiality," 24.

41. Ibid.

42. Ibid., 24–25.

43. SSHWC, "SSHWC Recommendations Regarding Privacy and Confidentiality," 11.

44. Ibid., 12.

45. Ibid.

Chapter XXVII

1. TCPS-2, 58.

2. TCPS-2, 59.

3. TCPS-2, 12.

4. TCPS-2, 58.

5. TCPS-2, 58.

Chapter XXVIII

1. "uOttawa Criminologists Go to Court to Protect Research Confidentiality," *CAUT/ ACPPU Bulletin* 60, no. 1 (2013), www.cautbulletin.ca/default.asp?SectionID=0&Sectio nName=&VolID=354&VolumeName=No%201&VolumeStartDate=January%2017,%20 2013&EditionID=38&EditionName=Vol%2060&EditionStartDate=January%2017,%20 2013&ArticleID=0.

2. "REB Members Deplore uOttawa's Refusal to Defend Confidentiality," *CAUT/ACPPU Bulletin* 60, no. 4 (2013), www.cautbulletin.ca/default.asp?SectionID=0&SectionN ame=&VolID=360&VolumeName=No%204&VolumeStartDate=April%2016,%20

2013&EditionID=38&EditionName=Vol%2060&EditionStartDate=January%2017,%20
2013&ArticleID=0.

3. Allan Rock, President and Vice-Chancellor of the University of Ottawa, to the
University of Ottawa Social Sciences and Humanities Research Ethics Board, Health
Sciences and Science Research Ethics Board, and Office of Research Ethics and Integrity
plus cc list, June 24, 2013.

4. Letter dated June 26, 2013, from James Turk, Executive Director, CAUT, to Mr. Allan
Rock, President, University of Ottawa.

5. Ibid.

6. TCPS2, 2010.

7. TCPS2, 2010, 12.

8. TCPS2, 2010, 12.

9. "Complaint Targets uOttawa for Failure to Defend Confidentiality," *CAUT/ACPPU
Bulletin* 60, no. 6 (2013), www.cautbulletin.ca/default.asp?SectionID=0&SectionN
ame=&VolID=364&VolumeName=No%206&VolumeStartDate=June%2018,%20
2013&EditionID=38&EditionName=Vol%2060&EditionStartDate=January%2017,%20
2013&ArticleID=0.

Chapter XXIX

1. See www.lexcanada.com/lb_jacobsen.html. Jacobsen was chosen because of his
extensive experience in cases dealing with journalist-source privilege (reporter's
privilege).

2. *See* www.lexcanada.com/lb_park.html.

3. *Dr. Colette Parent and Dr. Christine Bruckert v. Her Majesty the Queen and Luka Rocco
Magnotta.* No 500-36-006329-125; Judgment on a certiorari application to quash a
search warrant. Quebec Superior Court., at 1.

4. "Not Criminally Responsible" (because of insanity).

5. *R. v. National Post* [2010] S.C.J. No. 16, [2010] A.C.S. No. 16, 2010 SCC 16]. File no.
32601.

6. Globe & Mail *v. Canada* (Attorney General) [2010] SCC 41.

7. *R. v. National Post*, 28.

8. *Parent and Bruckert v. The Queen and Magnotta*, 93.

9. Ibid. 95–99.

10. Ibid.

11. Justice Bourque noted (at 103–104) that disclosure of their identities could expose
them to: risk of prosecution for criminal offences; personal harm as the result of
repercussions from family, friends, employers and numerous other parties; a safety
hazard should names and personal information be disclosed to clients; financial
risks should their relationships with clients be damaged; being ostracized by other
sex workers for failing to follow a professional code of conduct by participating in

interviews; exposing male escorts to homophobia; being cut off welfare as a result of not declaring their earnings; having Revenue Canada pursue them for unpaid taxes; and having their children bullied or harassed by other school children who find out their parent's occupation.

12. *Parent and Bruckert v. The Queen and Magnotta,* 112.

13. Ibid., 121–123.

14. Ibid., 130.

15. Ibid., 132.

16. Ibid., 133.

17. Ibid., 138.

18. Ibid., 139.

19. Ibid., 141.

20. Ibid., 142.

21. Ibid., 145.

22. Ibid., 148.

23. Ibid., 149.

24. Ibid., 150.

25. Ibid., 152.

26. Ibid., 156.

27. "16. (1) No person is criminally responsible for an act committed or an omission made while suffering from a mental disorder that rendered the person incapable of appreciating the nature and quality of the act or omission or of knowing that it was wrong."

28. *Parent and Bruckert v. The Queen and Magnotta,* 14, also at 160.

29. *Parent and Bruckert v. The Queen and Magnotta.* (Affidavit of Scott Woodside, at 2–7.)

30. Ibid., 165.

31. Ibid., 166.

32. Ibid., 168.

33. Ibid., 169.

34. Ibid., 171.

35. Ibid. 173.

36. Ibid. 190.

37. Ibid. 195.

38. Ibid. 198–200.

39. Ibid., 205.

40. Ibid., 209–212.

Chapter XXX

1. Ted Palys and John Lowman. "One Step Forward, Two Steps Back: Draft TCPS-2's Assault on Academic Freedom. A submission to the Interagency Advisory Panel on Research Ethics regarding their December 2008 draft 2nd edition of the *Tri-Council Policy Statement: Ethical Conduct for Research Involving Humans*" (2009); www.sfu.ca/~palys/Palys-LowmanCommentsOnDraftTCPS2.pdf; Ted Palys and John Lowman, "TCPS-2's Enduring Challenge: How to Provide Ethics Governance While Respecting Academic Freedom. A submission to the Interagency Advisory Panel on Research Ethics regarding their December 2009 draft 2nd edition of the Tri-Council Policy Statement: Ethical Conduct for Research Involving Humans" (2010). www.sfu.ca/~palys/PalysLowmanCommentsReTCPS2Draft2-final.pdf.

2. Will van den Hoonaard, *The Seduction of Ethics: Transforming the Social Sciences* (Toronto: University of Toronto Press, 2011).

3. See, for example, M. H. Fitzgerald, "Punctuated Equilibrium, Moral Panics and the Ethics Review Process," *Journal of Academic Ethics* 2 (2004): 315–38; J. Katz, "Towards a Natural History of Ethical Censorship," *Law & Society Review* 41, no. 4 (2007): 797–810; C. Shea, "Don't Talk to the Humans: The Crackdown on Social Science Research," *Linguafranca* 10, no. 6 (2000); SSHWC, "Giving Voice to the Spectrum." See also the collection of papers presented at a 2006 Symposium on Censorship and Institutional Review Boards that were later compiled in the *Northwestern Law Review* at www.law.northwestern.edu/journals/lawreview/issues/101.2.html. The international scope of the problem is evident when one notes that Katz's and Shea's articles focus primarily on the United States, Fitzgerald's article focuses on the "commonwealth countries" of Britain, Canada, Australia, and New Zealand, and SSHWC's monograph refers primarily to Canada.

4. See van den Hoonaard, *The Seduction of Ethics.*

5. A seminal paper here is Philip Hamburger, "The New Censorship: Institutional Review Boards," *The Supreme Court Review* (2005): 271–354.

6. R. Dingwall, "The Ethical Case Against Ethical Regulation in Humanities and Social Science Research," *21st Century Society* 3, no. 1 (2008): 1–12.

7. Ibid., 10.

8. Ibid.

9. John F. Galliher, "The Protection of Human Subjects: A Reexamination of the Professional Code of Ethics," *The American Sociologist* 8 (1973): 99.

10. In re: Request from the United Kingdom Pursuant to the Treaty Between the Government of the United States of America and the Government of the United Kingdom on Mutual Assistance in Criminal Matters in the Matter of Dolours Price. United States District Court, District of Massachusetts, M.B.D. No. 11-MC-91078. Motion of Trustees of Boston College to Quash Subpoenas. Filed June 7, 2011.

11. Beth McMurtrie, "Secrets from Belfast: How Boston College's Oral History of the Troubles Fell Victim to an International Murder Investigation, *The Chronicle of Higher Education*, (January 2014), www.chronicle.com/article/Secrets-From-Belfast/144059/

12. In re: Request from the United Kingdom Pursuant to the Treaty Between the Government of the United States of America and the Government of the United Kingdom on Mutual Assistance in Criminal Matters in the Matter of Dolours Price. United States District Court, District of Massachusetts, M.B.D. No. 11-MC-91078. Government's Opposition to Motion to Quash and Motion for an Order to Compel. Filed July 1, 2011. (emphasis added by government)

13. David Matthews, "Gerry Adams Arrest: Police Access to Boston Tapes Has Dealt 'Blow' to Research," *Times Higher Education*, May 1, 2014, www.timeshighereducation. co.uk/news/gerry-adams-arrest-surrender-of-interview-tapes-has-dealt-blow-to-research/2013038.article.

14. "Tout" is slang for "informer," which according to the IRA code, invokes a death sentence.

15. Henry McDonald, "Hate Campaign Against Me Has Ratcheted Up Since Adams Arrest, Says IRA Historian," the *Observer*, May 3, 2014, www.bostoncollegesubpoena. wordpress.com/2014/05/03/hate-campaign-against-me-has-ratcheted-up-since-adams-arrest-says-ira-historian/.

16. Gemma Murray, "Key Figures 'Upping the Ante' over Boston College Tapes," *News Letter*, May 5, 2014, www.bostoncollegesubpoena.wordpress.com/2014/05/05/key-figures-upping-the-ante-over-boston-college-tapes/; Jenny McCartney, "An American Oral History Project Makes Us Fear for Our Lives, Say Former IRA Members," the *Telegraph*, May 15, 2014, www.blogs.telegraph.co.uk/news/jennymccartney/100271584/an-american-oral-history-project-makes-us-fear-for-our-lives-say-former-ira-members/.

17. Liam Clarke, "Boston College Tapes: Archive That Turned into a Can of Worms," *Belfast Telegraph*, May 13, 2014, www.belfasttelegraph.co.uk/news/local-national/northern-ireland/boston-college-tapes-archive-that-turned-into-a-can-of-worms-30267260.html; Gerry Moriarty, "Boston College to Be Sued by Republicans over Troubles Tapes," *Irish Times*, May 13, 2014, www.irishtimes.com/news/politics/boston-college-to-be-sued-by-republicans-over-troubles-tapes-1.1793599.

18. Peter Schworm (May 18, 2014).

19. "Boston College Tapes: PSNI Bid to Obtain All Material," *BBC News Northern Ireland* website, May 22, 2014, www.bbc.com/news/uk-northern-ireland-27527213.

20. Andy Martin, "Boston College Tapes: US Network NBC Launches Legal Bid," *BBC News Northern Ireland* website, May 21, 2014, www.bbc.com/news/uk-northern-ireland-27505115.

21. Kevin Cullen, "BC exercise in idealism reopened old wounds," the *Boston Globe*, July 6, 2014, www.bostonglobe.com/news/world/2014/07/05/belfast-the-shadows-and-gunmen/D5yv4DdNIxaBXMl2Tlr6PL/story.html.

22. Paul Bew, "The Closure of the Boston College Troubles Archive Is Historical Loss," *Independent.ie* website, May 11, 2014, www.independent.ie/opinion/analysis/the-closure-of-the-boston-college-troubles-archive-is-historical-loss-30263223.html.

23. Joe Humphreys, "Historians Fear Boston Tapes Controversy Will Damage Research into the Troubles," *Irish Times*, May 10, 2014, www.bostoncollegesubpoena.wordpress.com/2014/05/10/historians-fear-boston-tapes-controversy-will-damage-research-into-

the-troubles/; Brendan O'Neill, *Boston College Subpoena News* website, "How the Adams Arrest Threatens Academic Freedom;" *Free Speech Now — Spiked*, May 6, 2014, www. bostoncollegesubpoena.wordpress.com/2014/05/11/how-the-adams-arrest-threatens-academic-freedom/; Andrew Sanders, "Deprived by the Actions of Malevolent Forces," *The Pensive Quill* website, May 17, 2014, www.thepensivequill.am/2014/05/deprived-by-actions-of-malevolent-forces.html.

24. Portions of our abbreviated discussion here regarding Bernhard and Young are taken from Ted Palys and John Lowman, "Going Boldly Where No One Has Gone Before? How Confidentiality Risk Aversion Is Killing Research on Sensitive Topics," *Journal of Academic Ethics* 8, no. 4 (2010): 265–284.

25. J. K. Bernhard and J. E. E. Young, "Gaining Institutional Permission: Researching Precarious Legal Status in Canada," *Journal of Academic Ethics* 7 (2009): 175–191.

26. Personal communication from Dr. Bernhard to Ted Palys, March 22, 2010.

27. For media accounts of these events, see, for example, www.kersplebedeb.com/nzinga/index.html, www.toronto.nooneisillegal.org/taxonomy/term/25, and www.toronto.nooneisillegal.org/node/390.

28. Bernhard and Young, "Gaining Institutional Permission: Researching Precarious Legal Status in Canada," 182–183.

29. Ibid., 186.

30. Palys and Lowman, "Ethical and Legal Strategies for Protecting Confidential Research Information"; Palys and Lowman, "Anticipating Law: Research Methods, Ethics and the Law of Privilege."

31. P. O'Neill, "Good intentions and awkward outcomes: Ethical gatekeeping in field research," in *Walking the Tightrope: Ethical Issues for Qualitative Researchers*, ed. Will C. van den Hoonaard (Toronto: University of Toronto Press, 2002), 17–25.

32. Palys and Lowman, "Ethical and Legal Strategies for Protecting Confidential Research Information."

33. SSHWC, "SSHWC Recommendations Regarding Privacy and Confidentiality," 10–12.

34. TCPS2 (2010), 56.

35. Ibid., 58.

36. Letter from Mona Nemer, C.Q., Ph.D., FRSC, Professor and Vice-President, Research at the University of Ottawa, to Susan Zimmerman, Executive Director, Secretariat on Responsible Conduct of research, July 25, 2013.

37. Ibid.

38. Letter from Alain Beaudet, M.D., Ph.D., President, Canadian Institutes of Health Research and Chair, Interagency Steering Committee for the Panel on Research Ethics, Panel on Responsible Conduct of Research and Secretariat on Responsible Conduct of Research, to Dr. Mona Nemer, Vice-President Research, University of Ottawa, January 28, 2013.

39. www.pre.ethics.gc.ca/eng/policy-politique/interpretations/privacy-privee/.

40. Ibid, 2B.

41. Letter dated January 20, 2014, 2.

42. www.pre.ethics.gc.ca/eng/policy-politique/interpretations/privacy-privee/ at 2E.

43. Letter from James Turk, Executive Director of CAUT to Mr. Allan Rock, President, University of Ottawa, dated October 17, 2013.

44. Email from Jennifer R. Fishman and Mary Ellen Macdonald to Russel Ogden inviting his participation, February 23, 2014.

45. Email from Russel Ogden to researcher Jennifer R. Fishman, February 24, 2014.

46. Email from Russel Ogden to Lynda McNeil, April 10, 2014.

47. Email from Jennifer R. Fishman and Mary Ellen Macdonald to Russel Ogden, April 13, 2014.

48. Email from Russel Ogden to researcher Jennifer R. Fishman, February 24, 2014.

49. Email from Russel Ogden to Jennifer R. Fishman and Mary Ellen Macdonald, April 13, 2014.

50. Email from Russel Ogden to Lynda McNeil, April 14, 2014.

51. The presidents posted their interpretation on April 15, 2014.

52. Email from Dr. Paul Brassard, Chair, Advisory Council on Human Research Ethics, McGill University, to Russel Ogden, May 23, 2014.

53. Palys and Lowman, "Ethical and Legal Strategies for Protecting Confidential Research Information," 31.

54. SSHWC, "Giving Voice to the Spectrum."

55. Thanks to Margaret Blakeney, the access to information coordinator at SSHRC, for her assistance. We also asked how many different scholarly associations were approached for their views, so we could have some indication of response rate, but were informed SSHRC had not retained that information.

56. Letter from Patrick O'Neill, President of the Canadian Psychological Association, to Janet E. Halliwell, Executive Vice-President, SSHRC, December 1, 2004.

57. Reply from Richard Moon, Canadian Law and Society Association to an October 27, 2003 memorandum from Janet E. Halliwell, Executive Vice-President, SSHRC, asking for the Association's views on the subject of "Statutory Confidentiality Protection for Legally Sensitive Research."

58. Response from Sarah Carter, Council member of the Canadian Historical Association, dated February 2, 2004, to a memorandum from Janet E. Halliwell, Executive Vice-President, SSHRC, asking for the Association's views on the subject of "Statutory Confidentiality Protection for Legally Sensitive Research."

Index